The Plural Society in the British West Indies

The Plural Society in the British West Indies

by M. *Michael Garfield* G. SMITH

UNIVERSITY OF CALIFORNIA PRESS

BERKELEY AND LOS ANGELES   1965

University of California Press
Berkeley and Los Angeles, California

Cambridge University Press
London, England

Library of Congress Catalog Card Number: 65-10236

Printed in the United States of America

To Mary

Preface

The essays in this book deal with certain problems in a common social field. Since the problems are of general importance and the field merits further study, it seems useful to bring these papers together here. From their joint concerns they derive many interconnections, and may prove useful as an introduction to the study of the Caribbean and similar mixed societies. It is this hope that has guided their selection for republication.

Written between 1952 and 1961 while I was attached to the University College of the West Indies, several of these articles are out of print, whereas others are relatively inaccessible. Only one has not yet appeared. In revising them for this volume, I have tried to improve and clarify their style, especially in the earlier pieces; but, although they were written over a fairly extended period, during which my ideas and knowledge of West Indian society developed considerably, I have found no reason to make any changes of substance.

The main subject with which these essays deal is the nature and character of West Indian society. However, in order to pursue the inquiry, it is necessary to examine certain general questions, such as the nature and variability of social order, the differing bases and modes of social integration, and the variety of societal types. In treating these questions, I have sought to develop and apply the work of J. S. Furnivall, especially his concept of the plural society as a unit of disparate parts which owes its existence to external factors, and lacks a common social will.[1]

Furnivall was an economist with first-hand experience of the colonial Far East before the Second World War. In these colonial societies, he observed groups of differing race and culture living side by side in economic symbiosis and mutual avoidance. He characterized such units as plural societies in contrast with the relatively unitary societies found among primitives or modern industrial peoples. Furnivall's ideas have evoked a negative response from various sociologists and anthropologists,[2] essentially on the ground that he "obscures the really important fact that no society can exist without a minimum sharing of common values—without a certain amount of social will."[3] Furnivall discussed this point explicitly. Of plural societies he said that

in each section the sectional common will is feeble, and in the society as a whole there is no common social will. There may be apathy, even on such a vital point as defence against aggression. Few recognize that, in fact, all the members of all sections have material interests in common, but most see that on many points their material interests are opposed.[4]

The apathy to which he referred was vividly demonstrated when these colonial peoples greeted the invading Japanese with no resistance. According to Furnivall, in plural societies, "all wants that all men want in common are those which they share in common with animal creation."[5] When Furnivall is criticized for minimizing the importance of shared common values by writers who also assert that in Trinidad "there was only one common value strongly held by the whole society, of a type inherently productive of tensions"[6]—that is, racial differentiation—then the need to examine the meaning of this postulate is obvious. Any orderly discussion of Furnivall's thesis should therefore begin by asking what precisely does it mean to say that no society can exist without a certain amount of common values. The following essays analyze West Indian pluralism, but none directly addresses this question, though it contains the central theoretical and practical issues. It is thus appropriate that I should discuss this problem briefly here.

Increasingly in recent years, Western sociologists have emphasized the thesis that, by necessity, societies are consensual normative systems. For Talcott Parsons

it is a condition of the stability of social systems that there should be an integration of the component units to constitute a "common value system." . . . The content of such a common value system, and the degree and modes of its integration with the actual actions of the units in a social system, vary empirically. But the existence of such a pattern system as a point of reference for the analysis of social phenomena is a central assumption which follows directly from the frame of reference of action as applied to the analysis of social systems.[7]

For Kingsley Davis and Wilbert Moore, "human society achieves its unity primarily through the possession by its members of certain ultimate values and ends in common."[8] Among the functional prerequisites of a society, these common values and norms hold a critical place. For Parsons, "this integration of a set of common value patterns with the internalized need-disposition structure of the constituent personalities is the core phenomenon of the dynamics of social systems . . . [It] . . . may be said to be the fundamental dynamic theorem of sociology." [9] According to other writers, "no society, however simple, can exist without shared symbolic modes of communication, because without them it cannot maintain the common value-structure or the protective sanctions which hold back the war of all against all." [10] For such sociologists, this Hobbesian "war of all against all," the deductively derived antithesis of their deductive consensual thesis, will inevitably appear "if the members of an aggregate pursue their ends by means selected only on the basis of instrumental efficiency." [11] In such a case, they hold that "a state of indeterminate flux rather than a system of action exists." [12]

The writers just cited are all committed to the analysis of social systems within the conceptual framework of the "theory of action." In this theory, the primary units of reference and analysis are the actions taken by actors in given situations to pursue particular ends. Clearly, any sociological theory which adopts this point of departure has to assume some general normative consensus in order to exclude "the war of all against all." But this heuristic assumption is a methodological necessity only for this particular theory; there is no reason to assume it is a general condition or requisite of all social systems. Any deductive theory with individualistic reference points will find some such assumption logically indispensable. But to give this axiom any substantive meaning it is necessary to translate it into specific terms, to define in operational language the minimum content, scope, intensity, and extension of the common values on which systems of social order are presumed to be always dependent. Once such questions are raised, differences in the logically possible bases and types of social order will immediately demand attention. But usually these problems are excluded under the general presumption of an indispensable and indefinable "common value system" without which societies cannot exist.

This type of social theory which assumes a normative consensual basis for social order has very distinguished antecedents. Emile Durkheim and Max Weber, the two main pillars of modern sociology, independently bequeathed the idea to their successors. Durkheim and Weber developed social theories which rested on the common assumption that all societies depend on normative consensus, or should be analyzed as if they did. Essentially this doctrine means that the members of society, or most of them, obey its rules and representatives because they feel it is right and good to do so. In consequence of this wide moral consensus, the social rules and representatives embody and enjoy an authority which is a mirror image of the members' willing submission. Without such willing submission—so runs the theory —societies could neither develop nor persist. Instead we should find the Hobbesian war of all against all. "Willing submission" is thus critical evidence for the prevalence of moral consensus; but no attempt is made to distinguish willing from unwilling submission.

According to Weber, "only in the limiting case of the slave is formal subjection to authority absolutely involuntary." [13] For Durkheim, even this exception seems too generous. In his view

. . . every society is despotic; there is nothing artificial in this despotism; it is natural because it is necessary, and also because in certain conditions societies cannot endure without it. Nor do I mean that there is anything intolerable about it; on the contrary, the individual does not feel it any more than we feel the atmosphere weighing on our shoulders. From the moment the individual has been raised in this way by the collectivity, he will naturally desire what it desires and accept without difficulty the state of subjection to which he finds himself reduced.[14]

Thus Durkheim, forgetting the French revolutionary tradition, argues that even slaves are happy to be slaves. His modern successors simply restate this thesis in rejecting Furnivall's observations; but a moment's glance will show that simple repetition of consensualist dogma cannot dissolve the basic problem. No one doubts "the necessity of looking at a plural society as a single social system." [15] The important question is whether the plural society does not represent a different type of system from that to which consensualist theses may properly apply.

Furnivall had argued that in the Far Eastern colonies, the union of differing racial and cultural elements was not voluntary, but "imposed by the colonial Power and by the force of economic circumstances." [16] History supports this statement fully. Furnivall also asserted that "the union cannot be dissolved without the whole society relapsing into anarchy." [17] Since he wrote, violent reactions against European rule in Indonesia, Malaya, Kenya, Algeria, India, the Congo, Palestine, and elsewhere have confirmed his first statement; and the more or less severe breakdowns of social order in several colonial units as they approach or achieve independence confirm the second. In the West Indies today, British Guiana is a striking example.

To "explain" these developments, advocates of the consensualist theory say that they show "that the identification with the superior social system has ceased, and [that] subordinate identification, whose strength has not been appreciated precisely because of this subordination, now assumes a major importance." [18] This statement simply assumes, despite all evidence to the contrary, that the subordinate colonial peoples had "identified" themselves with the "superior social system"—that is, the imperial power. But this assumption is indispensable only if this defective theory is to be applied to these situations. We are told that "there must be a certain minimum of common shared values if the unity of the society is to be maintained. In the case of Furnivall, this led to the neglect of ties of sentiment with the imperial Power, to an overstressing of economic elements, and to an overall view of the political structure as essentially one of force." [19] In brief, in order that the consensual theory may apply, we are required to interpret all modes of subordination as willing submission, and thus as prima facie evidence of shared moral sentiments between the subordinate and dominant group. By the same token we should regard racial conditions and Negro protests against them in Alabama and South Africa, or the Nazi extermination of European Jews, as indicating willing submission and moral consensus among all concerned.

The difficulties which this social theory faces are clear and important. From this viewpoint, the rejection of European rule by colonial peoples remains utterly incomprehensible; but so must any conflict which revolves around "subordinate identifications" and segmental loyalties, simply because the thesis that society rests on shared common values inevitably implies their dominance, and so minimizes the strength of "subordinate identifications" within segments of the total unit. It is perfectly clear that in any social system based on intense cleavages and discontinuity between differentiated segments, the community of values or social relations between these sections will be correspondingly low. This is precisely the structural condition of the plural society.

It is purely Pickwickian to assert that, since "no society can exist without a minimum sharing of common values," [20] societies based on conquest, slavery, or colonial domination must inevitably possess these common values, since they clearly exist. Yet this is what the theory really reduces to. The ultimate rationale for such dogma is the Hobbesian argument that "society based solely on force is a contradiction in terms." [21] But this principle, as stated, is as meaningless as true. In conquest states or slave systems we have to deal with at least two social categories or groups, one of which, sharing certain common values and interests, coöperates as a unit to dominate and control the other. Within either stratum, slave or free, ruler or ruled, the existence of shared values and understandings is not in question. The critical issue is the presence or absence of such normative consensus between these strata, and reliance on forceful regulation rather on than shared common norms to maintain the unit. Unless we choose to ignore onehalf of mankind and most of its history, we cannot deny the validity and significance of the distinction Furnivall made between those societies which derive their integration from normative consensus, and those which depend for their order on regulation by force. At the disciplinary level, the central issue this raises is whether sociology will remain a comparative, analytic science or become a normative one; whether sociologists will study societies as they are, or as they think they should be, in order that they might "exist" on dubious logicodeductive grounds.

West Indian slave society is a classic instance of the plural society identified by Furnivall. The West Indies were among the earliest areas that Europeans colonized after the Renaissance. On their discovery, the islands were thinly peopled by Carib and Arawak Indians. These aborigines were soon eliminated and replaced by African slaves whose general lot it was to provide field labor on the plantations which exported sugar, coffee, and other tropical crops to Europe. The economic rewards of this slave industrialism made the West Indian colonies a glittering prize in the imperial struggles of the eighteenth century when planter interests were prominent in the metropolitan states. Meanwhile, throughout the region, a peculiar type of society developed. The Caribbean colonies, whoever ruled them, were essentially similar in constitution. In all, the primary elements were white slave-masters and black slaves. In all, imperial claims and social order were based on force, *de jure* and *de facto*, and this was recognized by masters and slaves alike. Naval force transferred these units from one imperial power to another, as the fortunes of war dictated. Within the colonies, military force maintained their systems of slavery and order in the face of repeated revolts, not all of which were unsuccessful. Societies with such historical bases and constitutions merit very careful study. As we have seen, they provide social science with problems and data of the utmost importance.

If we care to regard as "normal" only those societies that depend for their integration on normal consensus, then at least until slavery was abolished, we must recognize the "abnormality" of these West Indian units. In that event, their present condition requires detailed study. We need to know whether these units are still "abnormal" and lack a consensual basis for their integration. If they are not, we need to know the processes and conditions in which their current consensus developed. We should also try to determine its present generality and intensity, and in this inquiry we shall have to find ways of identifying, demonstrating, and measuring consensus. On the other hand, if these societies continue to lack a moral consensus, we need to know the basis on which their present order rests, and their properties as social systems. The key questions here concern the levels and conditions of stability, the degrees of functional coherence, and the structural variety which these societies exhibit. Such problems are clearly important well beyond the bounds of this region; but so long as we begin by assuming the normative consensual integration of all social systems, they can scarcely be perceived, much less studied. From such presumptions absurdities often follow, as when sociologists emphasize "the processes making for unity and integration" [22] of plural societies within which social conflict steadily increases in scale and intensity. At that stage their deductive normative theory can only be maintained by asserting that conflict expresses consensus; but this deprives it of any meaning.

The order in which these essays are presented here differs from that in which they were written. The first two pieces are intended to introduce the reader to the West Indian scene and its leading problems. Both were written after various studies had shown the utility of the plural hypothesis. The opening essay, "West Indian Culture," was written in June, 1960, and published in December, 1961; the second, "Ethnic and Cultural Pluralism," was written in late 1956. Apart from its synoptic account of the West Indies, the main feature in this second essay is the discussion of ethnicity and of ethnic pluralism. The order in which the remaining papers were written will show how I came to adopt and apply this plural framework.

On beginning my study of the West Indies, I first soaked myself in the social history of certain colonies during the period between the abolition of the slave trade (1808) and the abolition of slavery itself (1838). I then tried to develop an account of those societies by analyzing an indexed selection of contemporary reports. This analytic reconstruction of West Indian slave society (essay 5) was important for several reasons. It provided a base against which continuity and change could be identified and studied. It revealed the principles which underlay the rigid structural forms of the old regime. It also revealed the shallowness of those reductionist theses which claimed to "explain" this social organization of slavery by reference to economic interests and motivations. This exploratory essay was written in 1952–1953 during a field study of Grenada in the South Caribbean, where I had the chance to witness a state of political unrest marked by arson, periodic strikes, and so forth. This experience suggested that Furnivall's thesis of plural societies defined by dissensus and pregnant with conflict was highly relevant to the West Indies.

On completing this Grenadian study, I pursued my early historical leads with a comparative analysis of slavery and its aftermath in Jamaica and among the Mohammedan Hausa of Zaria, Northern Nigeria, where I had worked in 1949–1950. This analysis (essay 6)

showed that in Hausaland and in the West Indies, slavery had dia-
metrically opposite structural effects which could not be explained
adequately on economic grounds. In Hausa society slavery provided
the institutional context and mode of acculturation; in Jamaica the
reverse was true. In consequence the institution of slavery distin-
guised two different types of society; one, Zaria, which was relatively
homogeneous and highly integrated; the other, Jamaica, which was
correspondingly plural and malintegrated. Such differing social systems could be expected to respond to the abolition of slavery in
sharply different ways. History shows that they did. From this inquiry
I saw how important it was to concentrate my attention on the problem of order and integration inherent in the diverse social and cultural
constitution of West Indian society.

The next step was quite clear. It seemed essential to examine the
anthropological and sociological literature on this region and on
nearby areas in order to see what light it might shed on the nature and
problems of society in the West Indies, and in those Caribbean countries with a parallel colonial past. Fortunately, modern Caribbean
sociology has an easily identifiable beginning with visits by Martha
Beckwith and the Herskovitses. From this base line I reviewed the
relevant literature and analyzed it in a short monograph (essay 3).
It seemed that I could identify certain approaches to this region, all
inadequate, due to their preoccupation with rather narrow segments
of social reality, but all indirectly suggesting the applicability of the
plural framework. In concluding that essay I drew on my Grenadian
experience and tried to put forward a plural model for the first time.
Later, in a working paper presented to the 30th Study Session of the
International Institute for Differing Civilizations (essay 2), I summarized the essentials of this analysis. When a further opportunity
arose in 1959 to develop this thesis formally, I tried to present it as
clearly and systematically as I could within the limits of a conference
paper (essay 4). In that essay, I also drew on a structural analysis of
the Jamaican milieu (essay 7), written in 1956, and published in 1961.
From this review it will be seen that the three early papers (essays 5,
6, and 3, in the order of writing) through which my recognition of West
Indian pluralism took shape, were all based on systematic analyses of the
relevant literature, both historical and contemporary. This literature
abounds with evidence of West Indian pluralism, both implicit and
explicit. The conclusions I derived from studying it were also reinforced by my own observations of the contemporary society. All that
was needed was the theoretical framework which Furnivall had
supplied.

In this collection, three essays (8 to 10) present descriptive analyses
of West Indian rural life based on field work. Because they describe

the peasants' situation, and also show how the plural thesis may orient and guide research, I think it worthwhile to include them. The questions that this plural theory raises generate inquiries focused on problems of social order and change, consistency and integration; but as a hypothesis it also imposes stringent conditions of field enquiry and analysis.

During 1955 I had made an extensive rural survey in Jamaica, and in this context had studied rural communities and official attempts to assist them. As might be inferred from the plural analysis, the nature of these rural communities was grossly misunderstood by the very people who were trying to promote their development and welfare, with the result that these and similar schemes used inappropriate methods to pursue their ends. It seemed worthwhile to try to pass on the knowledge gained from field work to these responsible persons; and I attempted this, without much success, in the account of community organizations (essay 8). This essay shows how the plural framework may be used in applied anthropology.

My analyses of Jamaican society in 1820 and in 1955 had shown the great importance of inequality in educational opportunities for the maintenance of this social structure. In 1958 I was able to examine some aspects of this problem in detail by combining data which Mr. P. C. C. Evans of London University kindly put at my disposal with materials I had gathered in 1955. Together, these surveys revealed the scale and nature of the gap between the desires of Jamaican countryfolk and the realities of their environment (essay 9). The degree of this divergence provides an index of the social malintegration that underlay Jamaican migration and social unrest during this period. At that time, many rural Jamaicans were leaving for Britain, while others were awaiting mystical transport to Africa.[23]

In Grenada during 1952–1953 I had studied a miniature replica of Jamaica at the southern end of the Antilles. Not far away was the tiny island of Carriacou, a dependency of Grenada occupied only by peasants. The better to understand and illuminate the nature of Grenadian society, I decided to study the contrasting society of Carriacou. There I found a homogeneous peasant population which differed sharply in its character and institutions from Grenada. To investigate certain features of their social order I compiled a detailed record of land transfers on a Carriacou settlement over the previous fifty years for comparison with certain features of peasant tenure which Miss Edith Clarke had recently reported in Jamaica.[24] The Carriacou data show how the peasant form of tenure develops as a set of functional adjustments to a very specific context and at a predictable rate. The analysis also shows that this peasant system of tenure is flexible and well adapted to communities with some measure of isolation and internal autonomy. In Jamaica, where the peasantry lack this isolation and autonomy, maladjustments may be common. But unless the peasants' situation changes radically, their system of tenure will persist, even though it diverges sharply from that which the law and the social elite recognize. Since Edith Clarke's paper describes similar conditions in Jamaica, these differing systems of tenure, the legal and the customary, can be regarded as a general feature of West Indian pluralism, and one aspect of the differing modes of property which distinguish its principal sections.

The selection concludes with two essays in political analysis written in 1961. The first of these discusses the context and character of the Grenadian upheavals of 1951–1953, while the other applies the framework of social pluralism to the immediate future of the West Indies. Both analyses have been amply substantiated by subsequent events. In Grenada Mr. Gairy has recently lost control of the legislature, having earlier forfeited his popular support in the industrial field. The West Indies Federation, with which the first and final essays deal, is now a historical episode. I include these political essays because they illustrate how the theory of the plural society applies to the study of current as well as future change. The objection that this framework is merely a static classificatory descriptive device is quite unsound. The reverse is the case. While consensualist analyses of West Indian societies such as British Guiana or the Federation have been falsified by later developments, projections derived from the plural interpretation have been confirmed by these events.[25] Its application to Jamaican developments after Emancipation and to the Grenadian crisis illustrates the dynamic capacity of plural analysis. The concluding paper also shows that this theory provides a serviceable basis for short-range prediction.

Pluralism explicitly enjoins a holistic view of societies and their cultures as units having historical continuity. Too often these historical and cultural dimensions are overlooked by writers who simply assume that all social systems must be integrated by normative consensus, and thereafter discuss only those sociological aspects of the present system which support their initial assumption. Since the basic postulate is probably unverifiable, it may be possible to maintain it only by some such procedures.

In these essays, which seek to test and apply Furnivall's ideas, I hope that I may stimulate their reëxamination, and also that critical reappraisal of consensualist social theory which is so urgently needed and so long overdue. In another book to be published shortly, I shall test these two opposed interpretations of West Indian society against a detailed analysis of social stratification in Grenada.[26] However, various essays in this collection set out the relevant West Indian data and key ideas of pluralism with sufficient detail for the reader to make his own assessment.

I wish to thank the following for their kind permission to reprint the papers listed: the Editors, *Caribbean Quarterly,* for "West Indian Culture" from *Caribbean Quarterly,* Vol. 7, No. 3 (December, 1961); the Secretary-General, International Institute of Differing Civilizations (INCIDI), Brussels, for "Ethnic and Cultural Pluralism in the British Caribbean" from *Ethnic and Cultural Pluralism in Intertropical Countries.* Brussels (1957); the Director, Extra-Mural Department, University College of the West Indies, Jamaica, for "A Framework for Caribbean Studies," *Caribbean Affairs Series* (1955); the Editor-in-Chief, New York Academy of Sciences, and Dr. Vera Rubin, Consultant Editor, for "Social and Cultural Pluralism," from *Social and Cultural Pluralism in the Caribbean,* Annals of The New York Academy of Sciences, Vol. 83, Art. 5 (1960); the Editors, *British Journal of Sociology,* for "The Plural Framework of Jamaican Society" from the *British Journal of Sociology,* Vol. XII, No. 3 (1961); the Editor, *Social and Economic Studies,* Institute of Social and Economic Research, University College of the West Indies, Jamaica, for "Some Aspects of Social Structure in the British Caribbean about 1820," Vol. 1, No. 4 (1953), "Slavery and Emancipation in Two Societies," Vol. 3, No. 3 (1954), "Community Organization in Plural Jamaica," Vol. 5, No. 3 (1956), "The Transformation of Land Rights by Transmission in Carriacou," Vol. 5, No. 2 (1956), "Education and Occupational Choice in Jamaica," Vol. 9, No. 3 (1960), "Short-range Prospects in the British Caribbean," Vol. 11, No. 4 (1962); and Dr. Vera Rubin, Director, Research Institute for the Study of Man, for "Structure and Crisis in Grenada, 1950–1954," background paper for Conference on the Political Sociology of the Caribbean, University College of the West Indies and Research Institute for the Study of Man (December, 1961, unpublished).

I also wish to thank my wife for her help during these years.

M. G. S.

Los Angeles, California

Contents

xix

Contents

[1

West Indian Culture

When people ask "Is there a West Indian culture?" a monosyllabic answer is rarely adequate. If there is a West Indian culture, we can surely define or at least identify it; if there is not, we should at least say what sort of culture West Indians have. It is also worth understanding why the question is raised at all, and what functions answers of either sort may serve. Instead of presenting a cultural inventory stressing provenience of cultural traits, I shall therefore discuss the factors that underlie this question of cultural identity, as well as the nature of this identity itself.

Alfred Mayer has shown that the culture concept first emerged in Germany and Russia as "a typical ideological expression of the rise of backward societies against the encroachments of the West on their traditional culture." [1] Thus the connection between cultural and political nationalism is evident in the history of this idea. After several decades, Sir Edward Tylor adopted the term culture to denote "that complex whole which includes knowledge, belief, art, law, morals, custom, and any other capabilities and habits acquired by man as a member of society." [2] Fifty years later English-speaking anthropologists defined their discipline as the study of culture. Since then, cultural theories and definitions have developed apace. In their recent review of these concepts, A. L. Kroeber and C. Kluckhohn cite 164 statements of somewhat differing emphases, content, and organization. After analyzing these formulas, they conclude that "culture is a product; is historical; includes ideas, patterns, and values; is selective; is learned; is based upon symbols; and is an abstraction from behaviour and the products of behaviour." [3]

There is then no single correct definition of culture, although there is an impressive correspondence among the many academic definitions. The culture concept moreover has two quite distinct functions, each

1

dominant in its own sphere: the ideological and the analytic. Since anthropologists have developed a specialized concept of culture, its meaning for them differs from that generally current; but since social ideas form part of the culture which anthropologists study, they are also concerned with the content, context, and functions of cultural ideologies.

As colonial peoples move to freedom, the connections between their culture and nationalism are important but various. Questions of cultural unity and distinctiveness typically emerge within contexts of nationalist action seeking autonomy. Where cultural diversity within the emerging group is too great to be ignored, several alternatives are available. The nationalist movement may claim the people's loyalty for itself on behalf of the state, as in Ghana; or the major cultural divisions within the emerging group may be given important margins of local autonomy, as in Nigeria. Where the "movement" is interterritorial and the range of cultural diversity is greatest, solidarity may be invoked in racial or metacultural terms. Thus, Pan-Africanism presently pursues African political unity to fulfill "the African personality." Although an important basis for nationalism, cultural unity is not indispensable after all. Race and communism offer adequate ideological alternatives.

Nonetheless, cultural distinctiveness has great values for nationalist movements. For a people emerging from tutelage, cultural distinctiveness may be used to justify demands for independence. Cultural homogeneity may also be used to promote political unity. For these reasons, nationalists often employ an ideology of culture to legitimate their movement—its methods and aims. Critics may make counter-charges of cultural diversity and unrepresentative leadership. The uncommitted public is then caught between two sets of conflicting assertions, and their political adherence depends on the answers they adopt to such questions as "Have we a separate culture? Are we a distinct nation or people?"

These questions are very much in people's minds in the British West Indies today (1960). Their principal spokesmen are politicians, educators, and journalists. "Before the West Indies can emerge as a nation, there must be a common culture. We must be West Indians first, and anything else afterwards." [4] Chaguaramas, selected as the site of the capital of the West Indies Federation, has often been cited as symbolic of West Indian and Trinidadian nationalism. Nationalism itself has few public critics in the West Indies; but the problems that beset federation indicate the uncertainty of many West Indians. Within the federated territories themselves, parallel cleavages are often present. To cite a recent article, "The two leading political parties of Trinidad —the People's National Movement and the Democratic Labour Party

—are accusing each other of preaching and practising racialism in Trinidad." [5] A nationalist movement may therefore flourish amid conditions of racial tension. Since race and nationalism are ideologies, consistency is essential to neither. The nationalist may invoke the nation during racial strife; the racialist may invoke race solidarity on cultural or other grounds.

For many West Indians, the problem of cultural identity is unusually acute. As our poets show, the question is often primarily personal. "What are we?" and "Who am I?" go together in this uncertain context. West Indians may intuitively sense something distinctive about themselves and their culture, without being able to define either satisfactorily. Especially because of their political implications, such definitions are unlikely to win a general consensus. West Indians also recognize the cultural diversity within their own and neighboring territories, without being clear how these differences fit into the larger schemes of national or cultural unity and distinctiveness.

When people ask "Is there a West Indian culture?" the short answer must always be positive. Since culture is a universal human attribute, every local group has a culture. If the group is fairly distinct or has a peculiar habitat, its culture will almost certainly reflect this in some particulars, and even if the group is part of a larger cultural and social unit, it may still be sufficiently distinctive to have its own subculture. Thus we can recognize subcultural variants of the more general British Caribbean culture in St. Kitt's, Barbuda, or Trinidad.

Culture is an abstraction from people's behavior. As an abstraction, the concept is serviceable to anthropologists and ideologues alike. For the anthropologist, its special importance lies in its patterning or regular standardized forms, its transmissibility as a tradition acquired by learning, and its intimate connections with society. As Nadel says, "Society means the totality of social facts projected onto the dimension of relationships and groupings; culture, the same totality in the dimension of action." [6] Like Nadel, Sir Edward Tylor also defined culture in terms of society.

The West Indies now (1960) has a common federal government, and so by one definition the component units form a single society. Yet it is clear that British Guiana and British Honduras, which do not belong to this polity, are culturally West Indian as much as those units that do. The prospect of Jamaica's forthcoming referendum on its federal association underlines this point. Should the Jamaicans vote for withdrawal from the Federation, will they cease to be West Indian?

Within the Caribbean, differences of history and metropolitan affiliation intensify local divisions; Guadeloupe and Martinique are no less West Indian than Barbados and Montserrat, but the two groups differ so sharply in consequence of their historical metropolitan affiliations that it is illusory at this stage to postulate their common cultural or national identity. Even within the British West Indies—to which I shall limit this discussion—important territorial differences reflect the course of history. Jamaica, St. Kitts, Antigua, and Barbardos are predominantly Protestant by virtue of unbroken British rule; St. Lucia, Grenada, Dominica, and Trinidad remain Catholic as their original rulers left them. In Grenada, St. Lucia, and Trinidad the popular dialect is a patois intelligible to Haitians or Martiniquans but quite beyond the Antiguan or Jamaican. The Shango cult is prevalent in some units, absent from others. The same staples, such as breadfruit, are cooked differently in different areas. In a sense, the large East Indian populations which differentiate British Guiana and Trinidad from other British Caribbean units are also historical accidents. Perhaps the specially dense population of Barbados is another.

Being learned, culture is derivative as well as transmissible; being transmitted, it is liable to change, even if this is selective rather than random. Being transmissible, it is not bound to particular society, although intimately involved in social life. Being an abstraction from behavior, it has an elastic reference according to problem and interest. Thus we may speak of West Indian or Trinidadian culture with equal relevance; the greater does not preclude the less, but rather assumes it. Moreover, although a system of patterns, cultures are in the process of change. Contemporary West Indian culture certainly differs from its future as well as its past condition. Its derivation from an earlier phase directs our attention to the history and composition of these societies. The intimate relations between culture as a way of life, and society as the people who live that way, indicate that West Indian culture at any moment is the sum of patterns, behaviors, ideas, and customs characteristic of West Indian societies.

I have already shown that the West Indies Federation in its present form does not correspond with the West Indian area whose common culture is my concern. This illustrates the distinctions between nationalism, political union, and cultural community. Despite the cultural continuities across imperial frontiers, I have also excluded the French, Dutch, American, and Latin units from my present field of interest. Political differences underlie and express the differences of language, history, economic, and social orientation which characterize the Caribbean dependencies of different metropolitan powers. Despite the best will in the world, these factors take precedence over regional coexistence and coöperation. British Guiana and Honduras were both invited to join the West Indies Federation; not so Martinique, Surinam, or Puerto Rico. If we are to answer that thorny question, "Who [or sometimes What] is a West Indian?" without setting any political restriction on the reply, it may well be "Anyone born in the West

Indies or adopting it as his home." Beyond this point we run into differences of citizenship and cultural model.

Properly speaking, we should distinguish here between British, Dutch, French, and other West Indians. It is an unhappy feature of the West Indies Federation that its name suggests it includes all West Indians; no doubt this is an effect of nationalism. By limiting the definition above to British West Indians, I include everyone native to this group of territories who has not transferred allegiance, as by naturalization in the United States, or by permanent emigration. I also include all immigrants who have adopted these territories as their home, whether formally or informally, provided they have developed local loyalties and attachments which take precedence over others elsewhere. These immigrants are subject to no racial restriction. In itself, this is a notable fact. But my definition excludes those immigrants whose primary loyalties to their homelands and native cultures undergo no major change. Such people may be described as expatriates; and within the British West Indies itself there is a sense in which Jamaicans in Trinidad, or Barbadians in Jamaica, may be expatriates; but this is subcultural. Once we have abstracted the distinctive West Indian pattern from their behavior, such intra-Caribbean migrants are distinguished mainly by in-group rather than cultural features.

The British Caribbean culture is one form of Creole culture; the French or Dutch West Indian cultures are other forms. Creoles are natives of the Caribbean; formerly, people born in Louisiana were Creoles also. Creole cultures vary a good deal, but all are sharply distinct from the mestizo cultures of Spanish-Amerindian derivation which dominate Middle America. The Creole complex has its historical base in slavery, plantation systems, and colonialism. Its cultural composition mirrors its racial mixture. European and African elements predominate in fairly standard combinations and relationships. The ideal forms of institutional life, such as government, religion, family and kinship, law, property, education, economy, and language are of European derivation; in consequence, differing metropolitan affiliations produce differing versions of Creole culture. But in their Creole contexts, these institutional forms diverge from their metropolitan models in greater or less degree to fit local conditions.[7] This local adaptation produces a Creole institutional complex which differs from the metropolitan model. Similar institutions function differently in Creole and metropolitan areas. In consequence, despite their shared traditions, Creoles and metropolitans differ culturally in orientations, values, habits and modes of activity. These differences alone would be quite sufficient to distinguish the Creole culture from its metropolitan model. The immigrant who adopts West Indian culture as a way of life "creolizes" in doing so.

The Creole culture, however, also contains many elements of African and slave derivation which are absent from metropolitan models. Perhaps this combination of European and African traditions is the most important feature of Creole life. As we know, slavery defined the initial circumstances of this cultural accommodation. European interests and institutions then predominated, but the functional problems of the slave society required adaptations which promoted a distinctive Creole version of the European parent culture. The African slaves made their own adaptations also, often in contraposition to those slaves born and reared as Creoles. Within this structural complex, the Creole society and culture emerged together, its white rulers having the highest status and their culture the greatest prestige. Things African were correspondingly devalued, including African racial traits. The basis of the "white bias" which characterizes West Indian society is thus cultural rather than racial.

Miscegenation complicated the picture, producing hybrids, some of whom were free and predominantly European in culture, while others were slave, acculturated to the Creole "African" complex. Emancipation removed the legal basis for this extreme form of racial domination; it neither could nor did establish social and cultural homogeneity. The Creole ruling class adapted to the changing conditions as best they could; so did the ex-slaves. The Creole culture area remained defined by the formative situation of African plantation slavery. Within this New World context, Old World cultural forms assumed new features and functions.

Professor and Mrs. Herskovits have shown the importance of African contributions to the Creole cultural complex.[8] "African" elements are observable in language, diet, folklore, family and kinship, property, marketing, medicine, magic and religion, exchange-labor, economic organizations such as the *susu*[9] or "partners."[10] In music, dress, dancing, and domestic life the African contribution is unmistakable. Only rarely however do we find African traits persisting in a pure form; more generally they are overlaid with Creole influences and situations, or they are associated with elements of European origin. Thus, the Shango cult is identified with Christian saints, "African" syntax underlies Creole dialects, and the Sixth and Seventh Books of Moses belong with herbal and animal medicines in the local obeah complex. The complex historical factors involved in this cultural accommodation are illustrated in the long debate about the derivation of Creole Negro family forms. Some scholars argue that the "matrifocal" New World Negro family is traceable to slavery; others admit the influence of slavery on its formation, but point to West African structural parallels. While I recognize the importance of both these historical influences, it seems clear that if we are to understand the persistence of these mating and kinship forms, we have to study them in their present context to determine their structural variability and functional correlates.[11] One reasonable hypothesis is that the structure of Creole society and culture is still sufficiently similar to that of its slave period for many old customs to retain functional value.

Without explicit recognition of this fundamental Negro-white combination within the Creole complex, it is difficult either to specify the distinctive features of West Indian life and culture, or to understand how other ethnic groups and traditions fit into it. This Negro-white complex which has been formative for the West Indies diverges sharply in its racial and cultural components. In this area Negroes outnumber whites markedly, and have done so for centuries; but European institutions and cultural models predominate. The Creole configuration which reflects the particulars of this association is unique because of this imbalance and historical depth. The West Indian-bred white is not culturally European, nor is the West Indian-bred black culturally African. Naturally, in view of its predominance, the European component in Creole culture has undergone less obvious modification than its African counterpart; but that it has been modified, there can be no doubt.

By 1838 the basic framework of West Indian society and culture was fully established. In Jamaica some Jewish elements had been partly assimilated to the British. After Emancipation, planters short of labor sought to import supplies. The greater their scope for economic expansion and their sense of labor shortage, the greater was their demand. Germans, Portuguese, Britons, Chinese, and Indians were imported. A certain number of African slaves liberated by the Royal Navy were also brought in at this time. The greatest scope for plantation operations then lay in Trinidad and British Guiana, and there the immigration was heavy and continuous. A few Indians came to Grenada but no Chinese. Barbados and Carriacou, already overpopulated, exported surplus workers instead of importing them. The economic depression in Jamaica discouraged immigration there, and the few Indians, Chinese, or Europeans brought in as workers presented no major problems. Naturally the immigrants sought to withdraw from their onerous situation as best they could. In Jamaica the Chinese rapidly acquired control of the grocery trade; the East Indians, although more numerous, have been less successful; the white immigrant laborers withdrew into rural enclaves, closed endogamous units, or, if Portuguese, into commercial urban activities. In Trinidad and British Guiana, where Indian immigration continued for decades on a substantial scale, the immigrants were concentrated on plantations in conditions which ensured social and ethnic isolation.

The cultural framework of Creole society governed the accommoda-

tion of these immigrant groups. The Creole cultural and social organization was a graduated hierarchy of European and African elements, crudely visualized in a white-black color scale. To participate
adequately in this system, immigrants had to learn the elements of
Creole life. This degree to which they adopted European cultural
forms set the upper limits of their place in the social hierarchy. On
their arrival, the indentured workers were therefore marginal to Creole
society in much the same way as the Dominican Caribs, Honduran
Maya, and Guianese Amerindians are marginal today. Being marginal,
the immigrants were free to abstain from Creole activities or to take
part in them. If participating, they were also theoretically free to enter
the Creole hierarchy at points of their own choice, providing only that
they manipulated the requisite cultural skills and had the necessary
economic backing. Being neither white nor black, both the Indians
and the Chinese escaped placement in the Creole color scale which
crudely equated race and culture. This position itself indicates their
marginal status in the Creole society not so long ago. Being white, the
European indentured laborers found themselves in an especially difficult situation, equated with Negro peasants economically and socially,
but with the white planter class in race and culture. It is therefore
quite understandable that they withdrew from this contradictory
structural context into the closed communities in which they presently
live. The variable degrees of acculturation and assimilation among
Chinese and Indian immigrants illustrate their opportunities and
attendant problems. The Jamaican Chinese exhibit different patterns
of assimilation from those in British Guiana.[12] For the large Indian
populations of British Guiana and Trinidad, the prospect of creolization—that is, the adoption of Creole culture and assimilation to Creole
society—still presents a number of problems, including the probable
loss of their Indian heritage and group solidarity. In British Guiana
the Indian population occupies an especially difficult position;
although the largest racial group, it had no clear alternative to becoming Creole. Under slavery the African majority were in a somewhat
similar situation. The current racial tensions of Guiana or Trinidad
may thus express changes presently under way as the Indians resolve
the problems presented by creolization, while the Creoles resolve the
problems of accommodating these Indian groups.

It is only with this multiracial Creole complex that West Indians can
identify as West Indians. Whatever their racial affiliation, self-declared
West Indians implicitly refer to this amalgam in which the basic racial
and cultural elements are white and Negro, and society is that mode of
their association to which important elements from other traditions are
selectively accommodated. The Lebanese colony in Jamaica merely
demonstrates this analysis; arriving late, they rapidly won a major

share of the trade in consumer goods. A generation ago, this group was distinguished from others as "Syrian"; today they are simply "Jamaican," partly assimilated to the urban upper class while remaining mainly endogamous. As indicated above, the Jamaican Jews went through a similar process long ago.

If my argument is correct, the characteristic West Indian complex combines two basic traditions, each of which is quite distinct and may persist more or less separately within the population. This is another way of saying that acculturation to the dominant Creole-European tradition varies widely among Creoles as well as immigrant groups. The problems presented by this cultural diversity are of special importance to student and nationalist alike, especially because the subordinate cultural tradition is that of the majority of the population whose social status and life chances differ radically from the minority acculturated to Creole "Europeanism." For the student, the demographic disbalance coupled with this cultural division presents important problems and conditions. For the nationalist, who is usually a member of the numerical minority, the issues are immediate and compelling.

People who are uncertain of their cultural or national status are unlikely to be clear about "national" cultural goals. To many West Indians of low status and predominantly "African" Creole culture, nationalism may have the initial appeal of promising full citizenship; if it does not deliver this, it will cease to retain their support and may be cynically regarded as of benefit primarily to the "middle class." Granted the social and cultural cleavages that are characteristic of Creole society, and the numerous factors that continuously reinforce them, "national" unity may be scarce, even within the Negro-white population, much less between this group and later immigrants. If this is so within separate territories, difficulties at the regional level can be expected. The common culture, without which West Indian nationalism cannot develop the dynamic to create a West Indian nation, may by its very nature and composition preclude the nationalism that invokes it. This is merely another way of saying that the Creole culture which West Indians share is the basis of their division. Hence present interest in the questions: "Is there a West Indian culture? What is it?"

[2

Ethnic and Cultural Pluralism in the British Caribbean

The British Caribbean consists of Jamaica, the Leeward Islands (St. Kitts, Nevis, Antigua, Montserrat, and the British Virgin Islands), the Windward Islands (St. Vincent, St. Lucia, Dominica, Grenada), Barbados, Trinidad, and Tobago, British Honduras in North America and British Guiana in South America. Except for these last two colonies, the remaining British Caribbean possessions are islands of the Antillean archipelago. Jamaica is over a thousand miles from Trinidad, and more than 500 miles east of British Honduras; British Guiana is larger in area than all the remaining units put together. Jamaica, with a population of one-and-a-half million, accounts for about 47 per cent of the total British Caribbean population. Despite such differences and distances, these colonies have much in common, historically and at present. They also differ among themselves in various ways.

The islands are overpopulated, while the two mainland territories contain large unsettled areas. All these territories depend on agriculture, and their urban ratios are relatively low. Industrialization is just beginning in Jamaica and Trinidad, nationalism has been slow to develop, and separatism is as pronounced within the colonies as between them. These territories are all depressingly poor, and despite their long histories of capital investment, they are still typical underdeveloped countries.

These societies are all multiracial. Except in the mainland territories, they contain no significant indigenous elements. Their present populations are descended from immigrants from the Old World: Europeans, Africans, Chinese, Indians, Lebanese, and others. Most of Caribbean history consists in the development of these areas by competing European nations through the exploitation of African labor, initially im-

10

ported as slaves. Negro-white associations have produced a large hybrid group which is culturally, as well as biologically, mixed. The approximate racial compositions of the various colonial populations in 1946 are given in table 1.

TABLE 1

APPROXIMATE RACIAL COMPOSITIONS OF VARIOUS
COLONIAL POPULATIONS, 1946
(Unit = per cent)

Territory	White	Black	Colored	East-Indian	Amer-indian	Chinese	Other
Jamaica.........	1	78	17.5	2	—	1	0.5
Barbados........	5	77	18	—	—	—	—
Br. Guiana.......	3	38.1	10	43.5	4.3	1	—
Br. Honduras.....	3.9	38	31.8	2.3	17	—	7*
Antigua.........	2	85	13	—	—	—	—
Montserrat.......	0.5	93	6.4	—	—	—	—
St. Kitts.........	2	86.5	11	—	—	—	—
Virgin Is.........	0.5	87.2	12.3	—	—	—	—
Trinidad.........	2.7	46.8	14.1	35.1	—	1	—
Dominica........	0.3	24.9	74.6	—	—	—	—
Grenada.........	0.9	73.6	20.4	4.8	—	—	—
St. Lucia........	0.5	58.1	37.6	3.8	—	—	—
St. Vincent......	3.1	73.1	20.5	3	—	—	—

* Black Caribs.

These percentages are based on the West Indian census of 1946 and reveal some of the ambiguities inherent in racial classification. Seventy-four per cent of the Dominican population, 37 per cent of the St. Lucian population, and 31 per cent of the British Hondurian population are classified as "colored." The reported racial composition of these colonies differs from that in the remaining territories; but to the best of our knowledge such figures do not connote genuine differences in the composition of these populations.

On the other hand, the East Indian ratios set out above do reflect genuine and very significant differences. It is commonly believed that East Indians now form about 50 per cent of the British Guianese population, and that they are rapidly approaching numerical parity with the Negroid groups of Trinidad. Some people see the recent political split between Dr. Cheddi Jagan and Mr. L. F. Burnham of British Guiana as essentially racial in character; both men were ministers in the short-lived government of the People's Progressive Party, the first government to be returned in British Guiana on a basis of universal suffrage. Jagan's strength lies with his East Indians, Burnham's with the black and colored groups. In Trinidad also, the East Indian population tends to have its own political organization, but the religious split between Hindus and Muslims has deprived it of unanimity. The refusal of British Guiana to join the British Caribbean Federation, and past hesitancy of Trinidad on this issue, together with the restrictions on immigration to Trinidad from the other colonies, have both been interpreted in other colonies as being due to East Indian political pressure. (The division between East Indians and Negro-colored elements in the populations of British Guiana and Trinidad is deeper and sharper than divisions between the Negro, white, and colored populations elsewhere. This may in part be associated with the lack of Indian-Negro miscegenation and the absence of any interstitial group.)

The heavy concentration of East Indians in British Guiana and Trinidad is an effect of the large-scale importations of indentured Indian labor to these colonies after the abolition of slavery in 1838. This in turn reflected the labor shortage suffered by planters in Trinidad and British Guiana at that time. In its turn, this labor shortage was an effect of the prohibition of the Atlantic slave trade and of intra-Caribbean slave movements by Britain shortly after she had acquired these fertile territories with their great sugar-producing capacities. Older colonies with played-out land, less profitable sugar production, and larger populations, neither needed nor were able to afford such large-scale labor imports as British Guiana and Trinidad; but as an effect of their differing historical situations, the contemporary social structures of the British West Indian colonies differ significantly as regards their East Indian components. Indian-organized schools now receive government aid in Trinidad, and the Hindu and Mohammedan religions are being increasingly recognized, for example, in matters of marriage. Little research has yet been done on these substantial East Indian populations, but it is known that Hindustani is spoken among them, and that the majority of these East Indians remain loyal to Indian culture and Indian nationalism. These loyalties are related to the slow growth of a Caribbean national sentiment.

The colonial ruling classes and traditions are also diverse. Trinidad, St. Lucia, Grenada, and Dominica have Catholic affiliations as evidence of past association with France and Spain. In these four colonies a French dialect, known as *patois*, is commonly used among the folk. In areas of continuous British rule, the dialect is based on English. The Roman-Dutch law of British Guiana is a relic of that country's old Dutch connection; in Trinidad, the European cultural section contains Spanish, French, and British elements, and the dominant white culture is a composite of these three traditions. Where Protestantism has been historically dominant, as in Jamaica, Barbados, St. Kitts, St. Vincent, and Antigua, aesthetically rich religious syncretisms such as Shango are absent; and Revivalism or Shakerism (Shouting Baptists) is the characteristic folk ritual form.

Small groups of Chinese, Portuguese, Syrians, and Jews are to be found in several of these territories, where they act as specialized occupational groups. Generally, they compete with one another for different sections of the retail and wholesale trade, and in Jamaica, Jews have long been prominent in the legal profession. Where East Indians are found in small numbers, they are assimilated to the black lower class and do not form a separate ethnic group. The Amerindians of British Guiana, British Honduras, and Dominica are not yet significant parts of these colonial populations, but are mainly administered on reservations.

In Trinidad and British Guiana, the East Indian segment is clearly differentiated from the remaining population. In the remaining colonies the whites, Negroes, and colored form a standard combination. This association of white, Negro, and colored groups is the historically primary and structurally dominant grouping in the British Caribbean. Despite the racial and cultural polarities within this Negro-white amalgam, miscegenation, acculturation, and assimilation have established a single continuum in racial, cultural, and social terms. The work of Professor Melville Herskovits and his colleagues in the study of Afro-American acculturation provides ample evidence of this cultural continuity; the racial distributions reported by the 1946 West Indian census indicate the extent of racial mixture; and the absence of any race or caste regulations indicates the permissive local attitude toward assimilation.

Nonetheless, there are significant cultural and social differences within this Negro-white combination. Jurors tend to be drawn from the propertied groups, and these tend to be of lighter pigmentation. Primary schools cater to the laboring classes, and these in turn tend to be mainly black. Family forms and mating patterns of the lower class differ remarkably from those of the white or colored elites, and so do lower-class religion, property forms, material culture, occupations, and economic organization.

People born within the West Indies are called "Creoles"; but East Indians are usually excluded from this reference. Thus Creoles are really persons of Negro, white, or mixed Negro-white ancestry who are natives of the Caribbean. Persons of Indian descent are described as "East Indian" (sic) or "coolies." Minorities such as the Chinese, that maintain their exclusive identity, are likewise distinguished from the Creole group, and are referred to in national terms.

It is possible to interpret the historical association between Africans and Europeans in the West Indies as an instance of symbiosis, but between West Indians of African or mixed stock and those of Indian ancestry, competition rather than symbiosis has hitherto prevailed.

To recapitulate, all these British Caribbean territories have a com-

mon Negro-white racial and cultural basis. In Trinidad and British
Guiana an Indian segment is also present, and in some of the colonies
there are also minorities of Jews, Syrians, or Chinese. Comparative
treatment of these different social and cultural amalgams directs attention to the differences between ethnic and cultural pluralism. Ethnicity
has a number of overlapping but different references, namely, racial
origin, nationality, language, and culture. These references invest the
idea of ethnic pluralism with an initial ambiguity. In contrast, the
idea of cultural pluralism is quite clear. I shall therefore discuss the
idea of cultural plurality before returning to the concept of ethnicity as
such.

By cultural plurality I understand a condition in which two or more
different cultural traditions characterize the population of a given
society. To discover whether or not this heterogeneity obtains, we must
make a detailed study of the institutions of the population in which we
are interested to discover their form, variety, and distribution. In a
culturally homogeneous society, such institutions as marriage, the
family, religion, property, and the like, are common to the total population. Where cultural plurality obtains, different sections of the total
population practice different forms of these common institutions; and,
because institutions involve patterned activities, social relations, and
idea-systems, in a condition of cultural plurality, the culturally differentiated sections will differ in their internal social organization, their
institutional activities, and their system of belief and value. Where this
condition of cultural plurality is found, the societies are plural societies. Where cultural homogeneity obtains, the societies are homogeneous units.

By virtue of their cultural and social constitution, plural societies
are only units in a political sense. Each is a political unit simply because
it has a single government. But the task of government can only be
discharged consistently within culturally diverse populations if one or
other of these sections dominates the political structure, or if some
form of federalism is adopted. In either case, the political structure of
plural societies consists largely of the relations between their component cultural sections, and changes in this system of intersectional
relations occur together with changes in the political constitution of
the unit as a whole. Democratic governmental forms appropriate to
plural societies are usually federal. Autocratic governmental forms
reserve the ultimate political functions for one or other of the constituent cultural sections, even where some sections are separated territorially—for instance on reservations—and are allowed some internal
autonomy. But some uniformity of laws and government is essential if
the society is to remain a political unit at all. Excluding government
and law, the institutional differences that indicate cultural plurality

relate to marriage, family, education, property, religion, economic institutions, language, and folklore. In all these particulars, there are differences within the Negro-white Caribbean community which indicate a condition of cultural plurality. Between the East Indian and Negro-white Creole segment, the cultural difference is still greater.

The idea of ethnic difference is less precise than that of cultural plurality. In some usages of the term, ethnicity refers to race, in others to culture, and in yet others to nationality. The first thing to note is that persons or groups of different races may share a common culture, as in the Mohammedan Hausa-Fulani societies of Northern Nigeria. Conversely, people of the same race may practice different cultures, as in the London of Disraeli, Dickens, and Mayhew, or in the many villages of India. Another important point is that as a rule, the social definition of race differs from the biological definition; moreover different societies may define the same racial groups differently. Thus the population of Guatemala distinguishes between its Spanish, mixed (Ladino), and Indian elements; but to some students these Ladino and Indian groups are racially similar. Similarly, the elite of Haiti reserve the term *Negre* for the subordinate population; but to the Americans, Haitians are Negro by race.

In the United States for instance, ethnicity connotes cultural differences that are quite compatible with the inclusive social order, either because they are differences within a common idiom or a permitted range, or because the groups which practice these variant cultures are numerically weak, and are dependent portions of the larger society. Insofar as nationality is the criterion of ethnicity, some cultural or linguistic difference is often implicit; but once again these differences may be minor variations on general cultural patterns, as for instance family organization, marriage rituals, language, and food habits among the Irish or Italians of New York. Bilingualism and acculturation of these groups is indicated by such terms as Irish-American, Italian-American, and the like. These cultural variations are thus neither inconsistent with one another nor with the wider American society and culture.

If compatibility of institutional norms characterizes ethnic pluralism, their incompatibility may be taken to distinguish cultural pluralism. Societies depend for integration primarily on the consistency and interdependence of their institutional systems. Hence special problems face a society that contains groups with incompatible institutional allegiances. These problems are most acute when a small ruling group has one cultural tradition and the mass of the population has another. This is the type-situation of British Caribbean history.

In discussing population composition I think race and nationality are appropriate terms. In discussing the cultural homogeneity or plurality of a given population, I think culture is the appropriate term. Where linguistic differences are under study, we can speak of linguistic groups. By isolating these variables and by referring to them directly, we avoid the need for ambiguous concepts, such as ethnicity, and can study the processes and forms of acculturation and assimilation as they occur.

In societies such as those of the British Caribbean which have long histories of acculturation, assimilation, and miscegenation, the concept of ethnicity has doubtful utility, even with regard to such minorities as Jews, Syrians, Portuguese, or Chinese. These are national minorities, and their further classification in terms of race or culture depends unambiguously on our definition of these terms. In analyzing the Negro-white Creole amalgam, we must deal directly with race, culture, and social relations, and seek to determine their covariation or independence. Relations between the East Indian and Creole segments of Trinidad and British Guiana can also be analyzed in these terms. Essentially we are concerned to understand the cultural character and social structure of multiracial populations, which may or may not contain national minorities also. It is difficult to conduct precise studies of these problems with such ambiguous concepts as ethnicity.

Government and the economic system are the two principal sources of social order in the Caribbean. Government acts to limit the chances of conflict, and to limit, maintain, or increase the opportunities for acculturation; the economic system embraces the entire population, although in different degrees and ways. In the first place, the peasantry practices a mixed economy of subsistence and exchange; the townsfolk are mainly involved in the exchange system. In the second place there is division of labor by race and cultural group. By and large East Indians form the bulk of the field-labor force on sugar plantations in Trinidad and British Guiana, Negroes in other colonies. Colored people are heavily represented in clerical occupations, whites in management and executive roles. The professions and the higher ranks of the local civil service now contain members of all racial groups. In occupational distributions, it is the fact of cultural performance and skill that is decisive rather than racial status; and the historic and continuing inequality of opportunities primarily attaches to cultural sections rather than to racial groups as such. Although most field hands are black, many are brown, and some are white. Although most executives are white, many are brown, and some are pure Negro. For analytic purposes the ratios of different racial groups in the same or different occupations do not tell the whole story, since none of these racial segments is culturally homogeneous.

One major preoccupation of plural societies is the choice between eliminating or maintaining their internal differences; and the social and cultural integration of such units is often mooted in terms of this choice. In the history of the British Caribbean possessions, drastic attempts to solve this riddle of integration have been made on three occasions.

In 1838 the abolition of slavery "freed a race, but failed to create a society." The numerically minute but politically dominant white planter class which then opposed Abolition, despite its experience that slave production of sugar was no longer economic, feared that social chaos would follow emancipation. With the aid of restrictive property franchises, this white cultural section retained control of the colonial governments for another thirty years, until the sense of their own weakness influenced them to surrender the reins of authority to the Crown and its officers. In Jamaica, this abrogation of the ancient representative constitution took place in 1865, and was openly heralded as the only alternative to a breakdown in the social structure.

Since 1945 this system of Crown Colony rule has been replaced by responsible government based on adult suffrage and operating through ministerial systems. Political parties and trade unions are now recognized institutions, and have flourished under the new regime. At the same time, the idea of a British Caribbean Federation has been actively publicized, and, with the exception of British Guiana, British Honduras, and the British Virgin Islands, these colonies have committed themselves to federation. Yet the chances are that such a federal structure will slow down the rate of change within each of its constituent territories, rather than accelerate it.

[3

A Framework for Caribbean Studies

Systematic social study of the British West Indies is a recent development, hence the slenderness of its sociological literature, and its dependent character. This dependent character reflects the fact that hitherto most of the researches in this area have been conducted by visiting social scientists from the United States or Britain, and have been guided by theories and themes of interest developed in studies of societies and cultures outside the British Caribbean. The resultant diversity of approaches has undoubted value for the systematic study of British West Indian society, as this diversity directs attention to a wide range of problems and aspects of local life. On the other hand, these researches have an *ad hoc,* exploratory character, and require careful sifting and collation if they are to form the background of a systematic program of area studies. Yet it is patent that to build soundly and quickly, we must use the old foundations, testing them first, and then assimilating all that proves useful and valid into the newer structure. The present paper is intended as a partial contribution toward that task.

It has not been entirely fortuitous that social studies of the British Caribbean reflect theories and themes of interest developed in the study of societies outside this area. This derivative character of Caribbean sociology partly reflects the comparative character of social science in general, and partly the fact that the British Caribbean has many elements and patterns which have been found and studied in a wider area. It is therefore necessary to consider those studies conducted within this wider area that have special significance for social research in the British Caribbean.

From the outset, Caribbean research is faced with problems of frames of reference. These are implicit in the dual bases of affiliation already mentioned. In the first place we have to face the problem of the

18

appropriate geographical frame of reference for such studies; that is to say, we shall have to delimit the area which forms the natural comparative context of Caribbean social research, and to define its most important characters. In the second place, we have to develop a system of concepts, orientations, and hypotheses, that is, a theory, which can act as an appropriate frame of reference for research in this area. In building this framework of theory, there is an obvious advantage in reviewing those studies carried out within the appropriate geographical frame of reference which have the most direct relevance for Caribbean research. We must begin therefore by delimiting the geographical frame of special comparative value to Caribbean studies, directing attention to its more significant features from our point of view. We shall then have to consider the various bodies of research and theory developed within this wider area which are of most importance in the present stage of Caribbean studies. On the basis of such a review of the literature, we shall then attempt to indicate the type of theoretical frame which seems appropriate for Caribbean social research.

Context

General historical processes define the regions from Brazil to the United States as the wider context of direct relevance for Caribbean area studies. This does not mean that all, or even the major part of, research into social and cultural conditions in this wider area possesses significance for the understanding of West Indian problems, but only that some studies in this wider area have already had considerable influence on Caribbean research by virtue of their local relevance, quite apart from their more general theoretical or methodological interests. This type of thing can be expected to continue.

The historical conditions that define the area from Brazil to the United States as the broad comparative context of Caribbean studies are well known. They consist in the expansion of Europe to the New World, the common historical patterns of conquest, colonization, peonage, or slavery, and the development of multiracial and multicultural societies throughout this area. Regional differences of a contemporary or historical nature are of obvious significance for comparative work within so vast a frame of reference. For present purposes the differences of habitat, economy, population composition, political history, and status are the most useful general guides in a preliminary subdivision of this wider area.

The Northern United States forms one region with an overwhelmingly high proportion of whites to Negroes in its population, a temperate continental habitat, high degrees of urbanization and industrialization, independent political status, and Anglo-Saxon Protestant affiliation. The Southern United States forms another region, having a higher ratio of Negroes in its population, lower degrees of urbanization and industrialization, greater reliance on agriculture, a subtropical habitat, and a political history and status differentiated from that of the North in certain respects, notably, by its defeat in the American Civil War of 1861–1865.

The Middle American states of Mexico, Guatemala, Honduras, Costa Rica, Nicaragua, Panama, Columbia, and Venezuela can be treated as a group having certain common characteristics, namely, populations composed principally of whites and Amerindian elements with minor representation of Negroes; tropical, continental habitats; low degrees of urbanization and industrialization; economies based on agriculture and mining; independent political systems of similar types; and Spanish and Catholic affiliations.

Cuba and Puerto Rico resemble these Middle American republics in certain features while differing in others. These two islands have been in closer association with the United States than the mainland countries, and occupy a politically independent position. They are also distinguished from the mainland republics by the absence of significant Amerindian elements from their population, and by the presence of Negroes in some numbers, although clearly as minority groups.

Haiti differs from other provinces in this geographical frame especially in its combination of French Catholic affiliation, political independence achieved long ago through a revolt of slave and free colored, the absence of whites and Amerindians from the native population, and its recent political association with the United States. Other Haitian characteristics include low urbanization, low industrialization, tropical habitat, an agricultural economy, and the island-wide border with its neighbor, the Dominican Republic, which resembles the Central American republics in certain respects.

Within the vast subcontinent of Brazil, as in the United States, several regional subtypes are distinguishable.[1] These regional differences primarily reflect significant variations of climate and habitat, racial population distributions, urbanization, industrialization, and agriculture. A general description of that country in terms of our present interest would note the white majority in its population, the variable racial distributions with Indian elements predominating over Negroes in the interior, while Negroes are numerous in such coastal areas as Maranhão, Bahia, and São Paulo. The political independence and Portuguese Catholic affiliation of Brazil are also distinctive as a combination of characters within this region.

This brings us to the Caribbean area proper, a region characterized by political dependency, and consisting mainly of small island territories, within which Amerindians are little represented, white elements form a numerical minority, and the overwhelming majority of the populations are of Negro descent. A general summary of this kind at once calls attention to diversity within this area. We have somewhat arbitrarily separated Haiti, the Dominican Republic, Cuba, and Puerto Rico from the rest of the Caribbean because of their distinguishing characteristics. Even so, our Caribbean area as it stands includes British Honduras, and the Guianas—British, French, and Dutch—all of which are continental territories with significant Amerindian elements in their population. Trinidad and British Guiana are also distinguished from the remaining British territories in the area by the presence of large East Indian populations. Surinam differs from other Caribbean colonies partly in its more varied ethnic composition, partly through the recent constitutional changes which have accorded that country an increased share in the management of its internal affairs.

The past and present associations of Caribbean territories with different metropolitan powers are clearly important for comparative work within the area. Present effects of previous association rule out the treatment of this aspect of Caribbean differentiation solely in terms of the contemporary distribution of territories among British, Americans, French, or Dutch. American St. Thomas still reveals the influences of its former masters, the Danes. Within the British Caribbean, islands such as Trinidad, Grenada, Dominica, and St. Lucia differ as a group from certain other territories by their continuing affiliation to Catholic tradition, a pattern laid down in earlier days by French or Spanish masters. The St. Lucia folk probably have more in common linguistically with French colonies such as Martinique or Guadeloupe, or with the former French possession, Haiti, than with islands such as Barbados or Antigua. If we attempt to classify Caribbean colonies in terms of their present association with metropolitan powers, we must therefore keep in mind present cultural variations and continuities within and across these divisions which reflect historical factors of various kinds. Within the British colonies, the main distinctions reflect differences of racial population ratios and composition, Protestant or Catholic affiliation, insularity, or its opposite. Together with the Caribbean colonies of other nations, these British territories share a multiracial composition from which Amerindian elements are largely absent, dependence on agriculture, low levels of industrialization, and low urban ratios.

It is clear that whatever the common patterns the British West Indies share with other Caribbean territories, or with countries outside this Caribbean region, these British colonies nonetheless form a separate area for social research, on the ground of their present political relations as well as history. Yet the patterns common to these British territories and other countries of the wider area delimited above are often of an order which cannot be ignored in the definition of Caribbean research problems except at one's peril. Perhaps within the geographical frame described above, the Middle American republics, with their Spanish and Amerindian populations, political independence, continental situation, and low population densities, have least in common with the British colonies. Yet it is clear that conditions in these countries provide useful comparisons with those of the British area, the populations of which differ from them in history as well as composition. The comparison of British Caribbean and Middle American conditions illuminates the study of either milieu separately by stimulating a variety of questions, hypotheses, and lines of investigation. Without delaying over this point unduly, we may mention such questions as the following which invite this comparison: what continuities of social structure obtain in multiracial societies which vary in their individual racial constitution as these do? With what structural variations does this continuity coexist? What differences are associated with the fact that on the one hand the subordinate race was settled in the area, while it was brought into it on the other? Or with the parallel fact that the dominant group settled in the one area, and tended to remain expatriate within the other? Or with the fact that subordination involved slavery in one case, and peonage in the other? Or with the development of plantation economies in one set of societies, and their absence in the other? Or in the different Catholic and Protestant traditions of the two areas? Or in their different political histories and conditions? It will be clear that Caribbean studies may gain greatly from adopting initial orientations which include these and parallel problems within a single comparative frame.

Racial and cultural intermixture and blending have gone on in both these Indian-white and Negro-white populations. Among the peoples of Middle America, this has given rise to a section of the population known as *mestizos* (mixed-bloods), or, in Guatemala, as Ladinos. Within the Caribbean islands, it has produced a hybrid group of mixed heritage and color. The same applies broadly to the United States and Brazil. What then are the similarities and differences of relations between these racially and culturally differentiated groups in the various societies of our comparative frame? What significant implications do these continuities and variations present for social research in the British territories? At what levels are they expressed, in what ways, in terms of what structures, and with what variable types of function? These are only a few of the problems which arise when Caribbean research is conceived in its natural comparative context.

Linkages between Caribbean studies and researches conducted within the broad geographical frame delimited above will become clear from a brief survey of such work over the past thirty years. We can date the development of current sociological interest in the British West Indies from 1924 when Martha Beckwith's first studies of folklore and life in Jamaica were published.[2] Two years later Puckett, from the same American university, published his definitive study of folk beliefs among the Negroes of Alabama, Mississippi, and Louisiana.[3] During these years also Nina Rodrigues and Arthur Ramos in Brazil, and Melville and Frances Herskovits in the United States, were being led from initial studies of the folklore and physical characteristics of Negro populations of their respective societies into the broader problems of Negro contributions to Brazilian and American culture, and their adaptation to these environments.[4] Herskovits' interest in this research field was greatly stimulated by an early visit with his wife to Surinam.[5] The broad problem of acculturation which Ramos and Herskovits formulated was approached by Redfield working among the Maya of Yucatan, from a different point of view, and led to the formulation of his dichotomy between folk and urban societies.[6] Within the United States studies of the assimilation of American Negroes by Franklin Frazier and Lloyd Warner were under way; and these approaches have also influenced research by later workers in other regions of our geographical area.[7]

Although Dollard's examination of caste and class in a Southern town of the United States acknowledges a debt to Warner and his school, it also marked a significant departure from previous research in this field by its thorough application of psychological analysis to the social conditions and relations in the community which he studied.[8] This psychological approach was also combined with an interest in cultural forms and development by Powdermaker in her independent study of the same community.[9] Psychological studies and interpretations of West Indian societies have since been published by Campbell, Simey, Hadley, Kruijer, Cohen, Rhoda Metraux, and Madeline Kerr.[10] Meanwhile those interested in the administrative and political aspects of Caribbean society were attracted by W. M. Macmillan's concise account, and were moved by the riots and strikes of 1937–1938 to reconsider the colonial situation, and to develop new policies and programs.[11] Since the end of the Second World War, there has been a sharp increase in the volume of social research in the British Caribbean, which has now come to be recognized as a separate unit for a program of area research. Clearly the guiding ideas of future studies will reflect the interests and approaches already developed in greater or less degree; and it is to the separate consideration of these relevant orientations severally that we must now turn our attention.

Afro-American Research

Afro-American research merits consideration first, not merely because it was the first major development with a direct Caribbean reference but also because it has been largely developed on the basis of materials from Caribbean societies, and therefore has a direct and obvious relevance for us. Afro-American studies owe a very great deal to Professor Herskovits, who has not been content to study African survivals in the New World, but has also sought to fill gaps in the ethnographic knowledge of parent societies on the West Coast of Africa by his own field work. Sociological literature on the Caribbean has also been enriched greatly by the accounts of Melville Herskovits and his wife of their field-work in Surinam, Trinidad, and Haiti; and by other researches of like orientation, falling within this area or its broader context.[12]

Briefly, Afro-American researches consist in the study of changes or persistence of African traditions and cultural forms that have marked the historical association between whites and persons of African origin or descent in the Americas. Culture here connotes the total body of learned and transmitted behavior that characterizes a population and distinguishes it from others. Thus Afro-American research is focused on the problem of "acculturation"; or cultural change in a situation of contacts between carriers of different cultures. In particular, such research studies the processes by which the African immigrants and their descendants have retained, lost, or adapted elements of their initial African cultures within the contact situation provided by association with whites in the New World. The method employed in pursuit of this inquiry is a combination of history and ethnology; and the general object is to contribute to the study of cultural persistence and change by unraveling some of the factors and processes of acculturation, through detailed studies of Negro-white contacts in the New World.

Now clearly the determination of results of this culture-contact must precede the investigation of the processes by which these effects developed. Hence, Afro-American research is initially concerned with an examination of contemporary Afro-American cultures to discover survivals, retentions, syncretisms, or reinterpretations of African cultural elements obtaining within them. As the results of such examination accumulate, they also raise problems about the processes of acculturation, especially with regard to the differential survival of African cultural elements of various kinds, and in differing environments. A useful tool developed to facilitate such comparative analysis is the concept of *a scale of intensity of Africanisms,* which permits a classificatory comparison of New World cultures from Brazil to the United States, distinguishing between Africanisms in economic, social, religious, and aesthetic life.[13] Such a scale shows a greater concentration of Africanisms in such fields as folklore, music, and religion, than in technology and economic life; but there is a notable absence of political and governmental institutions from this catalogue of Africanisms. The differential intensity of Africanisms in these various fields invites some explanation. This analysis is undertaken with the aid of various hypotheses and concepts, the most important of which distinguishes the focal aspects of cultures as those most tenacious in situations of contact, and of greatest interest to the populations concerned, and conceives of cultural persistence in terms of survivals or retentions on the one hand, syncretism and reinterpretation on the other. *Survivals* have greatest direct resemblance to original forms. *Syncretisms* involve a combination of parallel forms from the cultures in contact; while *reinterpretations* adhere to the substance or content of the original culture, although departing from its initial forms. Finally the concept of *cultural imponderables* connotes that category of Africanisms which are clearly not included in the *cultural focus,* but nonetheless have a high level of intensity in New World populations. It appears that values and automatic motor patterns constitute the bulk of these surviving cultural imponderables. Within this frame of research the ethnohistorical method has hitherto been employed principally to determine the cultural provenience from which Africans were recruited for the various New World slave-states, and the types of condition to which they were subjected under the slave regime. In the attack on problems of differential intensities of Africanisms, that is, the variable effects and processes of acculturation, the ethnohistorical method has played a less prominent part than the development of the hypotheses and concepts just mentioned.

This seems to constitute one of the major weaknesses of current Afro-American studies. Instead of undertaking the examination of those *processes* of acculturation which form the stated object of such research by the more vigorous employment of the ethnohistorical method which documentary materials, autobiographical, and other studies permit, with a view to the unraveling of detailed processes in limited fields, the tendency has been rather to develop and systematize a set of concepts which, taken together, obscure the problems of process rather than otherwise. We can illustrate some aspects of this weakness by a brief examination of these concepts and their interrelations, ignoring for the moment questions of variable distributions of African elements within the populations concerned, or the nature of Africanisms as such.

The scale of intensity of Africanisms shows a variable tenacity of African cultural elements distinguished in terms of technology, economy, social organization, nonkinship institutions, religion, magic, art, folklore, music, and language. The problem of variation in these different fields leads, after a discussion of syncretism, retention, and reinterpretation, to the following formulation by Herskovits:

Even under the compulsions of the dominant culture of the Whites, Negroes have retained African religious beliefs and practices far more than they have retained economic patterns. But when we examine the patterns of African cultures, we find that there is no activity of everyday living but that it is validated by supernatural sanctions. And consequently, these figure far more in the total life of the people than does any other single fact of the culture such as those matters having to do with making a living, or family structure, or political institutions. This weighting of the concerns of a people constitutes the focus of their culture. . . . The role of cultural focus is of such great importance in situations of cultural contact that a further hypothesis may be advanced to the effect that more elements which lie in the area of focus of a receiving culture will be retained than those appertaining to other aspects of the culture, acceptance being greater in those phases of culture further removed from the focal area. Where a culture is under pressure by a dominant group who seek to induce acceptance of its traditions, elements lying in the focal area will be retained longer than those outside it, though in this case retention will of necessity be manifested in syncretisms and reinterpretations.[14]

We can summarize the relations between the conceptual system and the scale of intensity in the following terms: greatest intensity of cultural survivals occurs in the area of cultural focus, if cultural imponderables are excluded. The cultural focus is the area of greatest tenacity in cultural retentions; consequently, assuming equal pressures on all fields of cultural activity from outside, it will show the highest degrees of purity in these retentions, and will also contain the last elements to disappear. Purity of retention diminishes as it passes from direct survival to syncretism, and so to reinterpretation. The relative proportions of these particular modes of persistence in different cultural spheres is reflected in the scale of intensity; and this illustrates or defines the focus. So the circle is completed; and the variable persistence of cultural elements of different kinds is simply restated in the form of a system of hypotheses and concepts, ostensibly developed to further the analysis of this variability, only to be canvassed thereafter as its explanation.

Even so, the distinction between cultural focus and periphery in terms of tenacity and persistence is not borne out by the scale of intensity on which it is based. Thus, Herskovits' comparison of folklore with magic or religion in terms of levels of intensity of African elements of these kinds for the fifteen areas concerning which materials were then available shows that folklore elements persist on an average to a higher degree than do either magic or religion. Similarly, Africanisms in music have a higher level of intensity than those in any other field, in terms of this scale.[15] Now it is possible to exclude music from the comparison effectively by treating it as a pattern of motor behavior of the type which is liable to persist in a very marked degree, even though marginal to the culture focus. But this treatment cannot be extended to cover folklore. Nor is it useful to define folklore, religion, and magic coterminously, although this would remove the problem of peripheral elements showing a higher degree of tenacity and persistence than focal ones. On the other hand, if folklore is included among the cultural imponderables on grounds of the value-systems which it often expresses, the question arises whether all other departments of culture are not equally open to similar treatment, notably of course, religion, and kinship. In such a case, the notion of cultural focus as distinct from periphery would cease to be of much use.

There is always grave danger in exaggerating the relative importance of one aspect of culture at the expense of others; and this difficulty is involved in the concept of cultural focus. The type of conclusion which emerges from Fortes' thorough study of an African society is relevant here.

To study Tale kinship institutions apart from the religious and moral ideas and values of the natives would be as one-sided as to leave out the facts of sex and procreation. On the other hand, our analysis has shown that it is equally impossible to understand Tale religious beliefs and moral norms apart from the context of kinship. A very close functional interdependence exists between these two categories of social facts.[16]

Similarly Forde, reviewing African cosmologies, finds that "belief and ritual tend, in other words, to mirror the scale and degree of social integration." [17] Fortes and Evans-Pritchard reach a parallel conclusion from their review of African political systems. "Myths, dogmas, ritual beliefs and activities make his social system intellectually tangible and coherent to an African and enable him to think and feel about it. Furthermore, these sacred symbols, which reflect the social system, endow it with mystical values which evoke acceptance of the social order." [18] These observations indicate the very great need for caution in the classification of cultural elements as focal or otherwise and direct attention to their close interdependence. Clearly, insofar as religion and kinship are essential to the understanding or practice of one another, their separation and ranking in terms of cultural priorities is liable to do violence to this relation.

We can perhaps more usefully and easily distinguish foci in the culture-contact situation itself than in the cultures themselves. Herskovits makes frequent reference to this variability in the pressures of the contact situation, but does not systematize concepts to treat it. In the historical situation of Afro-American culture-contact these foci of contact reflected the interests of the dominant group in its control of the subordinate as slaves. Consequently the social organization, technological, and economic practices of the subordinate Negroes were subject to pressure of a kind without parallel for intensity and continuity in such other fields as religion, music, or folklore. Language, the essential mode of communication between the dominant and subordinate groups, occupied an intermediate position in this variable pressure of cultural elements between the two groups. The advantages of conceiving the contact situation as a field of variable pressure over time as well as at any moment are many and varied. It directs attention consistently to the study of social relations between and within the two culturally differentiated groups as the matrix of these acculturation processes, and thereby invokes employment of historical and sociological research together to relate these processes to the structures and situations through which they matured. It allows relatively simple and precise determination of the focal and peripheral fields of culture-contact on the basis of documentary analysis. It thereby permits the study of persistence of different categories of elements in their differing degrees of intensity or purity to proceed without supplementary postulates which are hardly verifiable about focal and peripheral sectors within the cultures themselves. It directs attention to the fact that purity of form in survival might simply indicate marginality within the acculturative situation, rather than any central significance of the elements retained in the original culture; whereas relative impurity of form in persistence might simply indicate the relative intensity of pressure on the elements concerned, rather than their marginality to the original culture. A good many possible fallacies are ruled out at once by such conceptualization of the contact continuum, and effort is thereby redirected from the development of broad classificatory conceptions such as retention, reinterpretation, and syncretism, and imprecise and unverifiable hypotheses such as that of cultural focus, toward the formulation of more limited propositions capable of being tested against historical materials on the contact situation within the particular fields for which they are separately developed.

Hitherto we have been discussing certain aspects of Afro-American research which focus on the processes by which acculturation proceeded among New World Negroes. We must now turn to consider its conceptual system especially with reference to the classification and study of the forms produced by such processes. Here we are mainly concerned with the precision or generality of the principal concepts, although we must commence with the problem of attribution. Clearly, Afro-American research can only yield tentative ascriptions of provenience for contemporary custom, to the degree that the African centers from which

New World Negroes and their ancestors were recruited are unknown, or to the degree that parallel European practices, or the measure of influence exercised by these forms on the development of contemporary Africanisms are not fully determined. Systematic study has shown that the areas from which most of the New World Negro slaves were recruited lie along the densely populated West African Coast. This reduces the problem of the provenience of Africanisms, leaving only the question of their accretions of European or Amerindian elements. Amerindians, being largely peripheral to the areas of Negro-white contact, may be ignored in this general discussion.

Herskovits is careful to weigh the influence of European cultural practice on African tradition, particularly where elements of folklore are involved; but the issue is greatly obscured by his postulate of common denominators for European and African cultures in the concept of the Old World as a single cultural province.[19] A concept of this level of generality is of dubious value. It implies a division of the world into two cultural provinces, the New and the Old. Yet this could easily be criticized, partly on the evidence that points to the movement of Old World populations into the Americas to become their "aboriginals"; but more importantly on the ground that the absence of such elements as the wheel or writing from fifteenth-century America, or of tobacco from the Old World at that date, forms an inadequate basis for such a distinction, since cultural differences of a similar order have been overlooked within the cultures of the Old World province itself. Yet if this criticism was granted, it would place some strain on the conceptual framework of Afro-American studies.

It is difficult to reconcile specific studies of Afro-American acculturation with statements such as the following:

It is here we must turn for an explanation of the seemingly baffling fact, so often encountered, that given traits of New World Negro, and especially of American Negro behaviour, are ascribable equally to European and African origin. This may well be viewed as but a reflection of the fact that deep beneath the differences between these varied civilisations of the Old World lie common aspects which, in generalized form, might be expected to emerge in situations of close contact between peoples, such as Europeans and Africans, whose specialized cultural endowments are comprehended within the larger unity.[20]

Similarly, in comparing the wider persistence of Africanisms in magic than in religion, Herskovits notes the advantages of magic in being private and difficult of detection where pressures are brought to prohibit both practices; and concludes that Africanisms in magic "persisted in recognizable form everywhere, particularly since the similarity between African and European magic is so great that the one cultural stream must have operated to reinforce the other." [21] It is doubtful in what sense the predicated similarity of European and African magic can be taken to contribute to the survival of Africanisms in this field, as is clear from a glance at such patterns in West Indian Obeah. As is well known, a good deal of the magical rites of the Obeahman are taken in whole or in part from imported literature such as *The Sixth and Seventh Books of Moses, The Black Arts,* and the like. These books describe techniques which are significantly different from African practices, especially in the use of cabalistic signs, writing, and foreign languages. They present a type of magic which is distinguished locally in terms of its literary and learned pretensions as "book magic." In contrast, pure Africanisms in Obeah rely mainly on the employment of herbal or animal substances, and the casting of spells in dialects or African tongues. These two categories of Obeah, the literary and the "African," are at least as much in competition as they are active in reinforcing each other. Thus acceptance of the one form may mean displacement of the other. Something similar has been recently reported from Africa also by Nadel, who found the native pagan magic of Nupe being displaced by imported forms enjoying the higher prestige of Islamic civilization.[22] Now, unless a careful analysis of the magical systems of New World Negroes is made to determine exactly what proportion and type of practice has European or African provenience, the attribution of these forms to African culture whether as syncretisms, reinterpretations or retentions, begs the question of their "origin." The concept of a "generalized form" which permits this type of attribution is thus confusing rather than helpful to the analysis.

These observations direct attention to the levels of generality on which the search for Africanisms and their attribution proceeds; and these levels vary widely indeed, from meticulous correspondences between Haitian and Dahomean *vodun,* or Afro-Cuban and Yoruba divinatory practices on the one hand, to such conceptualizations as those which reduce "matriarchal" family patterns and loose mating associations among New World Negroes to the level of "reinterpretations" of African polygynous patterns by the device of successive, rather than simultaneous, plural matings.[23] Important questions concerning the levels of generality in such conceptualization of family-types, mating patterns, and reinterpretations remain to be answered before the attributions involved can be discussed profitably. An alternative approach to such problems as changing family structures present for acculturation studies may be made by comparing parallel situations and developments in other parts of the world.

Let us examine this matter of family forms for a moment since its handling by Afro-Americanists has promoted some controversy, their opponents attributing the contemporary "disorganization" of New World

Negro family forms to "the historic condition of slavery," under which, as is well known, stable matings among the Negro populations were inhibited by a variety of factors.[24] Afro-Americanists, as we have seen, derive these "deviant, disorganized" family patterns of New World Negroes from African practice by reinterpretation. Much ink has already been spilled on these conflicting ascriptions, and their antithesis has directly affected the study of family patterns in the British Caribbean.

Since, as we have seen, the level of generality in the ascription is imprecise, the only check on these competing theories is to compare West Indian conditions with those elsewhere; yet, obvious as this is, it has not yet been attempted. Among the South African Bantu living in Native Locations on the outskirts of European cities, "deviant, disorganized" family patterns strikingly similar to those found among New World Negroes are common. Yet clearly these South African Bantu families cannot be attributed to slavery on the one hand, nor to the persistence of aboriginal Bantu patterns by reinterpretation on the other, since there has been no experience of slavery among the urban populations, and since the new family types developing among them are as deviant from Bantu norms as from European.[25] A debate whether such family types among the urban Bantu are reducible to persistent Africanisms that have been reinterpreted, or to historical conditions such as slavery, would therefore have little to recommend it; and by extension this applies also to the debate about the derivation of the similar family patterns of New World Negroes. A more realistic analysis than either school of thought seems yet prepared to apply would involve the study of mating and family patterns in terms of particular social and economic contexts.

It is also unsatisfactory to attribute peculiar New World Negro family types to "historic conditions of slavery" without making a far more detailed comparative analysis of these than has yet been attempted. Among the Mohammedan Hausa and Fulani of Northern Nigeria who operated an institution of slavery similar in many respects to the historic New World pattern, religious conversion and marriage of slaves was an important obligation of their owners, and the abolition of slavery in this area has left no aftermath of deviant and disorganized family types.[26] What in fact passes under the name of "slavery" in the British West Indies and the New World generally, includes a great many factors which are not essentials of the institution. The Hausa sought to arrange marriages for their slaves; the New World masters on the whole did not. Slavery as an institution does not enjoin any particular mating pattern, for slave or slave-owner. This institution, like others, can only be fully understood by comparative studies of its structure and function in different and similar contexts. It is

therefore just as unsatisfactory to reduce "deviant" New World Negro
family types to "slavery" as to the reinterpretation of African polygynous forms.

It is worthwhile to dwell a little longer on this problem of family
derivation as handled in Afro-American studies. If our preceding observations are accepted, the problem is basically one of deviance, rather
than one of cultural survival or reinterpretation. Similarly, if our observations on the composite character of West Indian obeah are valid,
then obeah as a deviant pattern of behavior is more extensive than the
specifically Africanist magical practices of West Indian populations.
These distinctions between deviance and Africanism are surely of critical importance to Afro-American research. The deviant mating patterns of various Latin American populations, as implied by the statistics of illegitimacy, are obviously in some respects parallel to those
of New World Negroes, while in no way attributable to African culture.[27] The distinction between deviance and Africanism is however
somewhat difficult of construction in Afro-American studies, on three
main grounds: imprecision in the definition of traits as African or
other, which is partly related to the assumption of correspondences
between African and European cultures in the Old World; wide variability in the level of generality of the concept of reinterpretation,
which, together with the imprecise definition of Africanisms, allows of
extension equally to almost every field of social life; and most importantly, the formulation of problems of Afro-American contact and
research mainly in terms of culture and acculturation, without corresponding emphasis on the primarily sociological aspects of these processes. Deviance, for example, is easier to define in terms of social norms
than in terms of cultural form. On the other hand, where the deviant
practices are concentrated disproportionately among a particular
ethnic group, the culture of which forms a direct object of inquiry, it
is easy to conceive the differentiating behavior primarily, or even entirely, in cultural terms. This oversimplifies the problem and poses
questions of acculturation and culture-change which may be of little
direct relevance. Yet because culture is the total transmitted heritage
of a population, deviance in any form also invites consideration in
terms of a theory of culture-change. Now this is obviously a valid interest, but one liable to fail of attainment, unless it is accompanied by
a thorough study of the social structures and situations within and
with regard to which the deviation has developed.

Another characteristic of Afro-American theory which merits attention is the relatively great emphasis that it places on the acculturative
situation of slavery and the relatively marginal treatment that is given
to historical conditions following on emancipation. For this reason it
has been possible to debate the derivation of deviant Negro family

types in terms of slavery or African influences. Wittingly or not, in this matter as in certain others, Afro-American studies give the appearance of opposing African cultural conservatism and resilience on the one hand to the culturally destructive practices and organization of slavery on the other.[28] But the acculturative process is liable to serious misconstruction if handled in terms of such a simple dialectic. Many years have elapsed since emancipation in all parts of the Western world, and this period may well have an importance for the study of Negro acculturation equal to or greater than that of the slavery which preceded it. If we compare the distributions of Africanisms among the Negroes of the Northern and Southern United States with those of the Haitians, whether urban or peasant, on the other, we find the scale of Africanisms increasing in this order: Negroes of the Northern United States, those of the South, the Haitian town dwellers, the Haitian peasantry. Such a pattern of distribution directs attention to the variability of acculturative situations and influences experienced by these four groups in the postslavery period. Despite the relatively late emancipation of the American Negroes, they practice a culture containing fewer African elements than that of the Haitians, whose freedom was gained many years earlier. Within either population, moreover, the variation of African elements reflects differences of acculturative situation and exposure. Thus, urban Haitians are exposed to foreign cultural influences to a greater degree than the peasants, and the Northern American Negroes enjoy an environment more favorable to their acculturation than do those of the South. For some years after emancipation, Africans continued to arrive in the British West Indies as free indentured laborers; and the same is true in various other parts of the Afro-American area from Brazil to Haiti.[29] In Jamaica between 1834 and 1865, 11,380 free African immigrants settled, a number well in excess of the indentured laborers imported from India over this period.[30] More so than any other group of immigrants, these free Africans enjoyed cultural conditions which were favorable to the survival of certain of their practices. Quite often the decisive condition for this survival consisted in group cohesiveness, as well as in sympathetic attitudes in the Negro section of the host society. We can illustrate this process by a glance at the development and spread of the Shango cult in the island of Grenada.

At the turn of the present century, the representative African cult of the Grenadian folk was a type of ancestor ritual known locally as the Big Drum, the Nation Dance, or simply *saraca* (sacrifice).[31] The ritual dances of this cult normally lasted three days, from Wednesday to Saturday, and contained several elements which have since been assimilated by Grenadian Shango; but Big Drum rites were not associated with spirit-possession, which was not then practiced. Shango in Grenada was originally the ritual of certain closed communities of Africans and their descendants at Munich, Concorde, and La Mode. Over 1,000 of these Africans came from Ijesha in Yorubaland in 1849 after slavery had been abolished. On completion of their indentures they settled in the three communities named above. Within these communities, Yoruba was the spoken language, and numerous elements of Yoruba culture were preserved, including kinship elements, and the basic concepts and rites of Yoruba poytheism. Later, when the Africans and their descendants started to move out from these communities, Creole Grenadians showed great receptivity to their cult, and its spread outwards from these three centers was marked by syncretisms of form and content, numerous traits being taken over from the Nation Dance as well as from Catholicism, until Shango is now the representative form of African ritual among the Grenadians.

Here we see clearly the importance of group cohesion for the persistence and survival of a trait or complex of traits. Shango with its priesthood has displaced the Nation Dance, which lacked formal group organization in Grenada island, although Shango was a late arrival competing with a widely held cultural form. But until 1953, Shango remained quite unknown to the population of Carriacou, a dependency of the Grenada government, and only about 23 miles away. No groups of postemancipation immigrants from Africa had settled in Carriacou, and the Big Drum cult still flourishes as the representative folk ritual in that island.

To devote insufficient attention to the sociology of acculturative situations or to the role of organized and persistent groups in the preservation or transmission of culture is methodologically perilous since it is clear that the group as a carrier of culture is a natural unit far superior to the individual. It is also clear that the structural relations holding between, as well as within, each of the culturally differentiated groups involved in the acculturation process might well be of the utmost significance in understanding its development and effects. It seems likely for example that the Dahomean contingent imported to Haiti by Christophe after slavery and maintained by him as a unit with high prestige may have contributed to the present persistence of Dahomean patterns in Haiti in a degree disproportionate to their relative numbers.[32] The point to note here is that if acculturation is to be studied in terms of specific social contexts, then the implied opposition of slavery and African cultural conservatism must be replaced by a continuous study of the contact situation both within and since slavery, and particular attention must be devoted to the historical reconstruction of the social situations within which these developments occurred. This extension of interest would entail major revisions of the method, theory, and conceptual equipment of Afro-American research.

However, this conceptual equipment needs overhauling in any case. For example, let us briefly consider, first, the principle of reinterpretation, and then the concept of Africanisms:

Where it is not possible to set up syncretisms, the force of cultural conservatism seeks expression in the substance, rather than the form, in psychological value rather than in name, if the original culture is to survive at all. Here the importance of resemblance of the old element to the new is again involved. Though to a lesser degree than in the instance of syncretisms, reinterpretation also requires that some characteristic of the new cultural element be correlated with a corresponding part of the original one by those to whom it is presented, before the mechanism can operate effectively.[33]

Much of this is perilously like reification; and one of the dangers of acculturation studies that are not balanced by continuous examination of and reference to social process consists precisely in this tendency toward the reification of cultures and their component forces or parts. This danger is inherent in acculturation studies which are undertaken without adequate sociological emphasis since their field of interest is therefore defined purely in terms of two or more cultures, or bodies of tradition, in contact. But cultures do not carry themselves, nor do they of themselves have contacts, although their human carriers do.

The other notable point in this definition of reinterpretation is its inclusiveness, and its functional reference. Retention and syncretisms are the conceptual categories that focus directly on the survivals of cultural form. With reinterpretation however we are concerned with the survival of substance, that is, content and function, rather than with cultural form. Thus reinterpretation demarcates a category of persistence which cannot be defined or recognized in formal terms, but involves functional or valuational correspondences. From this point of view, it is somewhat difficult to set any bounds (other than the purely formal one already mentioned) to the ramification of the reinterpretative mechanism which expresses "the force of cultural conservatism" within any process of cultural exchange. Herskovits is well aware of this, but fails to face its implications. "This, of course, raises one of the most difficult problems in the entire field of cultural dynamics—whether any element of culture is ever taken over without some degree of reinterpretation, however free the borrowing." [34] The point is that, as defined, reinterpretation can apply to every cultural item observed among persons initially classified as bearers of any particular culture on grounds of race, descent, nationality, or otherwise. All that is necessary for this ascription is that there should be no formal parallels with practices of the "original" culture, and also that there should be a general tendency of human cultures to show some correspondences on the planes of function or value. Categories of such generality are liable to mean everything and nothing at once, and to invite questions as to whether particular reinterpretations may not be as validly attributed to a writer as to the African population itself.

The key concept of Africanism is similarly ambiguous. It applies equally to any particular trait, however minute, such as the word *ere*, to the thing or condition with which it is associated, and to the system within which the trait is found. It applies equally to relatively pure retentions on the one hand, or to reinterpretations which have dubious value on the other, and to minute elements or large behavioral systems, such as family-patterns, throughout all ranges of "persistence." It does not seem to permit easy attention to competing Africanisms, such as have been illustrated above from the development of folk ritual in Grenada, nor to compound formations of African tradition which develop through such processes, though here also the concepts of survival, syncretisms, and reinterpretation might apply. Taken together with the postulate of cultural conservatism and the general concept of reinterpretation it allows easy admission to a variety of possible types of deviant behaviors as Africanisms, although they may have no African provenience or parallels at all. In concert with the postulate of common denominators among the Old World cultures, it can also be applied to such institutions as the West Indian "wake" or "nine night," which Walter Scott reported among his countrymen. Similarly, although Haitian *vodun* is clearly African in inspiration and detail, there are elements in it, such as the pantheon of Creole gods headed by Dom Petro, which have different, perhaps Amerindian, provenience.[35] These Creole elements are at best African in a different sense from the more strictly Dahomean parts of the complex, and cannot adequately be handled in terms of syncretism or reinterpretation separately. The problem of independent developments among the New World Negroes, such as the Calypso music and steel bands of Trinidad, must also be faced. In some sense these new cultural forms are Africanisms, but little is to be gained by classifying them as retentions, syncretisms, or reinterpretations. Here Pearse's approach to the study of these and other musical forms in the South Caribbean in terms of their institutional settings, participants, and pattern, offers a more precise formulation of research problems and objectives which could also be applied to certain other areas of Afro-American cultural exchange.[36]

Studies of acculturation which are inadequately balanced by studies of the social situation, processes, and structures involved in such change, can hardly be expected to produce agreement, where social structures are the cultural traits involved. Careful reconstructions of past states of the societies with which Afro-American studies are concerned on the basis of indexed documentary materials, undertaken with the object of defining the structures, contexts, and functional characteristics of units and institutions in these past systems, are perhaps the only ways of determining how past social conditions and processes *may have* guided acculturation and contributed to the development of current social and cultural forms. Comparative studies of Afro-American societies focused on the detailed analysis of their structural and functional characteristics will also give rewarding leads about the role of social factors in present as well as past acculturative processes. Together such studies might serve to clarify the nature of cultural exchange and evolution, the types of context within which particular cultural developments occur, the distribution of Africanisms within delimited populations, and the relation of this distribution to contemporary social and economic factors on the one hand and historical process on the other.

Lack of any systematic study to date of the degrees and types of acculturation associated with different social and economic positions in Negro-white populations of the New World constitutes a serious weakness of Afro-American research. Until these studies of social and cultural differentiation within the populations from which Afro-American materials are drawn have been made, problems posed by the variable distribution of Africanisms within these populations, as well as between them, cannot even be defined, let alone receive attention; nor can the critical relations of social structure and acculturative process be analyzed. Yet variability in the incidence of Africanisms within a population is clearly an aspect of the internal differentiation of that unit, and implies the concurrence of acculturative processes between the differentiated sections, as well as of acculturative processes within each separately. Until such studies of internal differentiation are made, the representativeness and significance of the Africanisms reported from such populations remains open to question, and the core of the acculturative process cannot be exposed.

The Folk-Urban Continuum

Robert Redfield, who was also interested in the problem of acculturation, attacked it on a different front—in Central America —and from a different point of view. He worked in Yucatán, studying an important urban center, Mérida, and three rural Maya communities which were situated at different distances from the town. He found that differences in the cultural and social life of these rural communities seemed to form a developmental series which was matched by their relative distance from the common urban center, or conversely, by their immunity and isolation from modern influences. Redfield therefore raised the question whether in fact the significant feature of this acculturative process did not consist in a change of societal type; and on this basis he formulated an ideal-type dichotomy of folk and urban societies.[37] In terms of this polarity, the most isolated of his rural communities, Tusik, most nearly approximates the definition of the folk society, while Mérida is representative of the urban society in Yucatán, and other intermediate communities, such as Chan Kom, occupy a position on the cultural scale corresponding to their geographical situation between these two poles. This ideal-type antithesis allows Redfield to present a systematic comparative analysis of cultural changes to be found as one moves from Tusik toward Mérida in terms of increasing "disorganization", secularization, and individualization; and then to inquire into the functional relations between these aspects of the acculturation processes to which modern urbanization submits folk societies.

A brief comparison of Redfield's approach with that of Herskovits may be useful at this point since both sets of researches fall into the common field of acculturation studies, and these two workers once cooperated in producing an early memorandum on the study of acculturation.[38] Both writers employ comparative procedures in their studies of culture change or persistence, but whereas Herskovits devotes little attention to the variability of acculturation levels within a population, and compares societies on the basis of the distribution of African items between them, Redfield's emphasis is rather on the comparison of different levels of acculturation within a single continuum, and on the processes associated with acculturation as such. Unlike Redfield who takes the contemporary situation as his historical base line, and then proceeds to compare four differently situated communities in terms of certain selected indices and characters, Herskovits regards the initial situation of contact between the carriers of different cultures as the appropriate base line for his studies of Afro-American acculturation. Herskovits is therefore committed to ethnohistorical research, whereas Redfield's concern is with the incidence and processes of contemporary acculturation. Here it must be pointed out that Redfield's analysis of the cultural continuum of Yucatán is considerably weakened by the insufficient attention which he gives to the effects and processes of suppression of the great Maya rebellion in that area, as well as to the general history of Indian-Spanish relations in Mexico.

Redfield's approach directs greater attention to the structure of relations within and between groups as well as to impersonal media of communication than apparently does that of Herskovits; and this difference of orientation is reflected in the different conceptual systems of the two writers. Thus Redfield analyzes the acculturation continuum from Mérida to Tusik in terms of a *societal* polarity, and consequently employs concepts and categories which focus on the social aspects or concomitants of cultural change, such as "disorganization," individualization, or secularization. Herskovits, on the other hand, approaches problems of process through the initial study of forms, and therefore utilizes categories such as survival, syncretism, or reinterpretation, which reflect degrees of purity and independent persistence of the original cultural forms. Herskovits, in other words, has placed a primary emphasis on the cultural frame of analysis, whereas Redfield has tended to dovetail his studies of acculturation with the analysis of changing social forms.

Behind these differences of Herskovits and Redfield loom the historical differences of the areas with which each worker is concerned. The subordinate Maya of Yucatán were inducted into the wider society of their conquerors as communities, and their original social organization persisted in this new situation as far as the two were consistent. The African populations of the New World, however, were recruited on a basis which, in large measure destroyed their original social organization, and were then subjected to a mode of social reorganization in slavery which tended to continue that process. Consequently, the study of acculturation among the Maya can hardly be developed without devoting equal attention to social process and changing social forms, while the same study of acculturation in Afro-American populations would encounter many obstacles if it was initially conceived in terms of the concurrent study of social change. These important differences of milieu largely account for the hitherto divergent interests and procedures of the two sets of studies, but they do not by any means rule out the combination of their approaches within the framework of a general theory of sociocultural processes which may hold for both fields alike.

Redfield's approach, like that of Herskovits, has stimulated considerable interest and debate and will probably continue to do so for some time. Tax has shown that Redfield's ideal-type dichotomy is not mutually exclusive even in nearby Guatemala.[39] Steward has argued that the concept of levels of organization within a developmental continuum applies to the materials which Redfield uses, and that this makes the classification of any community in terms of the folk-urban continuum purely a problem in definition.[40] Herskovits has brought West African data to bear on the continuum.[41] Bascom, quoting Schwab, notes that some Yoruba cities are "urban" in terms of form, but "folk" in terms of process,[42] and it has often been pointed out that urban communities frequently contain folk elements and that folk societies also may exhibit urban elements. The position of certain societies such as the Hausa of Northern Nigeria in this continuum will vary according to the particular differentiae of the polar ideal-types which are under immediate consideration.[43]

It seems, however, that the principal criticism of Redfield's ideal-type analysis and approach to the study of cultural contact and change may consist in the incommensurability of the units between which his comparisons were actually made. One term of Redfield's dichotomy is given as the Folk Society, but it is only *communities* that he actually investigated, and there are crucial differences between communities and societies, particularly where the former are subordinate rural administrative units of a modern state whose governmental and economic life is centered in the urban areas.[44] Steward has recently called attention to this difference and to the problems of comparability which it presents. In terms of Redfield's ideal-types and empirical research, the urban unit, Mérida, more closely realizes the condition and status of a society therefore, than do any of the rural communities which are under its effective administration. For this reason also, the variation in degrees of urbanization, disorganization, and the like, which are exhibited by the several rural communities that Redfield studies, are more significantly analyzed in terms of the effective subordination and inclusion of these communities within the wider administrative unit, than as a function of linear distance from the town.

The root of this difficulty seems to lie in the failure to distinguish sufficiently between *social systems* and *societies*. Almost any group structure or activity can be conceived of as a social system of some particular kind or other, and this applies to schools, societies, and communities alike. But the society as a system is distinct from other social systems in many important ways.[45] The society is a system which includes all other types of social system as parts of itself. It is self-recruiting, theoretically self-sufficient, and is self-determining within the context of its relations with external societies. Communities differ from societies particularly with respect to inclusiveness, self-determination, and self-sufficiency. Communities also vary in the degree or level to which they control their own regulative institutions as self-sufficient units, and this variation corresponds directly with their subordination to and dependence on governmental, religious, and economic institutions and processes which regulate local life and integrate local groups within the framework of a wider society. It follows, therefore, that corresponding variability obtains between communities with respect to the levels of their integration as local units on the one hand, and their integration within the society on the other. This variability forms an important aspect of the processes of secularization, disorganization, and individualization, which Redfield noticed in the Yucatán communities that he studied. But it is clear that of themselves community studies provide an inadequate basis for the construction of a societal typology, since variability in the local control of regulative institutions, and scope of local integration, corresponds to variation of levels and degrees of integration within the societies of which communities are parts.

The significance of Redfield's work for British Caribbean sociology can hardly be overestimated. Beckwith, Edith Clarke, Cohen, Herskovits, Madeline Kerr, Matthews, Taylor, and R. T. Smith have all been concerned with problems of folk culture and its relation to the dominant traditions of various British Caribbean territories in one way or another.[46] Hadley and Macmillan have generalized distinctions on this basis, and applied them as exploratory categories in formulating general models of British West Indian society.[47] The Editors of *Caribbean Quarterly* have also directed attention to this cleavage, and Broom has indicated the necessity for specific studies of urbanization within the area.[48] On the other hand, analyses of society in Jamaica and Trinidad have been presented in terms of class, caste, and color concepts, without reference to the polarities of "folk" and "nonfolk";[49] and Henriques has challenged Kerr's statement that a cultural conflict obtains between folk and elite cultures in Jamaica.[50] It seems clear that differences of definition, research problems, and theory may all be involved in this conflict of analytic models, and that some conceptual and theoretical clarifications are requisite at this stage in the development of British Caribbean social research.

It is an indication of the general resemblances between British Caribbean societies and those of the wider area initially delimited that similar ambiguities about the appropriate analytic models for communities in this wider area should also obtain. Thus Haitian society has been analyzed in terms of class and caste stratification as well as cleavages between the urban and folk cultures.[51] Brazil and the Southern United States have received similar treatment.[52] So has Central American society.[53] The point at issue here is not simply the superiority of these competing models—stratification, and folk-elite cultural differences—since each may well be more appropriate for particular problems. Rather we are concerned with their combination to produce a richer and more balanced analysis than may be expected from researches conducted within either of these frames of reference separately. Where, as in Haiti, stratification coincides with marked cultural differences, there is almost no problem of the type we are now considering, and comparability of the research with other studies in the wider area of our concern is assured, whatever analytic model is employed. But to the extent that stratification and cultural differentiation are not patently coincident, then considerable problems of interpretation and conceptualization invest the analysis; and competition rather than comparability of models and materials may result.

At present, the debate over Redfield's theory seems to have shifted toward the question of the cultural status of the alternative poles of his dichotomy. The problem here is not whether the use of ideal-type constructs is valid or fruitful, but whether the particular constructs offered by Redfield are the most appropriate for field research. The criticism has been made that the culture of communities such as Chan

Kom is most appropriately handled in terms of the culture of the inclusive society, and hence may be regarded as the subculture of a community within that unit. Such a view recognizes the significance of cultural and political autonomy in theoretical typologies, and in comparative analysis of these types of data.

Recent work in Puerto Rico promises to clarify some of the problems raised by Redfield, together with many other themes in Caribbean sociology. Steward and Manners, working from an ecological basis, have indicated the existence of at least three types of regional culture in rural Puerto Rico, associated with the cultivation of sugar, coffee, and tobacco, respectively.[54] Mintz has directed attention to the plantation as a type of rural social unit with urban or industrial characteristics, and there are important differences between plantations themselves.[55] Edith Clarke and the Jamaica Social Survey team have found corresponding regional variations in culture, social organization, and ecology.[56] Accounts of Cuba and Haiti indicate regional differences there also;[57] and it is clear that the study of regional variations in ecological terms has much to recommend it methodologically and may yield significant comparable results.

Nonetheless we should give attention to the problem of conceptualization involved in these studies of regional culture variants. This problem is largely implicit in Redfield's distinction between urban and other cultures, since difference in localization characterizes culture and society in Redfield's dichotomy. Culture may vary on a regional basis while entailing no significant differences of kind or of societal type. Such regional culture variants must be distinguished sharply from that type of cultural variation which entails differences of societal type, and which are linked with horizontal stratification, where they obtain within a society culturally segmented on a regional basis also. If the term "subculture" is applied to these regional variants, then to avoid confusion between such local differences and the type of horizontal cultural differentiation, some other term must be adopted for the latter.[58] If we choose to describe these horizontal strata as classes or "castes," or in terms of folk and elite, and if they are found to exhibit cultural differences of an order sufficient to distinguish one culture from another, we could then apply terms such as class-culture, caste-culture, folk- and elite-cultures, to distinguish their ways of life. Clearly, where the two are found together, this type of cultural differentiation is of a different type from regional variation, and it invites confusion to treat them as equivalent.[59] Such an equivalence does violence to social space, reducing its contemporary dimensions from three to two. These problems of substance involved in this differentiation of vertical and horizontal cultural variations have been obscured in Redfield's formation of the folk-urban continuum; but concepts should aid rather than obscure investigation.

Psychological Studies and Interpretations

Problems of cultural and social differentiation, and of their handling, can be appreciated from a review of the psychologically oriented literature on the Caribbean and adjacent areas. Since more has been published on the psychological content and aspects of social relations among the Negro-white populations of the United States and the Caribbean than on the mixed Indian-white communities of Middle America, we shall confine our discussion to psychological studies and interpretations of mixed Negro-white societies. From the outset it is important to stress the distinction between psychological studies on the one hand, and interpretations which employ psychological concepts but do not represent the results of psychological field research on the other. A brief summary of the writings about to be examined will make clear this difference.

Since the pioneer studies by Dollard and Powdermaker of a cotton-producing area in Mississippi, formal studies of social psychology have been made in several Caribbean territories—in St. Thomas by Campbell, in Jamaica by Madeline Kerr and Yehudi Cohen, working independently, and apparently by Rhoda Metraux in Haiti. Psychological interpretations lacking bases of formal psychological research have been applied to St. Martin and St. Eustatius by Kruijer, to the British West Indies en bloc by Simey and Hadley, and to the Trinidadian middle class by Braithwaite.[60] Clearly these two sets of work rest on different foundations and require different treatment.

The geographical spread of these studies is almost matched by their differences of psychological orientation. Dollard and Powdermaker gave detailed treatment to the psychological content of race and caste relations without attempting to formulate overall personality configurations for the population studied. Lloyd Warner in an early study of Chicago Negroes developed a specialized concept of "social personality types" from the consideration of the individual life-chances of American Negroes, and found thirty-two such types among his sample.[61] Braithwaite applied the concept of the "authoritarian personality" to one social class in Trinidad. Campbell, Kerr, and Kruijer on the other hand, have attempted to define "basic personalities" in the populations which they studied, using methods and concepts formulated by Kardiner. Simey and Hadley have both written about British West Indian "basic personality" types, while employing the frustration-aggression theories of Dollard and others in their formulation. Campbell has also supplemented Kardiner's methodology by constructs derived from Lewin. Cohen's analysis of interpersonal relations within a Jamaica community represents yet another approach.

Problems of social and cultural differentiation are of central importance in the consideration of these psychologically oriented studies. They have received the clearest formulation in Warner's work. Since the determination of social structures, groups, and classes must precede their psychological investigation, it is necessary to consider the treatment of social differentiation before proceeding to discuss the psychological interpretations proposed for such patterns. In this respect, the first point to note is that the studies listed above were made in several different types of society. In Chicago, we are told, a system of informal caste operates. In Mississippi caste is traditional, highly formalized, and ubiquitous. In St. Thomas the Americans have recently introduced their caste pattern to a society formerly organized otherwise in terms of wealth, color, and culture. In Haiti, however much writers may dispute the nature of stratification in terms of caste or class, all agree that cultural and social differentiation coincide. In discussing stratification in Trinidad, Braithwaite describes it in terms of caste, semicaste, and class, while also assigning a prominent place to color differences. Kerr, whose psychological studies were mainly of the Jamaican folk, distinguishes three classes in Jamaican society, and points out that these are correlated with cultural and color differences, such that the conflicting cultural requirements which obtain are productive of personality disorientations and disorganizations under certain conditions. As mentioned above, this coexistence of diverse cultural traditions in Jamaica is questioned by Henriques, who submits no evidence to the contrary however, while his conceptualization of Jamaican culture in terms of "syncretism" would seem to indicate that Kerr's observations reflects concrete conditions.[62]

Within the small community of 270 souls studied by Cohen, three classes were distinguished, primarily in economic terms. Cohen also adds that even the upper class of this community would "occupy a lower class status in the urban areas." [63] Simey conceived of West Indian social stratification in terms of three classes, but described one "basic West Indian personality type," and has been criticized for this by Hadley on the basis of data from St. Vincent which indicate the existence of three major strata with marked cultural differences, and with personality types postulated to correspond.[64] It would seem therefore that outside the United States with its formal or informal caste systems, there is little unanimity about the nature and significance of differentiation within the societies examined.

A brief consideration of the two finest studies now under consideration, those by Dollard and Powdermaker, will serve to bring this issue into sharper focus. Both these workers conducted independent field researches in the same community of Mississippi, and attempted psychological analyses of the social milieu. Both recognized the importance of social differentiation within the community, and the necessity for determining its form and extent as a preliminary to the psychological study of social and race relations. The "caste" system was clearly indisputable, but within either caste both writers report differently the existence and extent of class divisions. Dollard regards the white population of the community as being mainly middle class, with no local representatives of the Southern upper class, and only "poor whites" or "red-necks," who live outside the township studied, in the white lower class. Powdermaker finds representatives of the white upper class present also. Among the Negroes Dollard finds two major divisions, a middle class, and a lower class, while Powdermaker reports the existence of a Negro upper class also, and implicitly subdivides the Negro middle and lower classes. It seems that whereas Dollard gives his classification a primary regional reference, Powdermaker's was primarily local; but there are other differences in the concepts of class with which these writers worked. Dollard's classes seem to have the same reference or connotations on both sides of the caste line, whereas it appears that the class subdivisions which Powdermaker employs have different meanings or referents on either side of the caste line.

These alternative schemes naturally have significant implications for the psychological analyses which these writers present. Thus Dollard defines the race problem as presented primarily by the patterned relations among and between middle-class whites and lower-class Negroes, although he also discusses the situation of middle-class Negroes. Powdermaker, on the other hand, finds a more diffuse, variable, and less dramatically articulated set of patterns, corresponding to her initial view of the greater degrees of internal differentiation of both groups.

This comparison is made here simply to highlight the critical importance of differentiation and stratification for social-psychological studies of communities, and to indicate that even after careful investigations by able workers carried out in an area of highly formalized social differentiation, disagreements concerning the nature and type of social differentiation remain which have significant influences on the psychological analyses themselves. Even admitting that different emphases or objectives may predispose workers to favor different systems of classification for the same population, we are simply left with the question of the expository, heuristic, or substantive nature of the categories involved, and their relations.[65]

Another aspect of these researches of Powdermaker and Dollard which is worthy of mention reflects the nature of the social system in which they worked. The system in the Southern United States presents a rigidly organized set of race relations, and equally rigid definitions of racial membership. In an important sense therefore, Dollard and Powdermaker were carrying out studies of "race relations" under conditions of their precise and elaborate articulation that are not usually found in other populations of the wider area that forms the natural frame of reference for Caribbean social research. On this ground alone it would seem quite likely that the conclusions reached by Dollard and Powdermaker in Mississippi would be unlikely to hold generally elsewhere in this area, and that their application to societies with less rigid systems of racial differentiation would be somewhat incautious. In fact, however, Simey has relied heavily and uncritically on Dollard's formulation of Southern Negro frustration-aggression reactions to their racial situation, and has applied this in a generalized form to the British Caribbean at large, with little attention to variations between or within colonies. This is simply one instance of the growing number of loose applications of concepts and theories developed by careful psychological studies of quite distinct field conditions to the description of West Indian social life. Social and psychological research will both suffer if this vogue should continue unchecked.

The fact that the frustration-aggression hypothesis lends itself to such facile application as that made by Simey is of itself sufficient to raise questions concerning its precision in the definition of key terms, or delimitation of processes and effects. Simey, for instance, argues that submissive behavior is a form of aggression.[66] Powdermaker writes of a young Negro girl who is "aggressive in her determination to hold her head high and break away from the lowly position to which the whites would condemn her." [67] Thus both self-respect and its opposite, self-abnegation, are instances of aggressive behavior in similar contexts; and one is left to wonder what is not. Key terms used helter-skelter in such a fashion are clearly of dubious analytic value.

Divergences in the psychological interpretations of West Indian social patterns as well as in the procedures of their investigation are probably as great as any community of method or findings among the psychologically oriented writers on this area. It seems to be generally assumed, probably on the basis of the two Mississippi studies just discussed, that aggressiveness characterizes a great many areas of social relations in the Caribbean, though relatively little attention is usually paid to the frustrations required by theory as correlates of this. Hadley and Campbell however point out that aggressiveness varies in its expression, incidence, and intensity according to the status of the individuals concerned. Kerr makes little use of this concept in her study of the Jamaican basic personality, by which she perhaps means the "peasant" personality type, and which she finds to be extra-punitive.[68] In his study of a small Jamaican community Cohen presents a picture of a group of persons markedly hostile, insecure, dependent, and fearful. Braithwaite, discussing authoritarian characteristics of the Trinidad middle class in a quasi-psychological manner, also stresses anxiety and insecurity, together with drives for power and submission. Rhoda Metraux traces Haitian individualism in political and social life back to certain traumatic adjustment situations of infancy and childhood. Campbell employs Lewin's concepts of aspiration and achievement levels to subdivide the population of St. Thomas into three groups, those with high aspiration and achievement, those with low aspiration and achievement, and those with high aspiration and low achievement, the last being a situation productive of both frustration and aggression. This attempt to extend the analysis beyond the circular frustration-aggression reaction by delimiting the types of situation under which frustration develops is commendable as an aim, though unsatisfactory in performance.[69] It is not easy to demonstrate that persons enjoying favorable conditions are any whit less aggressive than those who do not, although their frustrations may be less immediately obvious. Nor is Campbell's omission of the fourth category of Lewin's conceptual system, those with low aspiration but high achievement, entirely satisfactory. Social systems being what they are, such a category is not likely to be altogether devoid of empirical reference, and indeed, if aspiration is relative to the individual's situation, and if achievement is measurable in terms of social recognition, (how else?), then on Campbell's data, both the immigrant American and Creole groups of St. Thomas contain elements classifiable in those terms. On the whole, however, it would appear that such highly general categories could be applied a priori to any human or animal population whatsoever, yielding similar results, and thus saving a good deal of research.

As a group these psychological studies and interpretations are therefore subject to two main criticisms, the generality and vagueness of their various theoretical and conceptual systems, and the ambiguities in their classifications of the populations studied. It is also of interest to note how variously these students stress different aspects or stages of social life. Dollard and Powdermaker, for example, give the psychologically primordial infancy situation scant attention. Cohen deals with the early period most methodically and effectively, but largely ignores the school, which Kerr finds to be a fairly efficient agency for personality disorganization in Jamaica. Hadley regards the past and present situations of the British Caribbean populations as of such moment for understanding contemporary personality patterns that he devotes half of his paper to these topics, the remainder being a brief summary of the three main personality types as revealed by this survey. Simey indeed seems to have made little direct or systematic study of the West Indian situation with which his book deals, but was content to apply concepts drawn from studies in America to the Caribbean area in a manner not strikingly different from the application of stereotypes. In somewhat similar fashion, Kruijer has simply adopted Campbell's work on St. Thomas Negroes as a convenient frame for the discussion of St. Martin and St. Eustatius, while Braithwaite has done the same for Trinidad's middle class with the concept of the "authoritarian personality." The apparent ease with which these psychological concepts lend themselves to wholesale projections in alien areas without prior research strongly suggests that their formulations may be defective in rigor, or else they are not fully understood by those applying them; it also suggests that such concepts and interpretations may possess more significance as expository devices in the hands of certain writers, than as substantive statements about the populations referred to. Bearing this in mind, it is interesting to note the agreement in definition of West Indian personality patterns among these students who lay such different stresses on different phases of the psychogenetic process, or on different situations expressive of personality traits.

Stratification and Differentiation

Commencing with a review of studies that focus on cultural contact and change, we have moved gradually to the other plane of analysis offered by sociology and have now to deal directly with the problems of internal social differentiation. As a glance at the literature will show, these are among the most complex phases of social reality, and a great many conflicting views are held about their nature, interpretation, and appropriate methods of investigation.[70] However, we have found that without some adequate conceptualization of this phase of sociocultural reality, systematic comparative studies within the Caribbean or its geographical context are hardly possible on the one hand, while even the intensive studies of small districts and communities have unclear general implications and references on the other. Cultural variability and psychological problems gain in significance and precision from their definitions in terms of particular situations, structures, and groups. Thus, although alternative interpretations of social life might be offered by cultural, sociological, and psychological studies, the competition of these analytic planes, and of the models constructed within their separate frames, is ultimately more apparent than real; and in the last resort, we shall only approach an adequate and refined analysis of human problems or relations by a combination of these and other approaches. The need for this combined approach is well known of course; what differences of opinion exist on this subject mainly reflect divergences about the form or method of such interdisciplinary work.

We have seen that studies of cultural process and change lose a great deal when conducted without equally intense examination of the social milieu within which these developments occur; also that societal differentiation cannot be handled apart from equally intensive studies of the forms and processes of cultural differentiation which it implies; and finally that psychological analyses of social systems depend for their utility in large measure upon adequate prior analyses of the structure of such systems if they are to avoid errors of reference as well as interpretation. On these grounds it would seem that the order of objectives in a combined interdisciplinary study of society would give priority to the study of the social structure, defining its major units and their interrelations in a systematic fashion which would facilitate the integration of cultural and psychological studies. Clearly enough, the alternative to this procedure is the hit-or-miss method, which has already enjoyed an unhappy monopoly for too long. But there is little agreement about the nature and content of social stratification and differentiation. Since these dimensions are basic to the formulation of structural models of complex societies of the type with which we are concerned, lack of agreement here has been largely responsible for delay in the development of an integrated interdisciplinary approach to these problems.

Social stratification is nowadays conceived of as a continuous hierarchic ranking of social positions and roles.[71] It is sometimes also regarded as an inherent attribute of all societies; but this view is not empirically tenable. Such a postulate is only essential to general theories which seek to "explain" stratification as inherent and implicit in the concept of societies as systems of a particular type. If we look behind such theories to the problems which led to their formulation we shall arrive at a better understanding of both.

The recent history of thought about social stratification can be said to commence with the work of Karl Marx. He defined *classes* in terms of their relations to the means of production, that is, as economic categories within the society. Marx also postulated a continuous conflict between these economic classes, which thereby implied their existence as solidary and self-conscious social units in greater or less degree. That is to say, Marx commenced with an abstract operational classification of persons on the basis of economic criteria and concluded that these categories were substantive social units. Marx's procedure illustrates one of the critical problems in this field of study, the problem of distinguishing between operationally defined "classes," and actual social classes; or of ascertaining their correspondence.

In the past forty years, many alternative formulations of the class concept have been offered, some of which are presented in the recent book by Bendix and Lipset.[72] At the same time, dimensions other than those selected by Marx as important to the development and study of class systems have attracted notice; and problems of the interrelation of these dimensions have occupied a central place in theory and research alike. Terminological shifts have accompanied this refinement of the field of study; and nowadays one speaks of economic or social or political classes, of elites, estates, and status, of prestige classes and participation classes, of reference groups, and the like. Each of these terms and concepts reflects certain criteria relevant to the existence or study of classes, and these criteria are often closely related, so that the attribution of any single order of weighting and priority among them raises many problems.

This summary suggests the type of problems which lie behind certain current approaches to the study of stratification. There are problems inherent in the notion of classification itself. Are social classes simply analytic postulates of various writers? Do they have any substantive existence, and if so, how? There are further problems concerning the constitution of class-concepts themselves, which center upon the relation of the various criteria recognized as somehow associated with class organization. There are problems of the boundaries of social classes, of their functions as well as bases, and of their definition by objective indices of various kinds on the one hand, or by subjective identifications on the other. Above all, there is the question of their existence, implicit in disagreements about their definition and nature. One does not question the objective existence of lineage relations in an African tribe, however one disputes their interpretation, simply because these lineage relations recur constantly and in regular patterns during studies by different investigators. One does doubt the reality of the numerous human "instincts" postulated by various psychologists simply because their lists show so little agreement. Similar difficulties arise in the study of class, and the layman can rightly ask the sociologists, "How are you all so certain of the existence of class, when unable to agree among yourselves in what it consists?"

The type of theory which Parsons advances seeks to meet these problems, among others, by differentiating between value-systems in a way which is consistent with, and to some extent reflected in, the conflicting interpretations or models of class organization that currently obtain. Thus Parsons' four primary value-standards or systems allow of coexistent conflicting interpretations of the system of stratification within any society, to the degree that these value-standards are themselves tightly or loosely integrated. Different rank-orders may therefore obtain according to which of these standards are under consideration. But Parsons also holds that these standards themselves are always ranked in some order of priority, and that the distribution of power accords with this ranking between them, and with the prestige of persons or groups which also reflects this ranking. In other words, such a theory seeks to accept and explain differences of opinion about class boundaries and bases by postulating a system of multiple valuations, which is nonetheless itself hierarchic in structure. And this rank-order of the primary value-standards is conceived on analytic grounds as inherent in the notion of social systems as such. "The principal criterion of priority of evaluation of functions, hence differentiated sub-systems, is *strategic significance for system-process.*" [73] This simply means that insofar as societies are systems they must each have a continuous rank-ordering of roles and positions.

As already observed, however, this generalization is not always borne out, so that either some societies are not systems, or they are systems of a different type from Parsons' models. In certain tribal societies, for example, half the population—women—are often excluded from the ranking which obtains among males; and this ranking frequently, as among the Hausa, or in certain lineage systems, accords equal value to positions discharging different roles, as well as the contrary. Empirical materials of this type may be insufficient objection to Parsons' theory on either of two grounds: first, that such societies are not systems in the sense of his discussion; second, that, although they are, analysis has failed to define the four primary value-standards, as well as the content of each, or their interrelation. To these possible rejoinders, there are two replies. First, by what criteria other than field study itself can one establish whether any society is a system, or a system of the particular type under discussion? Second, by what criteria, other than the system of stratification itself, can one establish the rank-ordering of the various value-standards, or indeed their separateness and content? For clearly, if the theory which purports to "explain" certain phenomena assumes but cannot predict them, then it simply consists in their description from one particular point of view.

This is not the place for a detailed discussion of Parsons' theory of social stratification. It has been quoted merely to illustrate current thinking about these problems, and the complexity they present. But before proceeding to discuss empirical researches, three observations are necessary. First, Parsons discusses stratification in terms of roles or performances, which accords with the action frame of reference he adopts, but may not always be appropriate to or consistent with ranking as it goes on in empirical societies, some of which at least accord priority in rankings to positions, rather than roles, defining these consistently or otherwise in terms of one or more criteria. Because Parsons defines stratification problems in terms of roles, and ranks roles in terms of their "strategic significance for system-process," he implicitly assumes that stratification, besides being continuous with society, unidimensional, and integrative, also has positive functions essential to the system. None of these imputations is easily demonstrable by empirical materials, although each of them may be controverted by such data.

Second, Parsons' model of stratification develops from an abstract consideration of social systems as equilibrium systems with particular levels and types of integration. It seems however that levels and types of integration are properly a matter for empirical research, and that they cannot be postulated in any precise sense for societies at large, or for any single society at different points in time. Such postulation would lead to the treatment of a system in rapid and violent change, for example, during a period of revolution and counterrevolution, as exhibiting conditions of equilibrium and integration at all instants equally, and would also require the entire process to be conceptualized in these terms. Now clearly, predicates of this level of generality and imprecision are of dubious value as guides to empirical studies or analysis. And the same charge of generality and imprecision may be leveled at each of the value-standards in turn, not as formal categories, but with regard to their content and substance in any empirical society. Traits and functions classifiable in terms of each of these four standards in one context may be classifiable differently in another, and within the same society, as well as between societies. Such a condition simply reflects the multifunctional nature of institutional activities, the multiplicity of their goals, and their manifold interrelations. To conceptualize these diverse aspects in terms of phases reflecting basic differences of value-orientations involves abstractions of an order which are both so highly general as to be of doubtful value, and at the same time so constructed as to mutilate the organic structure and character of institutional activities.

Finally, the point must be made that the existence as well as the nature of a single continuous system of stratification must be established by field research in any particular society, rather than predicated as an implication of theory. Until such a single series is demonstrated, it is wiser to conceive the field of relations which involve ranking and distinctions in terms of social differentiation, which does not imply any particular form for the srtuctures under study, admits the possibility of a single hierarchy, reduces the theoretical problems and overtones that invade such studies, and also keeps empirical research alert to the many factors and aspects that are or may be involved.

Empirical studies of social stratification in America have been conducted on the basis of one or more indices of an objective kind, such as occupation, income, house-type, residential area, or association and group membership, as well as by the use of subjective evaluations and identifications of their own class position, or those of others, as given by informants. These approaches are sometimes combined, as in the work of Warner and his associates.[74] The criteria selected in these studies indicate the two primary orientations of the class concept, objectively toward an economic and social base, and subjectively, through identification and other references, as an expression of social psychology. Hence the frequent definition of such classes in terms of prestige, and the phenomenon of their ranking, as more or less prestigious. Naturally, as one would expect, even the most subjective classifications have a certain consistency in their objective referents; but this is by no means a uniformity, and cannot be reduced to invariant relations between any of the various dimensions, such as wealth, occupation, social participation, style of life, family history, power, or the like, which are involved in the general constructs.

As regards the relation of class-difference to culture, there has so far been little discussion. And this itself is one of the most revealing aspects of stratification studies. Class, in other words, assumes adherence of the groups which it differentiates to common institutions, and thereby, in the last resort to a common system of values. Classes are thus differentiated culturally with respect to noninstitutionalized behaviors, such as etiquette, standards of living, associational habits, and value-systems which may coexist as alternatives on the basis of the common values basic to the class-continuum. Classes differentiated in this manner reflect, besides their hereditary aspects, educational, economic, and other differences also. But they are not definable in terms of adherence to different systems of social institutions since that would imply their equation with societies, as distinct cultural groups.

Now in the United States, the criteria used in studies of stratification among whites have also been applied to Negroes. The sharp racial lines and frequently deviant patterns of American Negroes notwithstanding, there appears to be sufficiently general consensus about the validity of such studies to indicate that in America we have two parallel social segments, one white, the other black, linked together in various ways, among them by formal adherence to common institutions. The nature of this racial division itself calls for some consideration. It varies between regions and between states, but includes legal prohibition on intermarriage, occupational differentiation to a fair degree, bans on commensality in much of the area, provision of separate public facilities for the two racial groups, and the definition of a Negro as any person with one drop of Negro blood, or more. In terms of this definition Negroes are a residual social category, and as could be expected, under such conditions, pure Negroes form a minority within the American Negro group.[75] Warner and his fellow workers have labeled this type of race-differentiation, "color-caste," a term which directs attention simultaneously to its parallels with caste systems as obtaining in India for instance, and its differences. Caste implies uniformity in the ranking of units, and thus uniformity in ranking members of such groups, which does not always obtain in America. Thus across the American color-caste line, the poor white occupies an inferior social-class position to the middle-class Negro in many, though not in all, respects. Under a caste system moreover, occupational inheritance, which is lacking in America, obtains. Individual social mobility is ruled out by caste, theoretically, even where migrancy occurs, and the system of caste stratification enjoys the sanction of religion. In other words, caste is conceived of as a sacred structure, and disobedience to caste norms and interrelations is not merely unlawful, but also sinful. These latter features of the true caste-system are lacking from the American scene, and Warner's terminology seeks to reflect this.

Within the American Negro group, as many researches demonstrate, differences of color and shade are widespread and of great significance. This means that the number of criteria adequate for a study of class structure among American whites must be increased to include the color factor in parallel studies of American Negroes; and the correlation between color-ranking and other forms of status-determinant also requires investigation. Readaptations of this sort clearly reflect the ideological patterns associated with American race relations on the one hand, and the continuities of economic, cultural, and other factors which obtain between American Whites and Negroes on the other.

Within our area such conditions are distinctive of the United States. It follows therefore that to regard social differentiation in other racially mixed societies of this wider field in terms of American patterns may obscure factors of greater significance in the societies under study. Pierson's pioneer study of Bahia, Brazil, which was oriented toward the problem of race relations between the white, colored, and black groups of that city, illustrates the point very well.[76] Pierson's particular interest lay in the contrast between Brazilian and American race relations. This led him to treat social differentiation in terms of race, with little attention to the problems of cultural differentiation which are prominent in Bahia, though race differentiation or its absence is a cultural fact reflecting other cultural facts.

Pierson's application of American concepts of stratification and differentiation to Latin American conditions is not unique, as Beals' review article makes clear. Beals concludes that "the use of strictly economic or economic and political criteria for class analysis of Latin America is the least useful approach." [77] He directs attention to the differences in stratification and differentiation between North and Latin America, and especially to the cultural differences between the Indian and mestizo or Ladino groups within these Latin American societies. Redfield also has only touched on these problems of social differentiation within a community indirectly, so we shall have to look elsewhere for their direct analysis.

The Guatemalan village of San Luis, studied by Gillin and Tumin, is a suitable example.[78] Both workers were in the field together, but carried out independent researches, which although overlapping a good deal, were focused on different aspects of local life. In San Luis, two-thirds of the population are Indians, and the remainder, of mixed Spanish-Indian descent, are known as Ladinos. Within San Luis, Indians are subordinated to Ladinos, individually and as a group. Beals, in the article just cited, observes that "In Guatemala, an anomalous situation exists, for horizontal movement is often possible for the Indian when he leaves his community; within his community, however, movement into the mestizo (here called Ladino) group is regarded as vertical movement, and is virtually impossible." [79] Gillin and Tumin describe this system of stratification in terms of "caste," and both writers indicate that its posited racial basis is largely without objective foundation. Although Ladinos and Indians may not intermarry or eat together within the village, they sometimes do so beyond its perimeter. There are few other features at San Luis of the type usually associated with "caste" in comparative sociology, except uniformity of dominance-subordination relations. However, it is abundantly clear from both accounts that very marked differences of social status and culture obtain between Ladinos and Indians, and that the type and degree of their social differentiation is itself a cultural fact which is linked with and reflects these other cultural differences.

In America for example, color-caste obtains between whites and Negroes independently of cultural or class similarities or differences.[80] In San Luis, caste difference seems to consist in the social expression of cultural dissimilarity, and seeks to perpetuate this. The Haitian situation is structurally similar to that of San Luis. Although disagreements occur among students of Haiti concerning the definition of Haitian stratification in terms of caste or class, there is marked consensus on the existence of two different cultures in that country, and also on the definition of Haitian social stratification in terms of this cultural cleavage. In effect this means that cultural cleavages of a particular order, if associated with a rigid and traditional pattern of subordination, may give the appearance of caste, when they are really of a different nature. It also means that in populations characterized by wide cultural variability, the analysis of social differentiation must proceed together with the study of the cultural differentiation, in the same way that the study of acculturation must proceed also by the study of the social structures involved. Unless this coördination of cultural and sociological study obtains, then acculturation study is deprived of its social reference on the one hand, and stratification is inadequately conceived in terms of race, caste, or class on the other.

Few explicit studies of social differentiation have yet been made for British Caribbean societies, although there are several accounts of these populations which interpret them in terms of social and cultural divisions. Thus Martha Beckwith's study of Jamaican folk culture implicitly recognizes an important cultural cleavage within that society by its exclusion of a considerable section of the local population from its reference. Madeline Kerr's study reveals similar assumptions, and she explicitly states that this cultural cleavage, expressed as conflict, inhibits the development of healthy personality types among many Jamaicans. For Dutch Guiana and Trinidad, the researches of Herskovits into folk life have similar implications, many of which are explicitly formulated in terms of acculturation processes. Clearly any acculturative situation presupposes the contact and coexistence of two or more cultural traditions. Observations by other students such as Campbell, Reuter, Gordon, Hadley, Pearse, Kruijer, Cohen, Clarke, and Matthews, indicate that this condition is general among Caribbean societies.[81] In Central America comparable levels of cultural differentiation are reported by Redfield, Tumin, Wagley, Gillin, and others, although interpretations vary from the folk-urban continuum of Redfield to the caste constructs of Tumin.[82]

Writers with primary political or administrative orientations also face this problem of interpreting Caribbean social structures and culture. Blanshard, Proudfoot, Simey, and Macmillan direct attention to the complexity of their internal differentiation in both these fields, though differing about the significance of this condition.[83] Olivier writing about Jamaica gave less attention to these aspects of local society than to the community of social and cultural patterns laid down in its history. But publication of this work was followed by major social upheavals in the island, which contrast sharply with the implications of Olivier's study.[84] On the other hand, Macmillan's alternative interpretation of Jamaican society, which directed attention to the instability and internal tensions implicit in its differentiation, was borne out to a high degree by events of the year which followed its publication.

Explicit studies of social differentiation in British Caribbean societies have recently commenced with the work of Braithwaite, Henriques, and Broom.[85] All three writers are concerned primarily with the Creole populations, Braithwaite discussing Trinidad, the others Jamaica. Henriques and Braithwaite conceive the field in terms of stratification, but Broom prefers the more inclusive concept of differentiation. All three writers direct attention to ethnicity and color as criteria of importance in the social structure, but give little explicit attention to cultural differences within the population, or the relation of these factors to the patterns of stratification or differentiation. These three studies are therefore similar in their attack to the extent that they omit direct treatment of the cultural aspects.

Beyond this, they frequently differ, despite concentration on similar problems, and the use of common criteria such as color, occupation, and wealth. Henriques defines Jamaican stratification in terms of three "colour-classes," while Braithwaite speaks of a similar number of strata in Trinidad as castes, semi-castes, and classes. Henriques divides Jamaican society among these classes as follows: lower class, 85 per cent; middle-class, 10 per cent; upper class 5 per cent; and concludes with the candid observation that "The use of the class divisions, upper, middle, lower, is a necessary methodological device, and does not indicate the actual divisions in the society." [86] In other words his analysis may well have no objective reference. Braithwaite's position is very similar, and he simply dismisses the problem of objective reference in a "note on numbers," consisting of license totals of various kinds, and income tax assessments, which cannot themselves be equated directly with the type of variable, color, on which his analysis is principally based.[87] In other words, for both these writers the empirical boundaries of social classes, and thus their constitution, present little problem for stratification analysis.

Both writers agree that the system under discussion is one of continuous stratification, though one within which individual movement across the principal class or caste boundaries is extremely difficult. Both urge that this system is continuous for the population by virtue of the common valuations which it represents. Thus Henriques summarizes the Jamaican situation as follows: "Today the whole colour-class system is dependent upon the almost complete acceptance by *each* group of the superiority of the white, and the inferiority of the black." [88] Braithwaite's view of Trinidad is essentially similar: "Here again, we see that the key to the unity in the diversity of judgments is the acceptance of the upper class as the upper class. In this case, however, we have the main common values shared by all the groups in the society." [89] Now this really consists in explaining social stratification in terms of itself after first assuming that it forms the general framework of the social structure without detailed empirical examination of this question. Agreement upon these points however, does not rule out differences of their interpretation. Thus Henriques emphasizes the disnomic or disbalanced condition of Jamaican society, whereas Braithwaite sees Trinidad undergoing a process of change from adherence to a paramount common value system of a particularistic ascriptive type toward one stressing universalistic achievement. But Braithwaite notes cautiously that "the change may be expected to lead to a certain amount of conflict within the system; and the contradictions between the rival systems of values will be likely to lead to tendencies towards disintegration within the social system." [90] This can only be taken to indicate that the "common value-system" is not truly common at all, and such a view is supported by the data which Braithwaite provides illustrating the divisive effects of the caste, color, class patterns, and values obtaining in Trinidad. Given these divisions, the type of consensus which is presupposed by common values has marginal significance compared with the type of differentiation which obtains. It may well be the case that recent changes in the contemporary situation of Trinidad place primary emphasis on universalistic standards and even that certain elements of Trinidadian society would gain by these; but such conditions refer to the context of Trinidad, and do not directly warrant inferences about their acceptance by the society itself.

Henriques' conception of Jamaica as disnomic directs attention to the low level of integration within Jamaican society. This can only mean that the hierarchy of social divisions as a ranked series of white, brown, and black strata, has a primarily divisive rather than integrative function. Such a view does not conform to those theories of stratification which define it in terms of integrative functions. Now since social integration is an aspect of adherence to common institutions, the association of stratification with disnomic conditions such as Henriques observes in Jamaica would seem to indicate that institutional divergences characterize its different strata in greater or less degree. And this in turn would indicate that stratification is there definable to a large extent in terms of associated levels of cultural differentiation. However we find Henriques demurring to Kerr's conception of conflicting cultures in Jamaica and describing Jamaican "culture" in terms of synthesis and syncretism.[91]

The important question here concerns the form and level at which this synthesis or syncretism obtains. We can illustrate this point from the work of Herskovits. When Herskovits speaks of "the Old World cultural province" as a unit, he refers to certain generalized forms which obtain throughout that area. In a sense therefore, he presents a synthesis of Old World cultures of a very abstract character under the concept of a single cultural province. Of course, Herskovits is quite aware of the abstract and classificatory nature of such a synthesis. The question raised by Henriques' account of Jamaica is whether the cultural "synthesis" of which he speaks is not a conception of this kind, a classificatory, methodological device, subsuming or obscuring many diverse elements. On the evidence which he presents, this would seem to be the case. "Assimilation of European culture for the middle and upper classes has been successful. . . . The problem for the lower class in the elaboration of its institutions has been to endeavour to find avenues of expression denied it by the greater society." [92] This can only mean that the institutions of the lower class differ from those of the upper and middle classes, in which case the Jamaican cultural synthesis is a heuristic taxonomic device of the student, rather than a concrete observable field datum.

Similar problems of the level of generality and abstraction invest the concept of cultural syncretism, as used by Henriques. Cultural syncretism connotes the identification of elements from two or more different traditions. Defined in this way the concept has objective reference to defined complexes and traits, and is clearly valuable, as for instance in the work of Herskovits.[93] In contrast with this definition in terms of specific cultural patterns, Henriques seems to extend the notion of syncretism to all aspects and forms of cultural process simultaneously. Now even if this use of the concept was accepted, such a syncretism would have to be demonstrated in any particular case. But Henriques makes no effort to do this, and in fact, as can be seen from the quotation just given, recognizes the institutional differentiation characteristic of Jamaican society. It is clear therefore that when he postulates cultural syncretism in Jamaica, he does so on grounds which do not derive from field materials; and these grounds can only be theoretical or methodological in nature. Possibly these two conditions are integrated and require the conception of a single cultural field, whether as synthesis or syncretism, if the type of analysis Henriques offers is to be possible at all. "Complete disnomia is difficult to conceive as such a state implies an entire lack of order in which a society could not exist." [94]

Now the type of analysis which Henriques offers assumes a single continuous system of stratification. This in turn implies some level of consensus about values among the population, some integrative functions of the stratification, and some level of cultural synthesis or syncretism. The questions of interest here are whether these assumptions are liable to empirical demonstration; whether they derive from empirical materials or deductive theorems; whether in fact the nature and form of social differentiation in Caribbean colonies may not be more complex than such analytic schemes can handle adequately. Leonard Broom's view of Jamaica would seem to imply that this is the case:

Social stratification in Jamaica cannot be understood as an uninterrupted continuum of status positions. No matter what empirical criteria are employed, gross discontinuities are to be found. Given the historical forces briefly outlined, this fact should cause no surprise, but the extreme character of this status cleavage affects all facets of Jamaican society.[95]

Both Henriques and Braithwaite devote great attention to color differences in their studies of stratification. But neither appear to handle this problem consistently or systematically. Thus Braithwaite identifies his classes with castes, and defines both in terms of color factors; but his diagram of the color distributions obtaining in the contemporary stratification of Trinidad society indicate considerable departures from these definitions.[96] Henriques similarly defines his strata in terms of color-class, and notes that "this colour-class division is not at all rigid," [97] wealth being an important variable; but he gives a good deal of evidence which suggests rigidity in several spheres. "Each colour category has a series of stereotypes for all the other categories, and for itself";[98] and he concludes that "in fact colour can be said to pose the whole problem of 'cultural' values in the Caribbean." [99] If this is so, then a systematic analysis of the color complex would appear to form an essential preliminary to the development of any adequate model for the study of Caribbean societies. And it is to this analysis that we must now turn.

Color in the British Caribbean

In most mixed Negro-white populations, the concept of color is critical and pervasive, hence we can expect on general grounds that it may have several distinct though overlapping referents. A systematic analysis of the color concept therefore consists of isolating these different meanings, and of determining the relations between them.

As normally used in the British Caribbean, the term "color" connotes a combination of physical characters, such as skin-color, hair-type, form of facial features, prognathism or its absence, and so forth. This is the sense in which Braithwaite and Henriques use the term, and it will be referred to here as *phenotypical color*. The phenotypical color of an individual is simply his or her racial appearance. In British West Indian colonies there is a clear overt rank-order of different phenotypical colors in terms of a prestige scale, which places white phenotypes at the highest and black phenotypes at the lowest points. The phenotypical color of an individual is therefore a factor of importance in his status placement in these societies.

But the matter does not rest there. Often enough, someone who is phenotypically black will claim that he has "white blood," while someone who could be mistaken for white is known to have a mixed ancestry. These conditions direct attention to the biological variation of phenotype associated with varying degrees of racial mixture, and thus to the difference between *genealogical color*—the biological status of an individual as defined in terms of his purity or mixture of racial descent—and phenotypical color or appearance. The classic instance of status ascription on the basis of genealogical color in our field is of course the American system of color-caste; but although British Caribbean societies do not formalize status ascriptions solely in terms of this aspect of the color concept, it receives attention in all of them. Two phenotypically equivalent individuals may be dissimilar in terms of genealogical color, while two genealogically identical individuals, such as brothers, are frequently phenotypically distinct. This variability in the association of phenotype and genealogy guarantees that, where color values loom large in social organization, attention will be directed to both these conditions, even though they may not be generally distinguished with any consistency or precision. Between them, these two categories define and exhaust the genetic aspect of color.

By themselves, however, phenotypical and genealogical color can have no direct or necessary significance in society. This will be apparent immediately the lack of role differentiation on grounds of color in such racially mixed Mohammedan societies as Hausa-Fulani Zaria is brought to mind. In Zaria, light skin color is regarded as an attribute of beauty, but color differences as such form no basis for role differentiation or status ascription.[100] This example alone is sufficient to show the fact that status and role allocation on a basis of color difference is subject to cultural determination. It also suggests that the general concept of color may be an inadequate or misleading term of analysis unless its social and cultural components and their significance are clearly distinguished.

The social aspect of color differences refers to the part which they play in individual and group association. It is thus to be determined by empirical study of formal and informal associations within a society, and can therefore be expected to vary from one society to another. We can most briefly isolate this dimension of the color complex under the term *associational color*. The associational color of an individual is simply the expression of his associational habits in terms of the color of the persons with whom he typically associates on terms of equality, familiarity, and intimacy. Thus a white man who habitually associates with black persons is associationally black, while a black man who habitually associates with white persons is associationally white. Now there is room for misconception of the associational color of an individual, but this reflects misconceptions about the nature and type of his associational habits. Frequently enough, of course, an individual misconceives his own situation in this way, and this can be expected especially of mobile individuals. The point to note is that the associations which an individual forms, and in terms of which his associational color, or "class-color," is estimated, may vary at different times of his life, within limits which reflect the influence of other factors. For instance, as sometimes happens, a person whose fortunes change for better or worse may seek to change his associates correspondingly, and by this social mobility either acquires a new associational color, or has to reconcile himself to a position of relative isolation. The concept of associational color therefore permits a classification of individuals in terms of upward or downward mobility on the one hand, and static or isolated positions on the other. That is to say, besides allowing a formal classification of the population in terms of associational color categories, this concept focuses attention on the dynamics of such systems. It goes a long way toward making possible the direct and systematic study of differences between the observable phenotypes of persons and their classification in color terms within such societies. For, where color differences have social significance, although the color concept reflects this in its complexity, there is normally a ranking of persons in terms of color, a sort of chromatic status scale, and it is in these terms that the equation between an individual's associational and phenotypical color is defined.

So far nothing has been said about behavior, although associational patterns have behavioral content and aspects. Yet behavior per se—the institutions, mores, conventions, and value patterns, which together constitute the culture of a population, besides giving definition and cohesion to the social form—also defines the color complex itself. Hence behavioral patterns are clearly significant to the definition of individual and group statuses within society, and where social differentiation in terms of relativistic color concepts obtains, can be expected to influence or correspond with this differentiation in greater or less degree.

The relevance of this point of cultural identity or difference, real or assumed, for our present analysis can be readily appreciated by consideration of the lack of status ascription on color bases in multiracial Islamic societies which for religious reasons are intolerant of internal cultural differentiation. In contrast, role and status ascription on racial and color bases is characteristic of multiracial societies where, until recently, the racial divisions have formed culturally distinct groups. Under conditions of the latter type, the alternative to the complete disnomia that puzzled Henriques consists in a hierarchic organization of these culturally distinct groups, and the domination of one of these racial or cultural groups over the others provides the basis for a general prestige scale of their distinctive characters, phenotypical or other, such as we are now concerned to dissect. This simply means that, where culturally divergent groups together form a common society, the structural imperative for maintenance of this inclusive unit involves a type of political order in which one of these cultural sections is subordinated to the other. Such a condition derives from the structural requisites of society on the one hand, and the condition of wide cultural differences within some populations on the other. It is under such conditions that differences in race and color acquire general social significance.

We can illustrate the relation between race and culture briefly by considering the two opposite types of limiting cases. Mohammedan Zaria presents an instance of the type in which cultural uniformity obtains within a multiracial society, and race and color differences do not provide bases for status determination or role allocation. Although the governmental structures are hierarchic in type, office is open to members of all races within the society. Under conditions such as these differences of race and color lack social significance and hence are not socially systematized. Cultural community overrides racial differentiae.

The other type of limiting case obtains where culturally differentiated groups of the same race form a common society, characterized by the domination of one group by the other, and the expression of this cleavage in racial terms. This seems to be the position in contemporary Guatemala, since racial differences which lack biological foundations are postulated between Ladino and Indian. Similar conditions obtained in Britain after the Norman Conquest, and persisted until the Tudor Period. When the cultural differences of Norman and Anglo-Saxon lapsed, together with the form of feudalism in which they were expressed, the concept of a general English culture, and of the Englishman as distinct from either Norman or Anglo-Saxon, developed. Later, similar racial differences were mooted as an aspect of the cultural cleavage between the British and the Highland Scots, but attention to these racial factors also lapsed with the destruction of Scottish Highland culture in the years after 1745.

These instances show that race differences may be predicated even where they are of marginal character, provided that cultural cleavages of a certain order exist within a society. They also show that race differences lack formal expression where cultural uniformities obtain between the two groups within a single society. It is thus clear that hierarchic race relations reflect conditions of cultural heterogeneity in the societies in which they obtain, and that they tend to lapse or lose their hierarchic character as cultural uniformity increases. It follows that multiracial societies which invest racial or color differences with social status significance display cultural heterogeneity; and also that in such societies, the dominant culture will have high prestige, the subordinate less.

For societies such as those of the British Caribbean, this conclusion implies the existence of a scale of cultural color in which "white" and "black" cultures provide the poles. Moreover, it implies that all the members of such societies will be ranked in terms of their behavioral conformity to one or another of these traditions. Thus we arrive at the notion of *cultural* or *behavioral color*, that is, the extent to which an individual's behavior conforms to the norms associated with one or other of the hierarchically ranked cultural traditions of the society, as these norms themselves are associated with color-differentiated groups. Thus, in Jamaica for example, there is a set of expectations which define the behaviors of whites, browns, and blacks. In terms of these expectations, a white person whose behavior conforms more closely to that of the brown population is culturally brown. Similarly, a pure Negro may be culturally white or brown, which simply means that his behavior is analytically homologous with that distinguishing these color groups as cultural groups.

This type of color concept is implicit in much of the American literature, but requires explicit formulation for the analysis of societies in which color "can be said to pose the whole problem of cultural values." Powdermaker illustrates the concept when she introduces her discussion of Negro acculturation in Cottonville with the following remark, "some Whites deplore the process, and question how far it can go, believing the Negro incapable of becoming 'sociologically White.' " [101] Broom makes a similar point in his recent analysis of Jamaican social differentiation. "Certainly the differential statuses which are all too apparent in the 1943 census are reinforced by the selective perception of census takers. For example, a pheno-typically black civil servant of the upper categories is most likely to be classified as 'coloured.' A dark-coloured peasant is most likely to be classified as 'black.' " [102] In Grenada the folk use the term "African" to denote persons who adhere to African cultural traditions, as for instance ritual forms, such as the African Dance (Shango), whatever their racial or color characteristics. At the same time, Grenadians describe wealthy black persons who practice the same culture as that of the whites, as "white."

Where two cultural traditions coexist within a society, and their hierarchic relation does not closely approximate to caste, then social mobility and acculturation proceed simultaneously with sufficient volume to produce an intermediate cultural tradition, a sort of hybrid culture, which, although approximating more closely one of the two homogeneous original traditions, contains elements of both, and by virtue of its hybrid nature occupies a middle position in the cultural prestige scale. Where the two terms of this cultural scale are identified with white and black, this intermediate culture, the product of fusion, acculturation, and syncretism, is classified as colored or brown.

There is a tendency for genealogical and phenotypical color to correspond. There is also a tendency for associational and cultural color to correspond. This latter correspondence simply reflects the fact that people tend to associate with those whose behavior conforms to the norms which they themselves hold, rather than with those who hold different norms. But this latter convergence is at one and the same time more open to the influence of other factors and more variable than is the association of phenotype and racial composition, which, once given, remains unalterable. The nature, basis, and range of variability in this association of cultural and associational color forms an important aspect of the typological definition of the social systems in which such multiple stratifications obtain. The same point holds for the association between the cultural and social color-scales on the one hand, and the biological scales on the other. In conditions such as American color-caste, cultural uniformities between whites and Negroes are not yet recognized as an adequate ground for their equal association, although there is a trend toward revision of the caste line as acculturation proceeds; and in terms of our preceding discussion, we can expect "caste" to disappear as cultural uniformity extends to all levels of institutional behavior. Where color-caste does not obtain, cultural color, subject to certain other factors, such as wealth on the one hand, and genealogy, or phenotype on the other, tends to provide a basis for individual and group association of various kinds.

It is methodologically useful and revealing to assume initially that there is a complete correspondence of cultural with associational color, and of both with the biological dimension, in noncaste societies; and then to proceed to the empirical examination of this assumed correspondence, to determine the extent to which it in fact obtains, the conditions under which it does and does not obtain, and the variability of its actualization and associated conditions at different levels of the system. An empirical study of this type, focused on color-scale correspondences and divergences, will direct attention to the fifth and final dimension of the color concept, *structural color*. The structural dimension consists in those factors and aspects of social process, and the relations between them, that give the society its distinctive form as an arrangement of units and processes. Thus the structural dimension is an abstract analytic category reflecting the distributions and types of power, authority, knowledge, and wealth, which together define and constitute the social framework. When we speak of structural color, we imply an allocation of these variables among color-differentiated groups which obtains presently and reflects historical conditions. Thus structural color connotes the empirical distribution of these variables among the color-differentiated population. If we like, we can distinguish between contemporary and historical scales of structural color, and for certain purposes, such as the analysis of a rapidly changing situation, a distinction of this type may be essential. To the extent to which it is unnecessary, the society under study conforms to conditions of stationary equilibrium, under which the expected distributions of power, wealth, authority, and knowledge among the population are empirically confirmed. In such a scale, the structural color of an individual expresses his equation with the expected or empirical distribution of these controls among the population classified in a color scale. Thus a black man possessed of wealth and other structural criteria normally associated with the white population in such a scale is structurally white. Similarly the "poor white" as the term implies, is not structurally white, and for this reason, although he may adhere to white institutions, ceases to be associationally white, and forms a separate community of his own, where conditions permit. The analysis of discrepancies and consistencies between the empirical and the assumed correspondence of the first four color-scales will thus expose the fifth dimension of this complex, and at the same time lay bare the social dynamics to concrete analysis. For the reasons given above, it will be apparent that any society which is characterized by role ascription on a color basis is also characterized by a scale of structural color.

In the analysis of such social systems, we are therefore presented with the problem of determining by examination of the correspondences or lack of correspondences of the various color scales, the bases and conditions of superordination and subordination, and the relative significance of these forms and factors at different points of the system, by an inductive empirical study of deviant and typical cases together. This means simply that the definition of such social structures as a particular set of relations holding between certain critical variables, such as power, wealth, authority, and knowledge, and reflecting their distribution among the population, can only be approached after the position of a sufficient number of individuals within a composite color-scale representing the four dimensions of phenotype, genealogy, association, and institutional adherence, has been determined, and when the correspondences, or lack of correspondences, between these several distributions have been inductively analyzed in terms of the structural variables.

Analytic Models for Caribbean Societies

The type of theoretical model which emerges from this examination of color in the Caribbean has several interesting features. It is eclectic in the sense that it seeks to analyze and relate the parts played by such factors as race, culture, association, and power in the social system without predicating any initial priority or order among them. It is eclectic also in the sense that it provides a common framework for the integration and coördination of the various lines of research which we have been reviewing, and attempts their synthesis. It has heuristic values as a hypothesis about such societies; but the model is merely a guide to field studies, and its revision, elaboration, or abandonment will surely follow from the empirical researches which it may influence or stimulate. In other words, it is a goad to investigation, not a narcotic; and it defines the methods of field research as quantitatively and qualitatively inductive, their focus in terms of social and cultural differentiation, and their results and analyses as both the purpose and test of theory, and the ground for new, superior hypotheses. A brief consideration of such topics as social structure, social mobility, or acculturation, will serve to define the model more precisely, and illustrate its general comparative character.

Multiracial societies vary in the social significance that they ascribe to racial difference. In those societies where racial factors play a prominent part in status placement and role allocation, contemporary or historical conditions of cultural differentiation obtain. Thus such societies are characterized by a tradition of cultural plurality. To the extent that this condition persists as a contemporary fact, such societies approximate the model of plural societies. Thus the first problem of field research is the determination of the levels and areas of institutional differences and continuities within the population. Plurality is an aspect of cultural differentiation—not a finite thing, but a dimension, in terms of which some societies are more or less plural or homogeneous in their culture, and may be so variably in different fields. It is therefore essential in the comparative study of institutions and other cultural forms to ascertain their uniformity or difference, formally and functionally. Since such institutions as family, mating, kinship, religion, law, education, government, and property constitute the basic complexes and units of culture and society alike, the study of cultural and social differentiation must focus on the variability and distribution of their different forms throughout the population. Analysis of these results will show the degree to which and the fields in which the society under study approximates the extreme condition of cultural pluralism.

However, a word must be said about the structural limit of extreme differentiation. This structural limit is itself inherent in the nature and concept of society as an order or system of relations, that is, a type of unit. The unity of a population characterized by extreme differences of institutional culture is only possible where one of these culturally differentiated sections controls the destinies of the total unit. The alternative to this is disunity, that is, the existence of several societies as separate units having external relations with one another. Thus, within units characterized by such cultural pluralism, governmental institutions, such as law, administrative, political, and military systems, are by definition under the ultimate or exclusive control of one or other of the culturally differentiated groups. And in this way the maintenance of social unity is linked with hierarchic sectional relations of dominance and subordination. It follows, therefore, that within plural societies, plurality of form in political institutions cannot obtain. Such political pluralism really connotes the existence of different societies, each possessing internal autonomy in greater or less degree. Thus, the Hausa states of Northern Nigeria which were administered under the British policy of Indirect Rule through their own chiefs and political institutions are not part of an Anglo-Hausa plural society, but form separate societies of their own. Where cultural plurality obtains within a single polity however, it follows that the formal political institutions characteristic of subordinate cultural sections of that unit have been repressed as a condition of the political unity of the total society under the control of the dominant group.

We can describe that part of the population of a culturally heterogeneous society which practices a distinctive and uniform system of institutions, that is to say, a separate culture, as a *cultural section*. The boundaries of such a section, and the definition of its culture, are both matters for determination by field studies. Theory guides such investigations by directing attention to the problem of institutional variations, and their distribution within a population. It also provides a frame for the analysis of systems characterized by institutional variability of different types and orders, but does not predicate them. It is important to grasp this point, as it contains the difference between an ideology, which is often unverifiable by nature and may well hinder rather than help research, and a frame of hypotheses which defines field problems, systematizes their study, and is itself revised by their results.

Now, as we saw from our discussion of color, associational patterns may obtain within plural units between persons who practice different cultural traditions, and may also serve to distinguish persons who practice an identical culture. It is inherent in the nature of the hierarchic relations between culturally differentiated sections, which express and define the political order of a plural society, that the status divisions between these cultural sections should be of an extreme kind. Consequently the intimate and habitual association of members of different cultural sections on terms of equality will normally be absent in homogeneous societies, marginal within static pluralities, and of a changing range and character under conditions of structural change in plural societies. We can thus conceive of plural societies in terms of a series of associational continua, with marked status gaps between them. To the extent that these continua correspond with cultural divisions, class stratification may obtain within each continuum though not between them. We can describe these associational continua as *social* or *status sections,* and the marginal areas resulting from their bisection of cultural boundaries can be classified as *active* or *inactive margins,* in terms of their relation to the processes of structural change of such societies. Active margins will consist of groups associating primarily with adherents of different cultural traditions. Inactive margins are formed by groups associating primarily with members of

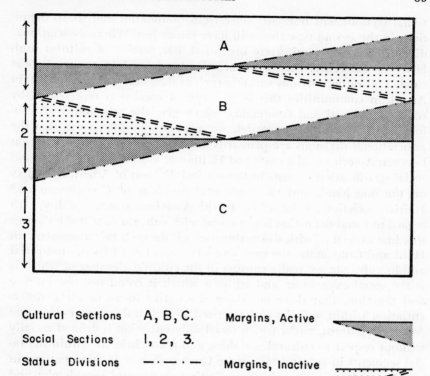

Cultural Sections	A, B, C.	Margins, Active
Social Sections	I, 2, 3.	
Status Divisions	— · — · —	Margins, Inactive
Culture Boundary	——————	

their own cultural section, but also with members of active margins. The accompanying diagram illustrates one set of possible relations between these structural categories in a plural society of three cultural and social sections. Despite its schematic character and oversimplification, such a model has the virtue of directing attention to certain features of decisive importance in the comparison and analysis of plural systems. These include the nature of the status gap, the nature of the cultural diversity, the number of social and cultural sections, the correspondence between them, the margins of their overlap, and the stability, change, and conditions associated with these margins.

In terms of such a model we can compare societies according to the number and arrangement of their cultural and social sections; and in this comparison variations in the correspondence and relations of these two dimensions of internal differentiation are clearly of critical importance. On this basis we can distinguish between those pluralities within which associational divisions are defined without respect to cultural differentiation in the one case, and those in which they are defined primarily in cultural terms. In the first of these types, associa-

tional sections will normally have rigid boundaries and sharp definition; in the second type they will have rather less. Where associational
discontinuities are uniformly instituted, irrespective of cultural similarity or difference, they will normally be defined in terms of some
single and rather obvious variable such as language or race. In certain
American communities this is the type of condition represented by
color-caste. Haiti and Guatemala, which give the appearance of con-
forming to this American model, are substantially different in that the
associational divisions are primarily cultural in base. The distinction
between American color-caste and Haitian or Guatemalan cultural and
social stratification consists in the vertical division of American society
on the one hand, and the horizontal divisions of Guatemalan and
Haitian societies on the other. In the American system rigidity with
regard to racial definition is consistent with cultural continuities across
this line as well as with discontinuities within each racial segment. In
Haiti and Guatemala, the caste-like structure, for all its posited racial
and linguistic bases, really consists in the cultural cleavage of which it
is the social expression, and without which it could not obtain. We
find therefore that there are three alternative forms of social differentiation within societies characterized by cultural heterogeneity: the
American pattern, under which social differentiation is defined racially
without respect to cultural variables, and relativistically within the racial segments in cultural terms; the Guatemalan or Haitian pattern in
which social and cultural differentiation correspond completely; and
the type of pattern represented by our diagram in which cultural and
social differentiation vary to some extent independently of each other,
although within limits set by other aspects of their interrelation within
a single structural unit. Where cultural differentiation provides the
general and historical basis for associational differentiation, but over-
laps and margins occur, then a system of multiple criteria provides the
basis of status ascription; and the relativism of individual ranking,
which contrasts with the rigidities of American or Guatemalan "caste,"
requires for its examination the type of concept and method outlined
above in our discussion of Caribbean color.

We have therefore to deal with culturally homogeneous or heterogeneous societies as well as those with relativistic or rigid systems of
social differentiation. It will at once be apparent that both forms of
social differentiation may coexist in either type of society. Thus, a
homogeneous society may contain two rigidly differentiated categories
of persons, within each of which ranking by multiple criteria of similar
or different kinds reflects relativism. This would appear to be the
American position, looked at from a national point of view. A plural
society may have similar structure. In the British Caribbean, for instance, it is possible that Barbados, Antigua, and St. Kitts, which share

a common ethnic and cultural composition, are examples of this structural type. Trinidad and British Guiana, which have a more complex ethnic and cultural composition, also belong in this category. In plural societies of this type, the racial variable, as culturally defined, provides a rigid uniform basis for the social differentiation of particular ethnic groups, within each of which relativistic ranking may obtain on similar or different lines, reflecting their internal cultural diversity.

In effect, therefore, we emerge with six possible structural types, looked at from our present point of view: plural or homogeneous societies having either rigid or relativistic ranking systems on the one hand, or those containing both types on the other. Clearly the coexistence of these two modes of differentiation within a society is only possible where a rigid division of the spheres and conditions in which each has significance for the other obtains. A similar point applies to the distinction between homogeneous and plural societies, which can be illustrated by consideration of the ambiguous position of Brazil and the United States.

There is evidence of pluralistic conditions in the United States, for instance, though these conditions occupy a minority status in terms of national American culture. This means that the significance of localized cultural plurality is marginal for the classification of American national culture or society in terms of homogeneity or plurality. Despite the sharp differences of Brazilian and American race relations, these two societies occupy a similar position in that both contain within their national framework localized pluralities having a minority status. This similarity between Brazil and America reduces to three related conditions. In both societies the dominant culture, which also enjoys the highest prestige, is practiced by the overwhelming majority of the population. Divergent cultures therefore have true minority status at the national plane, although their local significance is often great. It is very probable that the concept of a heterogeneous society containing culturally pluralistic elements is only applicable under the combination of limiting conditions which characterizes Brazil and the United States. It is notable that different patterns of race relations may obtain in such conditions, without in any way distinguishing between them at the present level of discussion.

Granted the presence of two or more cultural traditions in Caribbean and Middle American societies generally, that is to say, their pluralistic character, then—after the determination of these traditions—the first task in their comparison consists in the study of their various systems of differentiation and stratification, that is, the comparative analysis of their intersectional and intrasectional frameworks. Such study consists largely in an examination of the interrelation of cultural and social patterns within and among these various populations; and it focuses on the definition of relations holding between each of these systems separately, and both together, especially as these relations and their variability are essential to the understanding of particular social forms.

The appropriateness of such an approach is apparent from a consideration of social mobility in the Caribbean. In a plural society, social mobility has two forms, sectional mobility, and individual mobility. Sectional mobility is initially expressed through changes in the sizes and directions of intersectional margins, and is indicative of general structural change, such as may now be underway at different rates in the various British Caribbean colonies. Individual mobility in a plural society may be upward, downward, or lateral. Vertical individual mobility is of course found in many homogeneous societies, but both sectional and lateral individual mobility cannot by definition develop within them. Lateral mobility occurs when a person, usually already marginal in some degree, alters his behavioral pattern to conform with a culture different from that which he formerly practiced without effecting any corresponding alteration in his social position. In terms of the total society, the marriage of "peasants" after years of "faithful concubinage" is an instance of lateral mobility, even when associated with changes in other institutional patterns, such as religion, land-tenure, and the like. It is this difference between cultural movement and social mobility which, to a large degree, accounts for the failure of acculturation programs instituted by the dominant section of a plural society to win much acceptance from subordinate sections.

Individual upward mobility presents some interesting problems in the study of British Caribbean societies. It throws light on the relative significance of components in the structural color scale, and also on the variability of their relations at different structural levels. Let us briefly explore a set of hypothetical cases in which differently placed individuals all return to their homeland with equal increases of wealth. We have then a situation in which one factor, wealth, is constant, while others vary. Assuming a relativistic ranking system, our problem consists in the relative mobility of individuals drawn from different sections of the totality; for example, three brown men, one of whom is culturally white, another culturally intermediate or brown, and the third culturally black; or three white men, distinguished similarly; or three black men; or one white, one brown, and one black man, all belonging to the same cultural section—and so on. It is clear that the rate, range, and type of upward mobility will vary with respect to these differences. Similarly, if we considered the probabilities of downward mobility for such persons, consequent on an equal loss of wealth, similar differences of type, rate, and range would be noticeable; and the systematic character of the relations between color, cultural adherence, wealth, and individual mobility in such societies could be determined and subjected to predictive tests.

Acculturation as an aspect of process in the life of Middle American and Caribbean societies has received extensive attention. It has provided a field for such studies as those of Herskovits and Redfield. Of itself, this fact indicates the relevance of our pluralistic concepts for the analysis of such societies. As a process occurring within populations sharing common political institutions, acculturation implies a high degree of internal cultural differentiation, that is, a pluralistic character. Such acculturation processes define the societies in which they occur as pluralities of greater or less degree. Even where such societies show marginal plurality on the national plane, as is true of Brazil and America for instance, acculturation within them indicates significant pluralism at the local or community level. Thus, despite their differing orientations and problems, both Afro-American and Folk-Urban studies reflect and imply as their field of investigation, a type of social system containing culturally differentiated sections, that is to say, a condition of pluralism.

Other writers with less explicit theoretical interests than Redfield and Herskovits provide impressive evidence of the nature and extent of this cultural heterogeneity in the Caribbean and in Middle America, and sometimes distinguish clearly between *folk* and *elite* within such societies.[103] Such coincidence can hardly be accidental, and its theoretical implications cannot be ignored, considering the multiplicity of approaches that such studies represent: administrative, political, anthropological, folklorist, social psychology, and race relations. Their convergence provides most impressive evidence of the condition and nature of society in this region, and of the appropriateness of the plural framework to the analysis of such units. Such consensus is especially impressive in that it contains or reflects no hint of an explicit conception of the societies and cultures concerned in terms of plurality, as we have defined it. Yet we have shown that the deficiencies of the various approaches to the study of these societies all reflect an inadequate treatment of the interrelated planes of social and cultural differentiation; and that some conceptualization of these relations in terms of plural systems alone provides a basis for the systematic and detailed empirical study of such conditions. In such a program of studies, economist, historian, political scientist, anthropologist, social psychologist, folklorist, and sociologist can all contribute to one another's understanding of the common field equally and continuously. It is also worth mention here that concepts of pluralism such as we have just discussed have already been applied by Van Lier to Surinam, and by Beals to certain Middle American societies.[104]

Conclusion

Our analysis of the literature has revealed the principal current approaches to the social and cultural study of this area. These approaches consist in Afro-American studies, the Folk-Urban theory, studies of stratification, and psychological research which initially relies on concepts drawn from cultural and social analysis. We have seen how a competition of models tends to obtain, acculturation studies presenting one framework, while stratification theory offers another. We have seen that each of these separate models is inadequate for the systematic and comprehensive study of these societies, and that both try to disguise their inadequacies behind a screen of vague, unverifiable assumptions and indeterminate concepts. It has also been shown that when combined in terms of a theory of plural societies and cultures, these competing approaches may provide a unified and refined frame of concepts of equal use in defining the problems under study and in providing an integrated comparative framework for the study of this region.

[4

Social and Cultural Pluralism

In this essay I shall try to define the concepts and conditions of social and cultural pluralism and to indicate their importance for social theory and research. In order to focus attention on theoretical issues I avoid descriptive materials as far as possible.

J. S. Furnivall was the first to distinguish the plural society as a separate form of society. Furnivall was an economist with considerable experience of the colonial Far East. He summarized this experience as follows:

In Burma, as in Java, probably the first thing that strikes the visitor is the medley of peoples—European, Chinese, Indian, and native. It is in the strictest sense a medley, for they mix but do not combine. Each group holds by its own religion, its own culture and language, its own ideas and ways. As individuals they meet, but only in the market-place, in buying and selling. There is a plural society, with different sections of the community living side by side, but separately, within the same political unit. Even in the economic sphere, there is a division of labour along racial lines.[1]

Anyone with Caribbean experience will recognize the force and value of Furnivall's remarks, but during the years since he introduced it the idea of pluralism has undergone little refinement or systematization, although the term "plural society" now enjoys wide currency. Perhaps for this reason sociologists have tended to shy away from the concept, yet it is essential for comparative sociology, it is easily developed and applied, and without it a rigorous analysis of certain societies is extremely difficult, if not impossible. I shall therefore try to give this concept a suitable theoretical form.

It was the plural economies of the Far Eastern colonies that attracted Furnivall's attention. He saw clearly that this economic pluralism was simply an aspect of the social pluralism of these colonies, and said so in the passage already quoted. However, I wish to take the argument

75

back one step further, since this social pluralism is also correlated with cultural pluralism, and since the plural society itself develops in rather special, although by no means unusual, conditions. Accordingly, I shall begin by considering the most general problems of social science, namely, the nature of culture and society and their interrelation. To do so I shall quote some recent thinking on these topics.

Ever since Tylor defined culture as all those "capacities and habits acquired by man as a member of society," [2] there has been a fairly general agreement on the nature of culture. For the early anthropologists, culture was the proper subject matter of anthropology and, despite the work of L. H. Morgan, it was only with Émile Durkheim and his school that the nature of society and its relation to culture became an important focus of interest. By then Tylor's definition had become entrenched, and social organization was generally treated as one dimension of culture. The problem of defining society was thus complicated by the requirement that this definition should fit prevailing views of culture. For this reason, among others, Durkheim's method and theory at first failed to win wide support.

It is easy enough to define society generally, and Radcliffe-Brown's description of it as "the network of social relations" is perfectly adequate, social relations being distinguished by recurrent mutual adjustments. However, even this sort of definition tends to reduce society to social structure by telescoping quite different levels of abstraction. The real difficulty crops up when we try to define societies generally so as to distinguish between them. Since Tylor's view of culture implies that any particular culture is borne by a particular society, it is difficult to see how we can distinguish between cultures either, unless we have some agreed definition of societies.

By ignoring this anthropological concern with culture as primary and all-inclusive, sociologists tend to escape the difficulties of definition that arise from having to fit culture and society together; however, in trying to distinguish societies, they face much the same problems as do the anthropologists, and their solutions are not very different. Thus the current sociological preference for the study of social systems avoids the problem of defining societies themselves. Marion Levy makes this point very clearly, and bases his version of structural-functional theory on a definition of societies as theoretically self-sufficient systems of action, the members of which are mostly born into their respective units.[3] This definition has three features of special interest here. First, Levy's action has obvious affinities with that behavior that anthropologists regard as the content of culture. Second, the theoretically self-sufficient system is generally the most inclusive of its kind. Third, the view of societies as relatively closed reproductive units raises certain difficulties. In these terms, each Nuer tribe might well be a separate society.

Faced with this problem of distinguishing between societies, Rad-cliffe-Brown's response was an analytic evasion rather similar to the social system approach. In his view, "If we take any convenient locality of a suitable size, we can study the structural system as it appears in and from that region, *i.e.*, the network of relations connecting the inhabitants amongst themselves and with the people of other regions." [4] Radcliffe-Brown then equates "single societies" with the "structural systems observable in particular communities." [5] Despite this, he constantly encountered the problem of differentiating homogeneous and heterogeneous societies. Since he chose to study structural systems rather than societies, and since he conceived these systems as functional equilibria, they were homogeneous by assumption, and so heterogeneity was ruled out. Nevertheless, Radcliffe-Brown offered a useful criterion for distinguishing structural systems. In a homogeneous system each status and role has a uniform definition. When identical statuses and roles are defined differently we have a plurality of structural systems.[6]

For Raymond Firth, "No society can be given a definite limit," and he holds that "fields of social relations, not clear-cut societies, must be the more empirical notion of social aggregates." [7] On the other hand, Nadel, like Marion Levy, found it necessary to distinguish between societies, and he defines them as "the relatively widest effective groups," effectiveness being judged by "the quantitative range of institutional activities entered into by the group . . . and the nature and general relevance of these activities." [8] Nadel then points out that "mostly, when we look for a society, we find a political unit, and when speaking of the former, we mean in effect the latter." [9] There is an obvious correspondence between Marion Levy's "theoretically self-sufficient system of action" and Nadel's "relatively widest effective group"; both tend to be defined politically.

Since I am concerned with distinguishing between homogeneous, plural, and other types of society, I cannot avoid this problem of defining a society; neither can I ignore questions of the relation between society and culture. It is obvious that when societies are conceived as structural systems in equilibrium, their homogeneity is assumed, and heterogeneity is difficult to define, classify, or analyze. In consequence, one general model, namely, that of homogeneous structural systems, is applied to quite different types of society, thereby obscuring their differences, misleading their analyses, and blocking the development of social theory. It is perhaps worth noting here that the two main methods of field investigation, namely, community studies and sampling, both encourage assumptions of unity in the systems with which they deal.

Even so, their failure to distinguish societies has neither deterred anthropologists from distinguishing cultures nor from continuing to define culture in terms of society and vice versa. The current view is neatly stated by Firth:

The terms represent different facets or components in basic human situations. If, for instance, society is taken to mean an organized set of individuals with a given way of life, culture is that way of life. If society is taken to be an aggregate of social relations, culture is the content of those relations. Society emphasizes the human component, the aggregate of people and the relations between them. Culture emphasizes the component of accumulated resources, nonmaterial as well as material, which the people inherit, employ, transmute, add to, and transmit.[10]

David Bidney, in his recent review of anthropological theory, shares Firth's view.[11]

Failure to develop an agreed definition of societies ultimately may have the same basis as the continuing definition of culture and society in terms of one another. Analyses based on notions of system tend to avoid the problem of how a culture and a society are related. As we saw, Tylor initially defined culture as behavior learned in society but, oddly enough, social organization, which was taken to represent society, was regarded by Tylor, Malinowski, and others as one dimension of culture. The modern view, as stated by Firth is equally unsatisfactory, since it implies that a culture and a society are always coterminous and interdependent. This view also obstructs the recognition and analysis of culturally heterogeneous units.

In discussing their interrelation, Nadel, like Firth, at first treats culture and society as coterminous. "Society, as I see it, means the totality of social facts projected into the dimension of relationships and groupings; culture, the same totality in the dimension of action." [12] Nadel is here using the term "action" in much the same sense as Marion Levy or Talcott Parsons; but later on he distinguishes between the boundaries of culture, with its complex of language, idea systems, and activities, and society, with its complex of groupings and relationships. At this stage, culture and society cease to be coterminous for Nadel, since his category of "all-culture" includes forms of action such as language, building, or art styles, which are independent of social boundaries.

Nadel rests this distinction upon his concept of institutions as "standardized modes of co-activity," [13] for example, marriage, blood revenge, family, property, chieftainship, and the like. Although he claims that Radcliffe-Brown's definition of institutions is most like his own, it is probably to Malinowski that Nadel was most indebted for this concept. In fact, Nadel's institutions, like Malinowski's, involve a charter of values, a code of rules, set forms of social grouping and personal relationships, a set cycle of activities, a material apparatus, and a purposive character. These are the distinctive features of Malinowski's institutions, regarded as the "concrete isolates of organized behavior." [14]

Nadel shows that ideas, activities, and modes of grouping are interdependent elements of institutions, that they form a common system, although they can be separated for analysis, and that their interrelations can be studied. He then distinguishes between "regulative" and "operative" institutions, between those institutions that are "compulsory," "alternative," and "exclusive," [15] and between institutional and residual or noninstitutional forms of action, which he groups in four categories, namely, unique historical events, autonomous idea systems such as language or art styles, recurrent abnormalities such as suicide, and customary conventions and mores. Nadel includes these noninstitutional actions in his concept of culture. For him society consists of institutional social relations and groupings, and the main body of culture is also firmly rooted in the system of institutions.

The correspondence between Nadel's classification of institutions and Linton's analysis of culture into core, alternatives, and specialties is clear.[16] Linton's core consists of Nadel's compulsory institutions, and his specialties include Nadel's exclusive institutions, but Linton's scheme incorporates mores, conventions, language, and art styles as well.

This review of anthropological thinking provides the background for my argument. I think the views and positions just quoted are as representative as they are significant. The theory of pluralism seems to develop naturally on this basis.

In my view, only territorially distinct units having their own governmental institutions can be regarded as societies, or are in fact so regarded. Delegation of authority and governmental function is quite general and has many forms, but we do not normally treat an official structure as an independent government unless it settles all internal issues of law and order independently. By this criterion we can identify delegation and delimit societies. It often happens that a subordinate population group is permitted to exercise certain functions of internal administration; one does not thereby distinguish it as a separate society. However, colonial governments that discharge the full range of governmental functions within their territories regulate societies quite distinct from those of their imperial powers. In northern Nigeria the scattered communities of nomadic Fulani do not constitute a single Fulani society, but belong to the various emirates in which they reside; likewise, the general concept of Hausa society breaks down into the separate Hausa societies of these emirates.

I hold that the core of a culture is its institutional system. Each institution involves set forms of activity, grouping, rules, ideas, and values. The total system of institutions thus embraces three interdependent

systems of action, of idea and value, and of social relations. The interdependence of these three systems arises from the fact that their elements together form a common system of institutions. These institutions are integral wholes, as Malinowski would say, and their values,
activities, and social forms are mutually supporting. The institutions of
a people's culture form the matrix of their social structure, simply
because the institutional system defines and sanctions the persistent
forms of social life. To define the social structure, we must therefore
analyze the institutional system. Likewise, to define a system of social
value or action, we must first identify and analyze the institutional
framework.

It follows from this that a population that shares a single set of
institutions will be culturally and socially homogeneous. Provided that
it is also politically distinct, it will also form a homogeneous society.
The homogeneity of this unit will be evident in the uniformity of its
social structure, ideational systems, and action patterns. To determine
the forms and levels of integration within such a unit, we must pursue
the method of institutional analysis.

It also follows that institutional diversities involve differences of
social structure, ideational systems, and forms of social action. These
differences may conceivably hold for a single institution, such as the
family, or for an entire institutional system. Territorially distinct units
that practice differing institutional systems and that are politically
separate are culturally as well as socially distinct. In short, institutional
differences distinguish differing cultures and social units. When groups
that practice differing institutional systems live side by side under a
common government the cultural plurality of this inclusive unit corresponds with its social plurality, and the network of social relations
between these culturally distinct groups is wider and more complex
than those within them. In short, culture and society are not always
coterminous or interdependent. We do in fact find societies the
component sections of which have dissimilar ways of life and modes of
social organization. Such societies exhibit cultural and social pluralism
simultaneously.

Institutions have been treated as cultural forms by some writers and
as social forms by others. Actually, they combine social and cultural
aspects equally. Their social aspects consist of set forms of groupings
and relations. Their systems of norm and activity, together with their
material apparatus, properly belong to culture. Although institutions
form the core of culture and society alike, they do not exhaust either.
For our purpose, the important thing to note is that a group's institutional homogeneity involves its cultural and social homogeneity, while
institutional pluralism involves corresponding cultural and social
pluralism. A society the members of which share a common system of

basic or "compulsory" institutions but practice differing "alternative" and "exclusive" institutions is neither fully homogeneous nor fully plural. Such units are socially and culturally heterogeneous.

It is possible to compile an indefinite list of institutions if we adopt a very narrow definition. However, institutions dealing with the same phases of life tend to form a systematic cluster, and to forestall confusion I shall speak of these clusters as subsystems. Thus marriage, family, levirate, extended kinship forms, and the like, together constitute the kinship subsystem. Likewise, government is the subsystem of explicitly regulative institutions, such as law, parliament, police, and civil and military administration. Each of these institutional subsystems has many links with the others; thus the kinship institutions have prominent economic, educational, recreative, religious, and governmental aspects. We need not predicate any preëstablished harmony of institutions, as functional theory has tended to do. The available evidence suggests that consistency, interdependence, and coherence are necessarily greater within each institutional subsystem than between them. This set of institutional subsystems forms the institutional system, and this can vary widely in its mode and level of integration and equilibrium. Societies differ in their complement and distribution of institutional forms. Some lack such institutions as the army, the priesthood, chieftainship, markets, or age sets; but any given institutional system tends towards an internal integration and thus some closure. Thus in a culturally divided society, each cultural section has its own relatively exclusive way of life, with its own distinctive systems of action, ideas and values, and social relations. Often these cultural sections differ also in language, material culture, and technology. The culture concept is normally wider than that of society, since it includes conventions, language, and technology, but the presence of two or more culturally distinct groups within a single society shows that these two aspects of social reality may vary independently in their limits and interrelations.

To analyze a society that has a single uniform culture, we must define the component institutions and their interrelations. As already pointed out, this procedure includes the analysis of action patterns, ideational systems, and social structure. To analyze a society that contains culturally distinct groups we must make similar analyses of the institutional systems of each component group and then determine their interrelations within the inclusive unit. The culturally distinct components of a single society are its cultural sections. They are distinguished by practicing different forms of institution. Generally these cultural sections are highly exclusive social units, each constituting an area of common life, beyond which relations tend to be specific, segmental, and governed by structural factors. Under these conditions the boundaries of cultural and social sections correspond, and the discontinuity of value systems is most extreme. However, it sometimes happens that some members of different cultural sections associate more regularly with one another than with the sections to which they belong. In such cases the social and cultural sections have somewhat different boundaries, and their margins may be dynamic.

This brings me to the problem of defining the type and level of institutional variation sufficient to distinguish cultural groups. It is obvious that modern societies are culturally heterogeneous in many ways. They contain a wide range of occupational specialties, they exhibit stratification and class differences, they often contain ethnic minorities, and their rural and urban populations have somewhat different ways of life. Some writers describe modern society as pluralistic because of its occupational diversity. I prefer to say that it is culturally heterogeneous, and to reserve the term pluralism for that condition in which there is a formal diversity in the basic system of compulsory institutions. This basic institutional system embraces kinship, education, religion, property and economy, recreation, and certain sodalities. It does not normally include government in the full sense of the term for reasons given below. Occupations are simply specialties, in Linton's sense. The development of occupational groupings and institutions multiplies the host of specialties within the culture, but the resulting diversity leaves the basic institutional system untouched. Such a florescence of alternatives anchored in a common system of basic institutions therefore presents conditions of cultural and social heterogeneity without pluralism.

The same thing is true of class differences, which are differences within a single institutional framework. Their compatibility within this framework is essential for their comparison and ranking. Thus we can neither incorporate Hausa class patterns into our own system, nor can we amalgamate the two, simply because our own institutional system and social values differ radically from their Hausa counterparts. Class patterns represent differing styles of life, but the conceptual difference between such life styles and culture as a way of life is profound. Life styles can and do change without involving any change in the institutional system. Within class-stratified societies, such as those of the Hausa or of Britain, the various strata or classes hold common economic, religious, familial, political, and educational institutions; but the condition of cultural and social pluralism consists precisely in the systematic differentiation of these basic institutions themselves.

Within each cultural section of a plural society we may expect to find some differences of stratification or social class. These cultural sections themselves are usually ranked in a hierarchy, but the hierarchic arrangement of these sections differs profoundly in its basis and character from the hierarchic status organization within each severally.

The distribution of status within each cultural section rests on common values and criteria quite specific to that group, and this medley of sectional value systems rules out the value consensus that is prerequisite for any status continuum. Thus the plurality is a discontinuous status order, lacking any foundation in a system of common interests and values, while its component sections are genuine status continua, distinguished by their differing systems of value, action, and social relations. Accordingly, insofar as current theories assume or emphasize the integrative and continuous character of social stratification, they may apply to each cultural section, but not to the plurality as a whole. In class systems, for instance, social mobility and acceptance presuppose adoption of Linton's alternatives, that is, of new class conventions, linguistic habits, and life styles; in conditions of cultural pluralism, however, intersectional mobility involves adoption of a new institutional system, and for that reason it can rarely occur within an individual lifetime.

It is especially important to distinguish between pluralism and "class" stratification because of the profound differences that underlie their formal resemblance. Whereas the assumption of integration may be valid for a class system, it cannot normally hold for a plural hierarchy. In general, social stratification occurs without corresponding pluralism as, for example, among the British, the Hausa, or the Polynesians. There is also no inherent reason why all cultural sections of a plural society should be ranked hierarchically. It has been shown by van Lier that the Javanese, Chinese, Indian, and Negro sections of Surinam have parallel social status.[17] As I have pointed out elsewhere, status models must perform certain social functions, and they cannot do so if they are unduly complex.[18] Consequently, the status structure of a very complex plurality will often equate two or more distinct cultural sections. The point here is that cultural difference and social stratification vary independently. Thus they can neither be reduced to one another, nor can they be equated. Cultural pluralism is a special form of differentiation based on institutional divergences. It is therefore a serious error to equate pluralism with "class stratification," as Lloyd Braithwaite[19] and Raymond Smith[20] have done for Trinidad and British Guiana, respectively.

Like social classes, the rural and urban populations of a given society tend to differ in their life styles rather than in their institutional systems. However, as Redfield has pointed out, the institutions of a developing urban population may come to differ sharply from those of the rural folk.[21] This is a rather special case that involves pluralism only if the basic institutional system is affected. Otherwise the result is a condition of social and cultural heterogeneity.

The problems presented by ethnic minorities are somewhat more complex, largely because this term has been ambiguously applied to racial, national, linguistic, and cultural groups. Let us therefore consider specific cases. The Greeks, Italians, and Irish of New York each have their own religious and family practices, perhaps their own languages and sodalities also. If their institutional systems diverge from the general American model so as to be incompatible with the latter, then they must be regarded as cultural sections. Institutional incompatibility is indicated by differences of grouping, norms, activities, and functions. We have simply to ask, for instance, whether the paternal or maternal, the judicial or the priestly status and role have the same definitions and institutional contexts among differing groups, and whether these role incumbents could be exchanged without violating social practice. If they can, the groups share a common institutional system; if they cannot, the groups do not. Differences in the definitions of these specific statuses and roles imply differing forms of social grouping, of institutional action, and of ideational system. They cannot occur in conditions of institutional uniformity.

By this criterion, it seems clear that marriage and the family vary among Greeks, Italians, and Irish in content rather than in form, in their affective quality rather than in their social function, sanctions, and norms. Likewise, the Greek, Italian, and Irish variants of Christianity share common basic forms of organization, ritual, and belief. Their compatibility is evident as well in their common origin as in these common elements. We do not normally distinguish groups that observe different totems, or the same totem in different ways, as practicing different systems of totemism, and I think there is no case for treating Christianity otherwise. Unless ethnic traditions present incompatible institutional forms, they are, like social class patterns, stylistic variations within a common basic way of life, analytically similar to Linton's alternatives. Thus ethnic variations, like class styles, may produce cultural and social heterogeneity, but do not involve pluralism.

In certain parts of the United States it is possible that the Negro population practices a distinct institutional system in my sense of the term. There is evidence that certain Negro communities in the South differ sharply in their social, religious, and economic organization from those of the adjoining whites. Assuming this to be the case, we must regard such Negro-white populations as plural communities. They are communities, but not societies, even if they embrace entire member states of the Union. As events in Little Rock, Arkansas, have shown, these member states are not independent units, and therefore do not form separate societies. The point here is that federalism permits the presence of plural communities within a nation state that may not itself be a plural society. I discuss this point more fully below.

The whole process of Negro acculturation in the United States, the Caribbean, and other parts of the New World presupposed basic institutional differences between Negroes and whites. It stands to reason that some sections of the American Negro population will now be less fully acculturated than others. As a result, the American Negroes are culturally diverse and may be subdivided institutionally into two or more sections, the acculturated extreme consisting of those who have adopted white American culture as far as the present color-caste arrangement permits, while the opposite extreme consists of those whose religious, kinship, economic, and associational institutions are furthest removed from white norms. It follows that the American Negroes do not form a separate cultural section. They are a subordinate social segment of a culturally heterogeneous society, and may differ among themselves institutionally. Some groups of American Negroes belong to plural communities; others do not. Such a complex situation cannot be handled adequately in terms of race relations alone; pluralism and its alternatives must be defined institutionally rather than in racial or ethnic terms. Cultural heterogeneity has many forms and bases, while cultural pluralism has only one, namely, diversity of the basic institutional system. Plural societies are by no means the only alternatives to homogeneous societies. The United States and Brazil are heterogeneous societies that contain plural communities and evince pluralism without themselves being plural societies. Neither color-caste nor class stratification implies basic institutional differences and, in my view, the term ethnic minorities should be reserved for those national groups that share the same basic institutions as the host society, but preserve distinctive styles.

Several other points should be made before we leave this subject of institutional variation. As we have seen, each institutional subsystem tends to be integrated with other institutional subsystems. For this reason, it is rare for the institutional differences between groups to be limited to one particular institution. If these differences are at all significant, they will generally be associated with like differences in other institutions, and the cumulative effect will be basic cultural and social differences between the groups concerned. Such differentiated groups form separate cultural and social sections.

Institutional differences vary in degree, even when the institutions under comparison also differ in kind. Thus the kinship institutions of West Indian folk and elite form two distinct kinds of system, but the difference between these two systems is less than that between one based on patrilineal descent and polygyny and another based on bilateral kinship and monogamy. Although both paired comparisons reveal differences in kind, and thus belong to the same order, one set of differences exceeds the other. Clearly, the more obvious the set of institutional differences, the easier their identification and analysis. In this sense pluralism is a dimension, some societies being more sharply divided than others or having more subdivisions. Likewise, within a plurality, two sections may differ less obviously from one another than from a third; provided they all have different systems of basic institutions, however, all three are structural units of identical analytic status.

Since institutions are integral units, the elements of which are activities, ideas, and social relations, their differences involve differing systems of idea, action, and social grouping. To determine whether such differences exist in a given population is a simple matter of empirical research. Such study focuses on the institutional forms of grouping, idea, and action within the population. It seeks to determine their uniformity or difference by the criterion of compatibility already discussed and then to define their distribution. Given precise indices and hypotheses, the problems of social integration and change are also open to field study.

Even in a plural society, institutional diversity does not include differing systems of government. The reason for this is simple: the continuity of such societies as units is incompatible with an internal diversity of governmental institutions. Given the fundamental differences of belief, value, and organization that connote pluralism, the monopoly of power by one cultural section is the essential precondition for the maintenance of the total society in its current form. In short, the structural position and function of the regulative system differ sharply in plural and other societies. Institutionally homogeneous societies develop a variety of institutional motivations toward conformity with social norms; institutionally split societies lack these common motivations and tend to rely correspondingly on regulation. The dominant social section of these culturally split societies is simply the section that controls the apparatus of power and force, and this is the basis of the status hierarchies that characterize pluralism. Since the units of this hierarchic arrangement are the cultural sections, ranking applies initially to sections rather than individuals, and within each section it is therefore governed by other status factors.

In such situations the subordinate social sections often seek to regulate their own internal affairs independently of their superiors. Thus, in Grenada the peasants traditionally avoided the official authorities by settling their disputes through local "peacemakers" or magicians, by ignoring official forms of land transfer, marriage, divorce, wills, registration, and the like, and nowadays by appealing to their sectional leader, E. M. "Uncle" Gairy, for assistance in the most varied circumstances.[22] Such evasive adjustments are not necessary among the Bantu on South African reservations, who have their own officials appointed and controlled by the dominant whites. These Bantu are permitted to observe their traditional law as long as it does not conflict with the Union law. In Grenada, where there is only one legal code, the problem of the lower section is to maintain its customs by systematic evasion; the people there are fairly skillful in this respect, but it still remains true that, even within plural societies, we shall not find two equal and independent sets of governmental institutions.

Cultural pluralism is not confined to plural societies, although it is their basis. Furnivall noted this point long ago: "Outside the tropics a society may have plural features, notably in South Africa, Canada and the United States, . . . but in general these mixed populations have at least a common tradition of Western culture. . . . There is a society with plural features, but not a plural society." [23] This passage reveals some theoretical confusion; it would be difficult to name a more extreme case of a plural society than contemporary South Africa. Moreover, Furnivall seemed to think that plural societies were confined to the tropics. Nevertheless, I think that his main point here is very sound; in Brazil and the United States we have societies that evince cultural pluralism, but that are clearly different from plural societies. In Canada the French dominate Quebec, while Anglo-Saxons control the other provinces. Even if the French and British Canadians practiced different institutional systems, their provincial separateness would mean that the Canadian Federation is an association of groups differentiated territorially and institutionally. If this unit were dominated by a distinct cultural minority, it would then present a special form of plural society, the critical feature of which is that within it the cultural sections live side by side, a condition that in the Union of South Africa has given rise to *apartheid*.

In Brazil and the United States the culturally and politically dominant tradition is that shared by the overwhelming majority of the population. Under such conditions, even culturally distinct groups are minorities at the national level, although they may well include some local majorities. As national minorities, they present no threat to the current social order and, as long as their customs are tolerated by the dominant majority, these minorities may persist undisturbed. It is therefore necessary to distinguish such societies as Brazil and the United States from another and far larger group in which the dominant cultural section constitutes a small minority wielding power over the unit as a whole. Under such conditions, this dominant minority is inescapably preoccupied with problems of structural maintenance and economic and political control. For this reason it may actively seek to discourage acculturation among the subordinate majority, since the current incompatibility of their institutional systems is held to justify the status quo. This has happened in the British West Indies on several occasions, and is in 1960 the major issue in British East and

Central Africa. It is this latter group of societies that should be distinguished as plural societies. They are structurally peculiar, and they form a field worth special study. Federal constitutions may modify the significance of community pluralism when the sectional proportions of the community are reversed at the national level. They do not modify the effect of pluralism in the Union of South Africa because the dominant whites are a minority at both levels.

It is probably best to summarize my argument before proceeding. I have tried to show that the institutional system that forms the cultural core defines the social structure and value system of any given population. Thus populations that contain groups practicing different forms of institutional system exhibit a corresponding diversity of cultural, social, and ideational patterns. Since any institutional system tends toward internal integration and consistency, each of these differentiated groups will tend to form a closed socio-cultural unit. Such pluralistic conditions are far more widespread than are plural societies, the distinctive feature of which is their domination by a cultural minority. Pluralism is quite distinct from other forms of social heterogeneity, such as class stratification, in that it consists in the coexistence of incompatible institutional systems. Plural societies depend for their maintenance on the regulation of intersectional relations by one or another of the component cultural sections. When the dominant section is also a minority, the structural implications of cultural pluralism have their most extreme expression, and the dependence on regulation by force is greatest. A society whose members all share a single system of institutions is culturally and socially homogeneous. A society having one basic institutional system in a number of styles or one basic system and a number of institutional alternatives and specialties is culturally and socially heterogeneous. Since social integration develops institutionally, the structural conditions of societies vary according to their homogeneous, heterogeneous, or plural characters. Thus pluralism has three aspects of special significance for us: (1) on the theoretical plane, it directs attention to the need for refinement and variety of analytic models by presenting conditions that cannot be handled adequately with conventional models of homogeneous equilibrium systems or integrative stratification orders; (2) methodologically, there are the problems of studying such units holistically rather than in community segments, of classifying them structurally, and of assessing their relative integration in objective terms; and (3) analytically, the functional organization and development of such units also pose special problems that require historical study.

How do plural societies and other culturally pluralistic units originate? Furnivall thought that they were limited to the modern colonial tropics and were products of Western economic expansion. However, the Norman conquest of Britain, and the Roman conquest before it, certainly established plural societies, and there are many other instances that cannot be attributed to Western economic activity. Thus in Maradi, Niger, the former Habe rulers of Katsina, after being driven out by the Fulani in 1807, established a successor state that is also a plural society, since its Moslem rulers form a minority controlling pagans whose kinship, economic, magico-religious, educational, military, and political institutions are quite distinctive. In Uganda we also find plural societies founded before the Europeans arrived on the scene. Modern economic forces may account for colonial pluralities, but these are not the only ones. Perhaps the most general answer to this question of origin is migration, which also accounts for the development of ethnic minorities. This migration may be forced, as in Habe Maradi or West Indian slavery, or semivoluntary as in the movement of indentured East Indian labor into the West Indies, or voluntary as in the British penetration of Kenya and Burma, or the Dutch colonization of South Africa. It may involve conquest and consolidation, but this is not always the case.

It is a major error to conceive the conditions and problems of pluralism directly in terms of race relations. To do so is to mistake the social myth for reality, and thus to miss the structure that underlies it and gives it both force and form. It is quite true, by and large, that modern plural societies are multiracial, and that these racial groups tend also to be culturally distinct, but this is by no means always the case, as the cultural diversity of the American Negroes and the distinction between *evolué* and *indigène* in Africa makes clear. It often happens that racially distinct groups form a common homogeneous society, as for instance among the Hausa-Fulani of northern Nigeria. Conversely, we sometimes find culturally distinct groups that belong to the same racial stock expressing their differences in racial terms. This seems to be the case in Guatemala, Haiti, and among the Creole folk and elite of the British West Indies. History provides us with many other examples, such as the Normans and Anglo-Saxons, the English and the Scots or, most recently and most elaborately, the Nazi ideology. Race differences are stressed in contexts of social and cultural pluralism. They lack social significance in homogeneous units. As the Caribbean slave literature shows most clearly, the function of racism is merely to justify and perpetuate a pluralistic social order. This being the case, the rigorous analysis of race relations presupposes analyses of their context based on the theory of pluralism.

In class-stratified societies deference is demonstrated or exacted interpersonally, while in plural units it is often generalized by the dominant group and enforced on the subordinate sections. Such generalized obligatory deference is an important mode of social control. Normally, dress, manner, or speech serve to place individuals sectionally but, where racial differences obtain, they usually act as the most general indicators, being the most resistant to change. In this way the dominant minority seeks to perpetuate its dominion and the plural structure simultaneously. Racist ideology seeks to symbolize and legitimize intersectional relations.

Another common sociological error is the reduction of cultural and social pluralism to social stratification. Such equations misstate the character and implications of institutional differentiation where this is not entirely ignored. Thus the Haitian literature debates whether the Haitian cultural and social sections are castes or classes; Braithwaite applies both labels to the sections in Trinidad; Tumin[24] treats the Ladino and Indian sections of Guatemalan society as castes; and Lord Olivier[25] treats the Jamaican cultural sections as classes. Both Tumin and Olivier presented accounts of smooth change within well-integrated societies. Both analyses were discredited by violent upheavals in Guatemala and Jamaica shortly after the publication of the two works. The recent development of racism in Trinidad also questions Braithwaite's analysis. We cannot adequately analyze plurality as an integrated stratification order.

It is also misleading to suppose that the persistence of plural units is due to the predominance of common values between their cultural sections. Such common values and integrative mechanisms can hardly be claimed for societies like Kenya, Hungary, the Union of South Africa, British Guiana, Algeria, or Nyasaland. However, before their current disorders, did the value cohesion and regulative systems of these populations differ significantly from the present? Social quiescence and cohesion differ sharply, and so do regulation and integration but, if we begin by assuming that integration prevails, it is virtually impossible to distinguish these conditions. Here again, pluralism indicates the need for greater refinement in our structural models and social theory.

It is especially difficult to isolate the positive effect of common values in culturally split societies that owe their form and maintenance to a special concentration of regulative power within the dominant group. In the Congo the Belgians tried to solve the problems of political control and social justice intrinsic to these conditions by neutrality in its most extreme form. Accordingly, they denied all cultural sections the franchise, and this appearance of cultural impartiality was highly applauded for the stability it seemed to offer.[26] The reality was somewhat different, as the Belgian legislation affecting polygyny shows clearly, and recent events have shown the total inadequacy of this solution also. Whatever the form of the political system, the differing sectional values within a plural society are a profound source of instability. Since stratification is now assumed to be an integrative order, it is therefore misleading to represent the intersectional relations of a plural society in these terms.

Since the plural society depends for its structural form and continuity on the regulation of intersectional relations by government, changes in the social structure presuppose political changes, and these usually have a violent form. In desperation, the subordinate cultural section may either practice escapist religious rituals or create a charismatic leadership as the organ of sectional solidarity and protest. This sort of leadership develops only where people are desperate in the face of overwhelming odds. We have numerous examples of charismatic leadership in the West Indies.

The consequence of this mode of political change is often an increased instability, since the uncircumscribable powers of charismatic leaders are incompatible with modern bureaucratic organization and Western parliamentary practice. Either the charisma is routinized by ministerial roles and bureaucratic procedures, in which case the people may lose their leader, or both will probably proceed along the dictatorial path.

Recently the British have created several regional federations by uniting colonial pluralities. It is hoped that these federations will provide favorable conditions for the development of their populations, but these federal associations permit the elite minorities of formerly distinct societies to assist one another in controlling their subordinate social sections, as recently happened in Nyasaland, for example. Federalism may modify pluralities if these are absorbed into larger units with a different structure and composition, but these new colonial federations have much the same sectional compositions as their constituent units. Thus they face two critical tests. First, it remains to be seen whether the associated colonies will transfer decisive governmental power to their federations and thus cease to be separate societies. Second, it remains to be seen whether the federal form and association will facilitate structural changes within the component units.

Since institutional systems tend to be integrated, societies that include two or more institutional systems differ structurally, functionally, and in their modes of development from those that do not. Social science cannot ignore such societies, nor can it deal with them fully if they are treated as homogeneous units. Since the sociology and cultural constitution of these societies are unintelligible separately, both must be studied together to provide an adequate analysis. In this paper I have tried to put forward a theory of pluralism that may serve to guide field work and analysis alike. The utility of this theory depends on its capacity for development.

[5

Some Aspects of Social Structure in the British Caribbean about 1820

This essay is based on contemporary accounts of social conditions in the islands of St. Vincent and Jamaica about 1820. As the study is partly an experiment to show the utility of these old accounts for functional analysis of West Indian culture and society at that period, it seems more useful to restrict the number of contemporary sources to a few well-known documents than to make an exhaustive survey of the literature of the period. After careful reading, all references to social and cultural conditions by each of the authors selected were noted and indexed together to form the basis for the present summary. Such a compilation provides continual cross-checking of the various accounts, and makes obvious their various biases, while allowing deficiencies of data in any one description to be supplemented from another. Though the index compiled in this fashion is not printed here, the works used are cited in the Notes.

The substantive, apart from the methodological, interests of the present paper are twofold. It questions the common assumption that changing economic conditions determine changes in social structure in one particular instance; and, by providing a summary account of British West Indian society in structural terms at a point in time midway between the abolition of the slave trade and the Emancipation Act, it seeks to draw attention to certain structural conditions which are relevant to the study of the social development of the British Caribbean since that time.

The population of a British West Indian colony about 1820 was composed of several clearly differentiated categories of persons, as follows: whites, who were either Creoles (i.e., born in the West Indies) or immigrants, and were all free; free colored; free black; colored slaves, who

92

together with the free colored were all Creoles; black slaves, subdivided into Creoles and African immigrants. Calculations by various
writers agree in estimating the numbers of whites and free colored to
be approximately equal to one another in St. Vincent and Jamaica
respectively at this period. For Jamaica also, Stewart estimated that
there were 31,000 colored slaves—that is, 10 per cent of the slave population—as against 35,000 free persons of color.[1] Slaves formed the vast
majority of the population. In view of the social and cultural differences exhibited by each of these population classes, they will be
described separately.

The Whites

White society was not as homogeneous as its small size might
suggest (*ca.* 35,000 for Jamaica; *ca.* 4,000 for St. Vincent). Apart from
the distinction between Creole and immigrant whites, Carmichael and
Stewart distinguished two main categories based on socioeconomic
status which can be termed "principal" and "secondary" whites. Principal whites were those in authority over secondary whites, either as
plantation owners or senior officials. Secondary whites were either
lesser proprietors, landed or commercial, or employees. A further division among the whites followed national lines, principally between
English and Scots. Although figures are lacking, it seems clear that
there was a marked excess of males in the white colonial populations
at this period.

Creole whites are classifiable by occupation into three main groups:
"planters," the professional class, and merchants. Immigrants can be
subdivided into administrative, military, and "planter" groups. Immigrant planters fall into three subdivisions: plantation owners (e.g.,
"Monk" Lewis); their employees (e.g., overseers, bookkeepers, master
masons); and those who, having settled in the colonies with small estates after long years of employment, relied on the hire of their slaves
as jobbing gangs for more or less of their income. Absenteeism was an
important factor in plantation organization, in commerce, and also in
the most lucrative ranks of the administration, Established Church,
and judiciary, which were held as benefices by prominent persons resident in Britain, and administered by delegation of powers to their
employees locally. Absentee planters or their agents dealt with large
British firms, both in selling their produce and in ordering plantation
supplies. Among the Creole section of the white population, absenteeism gave rise to a combination of occupations in the role of attorney.
Two categories of attorney are distinguished: the "great attorney," often in charge of twenty or more estates in a colony at the same time,
and the "lesser attorney," who controlled only one or two, and was

sometimes appointed by a great attorney as his deputy, sometimes by
the proprietor directly. Attorneys were a class of professional planters,
the most prominent of whom sometimes engaged in commerce. Although not all attorneys were landed proprietors, the more successful
usually were. With few exceptions, attorneys at this period were white
Creoles.

The local clergy and missionaries were predominantly white expatriates. Bickell, Stewart and Mrs. Carmichael agree that the white
population was perfunctory in private and public religious observances, and all five accounts indicate antipathy among white planters
to missionary activity among their slaves. So deeply rooted was this
attitude to Christian proselytization among the colonial whites that
Bickell, an Anglican curate, based his advocacy of increased facilities
for the Established Church in Jamaica on the grounds that "conversion" of the slaves would make them more tractable.[2]

An important aspect of class in white society at this time refers to
the type of mating relations that white males practiced. Generally the
"principal" whites, who were the wealthier and politically dominant
class of white society, had white wives and white families, the children
being educated in the United Kingdom. "Secondary" whites, to use
Mrs. Carmichael's term, lacked white wives and white families, and
the legal sanction of marriage for their procreative relationships. Indeed, subordinate white employees on plantations seem to have been
inhibited from marrying by fear of loss of employment. It is apparent
that the status of a free father may determine the status of his children
by slave women. Thus, white subordinate employees, lacking the authority to manumit, or the income necessary to purchase the freedom
of their slave concubines or their children, tended to contribute, with
other groups, to the growing population of colored slaves. On the other
hand, it was taboo for white fathers legally or economically able to
free their offspring by slave women not to do so. In effect, paternity
norms in these extralegal matings differentiated the two main classes
of the white population. It seems, furthermore, that whereas "secondary" whites frequently had black slave concubines as (house)-"keepers,"
whites of the superior class preferred free colored women, and recognized the proper education of their offspring by such unions as an
obligation, frequently sending their sons to school in England, while
their daughters were educated locally in accordance with the notions
of differential education for the sexes current at the time.

It seems that the majority of white males whose white wives and
families were living with them, maintained unions with colored or
black concubines also, indicating that apart from the sex dispropor-
tions of the white population, there was a social preference for concubines, ideally free colored women, among white men. This prefer-

ence, in combination with other factors, conditioned the behavior of free colored women, with interesting effects. Free colored women sought, as a major goal of their life, to form concubinage or "keeper" relationships with white men, and hence avoided marriage to free colored men. Moreover, so well established was the norm of concubinage of white males and free colored females, that white women, who were themselves prohibited under the severest penalties of social ostracism from entering into extramarital sexual relationships, even with men of their own class, were expected by their male relatives and friends to recognize their colored concubines and to receive them socially on various occasions. Frequently, also, a colored concubine would ask her white protector's kinswomen to stand as godmothers to her children by him.

The internal differentiation of white society at this period has been indicated above by outlining the multiple variables of individual status from which the differentiation of subgroups and classes followed. Culturally, also, the white population was heterogeneous, with distinctions between the well educated and the poorly educated, while the immigrants and the creoles formed separate cultural groups.

At this period, also, white society exercised through its males a virtual monopoly of control of the major official institutions such as government in its various sectors—island administration, local government, legislature, law, the militia, and also the Established Church. Stewart, particularly, remarks on the desire of white men for office and title as a declaration and mode of maximizing status, and quotes several instances of military, religious, judicial, and administrative offices held by persons untrained in the exercise of these functions. In discussing the qualifications of the Jamaican clergy, and particularly the newly appointed curates, Bickell makes a similar point. This discrepancy between the duties of office and the capacities or training of the office-holder was most critical in military matters. On grounds of military efficiency a curious down-grading of militia titles was developed, to subordinate these to the command of less high-ranking regular officers on the declaration of martial law. Stewart bears quoting on this general interest in rank and office:

Such indeed is the fondness for dignified situations and high-sounding titles that one man sometimes holds the different situations of the Major-General of Militia, Assistant Judge of the Grand Court, and Custos Rotulorum and Chief Judge of the Court of Common Pleas, without being a soldier or a lawyer; as a safeguard against the danger of entrusting military command in actual service to men ignorant of the science of tactics and its practical details, a scale of Regular and Colonial rank is very properly established during martial law.[3]

Emphasis on status was obviously very great among the whites. De-

scribing the condition of the secondary class of whites, Mrs. Carmichael
states that through continuous association with black or colored folk,
a man of that class becomes "as the expression is, almost a 'white
negro.' " [4] Carmichael for St. Vincent and Stewart for Jamaica state
that the principal whites formed a closed social class. Association with
secondary whites, colored folk, and other social sections was rigorously
excluded, with the exception of the private "keeper" relationships previously noted. Linked with this social exclusiveness of the dominant
group of white society was the extensive use of ostracism as a mode of
social control of its members. The reactions to white women guilty of
extramarital relationships, or toward wealthy white men who allowed
their natural children to remain slaves, have already been noted. Monk
Lewis' experiences when attacked by the Custos of Trelawny in Jamaica in the Assize Court on grounds that he was interfering "with
our system, and by [his] insidious practices and dangerous doctrines
[calling] the peace of the Island in question" [5] because of his indul-
gences to the Negroes on his own estate and his view that their evidence against white persons ought at least to be heard, indicate another
field of behavior in which conformity was exacted under penalty of
ostracism.

Principal whites controlled the economic and political life of the
country. They exerted authority over secondary whites as employers,
in the militia, in local government and the law courts, and also through
differential political status consequent on the freehold property franchise. Instances occurred however, of white overseers rising gradually
through the ranks of managers and lesser attorneys to assimilate themselves in varying degrees to the dominant white class, and to enjoy the
increased privileges of that status. Incentives toward maximization of
status corresponding to those already noted among the principal whites
operated, however marginally, among the secondary whites also. As indicated above, between the two sections of white society, relationships
of superordination and subordination prevailed typically as a consequence of the delegation of authority in the administration of estates
and corporations; but promotion occurred with sufficient frequency to
furnish strong incentives.

Since the whites exercised a virtual monopoly of official institutions,
both in respect of their control and of participation in them, it is necessary to discuss these structures. Freehold real property, which included slaves, formed the basis of the parochial and colonial franchises.
Candidates for election to the legislature were further restricted by a
higher property qualification. The governor had legislative preroga-
tives, acted as chancellor, and was also commander-in-chief of the
regular troops and militia. At this period, the British West Indian
colonies were almost entirely self-governing in local affairs, and con-

tested the right of the British Parliament to legislate on West Indian issues. In view of the autonomy enjoyed by those colonies, the number of "dead-letter" laws enacted by the legislatures of both Jamaica and St. Vincent is significant. These dead-letter laws, in the main, relate directly to the relationships between masters and slaves, for example, sections of the various Consolidated Slave Acts, but also include laws which only have an indirect reference to them, such as acts ordering that parish vestries build chapels, and that rectors, together with the newly appointed curates, instruct the slaves in religion. The legal inability of slaves to give evidence against free persons, white or colored, rendered numerous provisions of the Consolidated Slave Acts and other ameliorative legislation nugatory from the start. As noted above, however, in the case of Monk Lewis, views on permitting slave evidence were strongly opposed by whites. Hence the paradoxical situation in which the ruling class rejected the only means of implementing legislation for which they themselves were responsible. To implement such legislation would require structural changes in the society, involving particularly surrender of status privileges by that section of the population to which legislative power was entrusted. Thus the apparent paradox is resolved. Structural realities made fiction of the law.

Similar attitudes centered about the issue of arming slaves. In 1795 Jamaica experienced a severe rebellion by the Maroons, an enclave composed of descendants of fugitive slaves who enjoyed freedom and local self-government under a treaty by which they acted as a military reserve at the disposal of the Jamaica Government for the suppression of slave rebellions. St. Vincent had a similar military reserve in its Carib population, who also revolted in 1795. Both governments were severely tested by these revolts, and it was suggested in both colonies that slaves be armed to assist in the struggle; white alarmism, however, was far too deeply rooted for such a measure to be acceptable, then or at any later period of slavery. In Jamaica a corps of free black rangers under the command of white officers was eventually mobilized against the Maroons by government in the face of hostile white opinion. This instance indicates the extent of white alarmism. The real cause for white alarm lay in the disproportion between the free and slave sections of the population, and also between the white and the black. The combination of these two dichotomies misled the whites into distrusting the loyalty of even the free black and colored population, when in point of fact these groups were more often in contraposition to the slaves than to the whites. However, alarmism of this type provided the ground for numerous arguments justifying punishment in various forms as the sole means of preserving the social structure by disciplining slaves; it also justified the restriction of civil and political rights of the free nonwhite population. Developments in Haiti (St.

Dominique) after the revolution were frequently cited as the only alternative social development.

Trinidad contrasted with Jamaica and St. Vincent in certain respects, as Mrs. Carmichael pointed out. Trinidad was a recent British acquisition and in 1820 still retained the Spanish code governing relations between master and slave, with certain other Latin institutions. Since its acquisition at the turn of the nineteenth century, Trinidad had been administered through its governors largely by Orders in Council originating in London, implementation of which was enforced by a set of area commandants empowered to investigate slave protests and hear slave evidence. One important consequence of this system which is quite clear from Mrs. Carmichael's account, was the disintegration of the authority enjoyed by masters when, as in Carmichael's case, they emigrated from an old British colony to Trinidad, bringing their slaves with them. Needless to say, in the older colonies conditions in Trinidad were cited as an undesirable consequence of any reduction of the authority of slave-owners.

The Colored Population

As pointed out above, the colored population in the British West Indies included both slave and free sections, which were approximately equal to each other in numbers at this period in both Jamaica and St. Vincent. As slaves, one section of the colored population was prohibited from giving evidence against free persons in a court of law, whereas free people of color were able to do so at this period, though they had not long enjoyed this right. Politically, however, the free colored were prohibited from offering themselves as candidates for election, and from voting, and were conscious of their inferior status vis-à-vis the whites, even in cases where they were the wealthier. The free colored were permitted to bear arms, and they participated in the militia under white officers. Consciousness of status and desire to maximize it were typical of both sections of the colored population; the free colored petitioned for increased civil and political rights in vain, while colored slaves sought their individual freedom in order to acquire the legal status of persons. Acculturation by adoption of white behavior and institutions was a prominent aspect of this preoccupation with improvement of status for colored males, and contributed to the great emphasis they laid on their differentiation as a group from black people, whether slave or free. This confusion of cultural difference with racial difference reminds one of the similar confusion already noted in discussing alarmism among the whites.

Acculturation for the colored slaves was facilitated at a technical level by the traditional plantation practice of employing them as estate craftsmen or domestics, and of keeping them out of the field gangs, a convention rationalized by the statement that they were no good as field laborers. In this way colored slaves enjoyed greater opportunities for purchasing their own freedom than the majority of the black slave population. Nevertheless, free persons of color often held slaves and land in their own right, mainly by inheritance from their white genitors. Some free colored males who had enjoyed education and training at their fathers' expense were also to be found acting as lawyers, accountants, or in other clerical professions. Owing, however, to the social exclusiveness of the white population and to the fact that the few physicians in each colony served the white population as well as other sections, it does not seem that free colored males entered the medical profession at this period. For other reasons, there were also no colored overseers or managers on plantations owned by whites. This was not so much a consequence of the Deficiency Acts,[6] which were such distinguished dead-letter laws that they had already come to be regarded simply as a mode of taxation, as of the refusal of black slaves to work under free colored overseers, and the suspicion of white management that free colored employees on estates were unreliable.

The harshness of free colored owners toward their slaves is remarked upon by all our sources. On general grounds it seems highly probable that the majority of slaves subjected to mistreatment by free colored people were black; in this case their masters can be regarded as expressing in exaggerated form the opposition between the free and the slave as well as that between the colored and the black.

Preoccupation with status can be expected to express itself preëminently in patterns of mating and association. As already pointed out, free colored women preferred concubinage with white men to marriage with free men of their own complexion, even where the latter enjoyed higher economic standing. Free colored fathers, moreover, as a paternity obligation sought settlements for their daughters about to enter into concubinage relationships with whites. A peculiar pattern arose in which free colored women would associate exclusively on one occasion with white males at parties, dances, and so forth, and in another context with men of their own color only. Kinship relations provided the basis of the second type of association, whereas mating was the basis of the first. Under these circumstances, free colored males tended to mate "downwards," that is, with females of darker complexion than themselves, or with cast-off colored concubines of white men. It seems that when free colored men mated with darker women, the relationship was not legalized by marriage, but that when they mated with free colored females marriage was usual. This parallels the taboo on marriage between white men and colored women at this period. It does not appear that there was any strong obligation on free colored fathers to free their children by slave women. Where color was important to the whites and the blacks, shade was important to the colored. This particularism regarding shade seems to have been true for colored slaves as well as for free colored persons with respect to mating, as Monk Lewis indicates. In effect the free colored constituted a class with particular political and civil disabilities and traditional limitations on occupations, as did the slave colored, though at a different level. Both free and slave colored tended to mate outside marriage, the slaves for reasons discussed later, the free colored mainly because of the preference of free colored women for "keeper" relationships with white men, who on no account would legalize these unions by marriage. Mating between free colored males and females appears to have been so rare, that Monk Lewis was at pains to quote two cases of it to disprove Long's statement that mulattoes (colored folk) cannot interbreed.

As an aspect of their aspirations to assimilate themselves to the whites and dissociate themselves from the blacks, both slave and free colored emphasized kinship with their white lines of descent and tended to repudiate kinsfolk on the black lines. Colored slaves frequently held their black mothers responsible for their own slave status, and in this way vindicated their white fathers and rationalized preferences for the white line. Among the free colored the motivations were similar. Desire of the free colored to assimilate white culture and hence raise their social status is indicated by the fact that they constituted the largest group represented in public worship, in proportion to their numbers, and also by the greater interest taken by colored men in European cultural developments which carried prestige value, such as literature, than was usual among the Creole whites. However, the utility of this assimilation of white culture by the colored was limited by the social practice of West Indian colonies, which at this period ruled out the possibility of social equality of free colored and white. For example, white women accepted the fact that free colored women dressed with greater elegance and more extravagance than they did themselves, without any desire to compete, though among themselves white women competed in dress display, just as white men competed in lavishness and scale of household and household entertainments. Competition between white and colored women could not arise because of their marked social inequality. Similarly, as noted above, although rigorous social taboos on extramarital sexual relations were imposed on white women at this period, they themselves were quite friendly toward free colored women, the concubines of their kinsmen and representatives of a class for whom it might almost be said that marriage was taboo.

The Free Blacks

Conditions in which black slaves acquired freedom largely determined their socioeconomic status in colonial society. If simultaneously endowed with real property on manumission by an affectionate master, they were enabled to strive for subsistence with some chance of success. But as a consequence of the abolition of the slave trade, the social and economic value of slaves in the British West Indies increased greatly, and acts were passed restricting the power of slave-owners to manumit, which severely limited this mode of obtaining freedom. In effect, therefore, at this period the majority of free blacks acquired their freedom mainly through purchase by their own efforts. Although incentives to free their families probably operated, the economic circumstances of the free blacks were usually such as to imperil their own subsistence and prevent this. On purchasing his freedom, the black slave surrendered all his rights to allowances of food, clothing, tools, housing, garden land, medical attention, and other benefits from his former master, and ceased to be a member of the estate community, setting forth, an isolated individual, with no rights in land on the grim task of earning his livelihood in a society which had little place for free labor. It is therefore not surprising to find harrowing descriptions of the conditions of the free blacks in triumphant contrast to those of the slaves, in these old accounts, and to hear that free blacks were accused of inciting slaves to rob their masters and sell them produce or goods, as a means of making a living in the markets.

The Slaves

Of all sections of colonial society at this period, the slaves probably showed the highest degree of internal differentiation. Occupation provided one basis for this. Thus, there were domestic slaves, estate craftsmen such as carpenters, coopers, masons and boilermen, field Negroes, jobbing gang slaves, "town Negroes" and those who were partially free, having begun but not yet completed purchase of their freedom from their master. In both St. Vincent and Jamaica the slaves on sugar plantations formed the overwhelming majority of the total slave population, and hence may be selected as modal for further discussion.

Plantation slaves fall into three clearly defined groups: tradesmen, those engaged in the production of sugar, and domestics. As observed above, openings for slave domestics or craftsmen (tradesmen) on plantations were wherever possible given to colored slaves. In the workshops these slave tradesmen operated as small productive units under appointed heads, who were themselves slaves and were responsible either to a white overseer or manager, or to a white tradesman practicing the same speciality.

The main body of plantation slaves was engaged in the production of sugar, and the bulk of this group is described in the literature as "field Negroes," indicating that field workers were thought of as black. Typical estates operated three gangs in the field, both sexes being represented in each, and each under an appointed slave driver who was responsible via the white bookkeeper to the overseer and manager. At crop time continuous shift work obtained in the boiling house, each shift being under its driver, but with the head boilerman and his assistants in charge of operations and responsible to the white supervisors. Other slaves involved in the sugar production processes included groups such as the waggoners or stockmen, which operated as small units under appointed slave heads, like the craft units.

However, plantation organization involved a great deal more than the simple production process. Care of the slaves during work and illness necessitated allocations of persons from among them to assist in the plantation hospital and in preparing food for the field gangs. Maternity conditions further reduced the numbers directly engaged in sugar production and gave rise to the female slave office of mid-wife or "graundee." In general it seems that malingering by pretended illness flourished on a considerable scale, and with other aspects of estate organization, reduced the number of effectives engaged in crop production and processing to roughly half the total body of plantation slaves.

Among domestics the hierarchic element was pronounced, each specialty, such as butler's work, washing, ironing, cooking, having a separate organization under an appointed head slave. The number of such specialized units, and indeed of the domestic staff as a whole, varied with the wealth and status of the white family they served, each member of which normally had an allocation of chamber personnel.

Differences between these three groups of slaves on plantations were expressed in various forms other than occupation. For example, field Negroes were unshod and the most poorly dressed, their huts the least adequately furnished. Domestics, on the other hand, were the most elegant in appearance and the most precise in speech, continuously displaying the higher degree of acculturation to white behavior which they had gained by their greater opportunities for contact and observation in the white household. Slave tradesmen occupied a middle position in these respects, but seem to have regarded themselves as a small select group in view of their greater familiarity with certain technical processes of white culture in great demand on the estate.

Senior members of the sugar production units, such as the "chief governor" and the "drivers" of each gang associated mainly with seniors of similar rank among the craftsmen and domestics, and displayed their high status by dress, housing, entertainments, and in other ways. Slaves appointed to supervisory positions enjoyed increased allowances of food, drink, clothing, garden land, and many other favors from the white management. Slaves of such high rank regarded manual work on their provision grounds and, indeed, manual work of any type, as unbecoming and beneath their dignity, with a consequent development of hired labor within the estate slave community for cultivation of these gardens, rewards being usually paid in kind and probably also in favors on the job.

All our accounts treating this subject remark on the great emphasis which slaves placed on authority as an aspect of status, both in the field of kinship and mating, and particularly with respect to quasi-occupational offices. Terms of address and reference were developed to reflect this, and rigid observation of the norms of their use was necessary by subordinate slaves if immediate punishment was to be avoided; the power of a slave superior to punish his inferior was subject to little control by the master. Subordinate slaves were subjected more immediately and continuously to the authority of their slave superiors, on and off the job, than were either group to the control and scrutiny of the white management, and this condition enabled slaves of high rank to enforce respect for their position by a variety of means, among which intimidation was prominent.

Great efforts were made by slave owners and their agents at this period to rear the progeny of their slave stock. These attempts were often defeated not only by disease, mainly tetanus, dysentery and malaria, and to some extent by the differing notions of proper child care held by the masters and the slaves, but also by the lack of stable mating patterns and family life among slaves, and by the heavy demands which the plantation system made on women's labor. In African fashion, slave mothers sought to postpone weaning of their children until they were two years old. This was opposed, even by such unusually enlightened persons as Monk Lewis, on the grounds that it was bad for the children and was a device of the mothers to continue drawing their nursing allowances. Other slave owners such as Mrs. Carmichael regarded this long nursing period simply as a form of malingering. White preoccupations with rearing slave infants, in the face of high mortality rates, and opposed conceptions of child care, mating and family life form the basis for the wide disagreement observable in the literature with respect to the strength of maternal sentiments among slave women, and the tendency to contrast this condition with the great fondness and care shown by free colored mothers for their offspring by white males.

Children were initiated into the organization of plantation activities gradually, proceeding from the vine-gang at the age of sixteen either to the field or to act as assistants to waggoners, pen-keepers, domestic staff, and so forth. Instances are reported which show that slaves of high rank, or those to whom the white managers were well disposed, sought employments with the minimum of manual labor for their maturing children.

Economically, slaves enjoyed a wide variety of rights, sufficient to insure a standard of living significantly above their socially ascribed subsistence margin. In the Consolidated Slave Acts certain of these slave rights were listed and given legal sanction. They included allowances of imported food of various types, clothing, and farm tools, together with usufructuary rights in garden land for the production of root crops and other provisions. By law, every Sunday and one Saturday each fortnight were given to the slaves for the cultivation of these plots. It appears also that the slaves traditionally kept stock of various types, with the probable exception of horses, and had recognized grazing rights on their masters' estates. From their provision grounds and stock rearing they supplied the master's household requirements for payment at market rates and themselves operated as the main contributors to the local Sunday markets, which were frequently condemned on religious grounds by immigrant whites. Various polemical estimates of the prosperity of plantation slaves and their superior economic situation when compared not only with free laborers in Britain, but with white management and ownership in the West Indies, are to be found in some of our authors. It is undeniable that the slaves enjoyed greater security at this period than did free blacks, or the poorer free persons of color, but white management did not seem to take seriously the idea that plantation production of sugar by a slave labor force organized in this way was highly uneconomic under prevailing market conditions.

All writers who discuss the rights of slaves agree that they were extremely tenacious and particularistic in this respect, usually refusing to accept as compensation substitutes of equal or greater value. It is thus not surprising that these legal and customary rights, which with certain material possessions constituted the complex of slave property, were subject to inheritance by categories of kin ordered in forms peculiar to the slave society. Similarly, alienation of moveables and certain types of rights by barter, exchange or sale were widely practiced between slaves.

There were two classes of slave property rights: rights *in rem* with respect to material possessions held against all other slaves in the plantation community, and rights *in personam* which held against the master or his agent for future allowances, usufruct, holidays and so forth.

The majority of rights *in rem* were customary, lacked legal sanction, and their infringement gave rise to, or followed on, disputes within the slave community. The majority of rights *in personam* were however sanctioned by law, and were conceived of by slaves as reciprocal returns for their labor. One consequence of this arrangement was that the master or his agent was not regarded as holding any rights *in rem* against the slaves, with the result that

to pilfer from their masters, they [the slaves] consider as no crime, though to rob a slave is accounted heinous. . . . When a slave makes free with his master's property, he thus ingeniously argues—*"What I take from my master, being for my use, who am his slave, or property, he loses nothing by its transfer."* [7]

Obviously this adjustment would suit the slave better than the master and has a direct relevance to post-Emanicipation developments of praedial larceny in the West Indies.

The internal political organization of an estate slave-community was defined by the hierarchic organization of occupational divisions, the offices of superior rank being conceived as statuses involving wide varieties of right over subordinate persons outside of the task situation, as well as superior perquisites from management. Consequently it is not surprising to find extralegal or illegal tribunals set up by and within estate slave communities in which the highest-ranking slaves adjudicated, advocacy being prominently by gift, and decisions, however unfair, being necessarily accepted. On some plantations the owner also presided as sole judge in a court of his own, when disputes were brought to his notice. Parties dissatisfied with decisions of either tribunal had little redress except running away, or recourse to obeah (magic, including poison).

Estate slave communities were internally segmented and also showed marked stratification by rank. There was also mutual hostility between Creole and African slaves within the estate and throughout each colony. It seems likely that Africans formed the majority of the field gangs at this period, and that the Creole and African slaves had a differential command of pidgin English. For the African immigrant, acculturation to his slave status in the West Indies was marked by two stages; arrival, followed by a period and process known as "seasoning," after which the lifelong acculturation process was voluntaristic, maladaptation expressing itself in running away, violence, or use of obeah at an individual level, and at the group level in plotting rebellion or murder of white managers. Creole slaves, subject from birth to a continual process of acculturation, were far better adjusted to their milieu, and accepted their situation more fully than the Africans. The suspicion with which Africans viewed Creole slaves was expressed in the exclusion of Creoles from rebellions that the Africans plotted against the whites, and reflected this basic cultural division of the slave population. Among the Africans themselves tribal differences underlined by linguistic barriers continued to be prominent, with the result that different tribal groups such as the Kromanti (Akan) or Ibo plotted rebellion separately, excluding persons of other tribes. Owing to this segmentation along cultural and tribal lines, slave rebellions failed to elicit sufficiently wide support to achieve their end.

Despite the internal divisions of the estate slave communities, there were strong sentiments of attachment to the community among the slaves; thus those who had purchased their freedom made frequent visits to their former community for longer or shorter periods, and when the Carmichaels, on the eve of their departure from St. Vincent for Trinidad, offered their slaves the choice of accompanying them or dispersing among new masters in St. Vincent, they all, with one exception, chose to accompany their owner because, as they put it, by so doing they would avoid separation. The fact that shortly afterwards these slaves twice attempted to murder Carmichael makes it clear that their attachment was not to their master. Similarly, slave views on freedom, which are frequently given in the literature, show a strong desire to retain membership in their community, as well as to keep the rights they enjoyed as slaves. The point to note is that the estate boundaries defined the limits of the slave community, the corporate solidarity of which was projected on to the estate, with the result that socially, as well as legally and economically, estates provided the basic corporate units on which the higher levels of social structure were founded.

Within the slave community, tensions between individuals centered mainly about positions in the ranking system and mating, and found their expression either in obeah or poison, fights or abscondment, separately or together. Complaints to white management were most frequent among domestic slaves, less so among the other groups which enjoyed less direct contact with the whites.

Established obeah men or obeah women in slave communities appear to have been persons maladjusted to their situation with respect to mating or status frustrations. Where physical violence was ruled out, obeah supplied a common mode of discharging tension, the obeah man often acting as a sorcerer or preparer of poisons at the request of his fellow-slaves. Though forbidden by law on penalty of transportation, obeah flourished on estates for two reasons. Fear of magical reprisals undoubtedly played its part in discouraging complaints, as did the unpredictability of the decisions of the official law courts in which these charges were tried; but apart from this there was a definite reluctance among the slaves to let white people know more about their affairs than was strictly necessary, as a protective adjustment to their cultural situation and their inferior social status.

In itself, obeah seems to have been a compound magical system into which certain practices of various tribes entered as components, and was used for a variety of purposes such as the protection of slave plots from interference, protection against the disfavor of white management or black drivers, obtaining promotion, love charms, and actual poisoning. Sorcerers were very important in the slave community by virtue of their reputed mastery of obeah technique.

Although to the whites it appeared that the slaves lacked formal religious worship, reports of funerals followed by feasts and dances, as in Africa, and of sacrifices on ancestral graves indicate that to some extent elements of ancestor cults were practiced by sections of the slave population. But if formal group ritual is rarely reported, an abundance of magico-religious conceptions was held by the slaves. *Jumbies* (place-spirits) and *duppies* (spirits of the dead) are recorded frequently. Names continued to carry magical significance even among Creoles, while Africans so confidently expected to rejoin their ancestors in Africa after death that they sometimes committed suicide in this expectation shortly after arriving in the West Indies. "Conversion" to Christianity and baptism was itself linked directly to this magico-religious system as the rite which provided the greatest possible protection against obeah. Superior white technology was also explained in magico-religious terms. Under these circumstances, Christian proselytization, whether by the owner, the Established Church or other sects, made little headway, though it seems that the sect of the owner was officially regarded as being that of his slaves. Baptism of slaves was not infrequent, but no formal marriages are reported by our sources.

A bond existed between Africans transported to West Indian slavery in the same vessel. Such companions in misfortune addressed and described one another as "shipmates." Although the shipmate relationship was lifelong, with certain recognized obligations such as hospitality, it had limited social use under conditions in which the slaves tended to be widely dispersed by sale after their disembarkation.

Apart from the internal stratification and segmentation of the slave community, mating and kinship provided the basis of the most durable and widely ramifying relationships. Marriage as a legal institution had no place in slave society for various reasons. As property, slaves were prohibited from forming legal relationships of marriage which would interfere with and restrict their owner's property rights. Originally, also, during the period of the slave trade, there were far more male slaves than females imported to the islands. But it must be pointed out that among themselves slaves lacked any generally accepted mode of establishing permanent mating relationships outside of legally recognized marriage. In the areas of their origin, permanent mating relationships were established for spouses by their kinship or lineage groups, which vary in type and constitution from one tribe to another, as do the ceremonial procedures and exchanges of property by virtue of which "marriage" is completed. It is obvious that such heterogeneous collections of individuals, shipped to slavery in the West Indies, would be unable to develop common procedures for establishing marriage since they would lack the lineage and kinship groupings by which the union was sanctioned and given permanence, the spouses controlled, and into which the offspring were incorporated in fixed descent lines. Wtih the dispersal of shipmates and the haphazard arrivals of Africans on the estates, the last possibility of permanent mating relationships for the slaves disappeared. It is also worth noting that whereas in Africa transfers of property or service are usual in contracting a marriage, the slaves, as property themselves, with few transferable resources at their disposal, would be unable to fulfil this cultural condition.

As a consequence of these various factors, mating of slaves was typically unstable. But their offspring were not regarded as either legitimate or illegitimate; the children of a slave woman were the lawful property of her owner, who could alienate them at will. The legitimacy-illegitimacy dichotomy only applied to persons born free, and was never applied to slaves, as it was meaningless in that context. If, therefore, after Emancipation for various reasons the majority of the slaves and their descendants continued to mate in unstable associations lacking legal recognition, the "illegitimate" status of the children had no significance among them. As in the instance of praedial larceny, another contemporary West Indian problem is elucidated by reference to historical conditions of social structure.

"Polygamous" mating associations were widely practiced among slaves and were most common for senior males of high rank. "Wives" were separated spatially, the majority living in their own huts, and some of them might belong, with their children, to adjoining estates. For the slave, not only was descent legally traceable through the mother to her owner, but he also provided her with allowances and assistance, and held her responsible for the care of the child. Under such circumstances the social role of the slave genitor toward his children differed widely from the obligations of paternity typical for the free section of West Indian society. Instances reported in our sources show that some fathers showed great pride in their children and strove to attend to their needs; generally such fathers were prominent slaves in some position of authority or trust, though two of the instances cited refer to men of the Ibo tribe, which is patrilineal.

Absence of any formal procedure for establishing unions, except for the house-building and feast on a girl's first mating, was paralleled by the informality with which these unions were dissolved. The owner being only interested in the children, his male and female slaves were free to mate as and how they pleased. Owing to the frequent change of mates by slaves of both sexes, half-siblingship predominated among them, with a consequent increase in the lateral spread of kinship, at the expense of sibling solidarity and the development of nuclear groups which might have provided a basis for continuous lines of descent, unilaterally or otherwise. Thus kinship was individualized to a great extent among slaves partly as a functional consequence of instability of mating.

Under these conditions, the woman normally acted as the sole permanent element in the slave family, whether or not her male partner was polygynous. Indications exist to suggest that in some instances females mated simultaneously with two or more men, making separate claims on each for gifts on account of the children they bore. Considering the prosperous condition of his slaves, Monk Lewis quotes a case in which an old slave hired from her owner a young woman to be his mistress "at a rate of £30 a year." [8] Normally the children resided with their mother, and the parents lived apart, singly or with different mates, but instances of slave parents and their children living together are also reported.

Interesting statements of slave attitudes to permanent monogamy are given by Carmichael and Lewis. Slaves of both sexes declared their determination never to marry people of their own kind when the idea was suggested to them, though they expressed willingness to marry white spouses, unaware of the part played by cultural, economic and social factors in the contrast between white and black behavior in mating. This attitude toward Christian marriage operated among the slaves to inhibit their receptivity to Christianity in other fields also.

In partial imitation of the whites, slaves held evening parties featuring music, dancing and feasting, attendance being by invitation on payment. As observed above, furniture and housing, speech, dress, occupation and rank reflected and marked the different stages of acculturation to white standards achieved by individuals and groups within the very clear social and legal limits which the condition of slavery imposed on that process. These limitations were so severe that slave society adapted itself to its social context, and developed a set of institutional patterns, as outlined above, in which its need for adjustment as the lowest section of a more inclusive society was stronger than the tendency to adopt white institutions and standards, thus inhibiting acculturation.

Masters and Slaves

The typical master was a white owner or his white agent, and the typical slave was black. Reference has already been made to relationships between colored owners and their slaves, which typically deviated from the norms of such relations in consequence of the deviant status of the owner.

The modal field of master-slave relations was the sugar estate or plantation. Whether the owner was resident or absentee, the slaves were subject to a white supervisor with wide authority and certain obligations. Legal definition of these obligations and limitations on the exercise of authority were not always observed in practice. Reprisals normally followed protests directed against superiors, whether slave or free, on the principle of delegated authority. Alternative modes of protest against white managements were abscondment, malingering in hospital, complaints to appointed trustees or important resident owners living nearby in cases of absentee ownership, and finally attempted poison or group violence.

On the other hand the power of masters over their slaves was to some extent restricted by their interdependence. Unless coercion was to be relied on as the sole principle of control, masters had to fulfil certain legal and customary obligations to their slaves in order that the estate community should function smoothly. Such obligations and expectations were of uniform character holding between a master and all his slaves. Apart from this, an important condition of harmonious master-slave relations was the degree of attention to individual requests and sympathy with members of the slave population shown by the master. Lewis's diary illustrates the tremendous range of such requests. To the extent that an owner or his agent fulfilled this condition of personal interest in the welfare of his dependants, individually and as a group, his authority ceased to depend purely on force, and came more and more to rest on the principle of reciprocity.

Contrasting instances of these alternative types of master-slave relationships are provided by the Carmichaels and Lewis. Eventually Mrs. Carmichael and her husband, having moved from St. Vincent to Trinidad, taking their slaves with them, abandoned their efforts to farm in the West Indies, after two plots to murder Mr. Carmichael had been discovered in fairly quick succession. Monk Lewis, on the other hand, doubled the legally required number of slave holidays on his estate and appointed others, abolished the use of the cart-whip, increased the provisions for medical care of slaves, instituted a scale of punishments for different categories of offence, and dismissed white bookkeepers summarily on the evidence of slaves. Yet when leaving Jamaica for the second and last time, Lewis concluded his diary with this observation: "What other negroes may be I will not pretend to guess, but I am certain that there cannot be more tractable or better disposed persons (take them for all in all) than my negroes of Cornwall. I only wish that in my future dealings with white persons, whether in Jamaica or out of it, I could but meet with half so much gratitude, affection and goodwill." [9] This statement by Lewis gains greater significance when it is remembered that on the eve of his departure, by his "New Agrarian Law," he had effected a summary redistribution of slave land holdings and rights at Cornwall to correct inequalities consequent on inheritance and differential family increase, had limited their grazing rights for pigs, and had acted as sole judge in a summary court clearing up all interpersonal disputes among the population of Cornwall. Of this court, Lewis says "Perhaps the most astonishing part of the whole business was, that after judgment was pronounced the losers as well as the gainers declared themselves perfectly satisfied with the justice of the sentence. I must acknowledge, however, that the negro principle that 'Massa can do no wrong' was of some little assistance." [10] Mrs. Carmichael's experience was quite the reverse. "We found that all instruction from the master was useless, since by the larger number of negroes all that came from the master was looked upon with distrust and aversion, the bad also intimidating the good." [11]

Clearly these different experiences reflect different relationships between owners and slaves. Assured of the master's goodwill, slaves placed little obstacle in the way of his power of innovation by "legislation" on his estate, provided that their legal rights were not interfered with. Unless this assurance existed, innovations exacerbated relations between masters and slaves, and tended after their failure, to be followed by recourse to coercion on the part of the master as the only means of control, and by antagonism on the part of the slaves.

One critically important observation by Mrs. Carmichael summarizes the situation and lays bare the basis of master-slave relationships. "In the present state of negro civilisation, all contracts between masters and slaves, whether entered into voluntarily or forced by Act of Parliament, are absurd, and incapable of being depended on." [12] No clearer declaration of the extent to which the social structure of the British Caribbean at this period emphasized the differential statuses of its component sections is possible.

Conclusion

From the preceding account of West Indian society about 1820, its complexity and internal differentiation emerges clearly. The three main social sections defined primarily by legal status, as free with full civil rights, free with limited civil rights, and unfree, are shown to have been composed in the main, but not universally, of persons who differed also in race and color. Thus the whites were all free but were internally differentiated, free persons with limited civil rights were in the main colored, but included some black, and the unfree were predominantly black but included some colored persons. Thus, though racial elements were of great prominence in the historical development of these social sections, at this period the two were not homologous.

The preceding account also makes clear the extent to which, and the ways in which, the three principal sections of colonial society at this period were differentiated culturally—that is, by their adherence to different institutions. To summarize, the whites, the free colored and blacks, and the slaves, differed from one another in their religious observances and concepts, their legal and political institutions, education, kinship and mating patterns, family organization, property rights, land tenure and use, division of labor, language, occupations and technology, community organization and associations, markets, value-systems, recreation, and folklore. The diversity of institutional subtypes characteristic of these different social sections has been documented to some extent above. In effect the population of a British West Indian colony at this period was culturally pluralistic—that is to say, it contained sections which practiced different forms of the same institutions. Thus the population constituted a plural society, that is, a society divided into sections, each of which practiced different cultures. Moreover, in the West Indies these social sections were organized in a rigid hierarchy and defined in terms of social and legal status differences, including the most extreme form, slavery.

This peculiar form of pluralism in the social structure of the British West Indian colonies at this period has never, to my knowledge, received the attention or emphasis that it deserves as a causal and explanatory principle. Hitherto, the earlier development of the West Indies has been studied mainly by economic historians, who assume tacitly, here as elsewhere, that economic factors determine processes of change and forms of social structure.

The basic fact to note about the West Indian economy in 1820 is that sugar production was uneconomic from the point of view of the principals engaged in the cultivation and processing of the sugar, though economically rewarding to the slave laborers. After calculating returns from investment in sugar production for Jamaica, Stewart says, "On the capital here stated, the owner has at present hardly one per cent (in 1821 prices) after all expenses are paid—such is the depreciated value of his produce. . . . Of all classes of persons holding property in the West Indies, the sugar planter, in short, is by far the severest sufferer." [13] Mrs. Carmichael observes, "There are few West Indian estates that are altogether out of debt, and some it is to be feared are involved beyond their value," [14] but discussing the use of free labor, or machinery such as plows, in sugar production she finds that "it is evident therefore that no sugar could ever be made were there a fixed hour for stopping the boiling; or if the planter had not the uncontrolled command of the negro's labour." [15]

This, despite an earlier observation that "they (the slaves) are so perfectly aware that you must give them all the necessaries of life, that if they determine not to work, or at least to do little, how are you to proceed in order to make them do more? for even if punishment, corporal punishment, were resorted to, it is not dreaded by them half so much as work." [16] Furthermore, the costs of living for whites in the West Indies at this period were notoriously high:

the common necessaries of life are also expensive; living costs three or four times as much as it does in England; besides, in the West Indies you lose a great deal from theft; the negroes plunder little by little, but still the annual loss is no trifle; neither can a man control his expenditures in that country, as he can do in England where there are retail shops for every article.[17]

As early as 1806, Sir William Young, after careful calculation based on exhaustive data, concluded that at the then prevailing market conditions a moderate estate producing 150 hogsheads of sugar per annum would provide an income £1,750 less than that obtained under the favorable market conditions of 1794–1799, the value of the hogshead having depreciated by £11 12s. 0d. from £32 since 1799.[18] During the years since Young had written, the downward trend of sugar had continued, and his observation that in the profitable sugar trade "the trader's profit is in ratio with the planter's loss!" [19] became fully justified.

If sugar production in the British West Indies at this period had been uneconomic for some time, in the sense that it provided investors with insufficient returns and often with losses, the question arises why no changes were carried out on a large scale to increase profits, or in the absence of any such possible changes, why did planters continue to engage in this uneconomic production of sugar.

Greater economies in the production process could have been achieved by the introduction of such machinery as plows, steam mills, and similar implements, or by a more rational organization of labor, particularly with a view to reducing the heavy costs of maintenance during the long out-of-crop season. While the increased investment in machinery required capital which the industry as a whole did not then possess, rationalization of the labor force was quite within their power. Yet significantly enough, the few known innovations in British West Indian sugar production at this period took the form of introducing machinery such as the plow and the steam engine, rather than reorganizing the labor force. In point of fact, as the literature abundantly indicates, any change in the structural relations between the white and nonwhite sections of the society, and particularly between white managements and their slaves, was never contemplated seriously. When discussed, the issues are clouded with polemical terms, ending in justification of the prevailing master-slave relationships based on coercion, as the only means of producing sugar "economically," and irrelevant comparisons are made showing how slave labor in the West Indies enjoyed better conditions than free labor in Britain.

Rationalization of labor costs could theoretically have been effected most easily by abolishing slavery and hiring free labor for specific tasks, thus at one stroke disencumbering the estate of the costs of "social security" for a large labor force only required urgently for the planting, harvesting, and boiling operations. This solution was dismissed summarily as impossible on the few occasions when it was suggested.

Monk Lewis, however, showed that increased output could be obtained from the slaves if the coercive type of master-slave relation was replaced by one stressing reciprocity. Lewis was a notable and probably unique exception. As mentioned above, his liberality toward his slaves was denounced as sedition by Jamaican planters, and the weapon of ostracism was leveled against him. Yet after doubling their holidays, abolishing the cartwhip, and limiting other punishments, he was able to record on his return to Jamaica in 1817 that "my trustee acknowledges that during my absence the negroes have been quiet and tractable, and have not only laboured as well as they used to do, but have done much more work than the negroes on an adjoining property, where the number is considerably larger, and where, moreover, a considerable sum is paid for hired assistance." [20]

In view of all this, it seems clear that considerations of status rather than economic forces maintained the social structure at this period. One might even go further and state that since a rational adjustment to their economic context would have led to changes in the social structure of West Indian colonies, this was prevented by the greater necessity to maintain the social structure in its current form. In this context it is significant that when slavery was abolished in the British colonies, it was by a fiat of the British Parliament, and not by local action.

Sufficient evidence is provided by our authors to show how considerations of status operated not only throughout all sections of Creole society, but also with great effect among the immigrant whites. It may seem paradoxical that preoccupation with status could maintain a social structure, since social structures are simply ordered relations of statuses defining the roles of individuals or groups within a population. The fact that this condition did obtain for West Indian society at the 1820 period may well be sufficient to suggest questions concerning the homogeneity of that society and its culture.

We have seen that status was even more important than race and color in the structure of British West Indian society at this period, and that quite rigid structural relations held between members of different social sections. This is probably the explanation of the West Indian preoccupation with status at this period, since any alteration in the statuses of different sections would be followed by structural changes in their relationships, thus endangering the unity and stability of the total society. Moreover, that different types of common institutions were manifested by sections of the society occupying sharply differentiated statuses in the total structure should now be apparent. In view of this marked cultural differentiation of the social sections of British Caribbean colonies, it seems clear that the total units were plural rather than homogeneous societies. Hence the preoccupation with structural relations between the principal social sections, and hence also the paradoxical preoccupation with status.

With such a historical background, investigation of the pluralistic and status aspects of contemporary West Indian social systems seems an urgent task of sociological research.

[6

Slavery and Emancipation in Two Societies

In this essay I shall compare the institution of slavery and the consequences of its abolition in two societies which formerly had this institution in common, but which were otherwise dissimilar. The two societies are Jamaica, British West Indies, and Zaria, a Hausa society of Northern Nigeria. To avoid burdening the account with lengthy and detailed descriptions of conditions in these two societies, references are made to published accounts where possible, and only a brief summary of the salient features of the institution and its contexts is given here.

1. CONTEXTS AND ORIENTATIONS

Before proceeding to the comparison of slavery in Zaria and Jamaica it is necessary to give a quick general sketch of the contexts and orientations of the two societies. The principal historical, demographic, economic, and political characteristics of these societies must, therefore, be summarized.

The history of the British Caribbean is relatively well-known. When discovered by Columbus the Caribbean islands were peopled by Arawak and Carib Indians, who were exterminated by the Spanish colonists and were replaced as a slave-labor force by importations from Africa. Numerous wars were fought between European nations for control of the various territories of this region, and most of the islands changed hands frequently.[1] But Jamaica remained under British control since its capture in 1655. This unbroken association between the colony and a single suzerain power, and hence one dominant cultural tradition, makes it simpler to use data from Jamaica in comparative

116

work of the present sort than from other Caribbean territories, such as Trinidad or Grenada, which were influenced by two or more competing European cultures.

The history of Zaria for present purposes can be pegged about two dates: 1804, when the nomadic Fulani, a pastoral people of different stock from the sedentary grain-cultivating Hausa, conquered the area;[2] and 1901, when Zaria was brought into the British Protectorate of Northern Nigeria by Sir Frederick (later Lord) Lugard, who by his Slavery Proclamation, withdrew the legal sanction from slavery.[3]

In 1950 the kingdom of Zaria had an area of roughly 13,000 square miles in the rolling orchard bush country of Northern Nigeria, latitudes 10° to 12° N., and longitudes 9° to 11° E. The southern half of this area is populated by some thirty-odd pagan tribes who formed the reservoir from which the Hausa settled in the north recruited their slaves by raids or as tribute annually. This northern area of relatively dense and continuous Hausa settlement in Zaria can be set at about 5,000 square miles, and probably had a population of about 200,000 at the start of the century.[4] Its population density of 30 to 35 persons per square mile is distinctly low when compared with Jamaican densities of approximately 100 per square mile, ca. 1808–1820.[5] This contrast is all the more significant, since most of the orchard bush country of Zaria is well suited to the cultivation of the staple crops, sorghum, millet, groundnuts, cotton, and so forth;[6] whereas Jamaica, like most other Caribbean islands, is mostly mountain land, with a much smaller area well adapted to the Caribbean staple, sugar.

British Caribbean societies were heavily engaged in the production of sugar for the British market during the period of slavery. The typical economic unit of the islands at this time was the estate, where the sugar cane was cultivated by the labor of slave gangs, and some part-processing of sugar was carried out in the boiling house. Subsistence cultivation was obligatory for slaves on the "mountain lands" of the estate, which were not suitable for sugar. Supplementary rations and essential clothing, together with medical facilities, were provided by the estate for its slaves. By 1820 numerous Jamaican estates were heavily encumbered, mortgaged, or otherwise operating at a low profit, under the prevailing system of absentee ownership and local management by attorneys.[7] An important difference in the economic contexts of Jamaica and Zaria is the dependence of the West Indian colony on long-distance overseas trade in markets outside its control, both in the export of the local product, and in the import of essential materials and manufactured goods.

Economically, Hausa Zazzau or Zaria was linked to the West Sudanic and Saharan areas by long-distance trade (*fatauci*), through camel caravans, conducted principally by the Tuareg.[8] Salt came from the desert, together with certain ores; slaves, grain, cloth, leather, and kolanuts went northwards. Metal was mined, smelted, and processed locally; cotton was cultivated, spun, and woven in sufficient quantities to provide surpluses for export; and, in contrast to the Jamaican colonists, the Hausa population cultivated enough to feed itself. Local building materials were also put to use by the Hausa, unlike the Jamaicans who imported timber and masons. In Zaria, a network of flourishing markets provided distributive channels along which goods and services flowed within and between communities, while wealthy traders handled bulk transfers of goods from areas with surpluses to those in need by the *fatauci* caravan. Unlike the British West Indies, Hausaland was virtually a self-subsistent unit. Unlike the West Indians, the Hausa controlled their market, which was located within their own country, and were not dependent on overseas markets; nor were the Hausa engaged in competition with rival producers, as Jamaica was, especially after 1815.[9] Furthermore, throughout the nineteenth century, as the evidence of various explorers indicates, the Hausa economic organization underwent little change.[10] In contrast the Jamaican economy was sharply affected by developments in industrial production and by changes in market relations overseas.

The West Indian colonies recruited their slaves principally from the western coast of Africa, under a trade, abolished in 1808, which was highly organized, and centered in London, Liverpool, and Bristol.[11] Hausa slave recruitment proceeded through government channels by raids or tribute.[12] In 1820, of a total population of about 380,000, in Jamaica, 310,000 were slaves.[13] Comparable statistics for Zaria are lacking because the early population records of the British administration made no distinction between the freeborn and those freed by the Slavery Proclamation of 1900.[14] However, it would not be rash, on the basis of other data, to put the number of slaves in northern Zaria—that is, in the region of continuous Hausa settlement—at roughly half the total population of that area.

Apart from this distinction between slave and free, the populations of both societies were also divided in racial or ethnic terms. Thus in Zaria, there were distinctions between the conquering Fulani, of Mediterranean racial stock, the Negroid Hamitic Habe of the conquered kingdom, and the slaves, recruited from Negroid tribes speaking Sudanic or semi-Bantu languages.[15] If the respective proportions of Hausa and Fulani in Zaria of 1948 are used as the basis for rough estimation of their ratios in the population of 1900, it would seem that of the free persons of northern Zaria at that date, roughly two-fifths may have been classified as Fulani.[16]

Jamaica, as a British colony with a large slave population of African stock, showed a comparable internal diversity. In 1820 there were in

Jamaica 35,000 whites, 35,000 free people of color, and 310,000 slaves, of whom one-tenth were also colored hybrids, while the remainder were black.[17] The two societies are therefore marked by a similar degree of racial heterogeneity.

Politically, the two societies also occupied fairly similar positions; both were dependent provincial governments of an empire, and although enjoying a high degree of internal autonomy, were nonetheless subject to enactments of the imperial authority.[18] For example, in the short space of thirty years, Jamaica experienced the direct effects of legislation by the Imperial Parliament, when first the slave trade, and then slavery, was abolished.[19] In Zaria, the suzerain power of Sokoto was exercised to appoint and depose kings, and after 1880, was applied to other appointments also.[20]

It is doubtful whether the existence of parliamentary institutions in Jamaica, and their absence in Zaria, can serve to differentiate the two societies in any significant sense. Legal restrictions on voting and candidacy served to render Jamaican representative institutions the organs of a class in the same way that councils of kinsmen and clients which surrounded a Hausa king also represented the interests of a class. There is also a striking parallel between the monopoly of administrative authority that was exercised in Jamaica by the governor, and in Zaria by the king.[21]

The political institution which most clearly serves to differentiate Zaria and Jamaica at this period is that of clientage, a relation holding between two socially unequal persons, which stresses their solidarity and involves mutual benefits. In the political system of Zaria, clientage operated to mobilize aggregates of followers around the various candidates competing for office, and at the same time institutionalized solidary relations between persons of widely different statuses within the society. No comparable institution is reported for Jamaica under slavery.[22]

Religion differentiates the two societies most sharply. The Hausa and Fulani of Zazzau were Mohammedans of the Malikite sect, and their slaves were recruited from non-Mohammedan communities. The Jamaican colonists, on the other hand, were professedly Christian, and were criticized by Nonconformists, such as Baptists and Methodists, for deviation from Christian standards.[23] In reply, Scripture was sometimes quoted to show that slavery had a divine sanction, and was beneficial for the slaves.[24] This type of disagreement among Christians concerning the status of slavery in religious doctrine may simply be an illustration of the fact that Christian standards are much less easily established from the Scriptures than Mohammedan standards can be from the Koran and the Hadith, or Traditions. The Mohammedan attitude is clear and simple. All non-Mohammedans, with the exception

of Christians and Jews, are fair game for the Faithful to convert or
eliminate, and the conversion prominently takes the form of a period of
slavery.[25] It was enjoined on the Mohammedan head of state to pursue
this method of proselytization in annual Holy Wars,[26] which resulted
in the recruitment of slaves to the Mohammedan community, at the
same time that they increased the size of the latter. The Mohammedan
slave law based on these religious principles is a refined and stable
structure, defining the manifold relations between slave recruits, their
masters, and the rest of the Mohammedan community, which neither
requires, nor can accommodate any great change.[27] On the other hand,
slavery occupied an ambiguous position in British law for over fifty
years before its abolition. After Lord Mansfield's famous verdict of
1772, all slaves entering England became free *ipso facto,* at the same
time that all Africans entering the British West Indian territories
became slaves.[28] This diversity of laws seems to indicate that whereas
British society could not accommodate the institution of slavery at
home, it could not subsist in its current form in the West Indies without such an institution.[29] Such a view implies that West Indian slavery
was rationalized as expedient or inevitable on one or more grounds,
and that this rationalization was an attempt to supply the institution
with some set of compelling sanctions.[30] Rationalizations of slavery
were unnecessary in Mohammedan Zaria, since religion provided a
firm ground for the institution in terms of the will of Allah.

2. SLAVERY IN ZARIA AND JAMAICA

Masters and Slaves

Slavery is a social institution in which one category of persons—
the slaves and their descendants—is placed under the control of another
—the masters and their heirs. Control exercised over slaves by their
masters is normally limited by law or custom. Since complete subordination of slaves to the will of their masters under the law is a definitive
feature of the institution, slaves are treated in many respects as if they
were their master's property, and may be alienated, pledged, or inherited. But this application of the forms of property law to slaves is a
consequence of the social requirement that they shall be regarded at
law as wholly subordinate to their masters. A relation of this kind
between persons or classes of persons can only be conveniently defined
in law in terms of the category of property.

Care must be taken with the analysis and interpretation of slavery
principally because the institution is legally defined in terms of
property. This definition constitutes a major trap for the unwary in
that it seems to lend the support of legal form to the treatment of the
institution primarily or even wholly in economic terms. This tendency

to regard slavery as an institution directly serving economic ends, in the way that banking, money, or marketing do, is prominent in cultures which stress economic values, and particularly so in the retrospective analyses of changing economies with a slave base which are made by economic historians and others.[31]

There seems to be an error of abstraction in the treatment of slavery as an economic institution, pure and simple, and in the application of economic theory and analysis directly to it. This error derives from the logical fallacy of misplaced concreteness, and consists in the reification of the economic aspect of slavery and its conversion into a unilateral causal or explanatory principle in terms that can only be described as economic determinism. However, the economic aspect of slavery, which is only one of its many important aspects—if a unilateral determinant of the institutional form—must operate with similar strength and effect wherever the institution obtains. As the data presented below indicate, this is not, however, the case. Given the initial situation in which outsiders are recruited into a society with the low social status of slaves, for purposes of economic production, the outcome is very different according to the structure and ethos of the recruiting group. In the West Indian situation it produced chattel slavery. Among the Hausa, although Mohammedan law defines the slave as a chattel, it resulted in progressive assimilation. The purity of strictly economic motivations in the recruitment and administration of slaves is certainly a variable factor, and there is a type of slavery which is not economically motivated in any strict sense, but which is aimed at the sheer increase in the size of social groups. The slaves, on recruitment, occupy the position of quasi children. Such an institution was fairly common in parts of West Africa until recently.[32] Among the Hausa, slave recruitment had a primarily religious motivation and military form. This religious background and aspect of the institution considerably reduced the effect of strict economic motivations in the employment and management of slaves, though it did not remove them. Instead of regarding slavery as a purely economic institution, the development of which reflects everywhere the workings of pure economic forces directly, it is therefore necessary to seek factors in other parts of the socio-cultural system which intensify or impede the rational employment of slaves as economic instruments.

It is necessary to demonstrate the inadequacy of interpretations of slavery based on economic determinism so that misconceptions resulting from the legal classification of slaves as property may be clearly removed. Two instances taken directly from our societies may prove sufficient. Among the Hausa, owners had not power to alienate those of their slaves who were born in captivity, the *dimajai,* though powers of alienation are obviously essential to the rational economic employment of property.[33] In 1820 the British West Indian societies provide a clear case of irrationality with regard to the economic employment of slave labor. At that period sugar production in the standard form was admittedly unprofitable for estate operators; nevertheless it was vigorously advocated and defended by planting interests in the United Kingdom and the Caribbean as the sole practicable method of producing sugar.[34] Yet those slave owners like Monk Lewis who successfully modified the relation of master to slave on their own estates—and by this means increased sugar output—were threatened with prosecution by other planters for subversion and sedition.[35] Arguments that the maintenance of West Indian slavery in the form then current depended on the indebtedness of the planters, or on their knowledge that sugar production by slave labor was profitable elsewhere, or on the entrenchment of its interests in the political and economic systems of Britain,[36] are therefore of little relevance. The issue was not simply emancipation or slavery, but also included modification of the existing form of slavery. The planters' objection was to any alteration in the then existing pattern of master-slave relations even though such alteration possessed economic utility.[37]

It should be clear that the economic utility of slavery is inadequate as an explanation for many of its characteristics; and also that the assimilation of slaves to property in law is a consequence of their subordination to particular persons who are invested with social recognition as their masters. A fuller understanding of the institution of slavery thus requires careful examination of the modes and consequences of subordination, and of the associated conditions. In such an examination it is essential to use the comparative method as a safeguard against those unsound generalizations based on the study of the single case which have for too long been a source of error in the analysis of Caribbean development. Provided that the validity of the comparison can be established, a simultaneous examination of Mohammedan slavery in West Africa and of Christian slavery in the West Indies should illuminate considerably the nature of the institution and the relations which hold between slavery and the social system of which it is part. It should also be possible to check the validity of such conclusions by examining developments which took place after the institution was abolished in both societies.

Subordination implies and is an aspect of authority. Authority is the socially recognized right to direct, control or manage some or all of the affairs of a person, or group, or thing. In this sense there is an overlap between property as a bundle of rights over things and the authority invested in some persons over others as their slaves, with the result that such types of authority are treated as property at law. But slavery is not the only instance of this legal assimilation of interpersonal rights to the norm of property rights over things. Among the Ashanti of the Gold Coast, the mother's brother traditionally enjoyed the right to pledge or pawn his sister's son.[38] In various African societies adultery is treated legally as infringement of the property rights vested in the husband over his wife at the establishment of marriage in consideration for the bridewealth transferred to the wife's kin on his behalf.[39] Among ourselves similar legal conditions obtain, even without such obligatory premarital economic transfers. Until the Antonines the Roman law of *patria potestas* invested the father with comprehensive property rights over his offspring.[40] These, and similar cases, reflect particular patterns of intrafamilial relationships, holding between guardians and wards. This widespread assimilation of guardian-ward relations to property right has a direct bearing on our present inquiry. It suggests that the analysis of slavery as an institutionalized form of subordination may be carried out briefly and appropriately if comparison is made between the actual patterns of familial and slave subordination in the societies concerned.

Parental authority is one aspect of a relation, the reciprocal of which is obligation and responsibility. A similar duality applies to relations of husband and wife, or masters and slaves. There are however considerable differences between the structural contexts of slavery and the two types of familial relation just mentioned. These differences of structural context may in turn entail differences in the types of subordination as effects. Of these structural differentiae, effective membership, or the lack of it, in descent groups of wider span than the individual family is probably the most important factor. On recruitment, slaves cease to be effective members of the descent groups into which they were born, and are attached to the descent group of their owner by legal form. Hence the hereditary nature of the slave status, which insures for the slave's descendants continuing linkage to such descent units, but may or may not involve modification of those subordinate relations which held between the slave's parent and the master. Among free persons, the authority vested in a husband, father, or person *in loco parentis,* is neither final nor unlimited, and remains exercisable only with the consensus of wider kin groups which include both the ward and his guardian. This is the normal condition for free persons, simply because membership in such wider kin groups is normal for free persons.

Familial authority thus has the status and form of guardianship, with consequent stress on the proper performance by the guardian of his obligations as these are evaluated and defined by the wider kin groupings to which both guardian and ward belong. Under slavery, however, the slave has lost membership in such wider kin groups at birth, and is only attached to that of his master by the condition of enslavement itself. Instead of the guardian's responsibility for his ward

to their common kinsfolk as is normal for free persons, the authority of
the slaveowner is limited by the law, and he is responsible for his treatment of the slave to the law-courts. With this difference in the responsibilities of guardianship for slave and free persons is associated the
greater range and variety of rights which masters exercise over their
slaves. Similarly, increases in the obligations of slaves to their masters,
and decreases in the reciprocal obligations of masters to slaves are
associated with this difference between guardianship of free and slave
persons when the two sets of norms are compared. This difference
between norms of free guardianship and master-slave relations may be
reduced by the development of new bonds of ceremonial or substitute
kinship between masters and slaves, either at the individual level, or as
a general pattern holding between particular categories of persons. To
summarize, whereas the slave at law belongs to an individual, the free
ward, whether junior kinsman or wife, belongs to a group, and it is
this initial difference which normally governs such differences between
familial and slave relations as are found in our two societies, for
instance.

As is well known, in the British Caribbean colonies, under the rules
that prohibited the evidence of slaves against free men in a court of
law, the elaborate slave codes were ineffective as protection for the
slave, where the obligations of ownership burdened or obstructed the
master or his agents.[41] For this reason the Jamaican slave codes are
unacceptable guides to the relations of master and slave which they
attempted to define and redefine.[42] For satisfactory data on this pattern
it is therefore necessary to turn to old contemporary accounts of conditions in Jamaica. In an earlier paper I gave a summary of such accounts,
and those interested in a fuller description are referred to that
essay.[43]

In 1820, Jamaican slave owners and their free agents distinguished
between their slaves on the one hand, and their wards, wives, or junior
kinsmen on the other, in treatment with regard to education, provision and care, property transference, employment, discipline, religion,
marriage, and association, as well as kinship. Further differences in the
treatment of free and slave wards were implicit in the legal codes, such
as prohibition of slave evidence against free whites, and the exclusion
of slaves from participation in the political or administrative systems
of government.[44] Apart from the minimal instruction essential to the
performance of their economic tasks, slaves were denied education by
their masters severally and as a group on grounds of policy, as contemporary accounts by dissenting missionaries, clergymen of the Established Church, and others with less direct factional interest in the type
of education to be administered all make clear.[45] Since at this time
education for the slaves was mooted by religious interests and con-

ceived in religious terms, its prohibition implied, and was in fact associated with, refusal to permit the slaves to share in the religion of their masters, with the result that on Emancipation, there were wide differences in the religious systems of masters and slaves.[46] Moreover, since marriage was then always established as a religious sacrament, denial of religion to the slaves further involved prohibition of marriages between them, and the resulting familial disorganization of the slave population was further intensified by dissolution of slave family units through the sale or other transference of their members. Unlike the free ward who could inherit property from his guardian and was not subject to conveyancing, the slaves, as property, were heritable and alienable, and around 1820, had little hope of manumission by their master, since the colonial laws severely discouraged this.[47] Care and provision for slaves was institutionalized in the form of allowances of clothing, fish, rum, and certain other commodities, provision of medical attendance, and the allocation of mountain lands for subsistence cultivation of "ground provisions," which formed the main bulk of the goods owned or consumed by slaves.[48] Whereas the obligations of guardianship stress adequate maintenance of the ward, the slave contributed largely to his own maintenance, and even more so to that of his master. Whereas wardship normally terminates on the maturity of the ward, the slave, even in old age, remained the dependent of his master. Slave employment typically meant labor in the sugar fields or the boiling house, and this was the dominating motif of slavery throughout the British Caribbean, despite the increasing unprofitableness of its later phase.[49] Incentives to labor ranged from solitary confinement to the cart whip and the treadmill, and though the maximum number of lashes which could be inflicted by a master or his agent on a slave was regulated by statute, these and similar regulations appear to have had little effect.[50] Finally, whereas the association of guardian and ward, though structured in terms of authority, is normally continuous, diffuse, and intimate, the association of masters and slaves was normally restricted to the processes of sugar production, domestic work, and asymmetrical concubinage, the relation normally being specific, limited, and expressing marked social distance and cleavage of interest.[51]

Relations between master and slave in Mohammedan Zaria differed appreciably from these Jamaican norms, and were assimilated in several critical respects without Caribbean parallels to the nexus between guardian and ward. If these differences are summarized institutionally for comparison with the Jamaican practice reported above, the contrasts are clearly evident, and certain factors associated with these differences may be perceived. To begin with, the education of his slaves was an obligation of the Mohammedan slaveowner, the education given being predominantly religious, as was also the elementary instruction proposed by missionaries for the West Indian slaves. For the Hausa-Fulani of Zaria, education was in fact identified with religious instruction and consisted of learning large parts of the Koran by heart, the study of Arabic, and the traditions of the Prophet, the Law, and the principal commentaries. Pursuit of this long educational process was marked by tests, celebrations, and the awards of titles or, occasionally, offices, such as *Mallam* (scholar), *Imam* (priest), *Mufti* (judicial assessor), or *Alkali* (judge).[52] Writing in a version of the Arabic script known as Ajemic was in great demand, not only for practical accounting, or for use in administration, but also because, in the absence of printing, local demand for copies of the Koran in part or as complete texts could only be met by trained copyists.[53] Naturally the majority of slave captives did not proceed far with this curriculum, since they faced severe linguistic and cultural difficulties as recruits from alien communities.[54] Nonetheless, the law stipulated that the owner of a captive slave should seek to convert the latter to Islam by chastisement if necessary.[55] This conversion required that the slave should learn the five daily prayers which are obligatory on Mohammedans. Some of the slaves born in Zaria must have proceeded far with this educational syllabus as their appointments to various prominent offices of state, for which these and related skills were requisite, attest. All slaves born in Zaria were also trained in the forms of the Mohammedan religion, at least to the stage at which they could say the five daily prayers.[56] Characteristically, the enrollment of slaves among the Faithful proceeded by a ritual equivalent to baptism, at which the slaves were given a new name, the owner providing the sheep for the sacrifice, and meeting various other expenses of the ceremony. By means of this ritual the relation between master and slave was assimilated to that between guardian and ward in many important respects.

This ritual assimilation was common for slave recruits, and was obligatory on the master for all slaves born in his ownership. It also had practical significance. Slaves recruited into Islam in this manner were less liable to alienation and were more liable to manumission than before, since the manumission of such slaves by the master during his lifetime, or posthumously, was an act of religious piety entailing rewards in *Lahira* (Paradise).[57] Adoption of Islam by the slave also obliged the master to arrange for the former's religious education and marriage, and to assist rather than hinder the maintenance of such unions as the slave contracted with his permission. Frequently enough the Islamized slaves were given further instruction in Mohammedan religious practice and doctrine by one of their owner's kin, and the assimilation of slaves to the position of wards was marked by the use

of kinship terms between the slave and his dependents on the one hand
and the master and his family on the other. Thus the slave would call
his owner *Baba* (father), and was referred to or addressed as son, other
kinship terms deriving from this relation. That this was not merely a
linguistic convention is illustrated by the effective moral limitations on
the owner's rights already cited, and also by the increased intimacy of
the associations between slaves and the families of their masters after
the naming ritual.[58]

For those persons born into slavery in the community, the securities
and liberties conveyed by such a nexus of wardship were both more
extensive and less subject to violation than was the case for purchased
or captive slaves. This category of native-born slaves, known as *dimajai*
(*s. dimajo*), could not be alienated or punished by mutilation on the
master's pleasure, but only through the courts for torts which generally
entailed such penalties. The owner was obliged to provide for their
religious education in a Koranic school from early childhood, and was
also expected to arrange for their marriages at the period when Hausa
of either sex normally make their first marriage, and to provide them
with living quarters, usually a separate compound for married slaves.
Dimajai also enjoyed greater freedom of movement than purchased or
captive slaves. Growing up as members of the master's household and
family, though of clearly subordinate status, *dimajai* established lifelong relations of privileged familiarity with their owner's children and
junior kin. They also acquired the technical skills of Hausa culture,
such as weaving, metal work, leather and tanning techniques, butchers'
and builders' skills, and other trades, and grew up as Hausa children
with a wide knowledge of the Hausa language, folklore, commercial
practice, and political organization.[59] This means simply that slaves
born in Hausaland practiced the same institutions and culture as their
owners and, though occupying a clearly subordinate status, were members of a common society with their owners, in the structural capacity
of wards. As we have seen, the position of captive slaves who adopted
Islam was somewhat similar.

This modal type of relation between Hausa master and slave figured
prominently in the structure and processes of government, as the
nature of the bond assured the master of the slave's loyalty and obedience to his wishes at the same time that it ruled out the possibility of
political rivalry since the slave was a legal minor, a status which he
shared with free children and women in Hausa culture.[60] The principal
political effects of this peculiar nexus between master and slave were
the allocation of slaves as property to certain titles on the one hand,
and the allocation of a wide and changing variety of titled offices of
state to slaves as administrative officials on the other.[61] A late development of this political system was expressed in the allocation of certain

principal military commands to slave generals on their appointment as administrative officers in charge of territorial fiefs.[62] Such authority allotted to slaves would clearly be exercised over slave and free alike. The political and administrative assignments to slaves of these military commands really shows that, in Hausa society at this date, the relation between chief and subordinate official of slave status was assimilated to that of clientage between the free senior and junior officials.[63] This also shows how freely and widely slaves and masters participated in the same culture and social systems, even to the point at which slaves were appointed to offices exercising authority over free men.

Such differences between the institution of slavery in Zaria and Jamaica as have just been reported may well raise the question whether we are really dealing with the same institution in both societies, or whether the term "slavery" is not misleading in that it refers to widely divergent social forms. The answer to this question is clear. On the legal evidence which defines the institution, we are dealing with a common social form in both these societies, but other social and cultural factors combined to produce these striking contrasts. In both societies the legal rights of master and slave are carefully defined, and treat of corresponding or of identical problems in a similar fashion.[64] Thus in both systems, the conveyancing of slaves, the rights of the master to punish slaves at his own pleasure, the ascription of usufructuary rights in real property to slaves, while recognizing their ownership of movable goods bequeathed or conveyed to them, are very similar, as is the treatment of abscondment, distraint on slaves for the bankruptcy of their masters, rights of ownership of the offspring of slaves, and the like. Other common features which occur in the institution at Zaria and in Jamaica include arrangements by which a slave redeemed himself over a long period by installment payments toward the ransom fee; the practice of manumission in various modes; the arrangement whereby certain slaves undertook to rent their freedom from their masters for periodic payments in cash or kind, being otherwise free to work or trade for themselves without restriction on their movements by their owner; or the owner's responsibility for their debts or commercial commitments, though under the law he retained responsibility for and authority over his slave where criminal offences (manyan shari'a) were the issue. The legal incapacity of slaves in Jamaica also recalls the defective legal capacity of slaves in Zaria, though the Jamaican code enjoined a more rigorous exclusion of slave evidence. These and other legal similarities of the definition of master-slave relations in our two societies, together with parallels in other aspects of the institution, make it clear that, despite the considerable functional differences noted above, we are dealing with a single institutional form in both cases. It is therefore necessary to examine the social and cultural contexts of slavery in these two societies if we are to understand the bases and significance of their remarkable functional differences.

The Demographic Aspect

Demographic factors require first attention. Whereas the Hausa pattern of slave recruitment gave priority to women and children and tended to reduce the number and proportion of adult males recruited as slaves,[65] slave immigrants to the British Caribbean were predominantly adult males.[66] Clearly these differing preferences in the age and sex of slave recruits are not accidental, and may reflect those basic differences of function we are now seeking to trace. In the Caribbean, plantation labor placed a high value on recruitment of adult males as slaves, and though the high slave mortality rate involved equally high expenditures to maintain an adequate supply of slave labor, in the eighteenth century returns from the exploitation of slave labor easily permitted this.[67]

Among the Hausa, preference for the recruitment of women and children as slaves derives from the military and religious nature of the process of recruitment itself. A variety of fates was possible for adult male prisoners of war, while enslavement was the only fate permitted by law for women and children who were captives.[68] In fact, however, the process of recruitment in Zaria, as in Jamaica, itself reflected basic social and cultural orientations toward slavery, which also found expression in the pattern of relation between master and slave. Slave recruitment for Jamaica was a commercial business, a matter of trade, with motivations and calculations of profit dominating the process.[69] Slave recruitment for Zaria was a military and administrative process, in fulfillment of a religious obligation to make war on the Unbelievers, and to administer or despatch them according to the Law.[70] Clearly, prior differences of sociocultural orientations to the institution of slavery in Jamaica and Zaria determine the notable differences in their patterns of slave recruitment. On the other hand, differences of practice in master-slave concubinage between Jamaica and Zaria together with other factors such as birth and mortality rates, worked toward the restoration of sexual parity among the slave population in either territory. Thus functional differences of Jamaican and Hausa slavery cannot be reduced directly to differences in the sex-ratios of the slaves recruited by these societies.

Two other aspects of their demographic situations require discussion; first, the relative proportions of the slave and free population of the two societies; and second, the ratios of local-born to immigrant slaves in either. Significant differences in these distributions could clearly influence the patterns of slave management in either society and thus could give rise to significant differences at that level.

Importation of slaves to the Caribbean on an increasing scale in the latter half of the eighteenth century continually increased the ratio of the slave population as against the free.[71] By 1820, as we have seen, roughly 80 per cent of the Jamaican population were slaves. From the data available for northern Zaria, the area of continuous Hausa settlement, we have estimated that some 50 per cent of the population were slaves. It is not so easy however to determine what significance this wide difference of the ratios of slave and free populations in the two states had for the differentiation of their patterns of master-slave relations. In Zaria slaves formed the main body of the military force, of the police, and of the administrative staff at a subordinate level.[72] In Jamaica they were forbidden to bear arms, excluded from the militia, and took no part in administration.[73] On the face of it, these differences in the military treatment of Jamaican and Hausa slaves might be attributed to the differences of slave-free ratios in the two populations; but closer examination shows that this is clearly not so. Slave-free population ratios are significant as determinants of master-slave relational patterns only by virtue of the military and administrative practice with which they are associated. In Jamaica this practice involved the exclusion of the slaves from military affairs, and the organization of the free population into a militia, supported by detachments of the regular army and navy, for the defense of the state against slave insurrection. In Zaria, conversely, slave generals were entrusted with military and administrative authority, and slave officers were the trusted guardians of the king. It is significant in this context that no insurrection of slaves is reported from Zaria during the period for which its history is known in considerable detail, the nineteenth century, and that there is no tradition of slave revolts before that time either.[74] In Jamaica however, where the slaves occupied a far more unfavorable military situation, there is a long history of slave revolt and conspiracy.[75] If the military situations of the Jamaican and Hausa slaves are compared, it is clear that the greater facilities for effective revolt which Hausa slaves enjoyed by virtue of their military and administrative training at the very least would place them as a potential military threat on a par with that which the slaves in Jamaica presented to their masters, canceling the differences of proportion between slave and free in the two societies.

Figures are lacking for precise comparison of the ratios of local-born to immigrant slaves in both Jamaica and Zaria. Failure of the natural increase of the Jamaican slave population to equal its mortality in the years between the abolition of the slave trade and Emancipation suggests that in 1838 the immigrant slaves were not far outnumbered by those born in the island.[76] Probably the ratio of immigrant to local-born slaves at Zaria in 1900 (when the legal sanction for the institution was withdrawn) was the reverse of the Jamaican ratio at Emancipation. Yet even if such relations could be established from population records, their interpretation and connection with these differing master-slave patterns of behavior would remain beset with difficulties. For instance mortality rates may be far more expressive as effects than as cause of social differentiation. Similarly, differences of ratio in local-born and immigrant slaves are more satisfactorily reduced to patterns of differential recruitment, reproduction, employment, and mortality among slaves in the two societies, than treated as an irreducible causal factor operating with any mathematical constancy to differentiate master-slave relations in societies. Thus, the demographic aspects of slavery in Jamaica and Zaria do not provide a basis for explaining the marked functional differences of the institution in these two societies.

The Ideological Aspect

It is likely that dissimilarities in the racial and economic circumstances of these two societies might be held to account for their differences in master-slave relations. It is therefore necessary to examine and compare separately the racial and economic circumstances of the two societies in some detail.

In terms of degree of racial heterogeneity, though not in actual ethnic composition, there is a striking similarity between Zaria and Jamaica. The ruling class of Zaria were Fulani, a light-boned, light-skinned people, classifiable as members of the Mediterranean division of the Caucasian race, whose culture as well as physical character differed from that of the Negroid Hausa population which they had conquered.[77] Both Hausa and Fulani were Mohammedans, and drew their slaves from still other racial and cultural stocks, the Sudanic and Bantu-speaking Negroes of the south and west. In Jamaica, the ruling class was British, and in 1820, 90 per cent of the slaves were of pure African descent, though drawn from a variety of areas and tribes, such as the Akan, the Ibo, Mandinka, Kongo, or Chamba.[78] There was also a class of persons whose cultural and biological status was midway between the whites and the slaves. This group, known as the "free persons of color," itself owned slaves, some of whom may have been hybrids like their masters; at this period in Jamaica the number of colored or hybrid slaves was approximately equal to the number of free persons of color.[79] That is to say, hybridization as such did not entail an unequivocal social status. Miscegenation on a considerable scale was practiced in both societies. Given this fact, and the similarity in the degrees of racial heterogeneity of Zaria and Jamaica, there is a strict limit to the type of racial hypothesis which can be mooted to explain their differing patterns of master-slave relations. Such a hypothesis would contain as its core the proposition that the maintenance of social and cultural distance between masters and slaves varies directly as the consciousness of racial distinctness among the masters, and the values which they place on its maintenance. Such a statement probably summarizes the crucial aspects of most racialist hypotheses which could be advanced to explain the differences between Zaria and Jamaica, despite variations of emphasis and form.

At first glance the correlation between greater astringency in master-slave relations and greater range of and emphasis on color differences of the Caribbean populations as against the Hausa would seem to support such a racialist explanation. Yet when we compare the respective relations of whites and "free persons of color" with their slaves in the Caribbean, it is clear that the free colored, who were biologically closer than the whites to the slaves, administered the latter with greater severity.[80] Such a pattern immediately illustrates how inadequate a simple explanation in terms of racial distance really is.

Similarly, the prevalence of miscegenation in British Caribbean societies shows that, however great the consciousness of racial distinctness among the masters may have been, no great store was set on the maintenance of racial purity, nor on the exclusion of hybrids from the society. Moreover, the definition of color differences as a significant variable, together with the emphasis placed on these distinctions, is a social fact, and not a biological necessity. In Zaria also, social significance is given to color distinctions; value is placed on lightness of skin as an attribute of beauty, and as a racial character, and a host of qualitative terms reflect this interest, such as *ja-jawur* (light-copper skin), *baki* (dark), *baki kirim* or *baki swal* (real black), and so forth.[81] The Fulani rulers of Zaria distinguish on racial grounds between themselves and their Hausa subjects, stressing such features as skin color, hair, and facial form, and also make similar distinctions among themselves, since past miscegenation has produced wide physical differences among them.[82] In 1900 however, such racial dilution did not prevent the Fulani or some of their British conquerors from declaring their racial affinity with one another. These protestations sometimes took the most bizarre forms, such as the doctrine advanced that the Fulani must be regarded as one of the lost tribes of Israel, from some reference in Deutero-Isaiah to a community called Pul, a doctrine which linked Fulani and British through the view that Britain is Israel.[83] The Caribbean has no monopoly on the color concept as a social value, though its elaboration and patterning in Caribbean societies may be unique. In effect, this means that race per se is only a possible ground for social differentiation and organization, just as are age and sex. By itself the fact of racial heterogeneity does not account for the particular form of racial differentiation current in any society, a pattern which is itself liable to wide changes over time.

Miscegenation has special interest in this context, as it may reveal the significance of racial factors as the determinants of institutional differences in the master-slave relations of Jamaica and Zaria. Three closely related aspects of miscegenation should be distinguished: the structure of the unions, their status, and the status of their offspring. Looking at racially mixed unions in Jamaica and Zaria under slavery from these points of view, we find a striking similarity in the asymmetrical structure of such unions. Wherever public, such unions were asymmetrical, in the sense that they held between a free man of superior status and a woman of inferior position, and this is true not only for unions which involved slaves as one of the parties, but for unions between free persons of different status-categories also. In the West Indies this asymmetrical structure of concubinage between free and slave persons distinguishes it sharply from the type in which slaves alone were involved.[84] In Zaria, a Fulani male might marry a Hausa woman and/or take a slave concubine, in much the same fashion that, among the Jamaicans, and according to his socioeconomic status, a white male would take a free or slave woman of brown or black color for his concubine. On the other hand, Fulani women were only rarely allowed to marry outside their own ethnic group, while Hausa women of free status could own but not marry slaves.[85] In much the same way, white women in Jamaica under slavery were prohibited from entering into sexual association with colored or black men of free or slave status, while free and unfree colored women sought mates of lighter complexion, usually without the mention of marriage.[86]

Despite the asymmetrical constitution of concubinage in both societies, there were significant differences in the institution as practised by the Hausa and the Jamaicans. These differences center about the status of the unions, and the status of the offspring to which they give rise. Among the West Indians marriage between a white man and any colored or black woman was taboo, and there was marked status superiority of whites to blacks or colored.[87] Among the colored population of Jamaica, the women showed a clear preference for extramarital associations with whites rather than marriage with their own kind.[88] The differing religious systems of the two societies is clearly significant here. Islam, with its permissive polygynous attitude and easy divorce, not only allows a man four wives simultaneously and many more in seriatim, but also an unlimited number of concubines, whose status approximates that of a wife in many respects, and whose unions enjoy legal definition and sanction.[89] Sexual association outside the bonds of marriage or concubinage is abhorred and repudiated by Islam, and legal penalties are attached in numerous cases.[90] In contrast, the Christian civilization to which both the white masters and the free colored members of British Caribbean society overtly belonged at this time prescribed a lifelong monogamous union in marriage, virtually excluded divorce, and set legal penalties on the husband for desertion or failure to support his spouse according to his means. Under such a system, white males already married and of senior status were unable to offer their mistresses respectability in its social form by undergoing the necessary religious rituals, whereas those who lacked wives were generally so young and of such low socioeconomic status that they feared to risk their future prospects by extending ritual guarantees to a relation obtainable without them anyway. Such conditions permit partial explanation of Jamaican mating patterns under slavery, and make it plausible to regard the behavior of colored women as an adjustment to a set of social circumstances. It fails however to explain the specific preference shown by these colored women for concubinage with whites, rather than marriage with their own kind. Such a preference remains puzzling even when the political and social inequality of the white and colored classes and the emphasis on "raising the color" of the children are taken into account;[91] it can only mean that asymmetrical concubinage rather than marriage was the norm of mating for all categories of free persons in Jamaica at this period, and that colored males by preference also recruited their concubines from women of a lower social level.

Yet despite its prevalence as the normal pattern of mating in the West Indies under slavery, concubinage lacked legal recognition and was a sin in religious terms. Per contra, among the Hausa, the relation was defined, regulated, and sanctioned by the religious and legal systems, within which contexts it was established and maintained. The marked dissimilarity of mating patterns in Zaria and Jamaica among women of free status reflects these factors. Among the Hausa women of free status were as loath to enter into relations of concubinage as colored women of free status in Jamaica were keen to do so. Among Hausa, therefore, concubines of free men were almost always women of slave status, at least to begin with; for in reality the concubinage of a slave woman with her master initiated a process of conditional enfranchisement. Such a woman ceased to be a slave when she bore a child for her master. If she proved barren, but remained his concubine until his death, she was enfranchised as a free person.[92] Like her master's wife or wives, the Hausa concubine was secluded in accordance with the requirements of purdah marriage, and was provided with her requirements of food, clothing, shelter, money, and other goods.[93]

Finally, British Caribbean concubinage, though prevalent, was an anomaly with respect to the religious and legal institutions of the dominant parent culture. It conferred on the offspring of concubines the anomalous status of illegitimates, whereas in the Islamic institution, such offspring were defined as lawful children of their father with rights of inheritance and succession similar to those of his children by marriage.[94] At least one king of Zaria in the last century was the son of a concubine.[95] In Zaria the child of a slave concubine by her master was free, of the same status as the father, and a member of the latter's kin-group. Among the Jamaicans, the child of such a union was illegitimate, took the mother's status, and was affiliated to her family.[96] If the mother was a slave, then such a child would be a slave, and would become free only if manumitted, a condition hardly likely unless the father owned the mother or was in a position to purchase or otherwise secure her manumission. There is not the least suggestion in the literature of Jamaican slavery that the slave concubine who bore her master a child was ever freed for this action; this is in striking contrast with the automatic change of her status for the better under Islam. In Jamaica therefore manumission of the child of a slave concubine must often have left the mother herself in slavery, thereby reversing the status norms of kinship, and severely straining the family tie.[97] The obligation to manumit their children by slave women was recognized among Jamaican whites in a position to accomplish this. However, the majority of white employees in the colony, bookkeepers, overseers, craftsmen, and the like, lacked both the authority and the funds necessary for such action, if not the desire as well. During this period also, it seems to have been common, on the evidence of contemporary accounts, for free colored males to leave their children by slave women in slavery.[98] Thus in effect, the obligation to remove one's illegitimate children from slavery was limited to wealthy members of the dominant white section of Jamaican society. Under these conditions, the number of colored slaves equaled the number of free colored persons in Jamaica by 1820;[99] and this really means that the chances of enjoying free or slave status were roughly equal for the products of all types of racially mixed unions. If it were possible to subtract from the aggregate number of free colored persons those who had been born of free mothers and thus arrive at a figure for the number of manumitted colored persons in the total of the free colored, we should be in a position to gauge more accurately the relative numbers and proportions of colored children borne by slave mothers for free fathers who were manumitted or kept as slaves. Howsoever, the numerical parity of colored slaves and free persons connotes a fairly frequent and comprehensive repudiation of paternity obligations by free males involved in such unions.

This contrast of mating patterns involving free men and slave women which obtained in Jamaica and Zaria is matched by an equally striking contrast in the mating patterns of slaves in the two societies. In

Jamaica, concubinage was the universal mode of slave matings because slaves were prohibited from marrying. In Zaria, marriage was the normal pattern for slave matings, although the owner had the legal power to terminate his slave's marriage as well as his own by unilateral repudiation. At the same time, under Mohammedan law, two persons of slave status were prohibited among the Hausa from entering into concubinage, and it was not permitted for male slaves to have more than two wives at the same time.[100]

The inadequacy of a strict racial explanation of the different conditions of slavery in Jamaica and Zaria is indicated by such patterns of behavior as those which obtained in Jamaica among the free colored folk as a class, in contrast to their relations with the whites and the slaves. In terms of the racialist hypothesis, the greater the racial distance, the greater should be the emphasis on social distance also; yet the mulattoes, who were biological hybrids, exaggerated the social distance between themselves and the slaves to a degree surpassing that which existed between themselves and the whites on the one hand, and the whites and the slaves on the other. To say that this exaggeration reflects the socially and psychologically ambiguous position of the free colored group is simply to admit the inadequacy of explanations in strictly racial terms. Such a view also rests on a general assumption concerning the stresses and strains of persons of intermediate status, racially and socially, which is of doubtful validity. It was not reported from Zaria that either the Habe, who were biologically and socially intermediate between the slaves and the ruling Fulani, or those persons descended from unions of free males and slave women, treated their slaves differently from the way in which the ruling Fulani did theirs. It is thus necessary to seek elsewhere for the basis of the difference in the slave systems of Jamaica and Zaria, and one key factor which has revealed itself as clearly worth consideration in this respect is the difference of religion.

Islam is a relatively coherent monotheism which holds that acceptance or nonacceptance is the crucial factor differentiating people. Those who accept Islam, the Faithful, are all members of one community, and as such have a basic equality of status.[101] Those who adhere to different rituals and creeds, the Unbelievers, are to be converted or subjugated by force, and, with the exception of members of the Jewish and Christian religious communities having historical links with Islam, exhibit little internal differentiation of interest to this system. Like certain other universalistic ideologies, Islam accords its adherence priority over racial or ethnic features which differentiate Believers.[102] The most general distinction that it recognizes among its adherents is that between those born into the Mohammedan community, and those who join it later on in life, whether voluntarily, or as captives, slaves, or recantors under duress. Thus among Mohammedans, adherence to Islam, with its religiously sanctioned and ordained law and social institutions, is a bond which overrides differences of cultural or racial origin; and this is effectively expressed and established by such obligatory and universal religious behaviors as the fast, the five daily prayers, and conformity to the code of social institutions laid down directly in the Koran, and indirectly in the Traditions, legal codes, commentaries, and teaching of the doctors (*ulama*).[103]

The ideological aspect of Western Christendom is both more complex and less static than that of Islam. Despite its universalism, Pauline Christianity, in its original religious distinctions between Jews, Gentiles, and Christians, contained elements which permitted future differentiation of Christians on racial and ethnic grounds. The medieval persecutions of the Jewry in Europe, though formulated in religious terms, also reflected racial and economic factors. During the fifteenth and sixteenth centuries, Western Christendom suffered a permanent schism in the developments known as the Reformation, and the differentiation of its Protestant and Catholic segments was intensified and accelerated by divergences of ideology and policy with respect to the economic aspect and processes of society. Weber,[104] Tawney,[105] and other writers, have shown that Protestant departures from the Catholic ethic which dominated the economic and political life of Europe in the feudal middle ages were ideologically associated and consistent with capitalistic developments then proceeding in the Protestant countries. And when industrial capitalism emerged in this context it was interpreted pragmatically as proving the validity of the ethic of economic laissez-faire which had developed under Protestantism to replace Catholic regulation of economic relations.[106]

The discovery, conquest, and colonization of the New World occurred within the context of these ideological and economic changes. The expansion of Europe to the Americas involved Protestant and Catholic alike, and reflected their rivalry. Catholic nations to whom the newly discovered territories were allotted by the Bull of Pope Alexander VI in 1494 played their part in opening them up by subjugating or exterminating the aboriginals, who differed in race and culture. The Protestant nations, under the leadership of Britain and Holland, increased the population of the territories by supplying them with people of yet another race and with another cultural heritage. The methods employed in this transfer of population—purchase and enslavement—accorded with extreme laissez-faire doctrines. "Rationalistic" commercial and industrial exploitation of these slave immigrants was incompatible with the old universalistic ethic which, even at this stage, influenced Catholic thought considerably. In the various Catholic colonies of the New World, differing reactions to the institution of slavery reflected different accommodations to, as well as developments of, the older Catholic ethic.[107] In Protestant slave colonies, care was taken to insulate the slaves against the incompatible influence of Christianity, and the morality of laissez-faire was for long unchallenged.[108]

Such a condition permitted and provided the necessary basis for the free and direct expression of economic motivations in the employment of slave labor by Protestant colonists and their backers in the home country and, initially, it yielded high rewards.[109] In effect, therefore, the values justifying and governing slavery in a Protestant colony such as Jamaica were instrumental and economic ones not heavily tainted by Christian universalism.

Such was the mental and moral climate of Jamaica during the eighteenth century heyday of prosperity for the sugar planters; but toward the end of that period new moral and intellectual movements, which had developed in Britain as part of the reaction against laissez-faire ideology, focused a continuous and systematic criticism on slavery, and succeeded, first, in securing the repudiation of the slave trade by the British government, and then in persuading Parliament to abolish the institution in territories under the British Crown.[110] During this long and vigorous debate, a variety of rationalizations were developed in support of the institution to supplement the *ad hoc* economic argument, and among these the argument from racial and cultural superiority figured prominently in this defense.[111] This debate on Negro slavery in the British Caribbean is the historical origin of the myth of the "white man's burden," the doctrine that it is a duty of culturally superior races to civilize the inferior for the latter's good, and if necessary, in their despite. In Jamaica, this rationalization of slavery, which had been mooted before by such earlier writers as Long,[112] was systematized in the early nineteenth century as dogma with a set of well-integrated attitudes attached to it.[113] This racialist dogma and set of attitudes outlived the institution they were elaborated to defend, and have colored relations between the dominant and subordinate sections of these societies for generations since Emancipation.[114]

It has been shown that religion and law so influenced the mode of establishing mixed unions in the British Caribbean as to make asymmetrical concubinage its typical form. But with systematization of the racialist justification of slavery, this set of dogma was extended to sanction the pattern of interracial concubinage also in terms of "raising the color" and cultural level;[115] and since asymmetrical concubinage was both supported and practiced by the dominant white section of colonial society, it was accepted as a "natural" social form by the free colored also who sought above all to assimilate their status and overt behavior to that of the whites, as far as this was convenient or rewarding.

This illustrates the manner in which the racial and cultural rationalizations were used to justify and sanction a variety of social practices concomitant with slavery in the British Caribbean. During the period between the abolition of the slave trade and the abolition of slavery itself, racial arguments gradually replaced economic ones in defense of the institution, since economic rationalizations became increasingly unserviceable because of the depression of the sugar industry in these years.[116] While Wilberforce, Clarkson, and the other abolitionists leveled their criticism in terms of the accepted religion and its moral code,[117] the defensive colonial interests pleaded expediency, or instrumental, economic, racial, or cultural obligations[118] and, even when justifying slavery by scriptural quotation, sought to avoid the stigma of directly repudiating the Christian religion and moral code.

Two further sets of factors require mention before our discussion of this racialist interpretation of slavery is complete. First, as an explanation of the conditions of Jamaican slavery, such a view is inadequate, not only because half of the colony's hybrid population was free, while the other half was enslaved; but also, and more importantly, because during the early period of British rule in Jamaica, thousands of Britons were brought to the island to labor for longer or shorter periods under conditions strikingly similar in many respects to those of the slaves.[119] Since the racial theory of slavery—that is, of colonial labor relations— could not 'explain' or accommodate such inconvenient patterns, they were tacitly forgotten or ignored.

The development of racism as a guide to economic and political action can be understood only in the context of the history of religion in Western Europe. The Reformation and the establishment of Protestantism provided conditions that have since permitted an extreme secularization of thought and practice in Europe, and have left the door open to many and various instrumental ideologies, such as laissez-faire, racism, nationalism, fascism, or others, to justify the ways of man to God. In effect therefore, normative doctrines based on cultural or racial superiority, Christianity, or economic values, all operated in the Caribbean colonies during slavery as systems of a similar nature, in much the same way, for example, that Islamic dogma functioned in Zaria. There is however a considerable difference between one social system supported by a single coherent system of belief and value, and another organized upon conflicting systems of the same order. Where societies are the systems concerned, it follows that the ways in which common institutions operate will reflect to some extent these differences of homogeneity, as well as kind, in their systems of belief and value.

The Economic Aspect

The racialist explanation of the notable differences of master-slave relations in Jamaica and Zaria having proved inadequate, it is now necessary to see whether these institutional differences can be reduced to an economic basis. This requires first, comparison of the two productive systems operated by slave labor, and then comparison of their general economic contexts.

We are particularly fortunate in commanding the data for this comparison, which consist in published contemporary accounts and more recent studies of slavery in Jamaica, and field materials collected on Hausa slavery in Zaria during 1949–1950, some of which, describing the slave village of Karo, have been published recently.[120] Karo may be taken as a typical instance of the organization of Hausa slave estates, since it conforms to the pattern discernible in other accounts given by Hausa informants.[121]

Karo was a village containing 250 slaves and the family of their owner. It was therefore comparable in size of population with the medium-sized Jamaican sugar estate of *ca.* 1820. Under Hausa rules of land tenure, usufructuary rights accrue to the man who clears virgin land by the labor of his own hands or that of his slaves.[122] The relative abundance of arable land permitted extensive holdings. It is possible to estimate the acreage under crop at Karo by use of data from surveys of land utilization and household composition carried out by the writer in Northern Zaria in 1949–1950, on the assumption that the average values yielded by such recent studies are similar to those of Karo in the 1890's.[123] Concerning changes in household size since then, it is not possible to guess, but certainly there has been no change in agricultural equipment or technique since then of the type liable to have an effect on crop acreage. The land utilization survey of 1949–1950 gave an average of 4.8 acres for 109 Hausa households of Zaria, while the household composition study, gave an average of 6.7 persons per household for 90 households. In these terms, the 250 slaves of Karo would form some 37 household units, farming a total of 178 acres between them, excluding fallow land, and the owner and his family. Such an estimate is sufficient to show that Hausa cultivation by slave labor is comparable in scale with Caribbean norms under slavery. There are also other striking parallels in the organization of labor itself:

This is how the slaves worked: Each slave had his own farming land; if he had a wife she helped him, if he had none he worked alone, and if he had children they helped him too. In the early morning the slaves and their sons would go to their own farms. At this time of day (9.30 A.M.) they came back, and went to the master's farm, the *gandu* fields, until Azahar (2.30 P.M.), when they returned. At noon food was taken out to them at the *gandu* farm. At

Azahar they came in and rested, then in the afternoon the men slaves went out to their own farm-plots, and their wives went to their little plots too. Everyone grew guinea-corn, cotton, millet, cowpeas, sweet potatoes, pumpkins, groundnuts, peppers, bitter tomatoes, sugar cane, rice, *iburu*, okras, tomatoes, and green peppers.[124]

We learn also that the slaves owned all the produce of their own farms, that they were frequently employed between the Azahar prayer (2.30 P.M.) and dusk in handicraft production or trade in the market; that they were fed by the owner at noon and in the evenings, but were otherwise responsible for their own subsistence though, as *gandu*-head (owner of the estate), the master was responsible for providing them with farmland, farm tools, marriage payments, and certain gifts at the main Mohammedan festivals; that the preparation of food in bulk for the slaves was allotted to groups of their wives in turn; and that they worked under the supervision of appointed persons, themselves usually slaves or ex-slaves, who were given such titles as *Sarkin Gandu,* the chief of the estate. The slaves were provided with separate compounds in Karo village, and strangers were excluded from the estate under the rule of land tenure mentioned above. Such was the Hausa *rinji* (slave-village) of which large numbers existed within Northern Zaria, some of them being said to contain well over a thousand persons.[125]

The organization of slave estates in Jamaica and Zaria is similar in the following respects: (1) There was a division of labor time for the slaves between their master's plantation, and their own gardens. (2) Food, separate housing, tools, certain allowances of clothing and farm-plots were allotted to slaves, and with the exception of these allocations they were held responsible for their own maintenance. (3) They were supervised directly by slave headmen or officials who were then responsible to free persons with managerial functions. (4) In Jamaica and Zaria, slave estates were economic and social units in which there was little place for strangers. (5) The principal occupation was agriculture. (6) There was a division between field gangs and slaves engaged in domestic work in both cases, the principal domestic tasks among the Hausa being the preparation of food in bulk for the slaves, and the care of the owner's household.

The following differences of organization must also be noted: (1) Among the Hausa, it was normal for the owner or a senior member of his family to reside at the estate, whereas absenteeism was the prevailing pattern in the British Caribbean, a hired white staff of overseer, bookkeepers, and skilled craftsmen being allocated supervisory tasks and powers under salaried or commissioned managers and attorneys. (2) The labor time allowed to slaves for cultivation of their own plots was less among the Jamaicans than among the Hausa; but the difference in time spent on their master's labor is less great than the preced-

ing account may suggest. Unlike Jamaican slaves, those of the Hausa
worked on their master's plantation during the farm season for seven
days per week. (3) The labor force of the typical West Indian slave
estate (the sugar plantation) had a more complex and permanent structuring than that found among the Hausa, there being divisions entrusted with field labor, domestic services, various craft activities, such
as masonry, woodwork, and so forth, or the care of stock. (4) The productive process on the West Indian estate was more complicated, particularly with respect to the boiling of sugar at crop time, which was
carried on in night and day work shifts till the crop was finished.

There are important differences of economic context and orientations which require attention. The Caribbean staples, sugar, rum,
molasses, coffee, indigo, and others, were produced almost entirely with
a view to sale and consumption overseas, in markets with which the
producer did not deal directly. Hausa production, however, was focused on local subsistence and marketing, though considerable surpluses of grain, cotton, hides, and other goods were sent northward to
desert communities in exchange for the salt, dates, minerals and other
products of such areas. Second, Islamic prohibition of interest on
debts,[126] together with the conservative orientation of Hausa economy
toward the satisfaction of traditional needs[127] served to reduce the role
of credit in capital formation among the Hausa, and thereby to give
capital in Zaria a meaning, use, and value different from that current
in the West Indian context. Given the low Hausa population density,
the relative abundance of arable land, and the rule which, by limiting
the modes and values of accumulation to certain commercial contexts,
excluded the chances of sufficient capital accumulation through credit
to initiate or support developments of large-scale production, the most
significant form of capital in Zaria consisted of slaves. Such slave capital was legitimate, and its accumulation was sanctioned by religion; it
was self-reproducing, self-supporting, and provided regular annual returns on investment; it was liquid, and could easily be sold; on the
whole it appreciated rather than otherwise, despite the rule against
the sale of local-born slaves (*dimajai*); it was eminently inheritable and
possessed political and military significance under prevalent patterns
of state organization.[128]

In the Caribbean, however, the costs of estate operations were far
higher, owing partly to the commercial value of arable land,[129] partly
to the expenses for the machinery and building required,[130] partly to
the greater market value of slaves,[131] partly to the high maintenance
charges associated with this type of labor force in sugar production,[132]
and partly to the expenses associated with long-distance trade and absentee ownership.[133] These various factors which pushed up estate costs
of operation in Jamaica cannot all be accepted at their face value as

necessary consequences of economic or situational determinants.[134] Better care of the slaves would in all probability have reduced their death rate, and so their replacement charges on the estate. Absenteeism can hardly be defended on grounds of necessity, and there are other reducible costs in this list of factors, especially costs involved in maintaining a labor force redundant for much of the year.[135] Nonetheless, the aim of the estate owner and management was the economic exploitation of the estate to secure high returns from the sale of its products overseas. And when after 1800, the returns obtained from such operations steadily diminished, there was a parallel decline in the market value of the estates themselves, and planters sought credit increasingly to maintain the colonial economic structure.[136]

It is difficult to believe that necessity, whether historical, economic, or technological, operated to produce such a pattern and state of affairs. Residence of the owners on the estates would have lowered the profit margins necessary for solvency by reducing costs, and might have prevented wholesale encumbrance. Where severity in the treatment of slaves was replaced by intelligent and considerate handling, increased output resulted.[137] Where attention was directed to the extraction of the maximum yields per acre, rather than to the cultivation of the maximum acreage per slave, greater efficiency was achieved.[138] A different organization of the estate labor force could also have increased the number of field workers, and so the output of sugar.[139] Had all Creole slaves been instructed in technical skills simultaneously with their training in sugar culture, estates would then have commanded sufficiently large bodies of skilled personnel to dispatch their requirements for this type of labor by group work rapidly, and there need have been no permanent withdrawals of craftsmen from the field labor force. Parallel reductions in the size of the domestic slave staff were also possible. Had all Creole slaves been given technical training on the estates while employed in agriculture, it is possible that those invidious prestige distinctions between agricultural or other forms of manual labor and clerical or supervisory activities, which were a source of wasted manpower under slavery as well as afterwards, would have lacked the necessary foundations for development.[140] Among the Hausa, where under slavery as now, most males practice some nonagricultural occupation as well as subsistence or commerical farming, no such invidious and crippling evaluation of types of work occurs; and "specialization" (sometimes taken as an index of economic progress without any careful definition or consideration of its types and contexts) there means a diversification of production to satisfy varied local wants, rather than monoculture for a foreign market.[141]

Clearly, the differences of productive organization which hold between Zaria and Jamaica can hardly be treated as necessary functions of their differing economic situations since the Jamaican adjustment to its economic context was a good deal less "rational" than that of the Hausa. If the annual processes of boiling sugar and transporting the products in bulk to the ports for shipment overseas are excluded, it is difficult to find any other features of productive organization or activity differentiating the Caribbean and Hausa systems which reflect differences of purely technological or economic conditions *as necessary adjustments or effects*. It is equally clear that neither the boiling process nor the bulk transportation of goods to port can possibly account for the very considerable differences in master-slave relations which existed between Jamaica and Zaria. This empirical comparison hardly bears out the basic principle of Marx, and the tacit assumption of sundry writers on Caribbean economic history,[142] that "in the social production of the means of life men enter into circumstances which are determined, necessary, and independent of their wills—circumstances of production which correspond to a definite stage in the development of the material powers of production." [143] Instead, our analysis directs attention to the manner in which the Jamaican system of slave production was governed and directed along economically irrational lines by noneconomic factors, which, since they are clearly neither biological nor environmental imperatives, can only be of a social or cultural character.

Such factors as the preference for absentee ownership; the conditions which permitted its establishment, initial "success," and maintenance at a later date when it was patently an economic handicap; the decisions to "specialize" slave factors as domestics, field or craft laborers, and to limit production to the monoculture of sugar; the organization of estate labor with its six-day week, and allocations of working time of the slaves between their own gardens and the master's plantation; even the evaluations of returns from estate operations as adequate or otherwise; the legality of interest on loans; the definition and uses of capital; marketing, and the structure of commerce—all these are clearly conditions of a social and cultural character, and give an expression to social valuations and beliefs less equivocally than to any necessary relations of supply and demand. In any event, cultural values and attitudes define and determine both demand and the modes of its satisfaction; and the economic processes of production, exchange, accumulation, and so forth take place within the limits and forms set by the culture. Instead of operating according to inexorable laws as an independent variable determining social relations, the economic structure is therefore simply one aspect of sociocultural reality, an abstraction, to which, on logical grounds, the remainder cannot be causally reduced. In effect, therefore, explanation of the form of British Caribbean slavery and its difference from that of the Hausa, in strictly eco-

nomic terms, is as inadequate and erroneous as its explanation in racial
terms. That this economic interpretation of slavery is inadequate may
be seen from the fact that the system was maintained in the British
Caribbean after 1808 with as little alteration as was possible, largely due
to the pressure of planters whose economic position steadily worsened
and who suffered losses by its maintenance and operation.[144] As
Merivale saw clearly, "slavery without the slave trade, and in the then
circumstances of the colonies, was rather a loss than a gain." [145] Neither
the technological processes of sugar production, nor the economic contexts of the British Caribbean colonies at this period, can provide a
necessary explanation of the pattern of slave organization and use in
those colonies, much less account for the peculiar patterns of master-
slave relations which differentiated West Indians from Hausa, among
whom similar modes of labor organization obtained.

The Structural Aspect

Since these differences between slavery in Jamaica and Zaria cannot be attributed directly to differences of racial composition or economic conditions, and since clearly, they are neither biologically ordained, nor ecological necessities, it is necessary to examine the social
and cultural contexts in which these differences were institutionalized
to seek their bases and functions. This is a less formidable task than
it may seem, as considerable reference has already been made to the
principal relevant conditions, including religion. What now follows is
thus largely a recapitulation, directing attention to the crucial differences of type in the two societies and their significance for our problem.

Among the Hausa, master and slave participated in the following
identical institutions: religion, marriage, kinship and family, marketing, education, and government. They also spoke the same language,
shared the same technology, and took part in common economic processes. Both groups had a common lore, a common classical language,
Arabic, in which the daily prayers were recited, common conventions,
etiquette, and value systems. Law provided further links between master and slave, including participation in common courts, and the code
of land tenure, which restricted rights in land to usufruct, placed both
slave and master on a similar footing.

Among Jamaicans, however, masters and slaves professed and practiced different forms of the following institutions: religion, marriage,
kinship, family, marketing, education, and government. They spoke
different languages, operated different technologies, and took part in
different economic processes. They were further differentiated as cultural sections in terms of lore, conventions, etiquette, and value systems.
Whereas Latin was the classical language of the masters, the slaves—
if they can be credited with any "classical" tongues—could have ac-

corded only the tribal languages of their ancestors such a degree of prestige. Law defined differences of master and slave sharply, underlining the latter's classification as a chattel by excluding him from the same courts as his master, thereby providing conditions favorable to the development of tribunals among the slaves to settle their internal differences, and of conspiracy or rebellion to settle accounts with their masters. Whereas it was forbidden for a slave to bear arms in Jamaica, the soldiery and command of Zaria included slaves in all ranks. Whereas the period 1804–1900, for which the history of Zaria is known in detail, contains no instance of slave rebellion, the Caribbean colonists lived in a perpetual state of siege of their own manufacture with somewhat uneasy periods of truce between slave revolts.[146] Neither racialist nor economic theories of slavery can account for these contrasting conditions of Jamaica and Hausaland.

As general regularities of behavior pattern, all institutions, such, for instance, as marriage, religion, or law, involve patterned sets of relations among the individuals and groups which practice them. Conversely, different forms of the same institution, for instance, different forms of marriage, kinship, or religion, will involve differences in the relations of the groups which practice them, and quite probably differences in the size and constitution of the groups themselves. This simply means that institutional divergences between populations define them as different societies, in the same way that institutional identities define the population in which they are found as a single society. And since institutional codes, values, relations, and processes are cultural forms, then the totality of such behaviors, and their interrelations, defines the culture of the group which practices them. Consequently we may speak of a population marked by institutional uniformity as culturally and socially homogeneous, and of a population marked by institutional diversities as culturally and socially heterogeneous. Cultural homogeneity or plurality thus distinguishes societal types. And to the extent that any single institution provides a basis for the societal differentiation of two systems in which it occurs, then despite its identity of form, it will show differences of an equivalent order in its social function and operation in these systems.

It is precisely in this condition that the very marked differences of slavery as an institution characteristic of Zaria and Jamaica are rooted. Hausa culture and society formed a single homogeneous field, to which slave recruits and their offspring were assimilated as fully as was possible, at the direction and through the instrumentality of the Mohammedan religion. However, in the British Caribbean, the cultural and social exclusion of slaves, which was facilitated and guided by the heterogeneous ethos of their masters, with its three conflicting sets of creed and value—racism, laissez-faire economic morality, and Christian universalism—operated to create and maintain a pattern of plural societies.

The Hausa slave by virtue of his assimilation to Islam found his relation to the master humanized and transmuted in the direction of guardian-ward relations, and was thereby further induced to assimilate Hausa culture voluntarily, to such an extent that he could be and, in fact, was entrusted with military command and territorial administration. In contrast, the exclusion of the Caribbean slaves from the Christian community to which their masters belonged involved and created differences of humanity and kind between the two groups which were expressed in the systematic exploitation of slaves as real property from which the maximum social and economic satisfactions were to be extracted. For Hausa, Islam prescribed an eclectic attitude toward race, and ordained cultural and social homogeneity. For the Caribbean, Christian ideology was only one of several competing systems of value and belief, and often enough it lent support to the ideologies of race or laissez-faire which sought to sanction and rationalize the plurality of Caribbean social and cultural systems.[147] Stated briefly, whereas the Mohammedan Hausa, having Islamized their slaves, treated them as Mohammedans, the Caribbean colonists, having denied Christianity to theirs, treated them as being outside the pale of Christian or "human" rights, and duly reaped their reward in thefts, malingering, abscondment, negligence, arson, rebellions, and the like.[148]

In effect, the part played by the common institution of slavery in the differentiation of Jamaica and Zaria as societal types completely explains all differences of the institution in these two societies. Among the Hausa, slavery was the principal means of recruiting persons of alien culture, who were then assimilated to Islam and Hausa culture by a variety of pressures, including force. Among the Jamaicans, the status of slavery defined and distinguished sections of the population which practiced widely different cultures, and formed distinct societies, assimilation being prevented by force.[149] For Hausa society as a whole, the function of slavery was integrative, and it operated as a channel of acculturation. For the Jamaicans, it had an opposite function in that it provided a basis for the cultural and social differentiation of the society along plural lines. Yet it also appeared integrative in that the maintenance of slavery was essential, if the hierarchical structure of the plural society was to persist in the current form. Hence, the bitter and protracted defense of slavery by the colonists and their supporters, and their legislative strike and other protests when it was formally abolished.[150] Rationalizations of slavery in terms of race and economic ideology were in fact simply arguments against actions which planters feared would destroy the social structure and plunge the territory into disorder.[151] Since a principal function of slavery in Mohammedan

Zaria was to expedite slave acculturation and assimilation to Hausa society, other things being equal, the distance between master and slave was minimized as far as possible. The converse is true of Jamaica. Since a principal function of slavery in Jamaica was to provide a basis for social and cultural differentiation of sections in a hierarchical plural society, the distance between master and slave was, other things being equal, as far as possible maximized, and the onus of maintaining this distance rested heavily upon the masters, to whom chaos seemed the most probable alternative. The defense of slavery in the British Caribbean was simply a plea to maintain the social structure in its current form.

3. EMANCIPATION AND ASSOCIATED CHANGES

If the difference between slavery in Jamaica and Zaria is functionally associated with the part it played in their differentiation as societal types, then the processes and effects of emancipation should also reflect these differences of function and context, and divergences in order and kind equal to and consistent with those already noted between the two slave systems should follow their abolition. Since the condition of slavery was a mode and channel of acculturation and assimilation among the Hausa, we should expect that its formal abolition would be effected without severe social dislocation or structural alteration, and would be followed by a smooth transition leading to a new society without this formal status but retaining many of the positively integrative aspects of the old institution. For the socially and culturally pluralistic British Caribbean colonies, we can expect an overall maintenance of the total social structure, with tensions focused on issues and forms of sociocultural assimilation and integration, particularly on the continuance or abrogation of these relations between social sections formerly distinguished in legal terms as slave or free. It is therefore necessary to test the validity of our analysis of slavery in these two societies by examining the processes and consequences of its abolition in both. I shall first compare the process of emancipation in the two societies, and then briefly treat postemancipation developments.

Slavery was abolished in the British Caribbean in 1838 after a four-year period of supervised "apprenticeship," by an act of the British Parliament, despite opposition from colonial interests, which a very substantial compensation did little to reduce.[152] Slavery was abolished in Northern Nigeria on its establishment as a British Protectorate in 1901, through Lugard's Slavery Proclamation, "which abolished the legal status of slavery, prohibited slave-dealing, and declared all children born after April 1, 1901 to be free. The proclamation did not make the holding of slaves illegal, the abolition of the legal status merely preventing a master from recovering a runaway slave through the medium of the courts, and enabling a slave to leave his master and claim his freedom whenever he chose." [153]

Between 1901 and 1910, 2,274 slaves were registered as free persons by the courts of Zaria, a peak occurring in 1911 when 1,075 slaves became free.[154] By the end of 1917, the total number liberated throughout Northern Nigeria since 1901 was some 55,000, the population of the region being estimated at 9 million, of whom nearly 6 million were Mohammedans. In the province of Sokoto, where the suzerain state of the large Fulani Empire

received tribute in slaves, and where at the time of its conquest in 1903 the great majority of the labouring class were slaves, and the masters most tenacious of their rights under Moslem law, the registers show 21,711 slaves freed by regular process up to the end of 1917. . . . Residents report that even as regards those who voluntarily remain, the old relation of master and slave is practically dead and is replaced by that of master and servant.[155]

Clearly, in view of the abundance of land, the legal protection offered slaves desirous of claiming freedom, and the relative numbers who claimed freedom or chose to remain in voluntary servitude, the Hausa slaves (who, in Zaria alone, must have numbered about 100,000 in 1900) were comparatively content with their lot.

That such was the case for a great many, though the precise proportion cannot be stated, is indicated by the continued residence of slaves and their descendants side by side with the owner and his family in numerous former slave-villages, or *rumada*, in Zaria in 1950, despite the persistence of many aspects of the old pattern of relations between the two groups. The proud self-description still given by persons hereditarily attached to the throne, *"Ni bawan Sarki ne"* ("I am the slave of the King"), is also indicative. In 1950, the slaves of Zaria and their descendants also recognized an obligation to send regular annual tithes of their principal crop, grain, to the family of their master, even where the two groups lived far apart. Conversely, the masters recognized obligations to assist, protect, and, on ceremonial occasions, make gifts to the representatives of those families formerly linked to theirs by ties of slavery, but now related by the triple bonds of wardship, quasi-kinship, and clientage. Each status-differentiated group participates in the familial ceremonies, such as marriage, the naming of children, and funeral rites, of the other, and visiting is frequent between them.[156] The proof of harmonious relations between master and slave, and of their sociocultural assimilation is the voluntary retention of these relations by the slaves in the overwhelming proportions indicated by the figures quoted above, when they were legally free to break the relation, and, under the conditions of Hausa economy, stood to gain economically from doing so.

These figures from the court registers may be incomplete, however, as it is likely that some slaves asserted their freedom without taking regular processes through the courts.[157] Such actions do not belie our analysis, but rather support it, since they imply tacit agreements between master and slave that the former would take no action through the courts to recover the value of services or goods due to him from the slave during the time which elapsed between the latter's "abscondment" and the filing of claim. If any material change in master-slave relations against the master's wishes was the slave's object, then he would either have to move a considerable distance, preferably to another state, to enjoy the freedom asserted, or he could seek registration as a free man by the courts.[158] Slaves who did neither of these things simply retained their master, even though leaving his immediate domicile.[159] Significantly enough also, the population returns of the villages and towns of Hausa Zaria during the first twenty-five years of British rule, give no indications of mass movement, such as an exodus of unregistered ex-slaves would present.[160] We may therefore conclude that the figures quoted above represent approximately the scale on which Hausa slaves effectively broke relations with their masters after 1901.

Even so, the figures from these registers are not unequivocal. They include numbers of slaves who were set free by the British in the early years, not at their own request, but as a punishment of the owners for selling and otherwise transferring slaves. By 1905 the bulk of the traffic in slaves had been suppressed through this policy.[161] Thereafter, the court registers also include among its numbers of liberated slaves those manumitted by their masters, since the manumissions were registered in court. Another group of slaves registered as free were women, whose future husbands by this means sought in advance to deny the former master any ground for claim to the issue of the unions such as he would hold in the old Mohammedan slave law, under which the child of a female slave was the slave of her owner. Of 106 slaves freed through process of court in Zaria during 1905–1906, it is simply stated that the majority were women whose intending husbands sought the registration to legalize paternity. Another 13 of these 106 were manumitted voluntarily by their masters. Of the 190 slaves freed in Zaria between January 1, 1900, and the end of 1905, 52 were women about to be married, 86 were "allowed to follow their own inclinations" (i.e., they were adults), 26 were restored to relatives, and 23 were "allotted to guardians" (i.e., children). The number manumitted or freed without request in suppressing the slave trade is not stated in the tabulation from which these figures are taken. For Zaria in 1905, the administration reported that "in some cases slaves have simply asserted their freedom without running away." [162] If this did not include registration, as the context makes clear, then it simply means that, instead of continuing to labor for their masters directly, such slaves maintained the relation by annual tithes and gifts. It seems quite likely that the number of slaves who terminated relations with their masters by effective abscondment during the two decades after Lugard's Proclamation is roughly balanced by the number who did not of themselves initiate the processes through which they were registered as free persons by the courts. This means that the substantial majority of Hausa slaves chose to continue as wards of their former masters.

Emancipation in the British West Indies provides a striking contrast with these Hausa data. There the abolition of slavery was followed by organized attempts of the masters to repudiate the legislative authority of the Crown,[163] and to reëstablish the former relation as far as possible by the enactment of stringent vagrancy laws; by a scale of charges for house and garden rent which penalized the ex-slaves for absence from, or negligence in, work; and particularly by attempts to deny the slaves access to land, except on contractual conditions not very different from the status conditions of slavery.[164] Ejectments from estates of ex-slaves whose attendance in plantation work was judged by their masters to be unsatisfactory were frequent, as were protests also. By 1846, when the British Sugar Duties Bill finally sealed the doom of the Jamaican planters, a considerable proportion of the former slaves had already withdrawn to the hills, either as squatters in single households and village groupings, or as organized communities, purchasing their land en bloc, usually under the leadership of some Nonconformist missionary, or some outstanding personality of the area.

Even before the British Parliament passed the Abolition Act of 1834, there was, as we have seen, considerable hostility to the idea of emancipation among the free classes of Jamaica. When the British Parliament decided to shorten the period of apprenticeship which linked slavery and freedom from six years to four, the opposition of Jamaican planters and their friends produced a severe constitutional crisis.[165] This was followed by organized efforts among the planters to coerce their former slaves to resume work under conditions similar to those of apprenticeship, and by combined opposition to government intervention.[166]

Those slaves who could afford to do so began to withdraw from the plantations in increasing numbers. Registered freeholders with less than 40 acres rose from 2,014 in 1838 to 7,848 in 1840.[167] By 1841 the planters were importing further supplies of free labor from Africa in considerable numbers (1,417 that year) to replace the withdrawing ex-slaves.[168] By 1844 the legislature had spent £128,000 on immigration intended to replace labor lost through withdrawal of the ex-slaves. Between 1838–1844, besides 2,000 free Africans, some 2,700 Britons, and 1,000 Germans had been imported.[169] In the following year, labor immigrants from India were brought in under the indenture system; and at the same time, Knibb, the Baptist missionary, reported that from the census of 1844, he found "full 19,000 persons, formerly slaves, who had purchased land on which they were erecting their own cottages." [170] The situation is reflected very clearly in the figures for sugar output. In the last year of apprenticeship, Jamaica produced 52,659 tons of sugar, in 1840, 26,453 tons and in 1846, 28,641 tons.[171] The planters protested bitterly that there was a labor shortage, and also that the ex-slaves were unsatisfactory laborers. In 1850 Bigelow estimated that there were probably 100,000 "coloured landholders" in Jamaica, "seven-tenths of them begotten in slavery," the colonial population then being approximately 400,000. He gives an estimate of the average size of these holdings as three acres.[172] In 1860, another American visitor, W. G. Sewell, who was concerned to discover whether free Negro laborers in the Caribbean were as unsatisfactory as their employers stated, reported that the lowest local estimate of land-owning ex-slaves placed them at 50,000, with an average of three acres each.[173] Such a figure might represent a peasant population of approximately 200,000. In 1861 Dr. Underhill of the Baptist Missionary Society, calculated, on the basis of the census of that year, and a study of contemporary landholding and use in the parish of Hanover, that the entire black population of the island formed 65,000 family units, owning 354,000 acres of land and property with a total value of approximately £2,200,000.[174] Another estimate places the number of free villages established by the ex-slaves between 1838 and 1865 as 200.[175] Clearly the withdrawal of the ex-slaves from the Jamaican estates was a continuous process and proceeded on a considerable scale. Could the contrast between this and Zaria be greater?

This continuing withdrawal took place in a tense political atmosphere. In 1841 there was a riot in Kingston.[176] In 1848 the government was urged to take steps to meet an anticipated rebellion of "Negroes" in the western part of the island, but the rebellion never materialized.[177] The year 1857 produced two riots. In 1859 there were further riots at Florence Hall, and, on the issue of tolls, at Savanna-la-Mar.[178] Finally, in 1865 a clash with bloodshed occurred at Morant Bay between the local militia and two groups of peasant workers. Governor Eyre proclaimed martial law, and, with support from the better-off white and colored sections of the community who felt that they were being threatened and in need of protection, suppressed this "revolt" rather harshly. A thousand homes were burned in the area, and 600 persons were killed—many without trial—and many, like Gordon, the colored liberal representative of that parish to the island legislature, after trials that were purely nominal. A great many more persons were publicly flogged, with or without cause, and sometimes with unnecessary cruelty.[179] The two chambers of the colonial legislature set the seal of their approval, and their terror, on the Governor's handling of "the Rebellion" at their next meeting, by rapidly acceding to his request that they should abolish the ancient constitution of the island and place the government of the country completely in the hands of the Crown.[180] In doing this the Assembly candidly expressed their "full conviction that nothing but the existence of strong government would prevent this island from lapsing into the condition of a second Haiti."[181] This was a reference to the successful slave revolt of Haiti under Toussaint, which defines the relation between Jamaica's "rebels" of 1865 and the social sections represented by these legislators in terms of master and slave, and gives a succinct statement of social distance and antagonism between the sections. In other words the superordinate sections of this society preferred to abandon all voice in the management of the island's affairs to a government which undertook to guarantee the status quo, rather than assimilate the unenfranchised majority of its population, who were mainly of slave descent.

At this period, 47 representatives were elected to the legislature from 23 constituencies by 1,903 registered voters, the device and cost of registration itself being intended to discourage voting among the landholding ex-slaves entitled to exercise this right. Of this electorate only 1,457 had voted at the last election, an average of 31 voters per representative.[182] But the delay of 18 years from 1865–1883 before any petition was presented by the population for restoration of political rights, and the terms in which such a petition was cast when it was ultimately made, indicate that the abandonment of the colony's ancient political liberties in 1865 enjoyed the approval of those persons of "education" and property who stood to benefit from an extended franchise, but who also feared the masses.[183] This means that the colored section of the community, who strove consistently under slavery and thereafter to assimilate their interests and status to that of the white, and simultaneously to exclude the black ex-slaves from these institutions, were here also identifying their interests with those of the whites and exchanging responsibility for protection. It is therefore of particular interest that both Dr. Underhill [184] and Lord Olivier,[185] who made careful studies of the circumstances of the 1865 Rebellion, conclude that one of its principal causes was the maladministration of justice suffered by the laborers, particularly with respect to rights in land, payment of wages, and other conditions of labor and tenancy at the hands of a magistracy principally composed of men actively engaged in estate management. Thus the surrender of colonial political rights followed on the rebellion of ex-slaves against a sectional definition and administration of justice which had been developed and employed by their former masters as a prime instrument of social control during the years after the abolition of slavery.

Between 1865 and 1937, the principal political events of Jamaican history have been the constitutional changes of 1883, 1895, and 1900, at the end of which a modified form of Crown Colony government was established, the governor commanding a permanent majority in the legislature, for which only persons with an annual income of £150 or more could canvass candidacy.[186] The right to vote was similarly restricted by property franchise to a fraction of the population. Such a system could not last forever,[187] and finally, a century after Emancipation, the riots of 1938 brought yet another Royal Commission to study the island's affairs.[188] Following on recommendations of this Commission, in 1944 universal suffrage was introduced, and with the organization of political parties based on trade union movements, the policy of sectional exclusion from government was formally abandoned.

The economy of Jamaica underwent marked change in the century after 1838, largely as an adjustment to, or as an effect of, changes in the conditions of overseas markets to which the colonial economy was linked, but also as an effect of internal developments initiated by emancipation. The abandonment of preferential tariff on colonial sugar by the British Parliament in 1846 was associated with a prolonged decline of the Jamaican sugar industry. This was marked by the abandonment of numerous estates, and the amalgamation of others around central factories to create more viable economic units.[189] Changes of tariff policy in Britain after 1890 gave an impetus to this development and to the related development of cane-farming, a pattern under which crops grown elsewhere were processed at the central factories. These changes brought about some recovery in the colonial sugar industry.

Among small holders there were three principal lines of development; first, the gradual replacement of cane cultivation by the banana after 1868; second, emigration, particularly to Cuba and Panama, at least equal in scale to the immigration of indentured Indian labor, which the government and the planters sponsored; and third, increases in the number of peasant or small holdings. In 1867 small and medium farms accounted for one-fifth of the cultivated acreage of the territory, then about 500,000 acres all told. By 1896 the acreage cultivated in small and medium farms had risen to 286,000.[190] In 1882 registrations amounted to 52,608, or one for every 11.4 persons in the island. In 1896 there were 92,979 taxed freeholds, or one for every 7.4 persons in the population; of the freeholds in 1896, 81,924 or 88 per cent were of 10 acres or less.[191]

These figures indicate the degree of continuity and pressure among descendants of the ex-slaves to acquire land, and thereby to win some measure of economic independence. To some extent they also indicate the intensity of the desire among this section of the Jamaican population to withdraw from intersectional relations expressed in economic terms as employment, tenancy, and the like, and uniformly characterized by status inequalities defined in sectional terms. Altogether this drive to land acquisition by Jamaican ex-slaves provides a most revealing contrast with the postemancipation developments of Zaria, where no comparable movement is found among the ex-slaves, although good land was freely available to all, and usufructuary rights accrued to the person who cleared it. In Jamaica, however, where the liberated slaves were faced with the alternatives of purchasing land, "squatting," or remaining in dependence on their former owners, the figures already given indicate the proportion which chose withdrawal.

Any account of postemancipation economic developments in Zaria must begin with the British Occupation in 1900. This was followed by three closely related developments; first, pacification, which includes the prohibition of raiding and the trade in slaves; second, formulation of the policy of Indirect Rule, under which the traditional northern rulers were confirmed in their previous powers, except where these conflicted with British norms, and the British Administration acted in an advisory and supervisory capacity with respect to the chiefs;[192] and finally, the gradual reorientation of Hausa trade and economic relations.[193] This economic reorientation was mediated through demands of the British market for such products of the region as hides and skins, cotton, groundnuts, and shea-nuts, in return for which manufactured textiles and metal products were exchanged. Gradually as the volume and significance of this trade for the Hausa economy increased, the direction of the external trade of Zaria shifted from its traditional northwestern orientation to the Sahara and West Sudan along the old caravan routes, southward to the sea along the new railway, and so to Britain. Income from this new overseas trade increased gradually at the same time that income from the capture, trade, and exploitation of slaves was declining. Yet it would be a serious error to attribute the smooth transition of Zaria from slave to "free" society solely to the introduction of new sources of income through trade with Britain. All local products exported from Zaria in this new trade had for long formed staples of the old economy.[194] With the exception of the traffic in hides, which presupposed ownership of cattle as herder or butcher, participation in these new commercial developments was equally open to all, under the terms of the Slavery Proclamation, and the prevailing code of land tenure.[195] The continuity of relations between former masters and slaves shows that these legal and economic changes which formed their common context, and which together provided the slaves with favorable opportunities for exercising independence, were significantly redefined by slave and master as conditions permitting retention of certain former patterns.

With the inauguration of elective councils having a voice in administrative affairs at all levels of society in 1948, Zaria, together with other northern Nigerian provinces, has entered on a new phase of political development, rather similar to that through which Jamaica passed in 1954. At the lowest level all adult males are now free to vote their representatives onto village councils. Above this level, delegates to higher bodies are chosen in electoral colleges. Criticism of the role that chiefs and Emirs sometimes take in these elections has been made both in London and Nigeria, but when one considers the traditionally autocratic organization of Hausa emirates, and the present persistence of former political practice and relations within them, such action is not surprising.[196] For our comparison it is more important to note that, in contrast with the Jamaican rebellion of 1865, and riots of 1938, both of which were followed by fundamental changes in the constitution, there has been no disturbance or riot among the Hausa associated with either of these two most important political changes: the Slavery Proclamation, or the introduction of democratic government. The sole outbreak of violence which has thus far taken place in Northern Nigeria, the riots at Kano in 1953, was a series of clashes between the Mohammedan Hausa and Ibo immigrants from Southern Nigeria, and so far from presenting an internecine dispute of Jamaican type, expressed the solidarity of the Hausa population.

The contrast between postemancipation political developments in Zaria and Jamaica is thus of the same order as the other differences found between them, first, in their conditions of slavery, and then, in the reactions of their slave populations when these were presented with the choice of quitting or remaining with their former masters. Clearly the association of these differences is not accidental, but forms a consistent logical pattern. Political instability in Jamaica during the century which followed Emancipation is linked with the pressure among Jamaican ex-slaves for independence from their former masters, and also with the reactions this movement evoked, in the same way that political stability in Zaria is linked with persistence of those integrative bonds formerly holding between masters and slaves. Together these different patterns of political and economic development cover the crucial fields of social adjustment which the abolition of slavery imposed on Zaria and Jamaica. These two different patterns of adjustment and social change were responses to an identical stimulus. In the logical contrast which they provide, and in the internal consistency which each severally exhibits, they indicate that the societal difference between Hausa homogeneity and Jamaican plurality which was basic to the differentiation of their systems of slavery, operated with equal effect to differentiate reactions in these two societies to the situation created by emancipation, and thus governed their developments.

There is an inescapable implication that this contrast may still hold good, and that this difference of societal type may continue in future to produce similar contrasting developments in response to common stimuli in these two societies. The most cursory reflection on the present heterogeneity of Jamaican culture, on its competing and conflicting forms of religion, family, mating patterns, value systems, or on its marked divergences in educational theory and practice, language, folklore, and participation in economic and technological processes, is sufficient to show that this plurality of culture and society is still the most distinctive and compelling character of the Jamaican scene.[197] Conversely, as the literature shows, all persons familiar with the Hausa way of life, in Zaria and elsewhere, remark strongly upon its balance, homogeneity, stability, coherence and integration.[198] These general impressions about Hausa culture are amply borne out by a detailed field study of Zaria, focused in particular on the problem of social and economic change.[199]

A question arises therefore concerning the significance of plural societal conditions for the stability, integration, or equilibrium of the total structure, and in particular, concerning the significance of sectional differentiation for relations between individuals or groups drawn from different social sections. These problems cannot be tackled here, though certain cues are decipherable from the conditions related above. For example, the relation between integration and plurality is important. Plural societies may or may not be highly integrated; but there is a significant difference in the type of integration that a plural or a homogeneous society can show. In homogeneous societies, integration connotes the maintenance and perpetuation of the system as a system by the functional relations of its institutions. This definition if applied to plural societies must be supplemented by distinctions between the integration of the totality, and each of its component sections. The same point applies to the concept of equilibrium, and, but only more so, to the notion of stability. In plural societies under certain conditions, the stability of the total social structure may be threatened by actions on the part of any of its sections which are oriented toward the preservation of their institutional patterns unchanged. In certain other conditions, attempts on the part of one or more sections to change these differential patterns may also jeopardize the total structure. Such a type of societal unit is therefore faced by the fact of change with problems of stability, which are different in kind as well as degree from the problems facing more unitary societies in comparable situations.

Preservation of the structure of the plural society under conditions of imminent change thus becomes a dominant value in itself, as we have shown was the case in Jamaica 1800–1838 and thereafter, simply because the stability of these units has such a narrow and precarious base. This in turn places a capital value in such societies on the rigid and durable ordering of intersectional relations on both the group and individual levels with the result that the structure of intersectional relations becomes and remains their distinctive political feature and practical problem. Yet, as each section is, by definition, differentiated in terms of ideational and value systems, the likelihood of establishing these intersectional relations on a freely consensual basis is normally remote, while the likelihood that such relations will rest on noncontractual bases, if durability and stability are major functions, is very high. In fact, the extent to which the intersectional relations of a plural society are indefinable and inconsistent in terms of contractual reciprocity is of necessity the precise degree to which they are defined by, and consist in, sectional differences of status, normally with a rigid hierarchic structure. Thus the total structure of these plural societies normally consists in a hierarchic pattern of intersectional relations.

Preservation of the total structure accordingly reduces to the preservation of this hierarchic pattern, and such an aim is unlikely to be given equal priority or legitimacy among the various component sections. Hence the peculiar position and role of authority and power in systems of this type, a factor which also serves to differentiate them societally from homogeneous units. Granted a society, the components of which are differentiated by ideational, relational, and behavioral norms, consensus becomes a remote probability, and authority and power have crucial significance and value as necessities in maintaining, controlling, and coördinating the whole. Under such conditions, and to the extent that the hierarchic organization of sectional statuses is not directly linked with the exercise of authority and power over subordinates on the one hand, and with responsibility upward on the other, instability obtains, and it seems imperative to exclude persons subordinated in terms of status, but not directly so in terms of authority, from participation in common processes of competition for power, that is, from the political system, if the hierarchic status-defined intersectional structure is to persist at all.

As we have seen, this was the condition of Jamaica between 1838 and 1938, and it is an implication of the present analysis that, with the extension of political processes to include all adults of the colony, an important step has been taken to establish a set of integrative mechanisms in place of those abandoned without the provision of any substitute, over a century ago at Emancipation. The empirical basis and significance of these observations may be appreciated by reconsideration of the data from Zaria. There the implicitly contractual bond of reciprocity between guardian and ward was substituted for the social distance involved in the legal differentiation of master and slave. This reduction of social distance and assimilation of different status groups contrasts directly with data from the West Indies, which reveal an opposite preoccupation with status distance both under conditions of slavery and since that normally produces strong motivations among persons of superior status toward the maximization of social distance between themselves and members of inferior social sections.

4. CONCLUSION

Our inquiry raises many problems and suggests some conclusions. The problems raised revolve about the use to which we have put the comparative method, and certain other aspects of our comparison. The comparative method has long occupied a controversial position in anthropology, and it merits attention since our substantive conclusions depend for their validity on the method by which we arrive at them. Recent developments of the comparative method revolve about distinctions of form and function, of cultural and social systems, and between the study of historical process and change on the one hand, and of synchronic systems on the other.

Despite formal similarities in their legal definition, the institutions of slavery in Mohammedan Zaria and Jamaica have been shown to bear markedly different functional relations with other institutions in the two societies. Analysis of these dissimilarities has involved some consideration of many different aspects of the two social contexts, such as the economic, religious, political, educational, demographic, and racial. Since the differences of these two systems could be reduced to none of these conditions, we were forced to inquire further into the nature and comparability of the two milieux. We then found the basis of functional differentiation of these formally similar systems to consist in the part which they played in the differentiation of Zaria and Jamaica as societal types; that is, in the definition and maintenance of a homogeneous culture and society in Zaria and of plurality in Jamaica. This conclusion contained two different hypotheses. First, that the differences between Jamaican plurality and Hausa homogeneity are differences of a societal order, that is to say, they are of an order distinguishing the two societies as members of different structural categories, with the implication that invariant relations between the elements in one of these systems may not obtain in the other. Our second hypothesis, which derived from that just stated, and which it was both necessary and possible to test, was that slavery was so directly linked with the differentiation of these two societies as societal types, that its abolition would produce divergences of their adjustment, which, being consistent with the structure of each, would correspond to their societal differences.

Our hypothesis emerged from this study of the effects of emancipation successful, not only as a general formula, but as an aid to the understanding of precise historical developments and patterns. Though this is far from constituting a "proof" of the validity of the societal distinctions between Zaria and Jamaica from which the hypothesis was derived, it suggests that this distinction of societal type has utility and significance. It also suggests, that the analysis of social change in a comparative context may be more rewarding than otherwise. It illustrates the value of distinctions between form and function in such analysis, and the necessity of pursuing a functional analysis of relations between the traits or institutions selected for comparison after their formal definition and similarity have been established. It shows too how data drawn from different time-levels by field and library research of one or more traditions may be usefully compared.

Comparison proceeds most fruitfully therefore through analysis of the functions of similar social forms. Where the trait isolated for comparison has direct and important links with some, but not all, of the social institutions, then it is only necessary to specify these less important connections, while giving detailed consideration to the more important.[200] Where, however, as in the present case, the institution selected for comparison is linked closely with most fields of social and cultural activity, then full treatment of the functional relations involved must be given. The fact that its comparison requires such treatment implies that the institution concerned is a formative organizing principle of the societies in which it is found. This is to say, at a certain level in the complexity of the traits under comparison, an adequate analysis of their functions and contexts must proceed on both the cultural and structural levels simultaneously, though, at still other levels of complexity or abstraction, only one or another of these frames of reference may be necessary or appropriate. The complexity of traits varies widely, and hence their analysis or comparison varies also. Murdock indeed has submitted relations of kinship to a statistical treatment. On the other hand, we have gained from this comparison first, a more adequate analysis of slavery for these two societies than might otherwise have been possible, and second, the notion of societal types differentiated in terms of cultural homogeneity or plurality. Whereas the comparative method as an inductive method applied to the study of synchronic systems yields purely formal propositions, its application to historical conditions of social change here as elsewhere has shown that it can also yield dynamic propositions which are capable of illuminating processes of social change.[201] When the comparison draws material from a limited number of societies, this comparative treatment of the milieu at different points in time is essential to check the validity of conclusions initially established about the traits concerned, by examining their reactions to processes of change.[202]

Finally, it may be observed that instead of treating similarities of functional relation, and seeking their basis in more generalized relations, we have been doing precisely the opposite. In the definition and analysis of difference the comparative method proves as necessary and valuable as in the study of parallels. It is equally serviceable in both these operations, not merely because it is a useful analytic method, but also because the data to which it applies sometimes determine and require such differences of treatment. By the same process that may enable it to produce social laws, comparison may also produce classifications, and these classifications may include distinctions of societal type, as well as distinctions between subsystems, such as kinship, political, or economic systems. Classification and generalization walk together and the pace of one is linked with that of the other. The comparative method is essential to either operation, and has equal validity when it raises such questions as those concerning the number and nature of societal types or when answering these and other questions by means of generalization or "laws."

Our substantive conclusions have been mentioned in the preceding discussion of method. It only remains to draw attention to two types of social interpretation our study has shown to be fallacious. First, there is a common saying in Jamaica and other British Caribbean territories that "Slavery has left its mark." [203] Stated thus, this view of the matter is really misleading, and the "mark" attributed to slavery in the West Indies was, and is, being made by, and in the context of, a state of cultural and social plurality, with which slavery was once historically linked in these islands as a formative principle of social structure. Slavery, *qua* slavery, has left no comparable mark among the homogeneous population of Zaria.

The other principle of social interpretation which our inquiry reveals to be fallacious has a more general interest and consists in the debate as to whether history is determined by "ideas" or by economic circumstances. Our data have shown that these categories are not mutually exclusive, that the antithesis suggested by such formulations is illusory, and that idealism and materialism each contains such significant components of its antithesis that the analysis of empirical situations of change in such exclusive terms is somewhat inappropriate.

[7

The Plural Framework
of Jamaican Society

Contemporary Jamaica is relatively complex and internally diverse. Although four-fifths of its population are black, and nine-tenths of the remainder are colored persons of mixed ancestry, there are structurally significant groups of Chinese, Syrian, Jewish, Portuguese, and British descent, and in several instances these ethnic groups are also differentiated by special statuses, organizations, and occupational interests.

Apart from this racial complexity, Jamaica includes a number of significantly different ecological areas: the expanding urban area around Kingston; the sugar belts with their large plantations and landless labor force; the rural highlands settled by small holders; and the tourist coast along the north shore. Community types and organization in each ecological area tend to be somewhat distinct. So do community interests, which now compete for influence on the island government. Of the 1.6 million persons who live in Jamaica, perhaps one-quarter are to be found in Kingston and the other main towns, and nearly one-half live in the hilly interior. The plainsfolk dependent on sugar probably exceed 400,000. Rural-urban differences are important already and will tend to become more so. The rate of population growth is very high.

Jamaica's racial diversity strikes the visitor immediately; but local "nationalism" has developed a convenient mythology of "progress" according to which race differences are held to be irrelevant in personal relations. Although it is difficult to state the precise significance of racial difference in a few words, it can be said categorically that race and its symbol, color, do play a very important part in structuring relations between individuals within Jamaica, and the study of this aspect of local life can throw a great deal of light on the island-society.[1] None-

162

theless, race concepts are cultural facts and their significance varies with social conditions.[2] To understand the local attitude to race, we must therefore begin with the society and its culture. Accordingly, in the following summary of Jamaican social structure, I shall avoid direct reference to ecological or racial differences as far as possible, while presenting a general account which incorporates this racial complexity fully within the frame of social and cultural difference. This procedure permits a shorter description than is otherwise possible, and reveals the basis of Jamaican thinking about race.

The most appropriate approach to the description of Jamaican society is that of institutional analysis. An institution is a form or system of activities characteristic of a given population. Institutional activities involve groups, and these groups generally have clearly defined forms of relations among their members. Moreover, institutional activities and forms of grouping are also sanctioned by normative beliefs and ideas, and social values are expressed in institutional rules. The basic institutions of a given population are the core of the people's culture; and since society consists of a system of institutionalized relations, a people's institutions form the matrix of their social structure. Thus the description of social structure consists in the analysis of the institutional system of the population under study.

In the following account of Jamaican social structure, I shall therefore describe the institutions of local society and their variety of alternative forms, as systematically and briefly as I can. In Jamaica, each institutional subsystem such as the family or religion is represented by a number of diverse alternatives. Moreover, each group of institutional alternatives characterizes a different segment of the local society. Although usually described as a social class, the population which practices a distinctive set of institutions is best described as a cultural or social section. The three distinctive institutional systems characteristic of contemporary Jamaica therefore define a society divided into three social sections. For initial reference, we may think of these sections as the white, the brown and the black, this being the order of their current and historical dominance, and the exact reverse of their relative numerical strength. Although these color coefficients are primarily heuristic, they indicate the racial majority and cultural ancestry of each section accurately. The white section which ranks highest locally represents the culture of mid-twentieth-century West European society. It is the dominant section, but also the smallest, and consists principally of persons reared abroad from early childhood. The black or lowest section may include four-fifths of the population, and practices a folk culture containing numerous elements reminiscent of African societies and Caribbean slavery. The brown intermediate section is culturally and biologically the most variable, and practices a general mixture of patterns from the higher and lower groups. This mixture seems to involve a combination of institutional forms as often as institutional syncretism. Thus the culture of the middle section includes coexistent institutional alternatives drawn from either of the two remaining traditions, as well as those forms which are peculiar to itself.

Kinship institutions differentiate the three sections clearly. The general pattern of kinship throughout this society is bilateral, but its operative range increases as we move from the first section to the second, and its matrilateral range and emphasis are predominant among the lowest group.[3] Differences in family types correspond with these differences in the kinship systems of the social sections; and these differences of family organization are both formal and functional. In the small dominant section, families have a bilateral authority structure and are small, tightly knit groups with important functions of status placement and training. In the intermediate section, families have a patriarchal authority structure, the division of labor between husband and wife is quite distinctive, and the composition and range of the family are more various. In the lowest-ranking section, family authority and responsibility is modally matriarchal, and the composition of domestic units reflects the primacy of uterine kinship and descent.

These sectional differences of family organization are linked with other differences of mating pattern. The small dominant section observes contemporary West European norms of marriage. It includes more divorcées than bastards. The intermediate section practices a creolized version of Victorian marriage, and distinguishes men's legal and illegitimate issue most sharply. The third section typically mates outside the context of marriage, which is usually postponed among them until middle age, very often after the birth of grandchildren. In the top section, mating, marriage and cohabitation imply one another; and family and household normally coincide. At the opposite social extreme, coresidence is certainly not a necessary condition of mating, marriage even less so; and there is no equation between family, household, and mating relation even as a social ideal. In the intermediate section, the mating and family forms characteristic of the other two sections are often found together, men living with their wives and lawful issue respectably, apart from their current or former mistresses and illegitimate children. These three differing forms of domestic organization, mating, family, and kinship are integrated as separate institutional systems which differentiate the three social sections. None fully understands or approves the kinship institutions of the others.

In their magico-religious systems, the three social sections are similarly differentiated. At one extreme, we find the agnostic attitudes characteristic of contemporary British society, and this religious agnosticism is coupled with operational faith and skill in modern science and administration, the dominant values of this world-view being those of materialism. At the other extreme, African-type ritual forms, such as spirit-possession, sacrifice, obeah or magic, are common, together with a liberal variety of beliefs in sorcery, witchcraft, divination, spirits and their manipulation, and several substitutes for *rites de passage*. Among the intermediate section, the typical religious form is denominational Christianity; and the church creed, ritual, theology, organization, and modes of recruiting members differ remarkably from the corresponding revivalist forms which are current among the lowest section.[4] The fundamentalist world-view of this intermediate section contrasts sharply with the moral and cosmological systems of the other two. Basically, these three types of magico-religious system are organized about competing principles of action and explanation. Agnosticism abides by materialist notions of causality and is normally coupled with faith in science. Fundamentalist Christianity believes in an omnipotent Christian God, whose actions are morally perfect, and who can be appealed to, but not manipulated. Revivalism and other Afro-Christian cults are based on a belief in good and bad spirits which can affect the living directly, and which may be manipulated for personal evil or good. In the agnostic view there is no room for revelation, but scientific method guides us to valid conclusions. In the fundamentalist view the decisive revelations occurred long ago in Palestine, especially during the life of Christ. In Revivalism and other folk cults, revelation occurs presently through dreams, divination, omens, and especially through spirit possession with its prophecy "in tongues." Agnosticism is an outlook which has no institutional organization or membership. Denominational Christianity normally recruits members by infant baptism. Revivalism and other Afro-Christian cults do so by adult conversion and baptism. The priesthood and organization of Christian denominations differ in like measure from that of the revivalist groups.

Education also differentiates the three sections sharply; and there is a positive correlation between the differing sectional experiences of education on the one hand, and their differing magico-religious or kinship practices on the other. The small dominant section consists mainly of professionals with university training, of entrepreneurs, and of landed proprietors, who could easily take such training if they wished, or finance it for their dependents independently. Members of the intermediate section normally undergo instruction in local secondary schools; while members of the third or lowest section have so far had little chance of formal education beyond the level of the elementary school. However, education and schooling are not coterminous, and among all sections the informal component in education varies inversely in its significance with the amount of schooling received. Thus the peasant's lore of herbal medicines, proverbs, folk stories, and the like, his skill in certain manual operations, and his knowledge of cultivation techniques have no parallel among the secondary school or college graduates. Thus the content as well as the form of these sectional educational experiences is quite dissimilar.

In adult life these differences find expression in differing occupational and employment patterns. The entrepreneur exercises managerial functions in personal or corporate organizations. The professional typically finds remunerative long-term appointment in some large corporation, such as government, or else conducts his own practice alone or in partnership. The secondary-school graduate whose education proceeds no further, typically finds clerical employment in business or government.

The great majority of Jamaica's school-leavers come from the elementary or primary schools, where tuition is provided free by government, and where efforts at ensuring attendance sometimes involve compulsion. Most of these elementary school children later find manual employment on the farms in the rural areas or in menial capacities in the towns. Recent surveys by the Jamaica Social Welfare Commission indicate that a high proportion of those persons who have only had elementary school education are unable to read or write. Another recent survey by Dr. C. A. Moser points out that less than one-quarter of the children attending elementary schools do so for the full eight years of the course.[5] A fair proportion of rural and urban children simply do not attend school at all. Certain militant cult-groups such as the Ras Tafarites[6] condemn these elementary schools as agencies of sectional propaganda, in much the same terms as Dr. Madeline Kerr, who found that they produced disorganized personalities.[7]

In effect, the technology which adults manipulate varies with their early educational experience. In Jamaica, these sectional differences of occupation are in part effects of the differing contents and significance of informal education in childhood, in part they are due to the historical inequalities of formal education. The longer a child stays in school receiving formal education, and the greater the stress on his proficiency therein, the shorter and less significant his informal training. The professional is normally just as ignorant of the peasant's knowledge and skills, as is the latter of the former's speciality.

The economic system places special emphasis on the techniques and knowledge transmitted by formal education, and the resulting occupational groups enjoy differing rewards of income and status. Proprietors and professionals who receive the largest incomes also enjoy higher status than other occupational groups; unskilled or semiskilled workers who receive very low incomes rank at the bottom of the occupational scales. These local scales of income and prestige are correlated with employment patterns; and, at least in recruitment, employment is closely related to the system of differential education. Thus the inequality of educational opportunities in Jamaica is an important condition of social and economic differentiation. The local system of differential education governs the distribution of those skills and aptitudes which are conditions of recruitment to occupations of different types. In this way the Jamaican educational system bolsters the social structure, and distinguishes three social sections.

The relation between the systems of occupational differentiation and education tends to be self-perpetuating, since the less-well-paid manual occupations do not allow parents to pay for their children's education at secondary schools. Moreover, children at elementary schools have not had adequate educational facilities or sufficient scholarship opportunities of free secondary education; these conditions have produced sufficient frustration to discourage many parents from sending their children to school regularly. Historically, the propertied sections of the Jamaican population have monopolized the local franchise on the basis of their educational and property qualifications. They have used their political influence to secure high government grants per pupil at the secondary schools while keeping expenditure on elementary education very low. Thus the differential allocation of political rights which was based on educational and economic differences was used by its beneficiaries to maximize the sectional differences in education which underlay these economic and political inequalities. Thus the educational system and the sectional order were integrated, and the one tended to perpetuate the other. Moreover, within Jamaica, the division of labor directly reflects these differences in the educational careers of the population, and serves to maintain them.

The three cultural sections already defined differ also in their economic institutions. Banking, currency, insurance, export-import commerce, and such large-scale agricultural undertakings as sugar or banana estates are controlled by that section which represents contemporary Western culture locally. Overseas marketing is controlled by overseas agencies, normally those of the metropolitan power. The forms of government finance and their development follow current metropolitan forms and changes. To a considerable degree, local branches of foreign economic organizations are managed by expatriates, or by persons of recent expatriate origin. Jews, Syrians, and Chinese are Jamaica's most important entrepreneurial groups; but the values which these groups attach to the maintenance of ethnic identity and cohesion only emphasize the extent to which economic control in Jamaica is separated from the "native" population, or Creoles as they are called.[8]

If we consider employment, saving, property, or marketing, the

differing institutional forms and roles of the three Jamaican sections
are equally clear. The top-ranking section consists of a hard core of
employers and own-account professionals, together with superior civil
servants, whose employment conditions are such that dismissal or
demotion are virtually inconceivable. Most members of the intermediate section are themselves either employees of "middle-income"
status, or small proprietors, businessmen, farmers, contractors or such
lesser professionals as teachers. The majority of this group are also
themselves employers, hiring domestic labor and other types of service
attendants by unwritten contracts and directing them in a personal
fashion which involves heavy reliance on prompt dismissal and casual
recruitment, but does not lend itself easily to trade-union action. In
the lowest section, the typical employment status is a combination of
wage and own-account work, and underemployment or unemployment
is widespread. Such institutions as partnership, lend-day, and morning
sport, which serve to redistribute labor on a coöperative reciprocal
basis, are as distinctive and typical of the lower section as are the systems of regular or casual recruitment for task, job or daywork used by
the first and second sections respectively.[9]

Saving and credit forms differ likewise. In urban areas, the lowest
section saves either by means of African-type credit-thrift associations,
such as "partner" or *susu*;[10] or individually by loans to market
vendors and others who "keep" the money placed in their care while
turning it over in trade; or cash is hoarded or put in government post-
office banks. For members of the lowest section credit facilities are
usually available only from those shops and persons with whom they
have regular business dealings. In the intermediate section, credit is
obtained through solicitors against security in property or insurance, or
by hire-purchase and other accounts with various firms. Among the
dominant section, credit is sought overseas or through local branches
of banks established overseas, and it is advanced by them typically on
mortgage, in the form of trading materials and stock, or against produce
designed for sale on the world market. Savings among the top section
are mainly invested in stocks, business, or land; at the intermediate
level the main forms of investment are in houses purchased for rent;
among the third section, animals or small holdings predominate.

The three sections differentiated by these economic characteristics
are also distinguished by the forms and roles of their economic associations. The dominant section is typically organized in employer
associations, chambers of commerce, certain farmers' societies, and the
like. Some of these associations have long histories. The lowest section
is now organized in trade unions and friendly societies, the former
being of recent growth. The intermediate section has hitherto avoided
explicit economic organizations of its own, and has also avoided direct

participation in the conflict between labor and capital. Its membership in these unions and associations is accordingly marginal, and in this respect its organization reflects its intermediate economic position. However, this intermediate section does control a number of important occupational societies, such as those for teachers, small farmers, or civil servants, which represent its major economic interest-groups.

Property concepts and distribution also differentiate these three sections. Among the economically dominant section, property takes the typical form of productive enterprise, such as commercial businesses, firms, factories, estates, or the like. Typically also these enterprises are limited liability companies, joint-stock or partnership organizations being in the majority, and in them the personalties of shareholders are sharply distinguished from their interests in the enterprise. Thus, for the dominant section, property principally connotes some interest or share in an enterprise, with corresponding rights to a fixed portion of the profits of its operation. Among the intermediate section, property is mainly held on an individual or family basis, by freehold or under mortgage; and it typically consists in land, homes and own-account enterprises, whether small businesses or professional practices. Among the lowest section, the dominant property form is "family land," that is, land held without proper legal title, and without precise personal distribution of rights, by the members of a family and their dependants.[11] At this level also, personalty consists mainly of small stock, tools, clothes and the like, while the homes which their owners regard as realty have the legal status of "chattels," being often movable structures, or otherwise of temporary character. The property concepts of each section are thus quite distinctive, those of the dominant section being defined mainly by company, contract, and commercial law; while those of the intermediate section are governed by the law of real property and debt; and the property concepts of the lowest section require such novel enactments as the 1955 Facilities for Titles Law to be accommodated to the prevailing legal code.

Similar differences characterize the sections in regard to marketing. Jamaican markets fall into three types: (a) the local shop or market, at which consumer meets vendor and in which "the Chinaman" or the "higgler" (market woman) are the specialist traders;[12] (b) intra-island produce marketing which is oriented to the collection of produce for shipment abroad, and wholesale shopkeeping which distributes imports; and (c) overseas import-export dealings which are controlled by large merchant houses that handle a variety of commodities traveling in either direction and typically operate a monopolistic system of commission agencies. There are also a number of recently developed crop associations, each exporting a particular commodity. The organization and processes of this large-scale overseas traffic are institutionally as

different from those of the intra-island produce trade in their details of
insurance, brokerage, shipping, customs, credit and commission agency,
and in their relation to the world market, as is the local produce trade
from the higgler-dominated trade in community markets. The specialist
personnel who dominate each of these three different marketing systems
are also drawn from distinct social sections.

The legal positions of the different sections are also different. Jamaican legal forms are typically imitations of the law of the metropolitan
power. These imitations have been locally administered by British
personnel. In their content and application Jamaican laws have
hitherto reflected the interests of the dominant section in controlling
the subordinate ones: and even today, when the political bases of this
historical order have been partly removed, local laws relating to obeah,
bastardy, praedial larceny, ganja (marijuana), and the like are sectional
in their orientation, content, and administration. The participation of
the intermediate section in law-making and administration is relatively
recent, and their typical role is still that of jurors or lawyers. Participation of the lowest section in legal administration has been limited to
subordinate police capacities, while the local police and law courts have
historically been administered by members of the dominant minority.

Both during and since slavery, the members of the lowest section of
Jamaican society have tried to settle their community disputes by informal arbitration or adjudication, in order to prevent such issues
from going to court. Obeah, family land, the village lawyer, the peace-
maker, or the revivalist priesthood are among the institutions which
serve these ends. During slavery, informal courts were held by the
slaves under their headmen;[13] after slavery, missionaries and other
prominent persons acted as arbitrators in community disputes.[14] Even
today court cases involving members of the lowest section only are
mainly criminal in character, and usually include some verbal or
physical violence. Cases brought by members of the intermediate section against their social inferiors are mainly for misdemeanor or for
recovery of debts. The judicial maladministration of intersectional
issues was especially important in producing the Jamaica "Rebellion"
of 1865.[15] Even today the high cost of legal advice and procedure
effectively deprives the lowest section of justice in civil issues against
their superiors. Illiteracy and widespread unfamiliarity with the details
of the law are equally disadvantageous to them. The dominant section
always employs legal aid in its litigation; the lower section can only do
so rarely; the middle section may do so half the time.[16] Like almshouses
and approved schools, prisons are primarily populated by the lowest
section and are administered by members of the intermediate section
under the supervision of the metropolitan power and its nationals.

Government is the institutional subsystem that expresses the conditions of social stability and change in Jamaica most directly. Historically, all important governmental institutions—law, the judiciary and magistracy, the militia and army, the administration and the legislature, were monopolized by the dominant section at the parochial and island levels, and these rulers were assisted in subordinate executive roles by members of the intermediate section. The lowest section remained outside the pale of political life until 1944. Until then they were denied the chance to develop their own political institutions or to imitate any other models. After Emancipation, restrictive property franchises maintained the disenfranchisement of the ex-slave section; and with this was associated control of administration and law by the other two sections. Under this system the dominant section directed policy, and the intermediate section executed it, while control of the lowest section was both the object and condition of many policy decisions.

In the historical development of Jamaican society the majority of its members have had no active role or status formally assigned to them in any phase of its political or legal systems. Under and since slavery, this massive subordinate section has only been able to express itself politically by riots, rebellions, and the like. The "disturbances" of 1937–1938 which produced Bustamante's charismatic leadership and hothouse unionism were the inevitable result of this political order and sociocultural pluralism. These social eruptions led to the introduction of adult suffrage, and this has since been followed by the establishment of the ministerial form of responsible government in the colony. However, the revocation of the British Guianese constitution in 1953 repeats the pattern of constitutional abrogation so familiar in Caribbean history, and shows that the formal transfer of power is hedged about by reservations and can be reversed by force if necessary.

One most interesting reservation held that economic independence is a prerequisite for political autonomy, and it is argued that since only a Federation of the British Caribbean colonies may develop this economic self-sufficiency, this is a *sine qua non* of Caribbean self-government. Within Jamaica, sectional sentiment has contributed greatly to acceptance of the federal idea, notwithstanding its contradiction of nationalism and certain other obvious disadvantages. From the popular point of view, perhaps the most far-reaching disadvantage is that the federal association will reduce the political power of the lowest section within Jamaica. This follows because the island government will now operate under surveillance of the federal legislature and administration, within limits set by federal policy, and under a federal constitution which places conservative political forces and values in a stronger position than they have recently occupied in Jamaica.

The question has been asked how the colonial elite can still maintain control of policy and their dominant status in the face of strong desires for rapid change among the newly enfranchised section. The answers to this question are many and various; they may do so, first, by capitalizing on their indispensability for the performance of certain elite functions, notably, of course, those of economic development and administration; second, by constitutional revisions of the type which promote the values of conservatism rather than popular movements; third, by federation, which involves simultaneous limitation of local power and the transfer of control from popular leaders to a federal executive which substantially represents the interests of elite sections throughout the Caribbean; fourth, by prolonging their dependence on the metropolitan power for economic aid, and therewith the colonial status; or, fifth, by stressing the need for imperial or federal forces to guarantee the current social structure to encourage overseas investors; or finally, by the technique of buying out the popular leaders, which is not unknown in Jamaica. The point to notice in all this is that the introduction of liberal franchises and constitutions has been followed by an extension of political action to a federal field, and that these federal developments tend to restore control to those two social sections which formerly monopolized it. Thus the abrupt reversal of the political order of 1937 may yet prove to be pure illusion; and an effective restoration of this order may now be under way, with federation as its basis. In such a case, the federal association would simply replace the metropolitan link.

So far we have discussed only those social forms which provide the institutional core of the society, namely, the systems of kinship and marriage, religion, government, law and economy, education and occupational differentiation. There are also important differences between Jamaica's social sections in language, material culture, sport, associational patterns and value systems. In Jamaica a complete linguistic dichotomy does not obtain; but it has been found that middle- and "upper-class" natives do not know the meaning of 30 per cent of the words current in the Anglicized folk dialect.[17] It would also be surprising if those Jamaicans who habitually speak this folk dialect should know more than 70 per cent of the words commonly used by those who do not. Bilingualism in such societies is a characteristic of cultural hybridism, and such hybrid cultural adjustment is most typical of the intermediate section. Thus, while the small top section speaks and understands English, but not dialect, and while the large bottom section only speaks and understands dialect fully, the intermediate section tends to employ either linguistic form according to the occasion.

Recreational patterns also distinguish the three social sections. To begin with, recreation is typically an intrasectional activity, and has different organizational and activity forms in each section, cricket being the outstanding exception to this rule. Clubs taking part in a variety of sport competitions, and organized therefor, are typical of the intermediate section and rare among the lowest, whose usual sport association is the single-purpose cricket club organized on a community basis in rural areas among populations that are not institutionally differentiated. Competition between clubs of the upper section is not usual, and those which provide sport facilities normally hold open-entry individual tournaments in games such as golf or tennis, occasionally inviting foreign professionals to participate. Proprietary clubs organized for gambling, dancing, and drinking are typical of the lowest section, while members' clubs are the typical forms of the upper two sections. Exclusive top-section clubs also offer facilities for the accommodation of members and guests, sometimes on a reciprocal exchange basis with certain of the London clubs. Club life among the top two sections is heterosexual and may include family units, but in the lowest section only men are members.

In their recreational activities the three sections differ even more strikingly than in their organization. Golf, polo, water-skiing, and certain other aquatic sports such as yachting are clearly limited to members of the top section, who do not take as active a part in track sports, football, or cricket as do the other two, especially the intermediate group. Tennis is commonly played among the upper and middle sections, together with billiards, bridge, and certain other indoor games which do not, however, include dominoes or those gambling games typical of the lower section. Boxing, cricket, track, bicycling, and to a lesser extent football, are the main outdoor games of the lower section. Such heterosexual activities as dancing and swimming are common to all groups, though the sex and age participation patterns, the forms of the activity, and the typical situations in which they occur also vary. It is almost a rule that intersectional participation in such activities as dancing, swimming, and the like should not take place. This restrictive sectional barrier has a considerable effect on the membership patterns of clubs in all sections.

Informal associations vary similarly among these social sections. Economic and political associations have already been mentioned. Excluding these, the clique is the typical form of association among the intermediate group, and is multifunctional in relation to occupation, mating, kinship, business, and recreation. Among the small dominant group, relations are both more specific and more widely distributed, the cocktail party attended by near-strangers and acquaintances being the stock alternative to the intimate dinner party. Among the lower section, cliques and parties are far less significant than are neighborhood, kinship, age-peer, and workmate relationships.

To an outsider, the most striking differences between these sections are seen in their material culture. The material culture of the lowest section is symbolized by a chattel-house, few but gaudy clothes, and the cutlass for a tool. That of the intermediate section may be symbolized by the concrete bungalow, gadgets such as washing-machines and refrigerators, and the motorcar or the typewriter for a tool. The upper section is characterized by "the Great House," of which modern versions are still being built (though in different style), the team of servants, and the checkbook or telephone for a tool. Although the intermediate and higher sections have many elements of material culture in common, they also differ significantly, and the differences between the material culture of these two sections and that of the third are even more striking. Technological aims and differences also correspond with these differences of material culture.

The study of value-systems presupposes an adequate semantic analysis and an adequate body of data. Neither of these exists for Jamaica; but values, beliefs, ideas, goals, and norms are of such fundamental moment in social and cultural organization that even in the absence of these investigations, one may tentatively indicate the principal value-foci which differentiate the several sections of Jamaican society. It has already been shown that these sections differ in the modes of action, explanation, and proof which they employ. It can also be said that materialism provides the formative principle or reference point in the value-system of the upper section, whereas social status dominates the value-system of the intermediate section, and values of immediate physical gratification are central among the third section, spiritual as well as secular values reflecting these principles. This tentative differentiation of the sectional value-systems by their foci has two important implications. First, the moral axioms of one section are not the axioms of another, so that the same events or patterns are generally interpreted and evaluated differently by each of the three Jamaican social sections. Thus, the values and implications of color are peculiar to the intermediate section in the same way that the notions and values of spirit possession and manipulation are peculiar to the lowest section. Second, the coexistence of these divergent value-systems within a single society involves continuous ideological conflict. The need to express these differences of value and morality governs and reflects intersectional relations, and this insistence on the incompatibility of the sectional moralities is incessantly activated by the differing sectional reactions to common events, especially of course those which involve intersectional relations.

It is not merely that the same event has different meanings or value for the different sections; these differing interpretations compete continuously, and their competition is inherent in their coexistence, and in the corresponding cultural and social plurality which they express and represent. It follows that interpretations of events by reference to one or another of these competing moral systems is the principal mode of thought that characterizes Jamaican society, and also that such sectional moralizations normally seek to define a negative, extrasectional and disvalued pole in contrast to a positive, intrasectional and esteemed one. Thus Jamaicans moralize incessantly about one another's actions in order to assert their cultural and social identity by expressing the appropriate sectional morality. For such self-identification, negation is far more essential and effective than is its opposite; hence the characteristic appeal of negativism within this society, and its prevalence.

This summary describes a society divided into three sections, each of which practices a different system of institutions. The integration of these three sections within the larger society has never been very high; and for cohesion Jamaica has depended mainly on those forms of social control implicit in the economic system and explicit in government. Even so, patterns of interpersonal relations do not always correspond with these cultural divisions; and in every cultural section there are some persons who habitually associate with others who carry a different cultural tradition more regularly than with those of their own cultural community. The fewness of these marginal individuals is no adequate guide to their importance.

It may be argued that this account only delineates two institutionally differentiated sections, and that the white and brown strata described above are really two social classes which form a common section because they have a number of institutions in common. Clearly, the greatest cultural gulf within this society lies between the two upper sections and the large lower one; but although these two upper sections do share certain institutions, each also practices a number of institutions which is quite specific to itself, and since these sectional systems of institutions each tend to be integrated separately, I have regarded them as quite distinct.

[8

Community Organization in Rural Jamaica

In this essay I present a tentative model of community organization in the Jamaican hill country, in the hope that it will be of practical use to persons working there on development and welfare projects. Since my aim is to provide a practical guide to community structure and dynamics, I shall avoid discussion of abstract sociological issues as far as possible, and concentrate on the methods and problems of studying community organization. The model and methods set out here derive from field work in eight "districts" during the Jamaican Rural Labour Survey, 1955.[1]

The Community Concept

Definitions of community vary. MacIver describes it as "any whole area of social life" and Ginsberg as "a group of social beings leading a common life, including all the infinite variety and complexity of relations which result from the common life or constitute it."[2] By a community, I shall mean a field of social relations based on regular face-to-face association between persons. Such face-to-face associations imply coexistence within a defined area; and the simple fact of recurrence in such social contacts, together with the likelihood that this will continue for some indefinite period, makes for some elements or levels of patterning.

Communities are local groups, and as local groups they fall into two main classes, those with compact settlement patterns and well-defined boundaries, and those which are dispersed in settlement pattern and overlap one another at the boundaries to a greater or lesser degree. Differences in the levels and types of formalization of community

176

structure are often related to these differences of settlement pattern. In this regard, isolation can be of special importance. Except where compact communities are also isolated, as in the case of certain Indian villages and rural Hausa settlements in Northern Nigeria, community boundaries are often difficult to establish, and the determination of community margins and membership presents a serious problem for sociologists as well as for field organizers working on programs of which the community is a constituent unit.[3]

The levels of intensity of social relations within a local group vary for spatial as well as other reasons. People living on the boundaries or margins of a local group may have their closest social ties with groups outside it. Class and wealth differentials are also important. The motorcar permits close and continuous social relationships between people who live at some distance from one another. The members of a particular class whose homes are quite dispersed may be divorced from the population among whom they dwell, and may really form a community of their own, in some senses of the term.

Jamaican Settlement Types

In contemporary Jamaica we must begin by distinguishing the urban area, the flourishing country towns, fishing villages, certain isolated settlements, recently established government land settlements, the sugar areas with their plantation economies and social organization, and rural communities proper. Each of these different types of settlement may well have its own peculiar form or level of community organization. I shall confine my remarks here to the last class of rural communities. Between one-third and one-half of the island's population live in settlements of this type.

In Jamaica it is further necessary to distinguish rural communities from certain other types of local units, with which they are sometimes confused. As I have defined it, a community is not a polling division, nor a market area, nor usually a village, and only in certain specific uses of the term is it a "district." Nor are these different types of units identical. "Districts" may include or cut across polling divisions, market areas, and village boundaries. Similarly, polling divisions may include segments of two or more communities, whereas a village may include several polling divisions. Polling divisions are purely functional units set up by the Electoral Office for the registration of voters and the holding of elections. Their boundaries are determined simply by these considerations.

As used by government officials, or with governmental organization in mind, the term "District" normally denotes an arbitrarily defined area which forms a unit in relation to some administrative scheme or function. Thus, we can speak of Districts of the Agricultural Department, or of the Jamaica Social Welfare Commission (JSWC); or of a proclaimed area or district under the laws to control praedial larceny, especially Law 30 of 1942 and Law 26 of 1949. As used by rural folk, however, the term "district" normally refers to a distinct community, members of which recognize certain bonds among themselves which do not extend to other groups nearby. Thus a person may say, "I am from 'Ridge' (district), Top Hill, South St. Elizabeth," meaning that he is a member of the community at Ridge which has its nearest post office, school, and governmental agencies at Top Hill, another district or community in South St. Elizabeth. To outsiders, however, including extension workers, Ridge might seem to be simply a portion of Top Hill District and community. Such misinterpretation of field realities by outsiders may promote difficulties in the achievement of their objectives, especially where these consist in the organization of community participation in development and welfare schemes. Whatever its administrative utility and reference, which may be various, the term *district,* as used by officials, does not refer directly to community units. As currently used by officials, this term sometimes refers to an area having some former historical and administrative unity, and at other times it denotes a unit within some present administrative framework. Despite its inappropriateness, however, this administrative usage has been widely adopted by organizations committed to working through communities and has been taken to distinguish them.

In rural Jamaica, villages are clusters of homes and shops, and typically contain the local primary school, post office, and other governmental agencies that service an official district. Where there is a market, it normally meets at the village center once a week, but unless it is sufficiently important, its limits may not be gazetted. The village is strung out along the road or intersecting roads that have promoted its growth. This pattern of ribbon development is similar to that characteristic of rural communities, but has a denser distribution of buildings consequent on the more favorable economic conditions and communications to be found in the village.

The village acts as the distributive and organizational center for the more dispersed settlements grouped around it, and which it serves. Unless completely isolated, it cannot be regarded as forming a community of its own separate from these dispersed settlements, since its sectors form parts of the communities immediately behind them. Nor is the village as a whole simply a part of the community formed by these dispersed settlements which surround it, since the dispersed settlements are themselves distinct communities. Thus, communal relations hold between sectors of the village and the settlements immediately adjoining them, but may not hold between segments at the opposite ends of the village. Nonetheless the village as a whole acts as the economic focus and agent of the communities immediately dependent upon it. Furthermore, if villages do not normally form distinct communities of their own except in cases of isolation, then the population living within the market limits of a village market is obviously not a single community. Market limits, it must be remembered, are recent administrative constructs in Jamaica.

Rural Community Characteristics

The following description of Jamaican rural communities summarizes those characteristics which distinguish them broadly as a distinct settlement type in the island, and also provides some guides to the determination of their boundaries.

Normally, these rural communities are established in hill areas, where estate operations are marginal, and the majority of the population is engaged in own-account farming on their own small holdings or on plots acquired under tenancy. Settlement pattern is dispersed within the conditions of local land relief and land holding. Where there are motor roads, ribbon development is characteristic but discontinuous, household clusters forming neighborhood foci for the dispersed homes beyond them.

Historically, as is well known, emancipation in Jamaica was followed by the withdrawal of large numbers of people from the sugar-producing plains, and this withdrawal has given rise to a permanent structural differentiation between hill and plain areas.[4] Plantation economies and social systems have persisted on the plains, while peasant-type economies and societies were developed among the population which settled the hills as squatters, freeholders, or with mission assistance. One often finds today a general denominational attachment in some of these hill communities, and to some extent this attachment reflects the historical conditions in which missions assisted their establishment. But today, church influence is probably dominant and integrative only where the community is considerably isolated.

Craft production is marginal within the rural community economies, and trade unionism is almost entirely absent. Markets are only to be found in the principal village centers. There is little wage-employment available locally except agricultural or domestic work. In terms of population movement, these rural areas attract little in-migration, but have substantial out-migrations of two types: relatively long-term movement out to other parts of Jamaica or abroad, and short-term seasonal flows of young people to the sugar-producing areas nearby. Thus we can conceive of them as relatively closed communities. Among the bulk of their population, the levels of education, income, and living are low, housing is generally substandard, and public facilities are rudimentary and poor.

Police supervision is generally exercised in somewhat personal fashion by a district constable who may or may not be resident within the community he serves. Where praedial larceny districts have been proclaimed, certain other persons are also authorized to make arrests under these laws, but these normally reside within the communities concerned. There may be a justice of the peace living in or near the area; but often there is none nearby; doctors or qualified dentists are hardly ever found resident in these regions. Weekly visits from a doctor lasting an hour or so, are as much as most of these districts can boast; and local herbal and magical specialists enjoy a high degree of freedom from local competition by the clergy as well as from the physicians.

Peasant holdings form the typical enterprises of these communities and in their organization and operation reflect the prime importance of kinship relations. Farm production is focused on provision of commodities for household subsistence as much as for exchange. Land is held under a system of customary tenure, involving conceptions and practices of family ownership.[5] In terms of the prevailing patterns of domestic economy, women have an important role as marketing agents, and the small holder without a mate or adult daughter often finds some difficulty in getting his provisions to market on his own account.

The basic unit within these communities is the household, a group which shares a common dwelling place, eating and sleeping together as a unit and coöperating in the provision of household needs by complementary or group activities, the latter typically involving the exploitation of certain common resources, notably land. Within any rural community, however, one will find several cases of single individuals living on their own, and there are other instances in which the definition of household membership may be quite ambiguous. For various purposes, different household types can be distinguished, the simplest and most usual breakdown consisting in a classification according to the sex of the household head. Household headship, however, is itself a composite concept, embracing such factors as age, health, formal or informal control of the principal resources of the household, ownership of the house, and taking into account the different positions of the senior household members with regard to the numbers and status of their kin within the household or in other units nearby.

It is reasonable to expect that church organization and leadership would provide communities of this type with some hierarchic patterns of integration, but these integrative capacities of religion are often latent and diffuse, due either to the nonresidence and infrequent attendance of the few ordained ministers who serve the country parts, or to the divisiveness generated by the claims of competing denominations and cults, especially as between Protestant Nonconformity, Revivalism, and Roman Catholicism.

The Problem of Boundaries and Membership

Having indicated the type of community under discussion, its characteristics and differences from other types of local unit, I now wish to deal with the problems of boundary determination which the dispersed settlement pattern presents.

Probably the most important factor governing community formation and separation in Jamaica is topography, especially land relief, water supplies, and roadways. Steep slopes make steep ascents, and this limits the intensity of social contacts across valleys, ridges and the like. Conversely, level patches or unbroken slopes make for easy and frequent social intercourse. These differences find expression in various ways, as for instance in mating relationships. Characteristically, rural folk tend to mate within their local group rather than with members of groups immediately adjoining theirs; and on the whole, the pattern of mating within a single community differs from that which crosses community boundaries. When members of immediately adjoining local groups mate, their relation normally begins by visiting and may continue to do so for years without the establishment of a common household, especially in those cases where both parties hold land or have cultivated plots in their several communities. By contrast, within the local group, the topographically distinct unit of mutually accessible homes, such mating normally leads to the early establishment of a common domestic unit, either separately or as part of the parental household of one of the partners, and normally this occurs in response to the pressures of kinsfolk who live nearby. Where intercommunity mating occurs, such kinship pressures are less effective, and other factors serve to keep the partners living in their different communities.

In looking over the countryside for the probable boundaries of rural communities, we must therefore begin with the principal topographic features that define local groups as community units, and which may further define neighborhoods within those local groups. These primary topographic features are water supplies, land relief, and the roads, motor or other, which lead through the area and beyond it to some village or town.

Other indicators of community boundaries in rural Jamaica strike the eye less immediately, if at all, but are nonetheless both important and easily documented. They include the local distributions of visiting, praedial larceny, kinship, leadership, free or exchange labor in farming, interest-free loans, religious affiliation, tradition, and interest. Since these patterns may be unfamiliar, I shall say a few words about them and try to indicate their cumulative significance.

Among Jamaican country folk, visiting practices are quite distinctive. In rural areas, males who are neither kin nor close neighbors rarely visit one another except "on needs occasion," that is, when illness or death occurs, or on matters of business, or by invitation to such ceremonies as baptism or marriage; but this restriction carries less weight within a community than might at first appear, since most members of the community are likely to be kinsfolk. Moreover, children move about freely between households, and women also visit one another easily, sometimes to arrange their marketing affairs. But across community boundaries, visits rarely occur except for specific business purposes.

Sometimes it is difficult to classify visits according to their purpose. Two friends who habitually "lend" one another a free day's work in farming may spend hours at each other's homes, ostensibly arranging their future work partnership. But cases of this kind are also extremely rare across community boundaries. Men who are "partners" in coöperative farm work, who regularly exchange free labor with one another, and may advance small sums of money or aid in kind, as occasion requires, to one another, are almost always members of the same community. Members of different communities rarely work one another's farms in partnership, or make these interest-free loans, except when purchases or rentals are involved, when the loan is understood to be time-limited.

Since the majority of community members who remain within their local group tend to mate therein, it follows that ties of kinship and affinity ramify widely among them, and these ties provide a broad and acceptable basis for mutual visiting. Children certainly make much of these opportunities, and because of their frequent movement between homes, they come to know and be known to their neighbors increasingly as they mature. The intimate knowledge of one another from childhood that is typical of persons who are members of the same community develops on this basis, and distinguishes them as a unit from the local groups on their boundaries who do not know them extensively or intensively, and of whom they also know little. Cases occur in which households are ignorant of their closest neighbors across a community boundary, and in a good many more instances such neighbors have never visited or spoken to one another. It is probable that this type of social discontinuity is most marked where the community boundary is clearly defined, as by a ridge or a portion of some estate. Yet, however indistinct the boundary may seem, familiarity with neighbors and kin who are members of one's own community contrasts vividly with the unfamiliarity across community boundaries. Moreover, this differential knowledge is quite easily ascertained. If local class divisions and relations are discussed with people in these areas in detail, and information is sought about individuals representative of different strata, the informant's range of knowledge can easily be mapped by suggesting the names of people drawn from different parts of the locality, and by testing the informant's capacity to give detailed information about these persons. People generally know their own community and its personnel in considerable detail, although they may be unwilling to talk or to tell the truth; but they tend to be vague and less well-informed about adjacent communities, since visits are rarely exchanged across these boundaries, and since intercommunity ties are individual and specific rather than general or diffuse.

As we shall see, there are a number of formal associations in most rural areas. As regards the problem of determination of community boundaries, the most revealing of these local associations is probably the cricket club. This is normally an informal organization, deriving most or all of its support from local personnel, and organizing weekly matches with teams from other communities, some of which may be at a considerable distance. When matches are played against distant teams, trucks are hired to take the local club members and their kinsfolk of both sexes from the community, and they often make a weekend of it. Where two or three cricket clubs occur in adjoining areas, the boundaries within which the members of each live, and from which its supporters are drawn, will almost always coincide closely with the divisions between these rural communities.

Similarly, where a wage rate changes sharply for a particular task, the place at which it changes normally marks a community division. For example, a man may do a day's work for another who is a member of the same community for a particular rate, but if asked to work for a third person who is a member of a different community, he will normally demand a higher rate.

Where two or three elementary schools are roughly equidistant from a given area, the children of that community will tend to go to the same school.

When a man calls for a free day's work, such as a "morning sport" on his plot of land, the majority of those who turn up to assist him are members of his own community. Similarly, men who exchange farm labor with one another on a regular basis through the institution of "partnership" or "lend-day," are almost always members of the same community.[6] Those men who receive most assistance at "morning sport" or a "digging" are clearly amongst the most popular in their community. Conversely, the men who receive least assistance, or none at all on these occasions, are among the least well liked. This simply means that each community recognizes within itself an informal local leadership. The character of this leadership is informal, since it is established, maintained, or discontinued solely through the movement of popular support and confidence; but this informal character does not make such leadership insignificant or ineffective.

When a man living in one community cultivates a plot within another solely for his own benefit, he often finds that losses by theft occur on this distant plot. These repeated thefts may continue even when he has no individual enemies in the community in which this plot is situated. But if he is merely working land on a share-cropping basis for some member of that community, such thefts are far less likely. Conditions such as these illustrate by contrast the strength, significance, and effects of community sentiments. Members of a community regard it as an especially heinous offence to steal one another's livestock or crops; and if such theft is found out, it normally gives rise to ejection from the community as an effect of local ridicule and ostracism. On the other hand, there does not appear to be any similar prohibition against larceny of crops or livestock belonging to members of other communities, or to strangers within the community. Persons who regularly suffer losses by theft from the holdings on which they live are not usually true members of that local community. They live within it, but are not *of* it. Either the community has not accepted them, or they have not accepted the community. In the latter case they are likely to be of a socioeconomic status superior to that of the community average. Where they are of average status and are not accepted, they are almost certainly immigrants or have a delinquent past. Persons of superior socioeconomic status rarely exchange visits with other households of inferior status in the neighborhood, nor do they attend the wakes and nine-night ceremonies which are customary after death. Such people are either representatives of a different section of Jamaican society from that to which most of the community belong, practice different forms of the same institutions, and have different beliefs, values and attitudes; or, erroneously, they see themselves in this light.

Communities are further distinguished in terms of tradition and quasi-political interests. For example, the people of any particular place will have demands for government assistance and complaints of government neglect which are specific to them and which normally evoke little sympathy outside their boundary. Thus, where different demands are juxtaposed and complaints are voiced, the community boundary lies in between. This identification of community members is often strengthened where there is a general attachment to a single denomination or cult leader, but as we have seen, this tends to be rare except in isolated districts.

It is not accidental that the critical indices of community solidarity and difference should consist in the differential incidence of particular types or forms of social relations in rural Jamaica, rather than in symbols of a more material type such as a church or a plaza, as in the Latin-American *municipios*. Unfortunately, upper-class Jamaicans tend to interpret community organization and boundaries in terms of such symbols, and to argue from the church or the market square to the district around it. In fact, however, noncorrespondence of community divisions with material symbols derives to some extent from past and present official preoccupation with local units of different character established for a variety of administrative purposes. Moreover, the rural communities now under discussion were typically established over a century ago by a population withdrawing from the Jamaican society which surrounded them. Consequently, from their establishment, emphasis on their identity and differentiation has rested on social relations rather than on material or cultural symbols such as churches, boundary marks, or community rituals of an obvious type. The real community rituals occur at the wake or the nine-night, when a death leads to a demonstration of community solidarity with the bereaved. Primacy of social relations in the differentiation of rural communities simply reflects the fact that communities are essentially social units constituted, defined and distinguished in terms of social relations.

Formal Associations and the Community

The principal characteristics of rural communities having been described, I now have to discuss the problem of their integration in terms of the principles on which they are organized.

The dispersal of households within a community, their economic and social distinctiveness, and the tenuousness and multiplicity of kinship relations within the community, raise certain problems for the integration of these household units on a community level. Granted that the community has boundaries, or even that we can speak of more and less communality, it is reasonable to begin the search for integrative mechanisms by looking to the agencies and associations that are formally designed to serve and to bind these household units into a distinctive group, or that are based on the assumptions that they form a distinctive group. Governmental agencies such as the school, post office, medical, or maternity services, and the like, could act as foci of common interests; so could the church. Children meet one another in school, their parents in church, and all share such common leadership as teachers, priests, or religious elders provide; normally too, all look

to a single nurse or midwife for modern medical assistance. Shopkeepers, produce dealers, government road headmen and foremen also
deal with the population of a community as a unit. Political party
organizations may either segment or consolidate social relationships
within the area, and certainly add another dimension to their organization. The owners or overseers of properties on the community
margins which offer relatively large employment opportunities are
important people locally, and may deal with labor drawn from the
area casually or on a regular basis.

Such formal associations as the Jamaica Agricultural Society branch,
the local branch of the Women's Federation, the Parent-Teachers'
Association, Banana Growers' Association (AIBGA), Pioneer or 4-H
Clubs, and various commodity or coöperative associations, normally
have teachers or other prominent local folk at their head. In areas
where the Jamaica Social Welfare Commission has been working for
some time, there may also be a Community Council, and one or two
special craft or project groups linked in with the welfare agency.
Since membership in these various formal associations does not usually
coincide with community boundaries, they tend to remain artificial
groupings of heterogeneous composition for specific ends. Weaknesses
in their functioning and operation reflect their constitution, and
weaknesses of this sort find greatest expression in the community
councils, of which the constituent units are normally these other formal associations.

The various voluntary associations to be found in rural areas break
down into a few simple classes: religious organizations, whether
churches or sects; associations attached to the Jamaica Agricultural
Society (JAS) and often organized by it, notably the registered co-
operatives and commodity associations such as the AIBGA, Citrus
Growers' Association, and the like, and Thrift Clubs; associations
organized by or within the framework of the Jamaica Social Welfare
Commission, such as the Community Council, 4-H Club, Pioneer Club,
Adult Literacy groups, and so forth; associations attached to, and organized about the school, namely the Parent-Teachers' Association,
school clubs and the like; political party groups; and those informal
associations which derive their entire leadership and support from
the community members themselves, such as unregistered coöperatives
or cricket clubs.

Excluding the religious bodies, the schools and the JAS itself, the
majority of these associations, although nationwide in character, are
of recent development. They are primarily focused on improving
rural welfare, standards of living, and farm practices, and at a national level they are either subsidized by government indirectly or
financed through the commodities they handle. Characteristically, each

of these organizations at the local level has a local president, treasurer, secretary and other officers; and keeps records, minute books, and the like. Leadership of each of the formal associations tends to be highly concentrated, the key positions in most associations in any area being held by a very few people. It is, therefore, interesting to notice that the majority of the positions of formal leadership in the associations now being discussed are commonly held by strangers to the community: teachers, welfare workers, and other persons who have come in to do a job.

In communities where there is a prominent middle-sized farmer, he and his wife may dominate most of the organizations in which they are interested. Such domination is often directed to some extent toward political targets with which the leaders are sympathetic. The parts which extension officers of the agricultural, welfare, coöperative, or other departments, play in the life of these improvement or commodity associations, vary a good deal according to the nature of the association, its membership, leadership, and significance for departmental policy objectives. Frequently, festival days, training days, or local exhibitions may be organized; attempts to build community halls may be made at the suggestion or request of the extension officer, whose role is conceived as catalysis rather than direction. The associations themselves vary a good deal in survival value. Some of them seem to go through continuous successions of death and rebirth without any increase of effectiveness. Attendance is also often depressingly low, notably in certain Parent-Teachers' Associations. Units like the Federation of Women, which link welfare and development work, depend to a high degree on the drive of the local leader, and correspondingly reflect her conceptions.

One frequently meets informal associations which spring up among the community natives on a neighborhood or community basis, often with multifunctional character, sometimes for specific purposes such as coöperation in the sale of eggs and poultry, savings, farm help, and the like. If these groups flourish and expand, they tend to fall within the orbit of one or another of the extension services which operate in the area, and to be organized formally, with a written constitution, procedural code and set of targets drawn up by some departmental officer. Frequently such a process of official organization stifles what was a thriving group. It does so probably because it removes the control of the association from the people themselves. Formalization of procedure and literacy requirements often present barriers to effective action by local folk who enjoy their neighbors' confidences. More importantly, registration often involves reduction and redefinition of group functions, and may destroy the values of association for former members. Consequently, interest and membership may lapse.

To the extent that the population of a rural community is engaged in diversified farming, the small holders will tend to be drawn into one or another coöperative and commodity association handling their major crops. Thus the enrollment within these farm service associations may be quite heavy. Enrollment and effective participation are, however, quite distinct. Branch meetings may be poorly attended unless some outstanding issues such as price are at stake. Multiple membership of male householders in these voluntary associations does not therefore indicate a corresponding degree of community organization or integration along these lines. Basically this is so because the leadership is foreign, and the objectives and methods of procedure and organization may also be unfamiliar. Dissatisfaction about bonuses, prices locally paid, and administrative mishaps of one type or another, serve to reduce enthusiasm and membership while the relative immobility of leadership at the local and national level in these associations blocks effective protest and change. Consequently community councils and the like, which are reared on the foundation of such associations, often fail to function effectively, since the constituent units themselves often lack local support.

Informal Organizing Principles

We have seen that the collection of individuals and households that forms the local community, does not gain much integration through specific associations. There are, however, other principles operating which serve to organize and structure community leadership.

The most general differences between community members are those of age, sex, and wealth. Color is of significance in most rural communities only where wealth permits status aspirations, and in such cases it serves to isolate the mobiles in ratio to their emphasis on color.[7] Sex differences provide a basis of family and mating relations which link the members of different households, and which also find expression in formal associations such as the Women's Federation, the 4-H, and the churches. In associations of direct political or economic purpose, however, women play a less prominent part than do their menfolk.

The primary age distinctions among rural folk are those between the children of school age; young folk who have left school, but have not entered into regular domestic unions; those who have domestic responsibilities of their own, but whose children have not yet started to work; and older people. Emphasis on age differences as a status factor is important within the family and leads to some separation of the elderly from the junior males. This often reduces the leadership value of age unless wealth or certain other conditions are present. Men of 35–50 years of age often exercise considerable influence over their juniors, simply by presenting the latter with personal models of successful adjustment.

Rural community organization is defined in terms of stratification and segmentation. We can think loosely in terms of a grid, the horizontal division consisting mostly of class and wealth variables, whereas the vertical divisions follow spheres of power and influence.

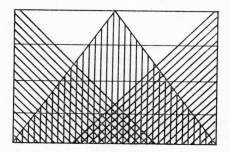

An outsider may fail to differentiate between the members of the local community in terms of class, but the members themselves do not. In the communities that I studied, locals would rank their neighbors in as many as six strata, distinguishing them partly in terms of behavior, partly in terms of wealth.[8] People not placed in adjacent strata rarely visit one another, while members of widely separated strata would not call at one another's homes even on "needs occasion," that is, at the time of serious illness or death. It is therefore important to determine the extent and character of local stratification if one is to understand the organization and process of the community life.

We can conceive of the local community as divided vertically in terms of power or influence. There is an overlap at the boundary of each of these pyramidal divisions, and the further down the community class system we go, the greater does this overlap become. The main segments reflect the principal economic and social forces operating within the community. The shopkeepers and produce dealers control credit and certain marketing facilities. Often also, they control transport and a considerable section of the locally available regular employment. They may straddle certain of the commodity or coöperative associations by providing these with necessary materials, stock feed, and so forth, and often occupy official positions within them. Their political sympathies are especially important, as most of the shopkeepers in the rural areas now under discussion are Creole rather than Chinese.

The teachers and civil servants control another set of facilities.

Those associated with the school are of a special interest to the community who feel that "teacher's" favor or disfavor makes a lot of difference to a child's educational chances. The school actually provides certain meals, educational supplies such as books, and employment opportunities as part-time pupil teachers, and it is the focus of certain teacher-dominated voluntary associations.[9] But the teachers themselves are often immigrants to the community and, except for the head teacher, may often remain divorced from it for years.

The head teacher occupies a different position and can hardly avoid entering into fairly close relations with the parents of his pupils. Often enough he may be acting as an incumbent for one or another of the denominations, in return for occupancy of the mission house, and thus may combine religious with educational leadership. As one of the most knowledgeable persons in the community about governmental procedure and the like, his advice may be requested on a variety of issues, and his services in this way may later inspire him to contest elections to the parochial or island legislatures. Where there is no local justice of the peace available, the teacher exercises a virtual monopoly of these advisory functions with respect to the needs of citizens. Parents also try to keep on his good side as a means of recommending their children to his attention. The teacher's area of power therefore spreads outward from the school to different levels of community life, both formally, through the associations, and informally, through his personal influence and knowledge.

Employment opportunities for unskilled labor are controlled by government foremen and road headmen on the one hand, and by the overseers or owners of nearby properties or estates on the other. The group to which these employment opportunities directly appeal is mainly that of the young men, but also includes those older men whose farming incomes are not sufficient to meet all their obligations. The influence that these labor recruiters can exert in local affairs is inversely proportionate to their social isolation from the community; for example, the overseer of a large property is often not concerned to exert any influence beyond that required by the strict task situation, whereas the road headman who disposes of far less employment, but who may be a community native, has greater importance in the eyes of people needing employment, some of whom will often undertake to work the headman's farm on a fairly regular basis at low rates in order to procure road work from him as occasion offers.

Headmen of the JAS and other farm organizations, whether those engaged under the recent Farm Recovery and Development Schemes or those otherwise engaged on crop inspection and development, together with those locals appointed to administer hurricane relief, similarly control significant economic opportunities and enjoy corresponding power. Under the prevailing party political pattern, there tends, for any area, to be an association between these unestablished quasi-officers and one or another of the party groups; and individual careers often reveal movements from one of these jobs to another. To some extent local administration of the American farm labor recruitment program was formerly integrated with this general area of activity.

The church does not form a separate segment; and the priest, even if resident, no longer controls a separate area of influence and power as before, although his personal prestige may be great, and he may sometimes act semi-officially as an electoral warden, a justice of the peace, or in sundry other capacities.

The principal pyramids of influence within a community are often linked up at their leadership level by informal contact between the heads. Teacher and shopkeeper may be friends, or they may avoid one another. Their spheres of operation do not directly clash, nor require coöperation, although for political or other reasons they may be drawn into open alliance or antagonism. Contraposition occurs mainly within each of these separate spheres of influence. Shopkeepers and produce dealers compete with one another. The teacher is in implicit contraposition to other quasi-official workers such as extension officers, JAS headmen, and the like. The extent to which these implicit contrapositions become explicit depends on a variety of personal and situational factors, but their latency must not be ignored. Because of this character, the structure of each segmentary sphere of influence consists in terms of loose fields of clientage and patronage, focused on the competing principals. The same thing holds, equally, where employment facilities are the values disposed.

The more important power structures operating within a community are controlled by or through local people, who are either native to or so long resident in the community as to be identified with it. For this reason the formal associations within which leadership is exercised mainly by salaried migrants, have less direct significance for the community structure than would appear on the surface. Influence and power rest with those who control economic resources and employment opportunities in the local community. But informal leadership, as distinct from economic power, is to be found among these men whose middling age and economic status arouse less envy and suspicion and whose position within the informal voluntary associations such as the cricket clubs, unregistered thrift or coöperative groups, or local political party groups, is strong by popular support. Such men, although not usually occupying official positions within the commodity and development associations, attend their meetings regularly, exercising a representative function on behalf of their juniors and seniors who do not attend. They hold, as it were, a watching brief on behalf of the community.

Since positions in the local systems of segmentation and stratification are closely related, between them these principles define the basic forms and levels of community organization. Moreover, even where contraposition develops along their various lines of cleavage, these systems of stratification and segmentation provide the only mechanisms serving to integrate rural communities above the level of household organization.

The Problem of Organizing Community Support

If this account is correct, rural community structure is informal in character. Formal organization of community interest and action must therefore present something of a problem, especially to those national associations committed to working through communities as units. In this concluding section I wish to set certain organizational patterns against our model to test its utility and fruitfulness.

Without singling out any particular agency, one can generalize their organizational patterns in the field in the following terms:

"A village is or should be a community. Its leaders are the educated, better-off members, such as the teacher, justice of the peace, parson, overseer, property owner, large shopkeeper, and the like. The village-community is as strong as its active groups. Hence to establish our branch or program in this village successfully, we must enlist the support of those persons who are the leaders of these established groups; or if no groups have yet been established, we must establish ours with those persons who would normally have been leaders of such groups."

Behind the variety of specific functions, purposes, names and forms of organization, behind the differences between the JAS branch, Community Council, Praedial Larceny District Committee, Federation of Women's branch, commodity or coöperative associations, and others, this is the common set of assumptions, the philosophy on which branches of national organizations are founded locally.

The serious misconceptions on which this approach is based are obvious immediately when reference is made to our model of community organization. It has been shown above that the village is not normally a true community, but rather a heterogeneous collection of sectors of the various communities which border upon it. In Jamaican rural areas, villages are the organizational and distributional centers for the hinterlands they service. Consequently community councils organized on the basis of villages service artificial units. Because the village is not a community, it does not provide a sound basis for the development of a community council.

Similarly, the proposition quoted above to the effect that the village is as strong as its active groups is a combination of fallacies. Since the village is not a true community its assessment in terms of strength or weakness of community integration or sentiment is scarcely relevant. Furthermore, the activity of active groups within villages normally bears little correspondence with actual community boundaries. Leadership of the interest groups concerned, whether "active" or not, is normally exercised by salaried immigrants such as teachers and others, who are often marginal to the community system of social relations. Consequently organization of village committees or community councils upon the basis of these formal associations multiplies the artificiality inherent in such structures, with consequent difficulties in enlisting or maintaining community interest and support.

In addition, it may be worth pointing out that where a community or development council is composed of representatives of voluntary associations themselves focused on specific interests, such as the Citrus Growers' Association, Boy Scouts movement, AIBGA, 4-H Clubs, JAS, and so forth, difficulties of program construction and implementation must follow. This remains likely even if membership of all the constituent associations of such a council coincides completely with the community boundaries, and follows from the fact that representation is based on a heterogeneity of single-purpose groups. As representatives of special interest groups the delegates from each of these constituent units are committed to the pursuit and support of policies favorable to the groups they represent, insofar as class considerations are not dominant. In other words misconceptions of the nature and form of Jamaican rural communities, combined with misconceptions of the relation of formal associations to these communities, have led to artificial organizations of councils for "communities" which are themselves artificial contructs. The difficulties such an approach imposes on effective field work by development and welfare officers are obvious.[10]

Since our model of community structure as an informal pattern provides the basis for these criticisms, it should also provide us with some constructive leads to the organization of community support.

Selection of the village as the *locus* of branches of national organizations and development efforts tends to bypass the large number of persons who do not live in villages, but live dispersed in the communities round about them. Consequently, if villages are retained as the centers of local branch activities and organizations, arrangements must be made to reach out beyond them into the neighborhoods and dispersed units where so many folk live.

Normally, the folk in these hillside communities cannot be reached effectively by the methods outlined above. In the first place, physical conditions rarely permit this approach, and in the second place, the conditions of social organization reject it. Instead of thinking initially in terms of specific single-purpose organizations or associations defined in terms of interests, we must therefore think of general groupings free to develop, define and pursue their own purposes, and based on locality and common community membership.

This second consideration, taken together with our information on the informal character of local leadership, suggests that club organizations based on community boundaries might provide the most appropriate method of commencing work.[11] It is especially important that such clubs should not be defined initially in terms of limited interests or procedures, but should be free to develop their own goals and forms. Within the club context, informal leadership can find full expression, and its capacities can be developed. The maintenance, control, and organization of such clubs should remain in the hands of their members if interest and participation are not to decline. After a period of initial experiment, during which the members find out what can be done with this new social form, it can be expected that subgroups will tend to develop within the club, defined partly by shifting interest, partly by social ties. With their emergence and differential pressures, the future of the club will become a matter of some concern and can be directly linked up with the future and improvement of the community as a whole. This should not be difficult, since the club is based on the community. At such a stage, it becomes possible for the local group to take an active interest through its club in certain of the formal organizations located at the nearest village, notably of course, the Development Area or Community Council. But if and when representation to these units is sought by the club, special care must be taken to insure that the informal leaders delegated to act on behalf of the club are not divested of their leadership capacities and support by formalization of their roles.

Frequently enough informal leaders have been rendered useless simply by appointment to positions of formal leadership within some community council or association branch. The reason for this is obvious. To formalize informal leadership is self-contradictory in the same way that it is self-contradictory to make formal authority informal. Formal leadership operates within a clearly defined structure and set of procedures, such as branch or council meetings. Informal leadership, on the other hand, can only operate in open situations lacking such defined structures and procedures, and in terms of community support based on presuppositions of equality and identity. Granted this, the informal leader acting as delegate for the multifunctional community club should be strictly limited to agency on its behalf, and should report back to the club his observations at the meetings attended, so that decisions of policy and action are taken by the club as a whole, and the capacity of leadership may be retained. As smaller groups within the club become differentiated in terms of interest, they should be encouraged to select their own delegates, plan their own programs informally, and to develop informal leadership within themselves.

These suggestions seem to be implicit in our model of rural community organization.

[9

Education and Occupational Choice in Rural Jamaica

Introduction

In this essay I seek to describe the patterns of occupational preference in rural Jamaica. To do so I draw on two independent surveys for my data. One of these inquiries was a study of elementary education made by Mr. P. C. C. Evans in 1957.[1] The other was a survey of conditions affecting rural labor supply which I made in 1955. Occupational choice was investigated in both studies, and by collating their data on this topic, we can explore the correspondence of career choices amongst peasant adults and children, and relate these aspirations to local prospects. The comparison depends for its value on the validity of this procedure. Various objections are possible, and I shall discuss these before analyzing the data.

In his study of rural elementary education in Jamaica, Mr. Evans administered a questionnaire to the children in forty-one schools, twelve of which were in rural townships, while five stood on the margins of sugar areas, and the remainder in the "open country" districts of dispersed peasant settlements. The schools were selected on the basis of current knowledge to represent the peasant populations settled on the margins of sugar plantations or further afield in the hills. The questionnaire was answered by 2,050 boys and 2,850 girls between the ages of 10 and 16.

The questionnaire contained two items of interest here. Question 28 asked, "What work do you want to do when you leave school?" Question 30 asked, "What work do your parents want you to do?" The questions were written on the classroom blackboard and read out to the children one at a time. The children wrote down their answers on sheets of paper which were then collected. The tabulation and

196

analysis of replies to Questions 28 and 30 were carried out under my direction so that I could compare these data with others in my possession.

The survey from which these earlier data were drawn was made in 1955. Its object was to study conditions affecting labor supply in the peasant areas of Jamaica. As part of this inquiry, I asked all individuals who lived in the districts visited whether or not they were then seeking work. Those who said they were, were then asked to name three types of work which they preferred. For the purposes of this labor survey, all individuals above the age of 15 were treated as adults, and, provided they lived within the areas under study, they were interviewed. However, for this paper, I shall deal only with the two junior-adult age groups, one between 15 and 24 years of age, the other between 25 and 39.

The eight districts in which I made censuses as part of this labor survey were selected by the Director of Statistics, Jamaica, so as to represent the peasant areas of Jamaica. They were scattered widely throughout the island, and are directly comparable with the rural areas in which the school survey was undertaken.

I have already reported on the economic conditions and occupational structure of my rural sample in considerable detail;[2] but in this paper some background data are necessary, so that readers may appreciate the context and character of the adult work-seekers whose preferences are presented below.

Of the total adult population of 2,593 in these eight survey districts, 360 males and 369 females were between 15 and 24 years of age; another 364 men and 378 women were 25 to 39 years of age. Of the men aged 15–24, 66.6 per cent declared themselves to be "looking for work." Of those between 25 and 39, 75 per cent did likewise. In both female age groups, 45 per cent of the women said they were "looking for work."

Such a high incidence of desire for work might be taken to indicate corresponding degrees of unemployment among the sample. This would not be quite correct. During the week preceding survey, of the young men under 24, 15 per cent did no work at all, 44 per cent did less than 28 hours of work, another 25 per cent worked between 28 and 42 hours, and 16 per cent worked 42 hours or more. Of the men aged 25 to 39 years, 11 per cent did no work that week, another 21 per cent worked less than 28 hours, 33 per cent worked between 28 and 42 hours, and 29 per cent did 42 hours or more. Except that women of these age groups tend to work somewhat longer hours than men, their distribution by numbers of hours worked that week is not very different. The great majority of the adults who said they were seeking work were therefore persons who already had work of some sort to do; yet even when allowance is made for weather, illness, social activities, and other factors which reduce available work time, it is clear that many of them were underemployed.

TABLE 2

ADULTS BELOW 39 YEARS OF AGE, CLASSIFIED BY SEX, AGE-GROUP, AND EMPLOYMENT STATUS DURING THE TWELVE MONTHS PRECEDING SURVEY
(Unit = per cent)

Employment status	Males		Females	
	15–24	25–39	15–24	25–39
Own-account employed*	24.8	17.4	52.5	67.0
Wage-employed only	32.7	13.5	10.3	5.5
Wage and own-account	36.7	66.6	21.5	26.4
No occupation	6.5	2.5	15.7	1.1
Totals	100.0	100.0	100.0	100.0

* Includes unpaid family labor.

The main occupation of these peasants is small-scale farming. Women report housekeeping as work, together with their other activities such as farming, marketing, dressmaking, shopkeeping, and the like. Of the total adult male population in these areas, 34 per cent were engaged in own-account farming, 46.1 per cent combined own-account activities with wage work, and 14.3 per cent were wage-employed solely. A further 5.6 per cent of these males had had no occupation during the twelve months preceding survey. For males, farming predominates among own-account activities. Wagework is predominantly road work, transport, or farm labor. Some employment is locally available in building and house-repairs, but this is small. The own-account category here includes unpaid family labor, which usually involves farming for the younger men and homemaking for women. Of the adult females in these areas, 63.8 per cent were own-account employed, a further 20.1 per cent combined own-account and wage-work, and 6.2 per cent were fully wage-employed. Over the preceding twelve months, 9.9 per cent reported no occupation. Only 8 per cent of these women worked at farming for wages, whether full or part-time. Another 6.3 per cent engaged in paid domestic service, on part or full-time basis.

Of the males, 78.3 per cent farmed full or part-time on their own account; and of this group, 66 per cent declared themselves to be "looking for work." Of those farmers who also undertook wagework, 80 per cent were looking for work; among the full-time farmers engaged purely on their own-account, 46 per cent said they were "looking for work." Of the wage-employed farm-workers, 82 per cent said they were seeking work; of those who worked for wages off the farms, 59 per cent said so. Table 2 shows how the members of these two age groups were distributed by employment status.

Full-time wagework has a higher incidence among males than females, and is greatest in each sex among the junior age group. For men of 25–39 the typical adjustment combines wage and own-account activities, the latter being mainly farming. For women concentration on homemaking is similar.

Given these conditions, it is worthwhile asking how many of those who wished work had taken steps to seek it. Here we encounter institutional arrangements that give local employers the main initiative in recruiting those workers they want as need arises. Farmers may keep work available for those persons they prefer. Preferred workers may have work offered them without their seeking it; but the same men may also seek work elsewhere, or, knowing of its local availability, may feel their applications fruitless, since the farmers involved have their own "regular" labor supplies. The same institutional context applies to female labor.

Of those men in either age group who declared themselves to be wanting work, 15 per cent had received offers of local employment during the previous twelve months, but had not sought work otherwise. Another 30 per cent of the men in the junior age group and 24 per cent in the senior one had neither sought nor been offered work. Of women between 15 and 24 who said they wanted work, nearly one-half had neither been offered nor sought any during the previous twelve months; of women in the senior age group, 54 per cent had the same record. Whereas only 37 per cent of both groups of women had actively sought work during the previous twelve months, 54 per cent of the men in the younger group, and 60 per cent in the older group had done so. Expressed desire for work is thus quite consistent with the fact that these people already have something to do. Underemployment, low wage rates, and poor returns from own-account farming together produce a general desire for additional or alternative employment and encourage many actively to seek it. This economic background is directly relevant to the preference patterns discussed below.

By comparing the occupational preferences of these adults with those of the school children, we may partly determine the correspondence between career wishes and prospects, and the changes of occupational preference which accompany maturation. One objection to this comparison may be that the groups compared were born at different times and do not belong to the same universe as regards careers or life chances. The force of this argument diminishes when the relevant time spans are examined. The school children who answered the questionnaire were born between 1941 and 1946. The junior adult age group were born between 1931 and 1940. The two groups accordingly contain successive cohorts, and no one could seriously argue that peasant circumstances had changed sufficiently within this interval of 15 years for this comparison of occupational preferences to be misleading. My own experience leads me to believe that the conditions of Jamaican peasant life changed very little during this period. From this view, life chances and patterns of occupational choice have remained constant, and we may assume that these junior adults had much the same career choices when at school as did the school children studied in 1957. It follows too that the occupational preferences of these school children will tend to change in much the same way and for much the same reasons as did those of the adults, providing rural conditions remain as they were. The same argument and assumptions underlie comparisons of the two adult age groups. Members of the senior age group were born between 1916 and 1931, and in this and the subsequent period, peasant Jamaica underwent little change. Readers who prefer to do so may ignore the senior age group when the preferences of adults and children are compared. In my view this restriction excludes significant insights, especially because the changing patterns of choice represent one aspect of maturation in the static peasant life cycle.

By comparing the children's statements of the occupational preferences which their parents have on their behalf with those of the children themselves on the one hand, and with those of the adults on the other, we may isolate the influences of home and school on the children's aspirations, and distinguish aspiration from expectation among the adults. Since the senior adult age group belongs to the same age range as do the parents of these school children, the two sets of responses bear directly on the difference between adults' aspirations for their children and expectations for themselves. The important proviso here is that the parental preferences which these children report are substantially correct. Persons familiar with Jamaica will not be surprised that these children know what sorts of occupation their parents would like them to follow. Adults frequently inform their children of these aspirations on their behalf, and for a variety of reasons. It is thus quite understandable that the majority of the school children questioned should have clear ideas of the careers their parents wish them to pursue. That these statements relate to parental preferences and not merely to the children's assumptions thereon is suggested by the large proportion of children who report their ignorance of the parents' preference. On these grounds I regard the children's statements of their parents' wishes as a correct record of the parents' views, and my use of these data is based on this assessment.

The following analysis accordingly focuses on occupational aspirations, expectations, and prospects among rural Jamaicans. These data are drawn from representative rural samples of some size, and I think that their comparative analysis can give a valid account of the patterns of occupational preference among Jamaican peasants, and of the conditions in which they change. Clearly, similar patterns of choice and change should not be assumed for the urban or plantation populations, nor for people of different socioeconomic status.

In tabulating these data, I have tried to observe uniformity, while isolating preferences with an incidence of more than 1 per cent. Residual choices are listed as "Other," except where comparability requires their separate entry. Activities of a similar type are grouped together, and this classification is kept constant for the four tables reporting on the school survey. In the two tables drawn from my 1955 sample, occupational groupings are slightly different, but their itemization allows easy adjustment.

Tables 3, 4, and 5 report the occupational preferences of males; tables 6, 7, and 8 deal with females. Table 3 summarizes the schoolboys' answers to the question, "What work do you want to do when you leave school?" Table 4 gives their replies to the question, "What work do your parents want you to do?" Table 5 reports the relative frequency with which different occupations were chosen by the young men whom I interviewed in 1955. Tables 6, 7, and 8 report the preferences of schoolgirls, of their parents, and of the young women in like manner. To simplify the discussion, I shall concentrate mainly on ratios of the totals, but among school children and adults alike, particular age groups will be mentioned where necessary.

Analysis

The occupational preferences itemized in table 3 represents 87 per cent of the schoolboys' responses; 9.4 per cent of the boys gave no answer, and 3.6 per cent gave miscellaneous replies. Beyond the twelfth year, the incidence of blank answers drops sharply, and miscellaneous replies increase. One-eighth of the boys from 10 to 12 years of age gave no answer.

Of the occupations preferred by these boys, mechanical work comes first with 29.2 per cent of the total, medicine follows with 11.3 per cent, then transport driving (9.6 per cent), teaching (7.1 per cent), carpentry (6.5 per cent), tailoring (3.7 per cent), farming (3.0 per cent), office work (2.7 per cent), police and soldiering (2.4 per cent). Road work and distributive trade are chosen by 0.6 per cent and 0.2 per cent respectively. No one selects farm labor or unskilled nonfarm labor as something they wish to do.

Of the boys aged 10, 13.5 per cent choose mechanical or electrical

TABLE 3

Rural Jamaica 1957: ELEMENTARY SCHOOLBOYS CLASSIFIED BY
AGE AND OCCUPATIONAL PREFERENCE*
(Unit = per cent)

Years of age	10	11	12	13	14	15	Total
(a) *Road headman P.W.D.*..........	1.3	0.3	0.5	0.3	0.5	—	0.6
Road work P.W.D..............	0.6	0.3	—	—	—	—	—
	1.9	0.6	0.5	0.3	0.5	—	0.6
(b) *Own-account farming:*							
Farming...................	2.6	2.0	2.2	2.9	3.5	11.3	3.0
Agricultural instructor.......	—	—	—	—	—	—	—
	2.6	2.0	2.2	2.9	3.5	11.3	3.0
(c) *Farm and field labor*.............							
(d) *Unskilled nonfarm labor:*							
Postman...................							
(e) *Crafts:*							
Tailor....................	3.2	4.1	4.1	3.9	2.3	3.7	3.7
Carpenter and cabinetmaker..	3.9	4.9	5.4	8.6	7.1	6.2	6.5
Mason....................	—	1.0	2.0	1.3	1.1	—	1.3
Plumber..................	—	—	—	0.2	—	—	—
Painter...................	—	—	0.7	0.2	1.2	1.2	0.3
Shoemaker................	0.6	0.7	0.7	0.5	0.7	—	0.6
Fisherman.................	—	—	—	—	—	—	—
Police and armed forces......	4.5	3.1	1.1	2.3	2.6	3.7	2.4
Other....................	—	—	2.0	0.7	0.5	1.3	0.9
	12.2	13.8	16.0	17.7	15.5	16.1	15.7
(f) *Distributive trade:*							
Shop assistant.............	—	0.3	—	0.3	0.3	—	0.2
(g) *Clerical:*							
Office work...............	3.2	4.1	2.5	2.2	2.4	2.5	2.7
Student...................	0.6	0.7	0.5	0.2	—	—	0.3
	3.8	4.8	3.0	2.4	2.4	2.5	3.0
(h) *Electrical and mechanical:*							
Electrician................	0.6	0.3	1.4	1.7	4.0	3.8	1.9
Mechanic.................	8.4	13.5	18.2	22.0	23.7	22.5	19.2
Mechanical engineer........	4.5	5.5	8.8	9.8	17.1	13.7	10.0
	13.5	19.3	28.4	33.5	44.8	40.0	31.1
(j) *Factory.*......................							
(k) *Transport:*							
Driver....................	9.7	8.2	12.1	11.1	6.7	2.5	9.6
(l) *Professional:*							
Doctor....................	20.0	21.1	9.2	9.6	7.7	6.3	11.3
Teacher...................	12.3	6.2	7.7	6.6	5.2	7.6	7.1
Dentist...................	0.6	1.0	0.2	0.2	—	1.3	0.3
Barrister, judge, and lawyer...	2.6	2.1	0.4	1.0	0.7	—	1.0
Artist....................	1.3	0.7	0.7	0.7	0.3	0.25	0.7
Civil servant and accountant..	1.4	1.4	1.1	1.0	1.0	—	1.1
Aero pilot.................	—	0.3	0.7	0.5	0.3	—	0.4
Engineer..................	—	—	—	—	—	—	—
Dispenser.................	1.9	0.3	0.5	0.2	0.3	1.2	0.5
Parson....................	2.6	2.4	1.1	1.0	1.1	—	1.3
Sanitary inspector..........	—	—	—	0.2	—	—	0.1
	42.7	35.5	21.6	21.0	16.6	18.9	23.8
(m) *No answer:*							
Miscellaneous..............	1.3	2.4	4.3	3.3	4.4	2.5	3.6
No answer................	12.3	13.1	11.9	7.5	5.3	6.2	9.4
	13.6	15.5	16.2	10.8	9.7	8.7	13.0
Totals in per cent...............	100	100	100	100	100	100	100
Totals in numbers...............	155	291	556	594	374	80	2,050

* Answers to Question: What work do you want to do when you leave school?

work. Of those aged 14 and 15 two out of every five boys do so. The proportion of boys choosing professional work drops from 42.7 per cent of the boys aged 10, to 16.6 per cent of those aged 14; and the choices in this broad category represent 23.8 per cent of the schoolboys' total. Few boys select electrical work. Of craft occupations, cabinet-making and carpentry are the most popular, and mason's work is seldom chosen. Only 0.3 per cent of these boys say they wish to be students. At the time when the survey was made, this may well have been the ratio of rural schoolboys who remained in school after their fifteenth year. In sum, there is a strong preference for mechanical and professional work, the former being the favorite of the older boys, the latter the favorite of the younger ones. Insofar as professional careers are unlikely for the boys in these rural elementary schools, the years in school do show a healthy move toward realism; but when we re-member that these schoolboys belong to a population of peasant pro-prietors, their marked preference for mechanical work and scant regard for farming is striking.

Law, the churches, and the civil service are selected as careers by 1 per cent, 1.3 per cent, and 1.1 per cent of these schoolboys respec-tively. Together with the police and armed forces, these occupations represent the principal agencies of social regulation in Jamaica. Their relative unpopularity among these schoolboys may reflect a recogni-tion that in Jamaica such occupations are usually held by people of a different background, the police excepted.

When asked to name the occupations which their parents wished them to pursue, 30.5 per cent of these boys could give no answer. Another 1.6 per cent reported that their parents wished them to pur-sue careers of their own choice. I have already shown why I regard the parental preferences reported by the remaining two-thirds of these schoolboys as probably accurate. Notably, few boys affirm that their parents wish them to follow their own preferences, and in no case do they say that their parents wish them to do farm labor, road or factory work, or other unskilled labor. Only 2.2 per cent say that their parents wish them to farm, although the majority of the parents were undoubtedly farmers. As against 31 per cent of the boys who chose electrical and mechanical trades for themselves, only 16 per cent re-ported that these were their parents' choices for them. Such differences, together with the large proportion of "don't know" responses to this question, strongly suggest that the boys were not projecting their own ideas onto their parents. Although the incidence of preferences for professions among boys and parents corresponds closely, the preference rates for various occupations differ, and so do the rates of preference in year groups. Only 19 per cent of the 15-year-olds themselves choose professions, whereas more than 27 per cent of them say this is their

TABLE 4

Rural Jamaica 1957: ELEMENTARY SCHOOLBOYS CLASSIFIED BY AGE AND THE
OCCUPATIONAL CAREER WHICH THEY SAY THEIR PARENTS
WISH THEM TO PURSUE
(Unit = per cent)

Years of age	10	11	12	13	14	15	Total
(a) *Road work:*							
Road headman............	—	—	—	—	—	—	—
(b) *Own-account farming, farming, and cultivating:*							
Farming...................	4.5	1.0	3.2	3.1	3.7	1.2	2.2
Agricultural instructor.......	1.3	0.7	0.4	1.3	1.1	5.0	1.1
	5.8	1.7	3.6	4.4	4.8	6.2	3.3
(c) *Farm and field labor*...........	—	—	—	—	—	—	—
(d) *Unskilled nonfarm labor:*							
Postman..................	0.6	—	—	—	—	—	—
(e) *Crafts:*							
Tailor.....................	2.7	2.0	4.8	3.2	4.6	5.0	3.9
Carpenter.................	1.9	3.0	4.0	5.6	4.8	6.3	4.4
Cabinetmaker.............	—	1.7	1.4	1.0	1.1	—	1.1
Mason....................	—	1.4	1.6	1.3	1.1	2.5	1.3
Plumber..................	—	0.3	0.2	0.2	0.5	—	0.2
Painter...................	—	—	0.2	0.2	0.3	—	0.1
Shoemaker................	0.6	0.3	1.1	0.5	1.1	2.5	0.8
Fisherman................	—	—	0.2	—	—	—	—
Police and armed forces......	3.9	1.0	0.7	2.0	2.2	1.2	1.6
Other....................	0.6	—	0.9	0.5	0.3	2.5	0.5
	9.7	9.7	15.1	14.5	16.0	20.0	13.9
(f) *Distributive trade:*							
Shop assistant............	0.6	0.7	0.7	0.3	0.3	—	0.5
(g) *Clerical:*							
Office work...............	4.5	2.4	3.7	2.4	5.9	3.8	3.6
Student..................	0.6	2.7	1.6	2.0	2.2	2.5	1.9
	5.1	5.1	5.3	4.4	8.1	6.3	5.5
(h) *Electrical and mechanical:*							
Electrician................	0.6	—	0.7	1.5	3.0	3.8	1.4
Mechanic.................	4.5	9.1	13.6	16.7	18.3	10.0	14.9
	5.1	9.1	14.3	18.2	21.3	13.8	16.3
(j) *Factory*							
(k) *Transport:*							
Driver....................	5.2	4.4	5.1	4.9	3.0	1.2	4.4
(l) *Professional:*							
Doctor....................	16.2	15.7	7.9	7.5	4.0	8.8	8.8
Teacher..................	11.0	7.1	4.5	4.8	3.5	3.8	5.2
Dentist...................	—	0.3	0.4	0.3	—	1.2	0.3
Barrister, judge, and lawyer...	2.5	3.0	0.8	1.0	2.2	3.7	1.6
Artist....................	—	0.7	0.5	0.5	0.3	1.2	0.5
Accountant...............	—	0.3	—	—	0.5	1.2	0.2
Civil servant..............	0.6	1.0	0.5	0.5	0.3	—	0.6
Aero pilot................	—	0.3	0.2	—	—	—	—
Engineer..................	3.3	2.0	4.4	4.9	9.4	5.0	5.0
Dispenser................	2.6	—	0.4	0.2	—	1.2	0.4
Parson...................	1.3	2.4	1.2	1.5	1.1	—	1.4
Sanitary inspector..........	—	—	0.2	—	—	1.2	—
	37.5	32.8	21.0	21.2	21.3	27.3	24.0
(m) *No answer:*							
What I choose.............	—	1.7	1.2	2.0	1.6	3.9	1.6
Don't know...............	13.5	16.3	16.7	16.5	14.5	12.6	15.9
No answer................	17.5	18.5	17.0	13.6	9.1	8.7	14.6
	31.0	36.5	34.9	32.1	25.2	25.2	32.1
Totals in per cent.............	100	100	100	100	100	100	100
Totals in numbers.............	155	296	556	594	374	80	2,050

parents' choice. As reported, parents prefer mechanical work (14.9 per cent), medicine (8.8 per cent), teaching (5.2 per cent), and engineering (5.0 per cent) for their boys in that order.

Despite the broad similarity of pattern in the choices of parents and children, details differ significantly for each year group and in the aggregate. Apparently these boys are guided by their parents' known preferences, but are not limited by them. Thus only 9.4 per cent of the boys gave no occupational choice of their own, whereas more than 30 per cent did not know their parents' preference. A favored occupation, such as medicine, mechanical work, or transport, always has a higher preference rate among the boys. An unpopular occupation is even more unpopular with the boys than with their parents. Presumably these differences reflect influences from school and elsewhere which are at work amongst the boys, reinforcing the general direction of parental choices while altering its details. Presumably the broad overlap in the preferences of parent and child represents values and sentiments common to both sets of influences. Since teachers in these schools and parents of these children are drawn from the same milieu and have been through the same school system,[3] the sentiments and values they share are many and important.

Table 5 reports the occupational preference rate among those young men between the ages of 15 and 24, and 25 and 39, who were looking for work when interviewed in 1955. All individuals who declared that they wanted work were asked to name three occupations they would like to pursue. Of the men interviewed, 58.4 per cent named three occupations, 22.1 per cent named two, 11.9 per cent named one, and 7.6 per cent named none at all. The responses of the women interviewed gave a similar distribution.

On the assumption of a peasant life cycle which is fairly fixed, we may follow the course of change in the career choices of rural school-leavers by comparing the occupational preferences of these two adult age groups with one another and with those of the children. Since the adults whose replies are tabulated here were looking for work at the time of survey, their job preferences have a special relevance.

Among young men between 15 and 24, craftwork is easily the most favored occupational category. Of all choices 28.9 per cent fell under this head. Farm labor follows with 15.9 per cent, then mechanical labor with 12.4 per cent. Preference rates for factory work and transport are 9.3 per cent and 9.6 per cent respectively. Road work and unskilled nonfarm labor have preference rates of 7.2 per cent each. Own-account farming and distributive trade account for 4.6 per cent and 3.2 per cent of the total preferences. The preference rate for clerical work is only 1.7 per cent, and nobody mentions professions. Thus 30.1 per cent of the young men's choices are for unskilled labor

TABLE 5

OCCUPATIONAL PREFERENCES OF YOUNG MEN LOOKING FOR WORK
IN RURAL JAMAICA, 1955
(Unit = per cent)

Occupational category	Specialty	15–24	25–39	All
1. *Road work*	(a) Road work	5.7	9.0	7.5
	(b) Road headman	0.9	0.7	0.8
	(c) Other	0.6	0.9	0.8
		7.2	10.6	9.1
2. *Own-account farming*	(a) Own-account farming	4.2	6.8	5.7
	(b) Cattle-rearing	0.4	1.1	0.8
	(c) Other	—	0.2	0.1
		4.6	8.1	6.6
3. *Farm and field labor*	(a) Farm labor	10.0	8.5	9.2
	(b) Cane farm labor	1.3	1.1	1.2
	(c) Farm headman	1.1	2.9	2.0
	(d) Gardener	1.7	1.3	1.5
	(e) U.S.A. farm labor	0.6	0.7	0.7
	(f) Other	1.2	2.7	2.0
		15.9	17.2	16.6
4. *Unskilled nonagricultural labor*	(a) Building labor	0.4	0.3	0.3
	(b) Yard boy	2.3	1.3	1.7
	(c) Watchman	—	0.2	0.1
	(d) General labor	0.6	0.9	0.8
	(e) Storeman	1.0	3.2	2.2
	(f) Hotel work	0.2	0.2	0.2
	(g) Bauxite labor	1.0	1.1	1.1
	(h) Government labor	1.3	1.5	1.4
	(i) Other	0.4	2.0	1.3
		7.2	10.7	9.1
5. *Crafts*	(a) Sawyer	—	1.1	0.6
	(b) Carpenter	6.9	5.4	5.8
	(c) Cabinetmaker	4.5	0.7	2.4
	(d) Mason work	7.7	6.3	6.9
	(e) Shoemaking	2.5	0.5	1.5
	(f) Butcher	0.9	0.3	0.6
	(g) Tailoring	2.3	1.1	1.6
	(h) Armed Forces and police	2.1	0.9	1.5
	(i) Fishing	1.1	1.8	1.5
	(j) Other	0.9	3.4	2.2
		28.9	21.5	24.6
6. *Distributive trade*	(a) Shop assistant	2.1	4.3	3.3
	(b) Other	1.1	1.4	1.3
		3.2	5.7	4.6
7. *Clerical*	(a) Office clerk	0.4	0.5	0.5
	(b) Other	1.3	0.9	1.1
		1.7	1.4	1.6
8. *Electrical and mechanical*	(a) Motor mechanic	10.4	3.6	6.7
	(b) Tractor driver	0.6	0.9	0.7
	(c) Other	1.4	1.6	1.5
		12.4	6.1	8.9
9. *Factory*	(a) Factory work	8.7	9.6	9.1
	(b) Other	0.6	1.4	1.1
		9.3	11.0	10.2
10. *Transport*	(a) Transportation	1.2	1.3	1.3
	(b) Chauffeur	6.8	4.7	5.7
	(c) Railway	0.2	1.1	0.7
	(d) Other	1.4	0.6	1.0
		9.6	7.7	8.7
Totals in per cent...................................		100	100	100
Totals in numbers...................................		470	556	1,026

on the farm, the road, or elsewhere. A similar ratio is for transport, mechanical and factory work combined, and almost as much is for craftwork. Own-account farming is preferred by 4.6 per cent.

It is instructive to compare the preferences of the young men of 15–24 years of age with those of the men 25–39. Among this senior age group, unskilled labor on the farm, the road, or elsewhere, accounts for 38.5 per cent of all preferences. Own-account farming has a rate of 8.1 per cent. Preference rates for factory work and distributive trades increase, while the rates for transport and craftwork decline. The preference for mechanical work falls from 12.4 per cent among the junior age group to 6.1 per cent among their seniors, that for craftwork from 28.9 per cent to 21.5 per cent. Neither age group includes professions or electrical work in its preferences; and the preference rate for clerical work is low but constant in both.

The occupational preferences of these adult males contain few strictly urban choices. Occupations such as hotel work, factory work, shop assistant, store man, or chauffeur are pursued within or near their districts. The term chauffeur in this context refers mainly to truck-driving. Except for the category of mechanical work, the great majority of the occupational choices made by these adults relate to activities which form part of rural life.

We have seen that 42.7 per cent of the schoolboys aged 10 wanted to pursue professions. Among those aged 13 to 15, the preference for professions is not quite half as great; even so, nearly one-fifth of the boys in their final year at school still want such work. Among 10-year-olds, 13.5 per cent prefer the urban occupations of electrical or mechanical work. Among the 15-year-olds, 40 per cent do so. However the line is drawn, roughly 60 per cent of the occupational preferences of the schoolboys of each year group are for urban occupations, the younger ones preferring white-collar activities, while the older ones choose industrial trades. Whatever their age, the boys' aspirations exclude own-account farming, unskilled work on or off the farm, road work, factory work, and distributive trade. The activities thus excluded are precisely those which have first preference among the young men of these districts. Moreover, the older the men become, the greater is their preference for these formerly disvalued occupations. The unrealism which characterizes occupational preferences among the schoolboys is matched by the realism shown by the senior men. Among young men below 25 years of age some unrealistic preferences persist. Thereafter these decline sharply, perhaps under economic pressures of maintaining a family. The realistic appraisal of career opportunities that guides occupational preference among late adolescents in other societies seems to be delayed among the Jamaican peasants until near their twenty-fifth year.

Of these young men below 24 years who had actively sought work during the twelve months preceding my survey, 37.7 per cent had sought farm labor, 8.3 per cent factory work, 4.7 per cent employment in trade, 1.8 per cent domestic service, 12.8 per cent some form of government work as unskilled labor, and 34.7 per cent a miscellaneous collection of jobs, such as building labor, truck-sideman, mason, carpenter, mechanic's assistant, and the like. Of these young men, nearly 30 per cent had sought employment in other parts of Jamaica, and another 2 per cent had applied for farm work in the United States. Of those men between 25 and 39 years who had actively sought work during the preceding twelve months, 32.7 per cent had sought farm labor, 8.2 per cent factory work, 9.9 per cent some employment in trading, 23.0 per cent unskilled labor from the government—mainly on road repairs—and the remaining 26.2 per cent miscellaneous employments. Only 26 per cent of these senior men had sought work elsewhere in Jamaica that year, and 2 per cent had applied for work in the United States. There is, in short, a reasonable correspondence between the distribution of efforts in search of different types of work made by these men and their statements about the sort of work they would prefer. Rather higher proportions seek farm work than volunteer it as their choice; economic pressures may account for this divergence. Very much the same ratio of active applications and of preferences go to factory work, trade, and perhaps to road work also. The expressed preferences of male adults to this extent at least correspond with their directed efforts.

As revealed by these figures, the occupational aspirations of the rural schoolboys and the prospects they face as adults could hardly differ more sharply. Where the schoolboys exclude some occupations and emphasize their preference for others, the reverse is true of the men. The preferential drift among schoolboys of increasing age from professional to mechanical work continues in early adulthood as a drift first from mechanical work to crafts, and then from crafts to unskilled labor. Throughout the entire age-span under study, own-account farming is seldom chosen; yet the overwhelming majority of these rural folk derive their livelihood from own-account farming, and both the men who seek other occupations and the parents of these school children are predominantly small holders. When they leave school, these rural boys abandon their professional aspirations. As the young men grow older and their realistic assessment of local opportunities increases, there is a further drop in their preference for mechanical work, transport, and crafts. Own-account farming or unskilled labor—the two least desired types of occupation—are almost the only alternatives before them.

Nowadays, in consequence of a new program of government scholarships, increasing industrial activities in rural Jamaica, and the steady emigration to Britain—which began in 1955—this picture may have changed slightly; but when the relative numbers of the peasant population, peasant emigrants, the new industrial jobs, and scholarships are compared, it is clear that this basic picture cannot have changed much.

It may be argued that the low incidence of preferences for urban occupations among these rural adults simply reflects the fact that young people with these aspirations have already left the districts and gone to the town. Undoubtedly some will have done so; and many of the men interviewed had themselves sought work in other Jamaican areas, including towns, during the preceding year. However, since 60 per cent of the schoolboys choose urban occupations, it is clear that few of them do move to the towns, simply because the rate of urban growth in Jamaica is so low. In addition, we still find high rates of preference for mechanical and transport work among junior adults in the rural areas. Clearly, it is probable on other grounds, as well as on the data before us, that the majority of these urban-oriented boys remain in their home districts on leaving school, and gradually revise their aspirations to fit their prospects.

We may now compare the occupational aspirations of young men looking for work with the schoolboys' reports of their parents' aspirations for them. Whereas 9.1 per cent of the young men want road work, no parent is reported to want this for his son. Whereas 16.6 per cent of the young men want farm or field labor, no parents is reported to want this for his son. Whereas 9.1 per cent of the young men want unskilled nonfarm labor, hardly any parents were reported to want this for their sons. Only 13.9 per cent of the reported parental preferences were for careers as craftsmen, while 24.6 per cent of the young men want such work. Whereas 10.2 per cent of the young men want factory work, no parent is reported to want this for his son. In detail as well as in sum, the contrast could hardly be greater.

Tables 6, 7, and 8 describe the girls' position in the same order as has been done for the boys'. Table 6 gives the girls' own preferences. Of these schoolgirls, only 5.4 per cent gave no answer, only 0.3 per cent wished to stay at home. Occupations loosely labeled as clerical attracted 46.2 per cent, and nursing appealed to 33.0 per cent. Another 22.4 per cent selected professions, 19.5 per cent wishing to become teachers. Dressmaking was chosen by 22 per cent. Essentially the schoolgirls prefer nursing, dressmaking, and teaching in that order. Only 1.5 per cent chose domestic work; 1.6 per cent, crafts; and 0.6 per cent, trade. None wanted unskilled labor of any sort.

Of these girls, 22.9 per cent said they did not know what occupations their parents wanted them to pursue. One and six-tenths per cent said that their parents wanted them to pursue their own choice, and 0.5

TABLE 6

Rural Jamaica 1957: ELEMENTARY SCHOOLGIRLS CLASSIFIED BY AGE AND
OCCUPATIONAL PREFERENCE*
(Unit = per cent)

Years of age	10	11	12	13	14	15	Total
(a) *Road work*................	—	—	—	—	—	—	—
(b) *Domestic*.................	2.8	1.7	1.4	1.5	0.8	2.5	1.5
(c) *Light unskilled labor*........	—	—	—	—	—	—	—
(d) *Manual labor*..............	—	—	—	—	—	—	—
(e) *Farm work:*							
Own-account farm......	—	—	—	—	—	—	—
(f) *Distributive trade:*							
Shopkeeping...........	0.7	0.6	0.2	1.0	0.4	—	0.6
(g) *Clerical:*							
Commercial...........	0.4	0.4	0.3	0.1	0.4	—	0.3
Typist (shorthand)......	1.0	1.8	2.8	3.7	5.7	4.9	3.2
Office work...........	1.4	0.8	1.3	1.0	3.3	3.7	1.5
Postmistress...........	6.7	5.9	8.7	6.7	6.7	1.2	7.0
Nursing..............	35.6	32.2	26.7	31.9	40.0	58.0	33.0
Student..............	1.7	1.8	1.3	1.2	0.4	—	1.2
	46.8	42.9	41.1	44.6	56.5	67.8	46.2
(h) *Crafts:*							
Hairdresser...........	0.4	0.8	2.0	1.9	1.4	—	1.4
Police................	0.4	0.2	0.2	—	0.2	—	0.2
	0.8	1.0	2.2	1.9	1.6	—	1.6
(j) *Transport:*							
Bus conductress........	—	0.2	—	—	—	—	—
(k) *Factory*.................	—	—	—	—	—	—	—
(l) *Sewing:*							
Dressmaker...........	12.2	19.2	25.0	25.3	22.1	13.6	22.0
(m) *Professional:*							
Doctor...............	5.2	2.3	1.8	1.5	0.6	3.7	2.0
Dispenser.............	—	0.4	0.4	0.4	0.2	—	0.3
Teacher..............	25.1	24.9	18.4	17.9	16.0	12.4	19.5
Artist................	—	0.2	0.1	0.1	0.2	—	0.1
Law.................	0.4	0.4	0.2	—	—	—	0.2
Other................	0.4	—	0.6	0.2	0.2	—	0.3
	31.1	28.2	21.5	20.1	17.2	16.1	22.4
(n) *Miscellaneous:*							
Stay home............	0.7	0.2	0.5	0.3	—	—	0.3
No answer............	4.5	6.0	7.4	4.7	1.0	—	4.9
Don't know...........	0.4	—	0.7	0.6	0.4	—	0.5
Totals in per cent.............	100	100	100	100	100	100	100
Totals in numbers...........	286	510	804	677	492	81	2850

* Answers to Question: What work do you want to do when you leave school?

per cent said their parents wanted them to stay at home. Over 24 per cent said that their parents wished them to be nurses; 16 per cent and 14.8 per cent said their parents wanted them to become dressmakers and teachers respectively. As among the boys, the girls' own preference for a popular occupation exceeds that reported for their parents. Likewise, the avoidance of an unpopular occupation by the girls exceeds that reported for their parents. Thus 3.3 per cent of the parents were reported to have chosen domestic work, as against 1.5 per cent of the girls; 0.1 per cent of the parents were reported to favor own-account farming, but none of the girls. If parental preferences as reported here are somewhat unrealistic, the girls' own preferences are even more so.

Year group by year group, we can follow changes and differences in the preferences reported by the girls for themselves and their parents. Of girls aged 10, only 7.8 per cent say their parents wish them to become dressmakers, as against 17.4 per cent of those aged 15. Only 21.6 per cent of the 10-year-olds say their parents wish them to be nurses, as against 41.4 per cent of those aged 15. Of the 10-year-olds, 19.1 per cent say their parents wish them to be teachers, but of those aged 15, only 6.6 per cent. On entering school, 12.2 per cent of these girls choose dressmaking as a career, but after two years the ratio doubles, falling again to 13.6 per cent in the final year. Whereas nursing is the choice of 35.6 per cent of the 10-year-olds, 58 per cent of the girls aged 15 choose this. The preference rate for teaching is 25.1 per cent among 10-year-old girls, but falls to 12.4 per cent among those about to leave school.

These patterns of choice show that both the girls and their parents prefer occupations which offer some assurance of escape from peasant circumstances. This desire for escape seems to dictate the direction of occupational choice. Variations in these choices for children of different ages seem to be governed by estimates of their probable achievement, however unreal these may be. Thus the changing preference rates among children of different ages, and the differences observable between preferences of parents and children, simply express differing estimates of the chances of escaping rural poverty by means of particular occupations. Since conditions among the sugar-working proletariat are not notably better than those among small holders, in Jamaican terms the urban areas and their occupations offered the only acceptable escape from peasant life until emigration assumed its recent proportions. This escape goal provides the basis of the career choices made by and for children; but the conception of occupational careers primarily as the means of escape severely limits the realism of the choices to be made, and of the estimates of probable achievement on which particular choices are made or changed.

As against 1.8 per cent of the 10-year-olds who say their parents

TABLE 7

Rural Jamaica 1957: ELEMENTARY SCHOOLGIRLS CLASSIFIED BY AGE AND THE
OCCUPATIONAL CAREER WHICH THEY SAY THEIR PARENTS
WISH THEM TO PURSUE*
(Unit = per cent)

Years of age	10	11	12	13	14	15	Total
(a) *Road work*	—	—	—	—	—	—	—
(b) *Domestic*	4.2	3.4	3.1	4.6	2.4	2.7	3.5
(c) *Light unskilled labor*	—	—	—	—	—	—	—
(d) *Manual labor*	—	—	—	—	—	—	—
(e) *Farm work:*							
Own-account farm	—	—	0.1	0.3	0.2	—	0.1
(f) *Distributive trade:*							
Shopkeeping	1.8	0.6	0.2	1.2	0.8	—	0.8
(g) *Clerical:*							
Commercial	—	—	0.1	0.1	0.4	—	0.1
Typist (shorthand)	1.8	1.4	2.4	2.7	3.2	5.3	2.4
Office work	0.7	2.2	1.0	1.2	1.2	2.7	1.3
Postmistress	5.0	4.4	6.0	4.3	5.9	2.7	5.5
Nursing	21.6	26.7	19.8	24.6	29.6	41.4	24.5
Student	3.2	1.8	2.7	2.9	2.4	—	2.6
	32.3	36.5	32.0	35.8	42.7	52.1	36.4
(h) *Crafts:*							
Hairdresser	0.3	0.4	0.9	1.7	1.0	1.3	1.0
Police	—	—	0.2	0.1	—	—	0.1
	0.3	0.4	1.1	1.8	1.0	1.3	1.1
(j) *Transport:*							
Bus conductress	—	—	—	—	—	—	—
(k) *Factory*	—	—	—	—	—	—	—
(l) *Sewing:*							
Dressmaker	7.8	11.9	19.5	17.4	18.1	17.4	16.0
(m) *Professional:*							
Doctor	4.6	1.4	1.3	1.2	1.0	1.3	1.6
Dispenser	—	0.2	0.4	0.4	0.2	—	0.3
Teacher	19.1	18.4	15.3	12.6	12.5	6.6	14.8
Artist	0.3	—	0.2	—	0.2	—	0.1
Law	—	0.2	0.2	—	—	—	0.1
Other	0.6	0.2	0.3	0.1	—	—	0.2
	24.6	20.4	17.7	14.3	13.9	7.9	17.1
(n) *Miscellaneous:*							
Stay home	2.1	0.2	0.4	0.7	—	—	0.5
No answer	15.6	12.3	12.5	10.2	7.7	1.3	11.0
Don't know	10.6	13.5	11.7	12.0	10.8	13.3	11.9
What I choose	0.7	0.8	1.7	1.7	2.4	4.0	1.6
Totals in per cent	100	100	100	100	100	100	100
Totals in numbers	286	510	804	677	492	81	2850

* Answers to Question: What work do your parents want you to do?

would like them to be typists, 5.3 per cent of the girls about to leave school say so. Whereas 4.6 per cent of the 10-year-olds say their parents wish them to be doctors, only 1.5 per cent of those aged 15 say so. The overwhelming vote by parents and daughters in favor of nursing, teaching, and dressmaking simply declares how restricted is the range of occupational choice for rural women, granted this urban orientation. In the sense that they are based on tradition and experience which show that such careers are almost the only means of social mobility open to Jamaican peasant girls, these choices are not wholly unrealistic; but when the volume of mobility which these occupations actually provide is compared with the demand, the situation seems pathetic.

What happens to rural girls when they leave school? Very few of them actually becomes nurses or teachers. Many start to learn sewing but abandon it after becoming pregnant in later adolescence. In any event, these peasant communities hardly offer many dressmakers profitable employment. We have already seen that 45 per cent of the rural women aged between 15 and 39 were looking for work at the time of my survey; and table 2 describes their position in regard to employment.

Of the job preferences of young women aged between 15 and 24, domestic work is by far the most important, with a preference rate of 36.9 per cent. Farm work, mainly farm labor, accounts for 5.8 per cent of these choices, light unskilled labor for another 12.8 per cent. Clerical work of all kinds has a preference rate of 6.1 per cent. Nursing, which is the preferred occupation of one-third of the rural schoolgirls, is chosen by 2 per cent of the young women under 24. Sewing is preferred by 13.2 per cent and teaching by 1.1 per cent.

Job avoidances are equally significant. Of the preferences reported by the young women 15–24, 5.8 per cent mention farm work, and only 0.3 per cent mention manual labor off the farm. Factory work has a preference rate of 4.4 per cent; crafts, mainly straw-work, of 2.4 per cent. Distributive trade enlists 17.1 per cent of the preferences, and 12.8 per cent goes to light unskilled labor in bars, offices, restaurants, or hospitals. Road work rates 1 per cent.

The occupational-preference scale current among young women of 15–24 changes little among the senior age group. The proportions of women in these age groups who are looking for work in rural areas also remains constant. There is some increase in the desire for domestic work, which represents 42.1 per cent of the choices made by women aged 25–39. Farm and road work, manual and factory work, also show slight increases, and preference rates fall slightly for light unskilled labor, distributive trade, and sewing, but steeply for clerical work. Since individual aptitudes and economic circumstances are largely

TABLE 8

OCCUPATIONAL PREFERENCES OF YOUNG WOMEN LOOKING FOR WORK
IN RURAL JAMAICA, 1955
(Unit = per cent)

Occupational category	Subdivision	15–24	25–39	All
1. *Road work*	(a) Road work	0.7	1.4	1.0
	(b) Other	—	—	—
		0.7	1.4	1.0
2. *Domestic*	(a) Domestic	16.9	22.4	19.7
	(b) Cook	3.4	3.4	3.4
	(c) Nursemaid	12.2	9.5	10.8
	(d) Laundress	2.4	4.4	3.4
	(e) Other	2.0	2.4	2.2
		36.9	42.1	39.5
3. *Light unskilled labor*	(a) Office maid	4.4	1.4	2.9
	(b) Hospital maid	0.7	—	0.3
	(c) Waitress	3.0	3.7	3.4
	(d) Barmaid	3.7	4.1	3.9
	(e) Other	1.0	1.0	1.0
		12.8	10.2	11.5
4. *Manual labor*	(a) Manual labor, nonfarm	0.3	1.0	10.7
	(b) Other	—	—	—
		0.3	1.0	0.7
5. *Farm work*	(a) Own-account farm	0.7	1.0	0.8
	(b) Weeding	0.3	0.3	0.3
	(c) Farm labor	4.1	5.8	4.9
	(d) Other	0.7	0.7	0.7
		5.8	7.8	6.7
6. *Distributive trade*	(a) Shop assistant	12.2	12.5	12.4
	(b) Fish-selling	1.0	0.3	0.7
	(c) Higgler	3.7	3.0	3.4
	(d) Other	0.2	—	0.1
		17.1	15.8	16.6
7. *Clerical*	(a) Teacher	1.1	—	0.6
	(b) Nursing	2.0	0.7	1.3
	(c) Typist	2.1	—	1.1
	(d) Other	0.9	1.0	0.9
		6.1	1.7	3.9
8. *Crafts*	(a) Straw work	0.7	1.4	1.0
	(b) Other	1.7	1.0	1.3
		2.4	2.4	2.3
9. *Transport*	(a) Transport	0.3	1.0	0.7
	(b) Other	—	—	—
		0.3	1.0	0.7
10. *Factory*	(a) Factory work	4.4	7.8	6.1
	(b) Other	—	—	—
		4.4	7.8	6.1
11. *Sewing*	(a) Sewing	13.2	8.8	11.0
	(b) Other	—	—	—
		13.2	8.8	11.0
Totals in per cent..		100	100	100
Totals in numbers..		296	295	591

fixed by the time these women enter their twenty-fifth year, changes in
the occupational preferences of the senior age group reflect increasing
realism in the estimates of probable fulfilment. In this respect the rise
in the preference rate for domestic work, from 1.5 per cent among
schoolgirls to 36.9 per cent in the junior and 42.1 per cent in the
senior adult age group, is especially significant, the more so when
compared with the rate of 3.5 per cent that schoolgirls gave as their
parents' choice of this occupation for them. Most of the young women
who say they want such work already have children. They do not
select domestic work because they especially like it, but because it is
perhaps the most generally available employment, and, given their
lack of skills, in their circumstances, offers the likeliest means of escape
from the rural environment. When women give this occupation as
their choice, they set their sights on the towns.

This in itself indicates that many of the urban-oriented schoolgirls
remain in these rural areas after leaving school. Some certainly go to
the townships, and of these many may settle there; but as indicated
above, those who move to town are at most a fraction of the number
whose occupational choices show that they want to do so.

To compare the job preferences which adult women give for themselves with those which girls report their parents to have on their
behalf is to contrast expectations with aspirations. Our tables show a
fair correspondence between the girls' own occupational choices and
those which they report their parents hold for them. The contrast between the occupational preferences of adult women and those of the
schoolgirls is thus largely the same as that between adult preferences
for themselves and for their daughters. This contrast can only be
accounted for on the hypothesis that the frustration these adults experience in their own lives makes them want their children to pursue
occupations that offer escape from a similar lot. Thus the cycle of
childhood aspiration and adult despair perpetuates itself; hence too
the peasants' esteem for those persons whose children have "moved
out," [4] initially by occupational means, nowadays by emigration also.
The snag in this system of occupational preference is that, although
the preferred occupations may guarantee the escape and mobility that
determine their choice, there may be very little chance of access to
them.

The gap between the schoolgirls' occupational aspirations and the
prospects presented by their environment is just as great as that observed among the boys. Both girls and boys exclude all forms of unskilled labor, own-account farming, factory work, and distributive
trade from their occupational horizons and say that their parents do
likewise on their behalf. But as these young people leave school, they
are compelled to abandon their ambitions to become teachers, nurses,

dressmakers, doctors, mechanics, or engineers. Instead they have to look for the very forms of work which they previously rejected. It follows that until economic pressures override distaste, these young people can hardly show much interest in work they dislike and still seek to escape.

To clarify this contrast between aspirations and prospects, I shall summarize the statements of adults interviewed regarding the number of hours per week they were willing to work and the minimum weekly wages they would accept. These statements indirectly describe peasant conditions.

Of the young men between 15 and 39 who were looking for work in the areas I studied, 11.8 per cent were unwilling to work more than 38 hours per week, although 16.5 per cent were willing to work 54 hours a week or more, and 70 per cent had in mind a working week of 38 to 54 hours. Of these men, 22.7 per cent were willing to work for less than 35s. ($5 U.S.) per week, and another 18 per cent wanted between 35s. and 40s. per week. Almost 32 per cent wanted between 41s. and 60s. per week. Thus 70 per cent of these men would accept wages of less than £3 ($8.40 U.S.) per week. Such levels of demand may seem depressingly low, yet many employers in these rural areas would consider requests for 40s. a week outrageous, and would scoff at a work week of less than 50 hours.

Of the young women between 15 and 39 who were looking for work, only 9.2 per cent rejected a work week which exceeded 38 hours, while 31.2 per cent were willing to work 63 hours a week or more, presumably as full-time domestics. Of these women, 12.1 per cent were willing to work for 10s. ($1.40 U.S.) per week, and another 34.7 per cent for wages between 11s. and 20s. per week. Almost 21 per cent wanted from 20s. to 30s. per week. Thus two-thirds of the women would accept wages of less than 30s. ($4.20 U.S.) per week. The aspirations of parents for their children and those of the children themselves should be interpreted against the background of adult accommodations revealed by these data.

Discussion

The facts presented reveal a formidable gap between reality and desire. Apparently the conditions of rural life are so depressing that peasants greatly desire that their children should escape them and hope that this will be achieved by occupational means. The parents' ambitions on behalf of their children are reinforced in some ways and modified in others by the children's years at school. The most unrealistic aspirations are thus partly corrected, but the basis on which occupations are chosen remains untouched. The elementary schools can merely modify details but cannot challenge this occupational preference scale or its basis, because both are cast in the image of the school.

The school presents peasants with the idea and prospect of alternative occupations. Traditionally it has been the principal avenue of social mobility open to them in Jamaica, and in some periods perhaps the sole important one. In addition the school presents a curriculum based on others designed for urban populations in industrial countries. This disvalues the peasant way of life, inexplicitly but profoundly. In the content of the education it offers, the school directs the children's attention away from their peasant community to the preindustrial towns with their wide range of prestigious occupations and seemingly endless opportunities.

We have seen that the young folk who leave school in these districts seem to need several years in which to readjust realistically to their environment. In one sphere at least they never do adjust fully, since they heap their own frustrated ambitions on their children, to bring further frustration. The school, by virtue of its curriculum and its role as the primary instrument and channel of a social mobility which is occupational in means, may modify the particulars of this ambition, but can neither challenge nor alter its direction. The occupational values that parents and children hold in common are those that the school represents.

Before proceeding, I wish to consider certain objections that may be raised to this interpretation. First, it can be argued that children in any country have high aspirations and prefer unusual occupations. This is not quite correct, as my own inquiries into the occupational preferences of Hausa school children in Northern Nigeria indicate. Moreover, in no case do these Jamaican schoolboys wish to be cowboys, engine-drivers, sailors, or airmen; nor do the girls wish to become air-hostesses, models, or to go on the stage. There is nothing unusual about nursing, dressmaking, teaching, or mechanic's work. Even so, the important point is surely that when an English or American boy wants to be a mechanic or a doctor, or when an Australian or German girl wants to nurse or teach, they usually have good opportunities for doing so, simply because they participate in an educational system that provides these opportunities, and belong to an industrial society that values such skills.

It may be argued that the children do not fully understand the occupations which they select, and that in any case their preferences change as a normal part of the process of growing up. These arguments should be discussed separately. If the school children of 14 or 15 do not understand the nature of medicine or machinery, dressmaking, nursing, or teaching, the schools must accept responsibility. However, as we have seen, there is a fair correspondence between the children's own choices and those which they report their parents to have on their behalf. Even if the child does not know what he chooses, the parent should; and the correspondence of parental and children's choices is only matched by the divergence in the choices of adults for themselves and for their children.

It is quite true that children often change their occupational preferences as part of the process of growing up; and we have seen examples of this at various places above. But the shifts that take place in the preferences of these children are shifts within a limited framework of implicitly urban character. When professional aspirations are too clearly unrealistic to be retained, nursing or mechanic's work takes the lead. Only after the child has left school is there a shift toward available rural occupations. To say that the changing career preferences which accompany maturation normally involve careers that are not available would be to stretch this objection too far; but unless it is stretched that far, it does not apply in this case, since it is precisely this choice of the unavailable that is so striking in our sample.

Yet another argument might be that a certain volume of occupational frustration is inevitable, and indeed desirable, in societies that value mobility and change. Without disputing this general proposition, it is clear that the volume of frustration we have been measuring here is both excessive and self-perpetuating. To compare these conditions with occupational frustration among the Hausa, British, or Americans is absurd.

Our data show that rural school children nourish bright aspirations in school and face a grim period of disappointment when they leave. The educational system which permits or encourages these aspirations cannot avoid some responsibility for the disorientation and disillusion which is their result. Dr. Madeline Kerr, in her study of Jamaican country folk, has attributed some of the cultural confusion which she observed among rural people to their experience of elementary education.[5] The gap between occupational choice and prospects discussed in this paper represents one aspect of the confusion Kerr described.

Our data have implications for the program of social and economic development which Jamaica is now pursuing. In so far as a program of agricultural development depends on peasant support for success or seeks to improve their economic conditions, it is useful to know what their occupational orientations may be. Programs which, for their success, presuppose the farmers' interest also presuppose that the farmer wishes to remain a farmer, and typically wishes his children to do likewise. Our data have shown an impressive preference for urban-type occupations among rural folk, together with an underlying desire to escape from the peasant environment. It seems self-contradictory to

foster an educational system that permits or encourages such pronounced urban orientations among rural folk at the same time that
one subsidizes farm programs which presuppose that the peasants'
heart is in his land.

Since the preceding data were collected, the government of Jamaica
has initiated a program of scholarships to secondary schools, which is
designed to raise the secondary school population from 10,000 in 1957
to 26,000 ten years later. By 1967 the population of Jamaica may be
about 1.8 million, and the school-age population about 500,000. Thus
even when this scholarship program is fulfilled, only one child in
every twenty may expect a secondary education. Despite its generous
intention, this scheme will do little to alleviate occupational frustration among rural Jamaicans.

Finally, it has been argued that the integration of a society is not
affected by the fact that many people within it have high levels of aspiration but low expectations.[6] Without careful documentation and
qualification this proposition is unacceptable. Its chief novelty is to
assume social integration under any conditions whatever their measure, cause or form.

Our data reveal a considerable difference between occupational
choices among rural adults and children. Since this difference is
matched by others between the choices of adults for themselves and
for their children, we are clearly dealing with divergent aspirations
and expectations. The children's preferences and those of their parents
for them express aspirations. Those of adults for themselves express
expectations, in the sense that they represent accommodations to local
realities. The gap between these scales is the difference between aspirations and expectations. It provides a useful measure of the inconsistency of the social system which promotes them in its adaptive phases.

Recent studies in America have shown that "anomia results when
individuals lack access to means for the achievement of life goals."[7]
Anomie, the "polar opposite" of full social integration,[8] is that condition of the social system in which the individual disorganization called
anomia is widespread. The data just presented indicate a sufficiently
high incidence of anomia among Jamaican peasants for anomie to be
more probable than social integration.

There is little symbolism about the occupational preferences parents
hold for their children. In rural Jamaica these choices express the
parents' frustration and desire for their children's success by means
of escape from the peasant environment. To the parents, occupational
advancement alone offers social mobility. The measure of the adults'
disappointment with their own lives is their aspiration on behalf of
their children. The low level of expectation and high level of aspiration are two sides of the same coin, in this case bound together by

the frustration which ensure their perpetuation from parent to child.

The element of motivation is missing from the argument of the integrationists. Where aspiration and expectation correspond, motivation and performance may do likewise, and the integration of the system concerned consists in the mutually reinforcing relations of these four variables. Where aspiration and expectation differ sharply, so do motivation and performance as a rule, and the lack of coherence among these variables expresses the internal inconsistency of the system of which all are part. Social systems that foster and then frustrate the chosen life-goals of their members are correspondingly incoherent and ill-integrated. When the volume of this frustration reaches the levels with which we have been dealing, it is pertinent to ask in what sense is the society integrated at all. This question suggests that we may have isolated an index of social integration by comparing occupational aspirations and prospects. Such an index would have obvious comparative values, and could also be used to measure certain aspects of structural change which accompany programs of economic development.

[10

The Transformation of Land Rights by Transmission in Carriacou

Two highly distinct systems of land tenure are to be found side by side in many British Caribbean societies.[1] One system is defined by statute and common law, and guides official policy in relation to land. The other system, which has recently been described for Jamaica by Miss Edith Clarke,[2] is of a customary and traditional character which neither observes the forms nor directly invites the sanctions of law. These differing systems of tenure are normally practiced by different social sections, and for holdings of disparate value.

In the present essay I shall show how the official, legal system of tenure has been transformed in one instance into its rival, the customary system. I shall also attempt to isolate and define the most important conditions of this change, and the forces which gave it form. Starting with a situation in which all persons holding land in a given area were officially provided with legally valid titles, I want to show how it has come about that many occupants presently hold land without such title, and to estimate the number of such occupancies. Further, since this changeover from legal to customary tenure has proceeded by the transmission of rights to land in the area, I shall devote special attention to these processes of transmission, their contexts, and conditions.

To these ends I present below a detailed account of landholding and transfer on a government land settlement at Harvey Vale in the island of Carriacou. The data on which this account is based consists of field and official records of all land transfers and occupancies on 77 of the 79 allotments of the settlement, for the period 1904 to 1954. This record of occupancy and transmission is tied to a detailed genealogy of the family lines involved in each allotment. The method is thus

221

essentially a case study, but here it is applied to an area, the settlement, on the one hand, and to a population, the allottees, and their
successors, on the other.

When systems of land tenure are conceived in static terms, only
formal analyses are possible, and these must center on the prevailing
classification and distribution of types of right. But of themselves such
analyses cannot provide a complete understanding of the bases and
functions of the systems concerned. To achieve this, it is first necessary
to focus attention on the ways in which rights are transmitted before
proceeding to the forms of right themselves. This is obvious, since the
form of a right is the product of the process by which it developed,
that is, the transmitted effect.

1. CARRIACOU

Carriacou, with an area of 13 square miles is the largest of the
Grenadines, the chain of rocks and islets stretching over the 60 miles
between St. Vincent and Grenada. The island lies about 23 miles
northeast of Grenada, and is now administered as a dependency of the
government of Grenada by a resident district officer, and, formerly,
by a district commissioner who exercised magisterial powers. Under
Grenadian law, however, issues affecting the possession or ownership
of land are beyond the scope of magisterial powers and must be referred to the High Court which meets in St. George's, Grenada, the
colony capital, about 40 miles by sea from Carriacou.

Carriacou differs from Grenada climatically and socially more than
its proximity would seem to make probable. Grenada, with its steep
slopes, has a high rainfall, and produces considerable quantities of
nutmegs, cloves, cinnamon, cocoa, and copra for export. Dense rain
forests of timber and food-bearing trees are characteristic of its high
interior. Carriacou, with no land over 1,000 feet high, has a far lower
rainfall than Grenada, together with a shorter and more irregular
rainy season. Breadfruit, "bluggo" (a variety of plantain, *Musa para-
daisica*), avocado pear, yam, dasheen, and other Grenadian food staples
are almost entirely lacking in Carriacou, together with cocoa and the
export spices. Instead, the Carriacou people farm maize, pigeon peas,
and sea-island cotton, and rear considerable numbers of stock. Men are
heavily engaged in fishing and sailing, and work overseas for periods
of varying lengths.

These differences of economy between Grenada and Carriacou are
paralleled by differences in the two societies. In 1953 there were over
a hundred working estates of more than a hundred acres each in
Grenada, but none in Carriacou. Equally important, the cleavage between folk and elite which is so characteristic of Grenada is completely

absent from Carriacou, the population of which practices a common culture, in certain respects similar to that of the Grenadian folk.[3]

According to the 1946 census, the population of Carriacou was then approximately 6,700.[4] At that time, too, there were over 1,200 natives of Carriacou living in Trinidad, more than a thousand of them having been there since 1941.[5] It is generally accepted that a high proportion of the natives of Carriacou are absent from the island at any time. The 1946 census also reports that there were then 1,366 farms and small plots in Carriacou at that time, 249 of these being less than one acre in extent. The total number of holdings composing these 1,366 farms amounted to 2,571, or on an average 1.88 holdings per farm, and one farm to every 4.9 residents.[6]

In Carriacou the most important kinship units are individual families and larger groups of kinsfolk who trace relationship to one another through males, commonly to a depth of three or four generations. This larger patrilineal group is known locally as a "blood," and normally most male members of such a group have a common surname. But even if a child does not receive its father's name, it takes its "blood" from him, and is a member of the lineage to which he belongs. In Carriacou, patrilineal descent is of importance in the inheritance of land as well as the transmission of status and lineage membership.

2. ESTABLISHMENT OF THE LAND SETTLEMENT

During the sugar centuries, Harvey Vale was a flourishing estate, but toward the latter half of the nineteenth century, it ceased to operate as a cane plantation, and after a brief period of *metayage,* was taken over by the government of Grenada in 1892 and prepared for allocation to the land-hungry folk of the area under the contemporary conventions of land settlement. In 1904 the estate totaled 331 acres, 2 roods, and 30 perches. It is situated at the western end of the island, and consists almost entirely of flat land, only the most inward sections that lie on the lower slopes of the island-spine having gradients of 15 degrees or more.

In 1904 a total of 252 acres, 2 roods, and 4 perches was subdivided by the government for distribution in 79 allotments. The accompanying map presents the settlement layout and system of plot-referencing used here, together with a schematic picture of the distribution and relative sizes of all occupancies on these plots at the time of the survey.[7] It was the aim of our field inquiries to make a complete census of the allotments at Harvey Vale, but owing to an unfortunate oversight no information was collected about two of the plots and their owners.

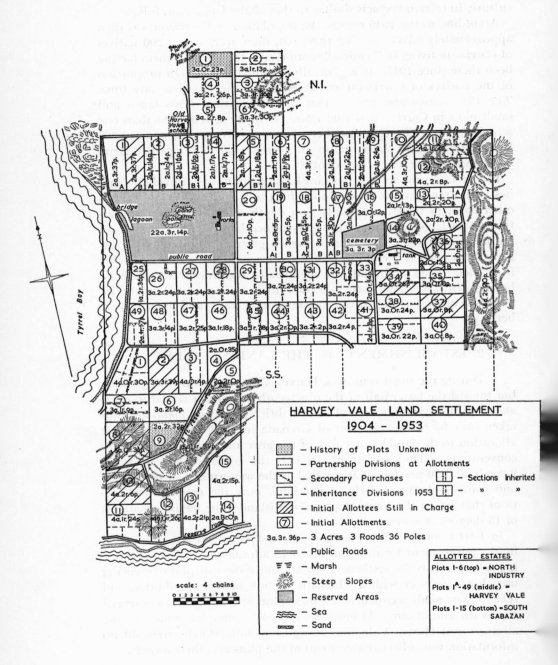

HARVEY VALE LAND SETTLEMENT
1904 - 1953

▨ — History of Plots Unknown
⋯⋯ — Partnership Divisions at Allotments
⧄ — Secondary Purchases   ⊞ — Sections Inherited
— ⋅ — Inheritance Divisions 1953   ▥ — "   "
▨ — Initial Allottees Still in Charge
⑦ — Initial Allottments

3a.3r.36p — 3 Acres 3 Roods 36 Poles

═══ — Public Roads
⋎ ⋎ — Marsh
✺ — Steep Slopes
▨ — Reserved Areas
≈≈ — Sea
⋯⋯ — Sand

scale: 4 chains
0 1 2 3 4 5 6 7 8 9 10

ALLOTTED ESTATES
Plots 1-6 (top) = NORTH
                  INDUSTRY
Plots 1^A-49 (middle) =
              HARVEY VALE
Plots 1-15 (bottom) = SOUTH
                  SABAZAN

The Official Allocation

Plots were allocated at an average price of £10 per acre, payable by annual installments over a period of 12–15 years. An initial deposit was also required. On completion of payment, the allottee or his heir was given a diagram of his allotment, together with a deed of ownership by the government in accordance with legal requirements. Until an allotment had been fully paid for, the allottee was required to obtain permission from the government before he could sell any portion of his holding. On the completion of payment, this restriction lapsed. Administration of the scheme included certain other types of supervision; and forfeitures for infraction of certain policy rules or for failure to pay the annual installments, occurred in 6 cases—3 in 1908, and the remainder in 1910. By 1920 the majority of the plots had been fully paid for, and title deeds were held by the allottees or their successors.

The 79 allotments varied in size as follows: 1 plot was less than 2 acres, 23 plots ranged between 2 and 2.5 acres, 7 between 2.5 and 3 acres, 16 plots between 3 and 3.5 acres, 19 between 3.5 and 4 acres, 5 between 4 and 4.5 acres, 6 between 4.5 and 5 acres, while 1 plot was over 5 acres but less than 5.5, and another, plot 20, was over 6 acres when allocated.

In 1904, 59 of the 79 plots were allotted. Between 1905 and 1911, the remaining 20 plots were distributed. Of these later allocations, 6 plots lay on the inland hill slopes, and another 4 contained floodwater courses, which have since been considerably enlarged. Delays in the remaining 10 later allocations must be attributed either to government policy, or to lack of suitable purchasers near the settlement. Most of the allottees lived on the borders of the former estate in the villages of Belmont, Bellevue South, and Six Roads, as well as in the village at Harvey Vale itself.

Of the final allottees, 11 were women, 68 men. All 6 forfeitures involved male allottees. Of the female allottees, 7 were independent purchasers. In 2 cases the real purchasers were the women's fathers; in one the woman had a female partner; and in another, the woman's husband had also taken a plot in his own name with the ostensible intention of going into partnership with his wife with both their plots, a plan that broke down when the marriage later dissolved, each spouse taking a part.

Administrative supervision of the holdings does not appear to have included promotion of planned land use, but was focused on the prevention of speculation in land on the settlement. Tax payment was enforced where necessary by putting up for sale those allotments for which tax was overdue.

The Actual Allocation: (a) Partnership

There are important differences between the initial allocation as registered in the government files, and the distribution of plots which actually occurred. These differences mainly reflect the operation of two principles and types of relation among the allottees, partnership and kinship, both of which also involve disguised purchases.

A total of 15 partnerships, none of which was officially recorded, were involved in the initial allocation. Of these, 9 have since been acknowledged without dispute by the parties involved or their heirs; 3 partnerships are alleged on one side to have been established when the government first distributed the allotments, but these claims are contested by the other side, although so far without litigation arising; in the 3 remaining cases, conflicting allegations about initial partnership have led to disputes, litigation, and may continue to do so.

Apart from these unrecorded partnerships, and those cases in which allotments were made to women who were not the real purchasers, 11 disguised purchases were effected at the initial allocation. Of these, 10 were cases in which the real purchasers were the allottees' fathers, and in more than half of these cases the older men already had plots of their own, often in their own name on the settlement at Harvey Vale.

The 15 partnerships varied in constitution as follows: between spouses or kin within the range of first ortho-cousins, 8; between persons linked indirectly to one another through mating relations, 3, of which 2 have already given rise to long disputes; between persons not linked by kinship or affinity in any way, 4, in 2 of these cases the partners being male, in 1 case a man and a woman forming the partnership, and in the fourth case, which has also produced disputes, the partners being 2 women. From this record it is clear that harmonious partnerships most commonly develop between people who are either close kin or are already married to each other.

When these 15 partnerships are taken into account, the number of allocations actually effected by official action becomes 94 for the settlement as a whole; but of these we only have information on 92.

The normal arrangements of partnership involved sharing the plot and its cost equally; similarly, although tax continued to be paid in the name of the registered allottee, each partner contributed in proportion to his share. On the day following its official allocation, the partners subdivided the plot after a rough, unofficial survey. Certain boundary marks were planted then or shortly after. In only three of the fifteen cases were plots divided unequally between the partners to their purchase; since contributions toward purchase and tax payment varied proportionally, and the partners were close kin, none of these cases of unequal division has given rise to dispute. In two of these three cases the registered purchaser had for a partner an individual who already held one of the plots on the settlement in his own name.

Various types of devices were used to record the partnerships. In five cases the registered purchaser made a will which recorded the partnership, and formally transferred rights in half the plot to the partner and his heirs; but generally transfer by will was linked to some statement that limited the partner's rights of sale to the descendants of the registered purchaser, and froze the price at the level of the original purchase from the government. In three cases the registered purchaser went through the formality of arranging the sale of a share of the plot to his partner with official permission and record. In such a way the informal partnership was terminated, and the informal subdivision of the plot between the partners was later made official. In other words, partnership ceases when it is ratified officially in accordance with the forms of law.

In three cases of partnership between spouses, no record of the partnership exists either in the settlement files or in the form of a will, though the land has since come under inheritance. In another case of partnership between two unrelated women, one, who was married, asked her husband, who held another allotment in his own name, to dispose of the portion under her partnership in his will. This has since given rise to some dispute among the heirs of the two women initially concerned in the partnership, as there is no official record that the woman whose husband's will transmits rights in this plot had any claim in her lifetime to its ownership. But the case shows how wills may be used to register the fact of partnership by persons whose claims are otherwise unrecorded, after they have waited in vain for their partners or the latter's heirs to put the relation on record.

Recording the partnership does not of itself prevent disputes arising, except where such recording, as in the case of sham sale under official permit, terminates the partnership in effect. Two of the five cases in which wills have been used to record partnerships and transfer land rights to the unregistered partners or their heirs have been followed by disputes among the parties concerned. In none of the cases in which the partnerships have remained completely unrecorded has any dispute developed. Since, with only one exception, all these unrecorded partnerships involve people who are close kin or spouses of one another, and partnership runs smoothly within the context of these basic institutional relations, nothing is gained by recording. Rather, it seems that recording of partnership may be attempted after strains have already developed within the partnership, and as often as not leads to an open breach.

This really means that apart from the simple conditions of partnership set out above, there are other less easily formulated notions and norms which govern the relation. Probably the most important of these relate to the reversionary rights which partners or their heirs hold in one another's share of land, and to the limitation that partnership imposes on the price or type of sale. When dealing with land reportedly held in partnership, government officers in Carriacou act in harmony with these customary notions, as far as conditions permit. Thus, when one heiress to a partnership was unable to meet tax commitments, the District Commissioner sold her plot to the heir of her father's partner. The defaulting heiress announced at once that she would repay her partner's heir, and retake her land, as soon as she was able. The new purchaser raised no objection, but the heiress died childless in Trinidad before paying off the debt, thus leaving him with undisputed right to the entire plot.

Another case that illustrates the way in which the relation of partnership is extended and reinterprets conveyance to conform to the intention of the partnership may be mentioned here. Two men whose mates were full sisters took a plot, 30, in partnership, making the usual rough survey and subdivision on the day after its allocation. Together they paid off the price. To record the partnership, the registered purchaser made a will, in which he allotted half of the plot to his partner in these terms: "And the 3 acres, 2 roods, 24 poles at Harvey Vale, A.B. possesses half of it, if he fail and be unable, the land is to return back to the said owner, no stranger to get any, my wife or my son are to pay the said amount what I paid for per acre, and to take back the land." A. B. duly failed during the great depression, and transferred his share back to the sole heir of the deceased purchaser resident in Carriacou at that time for an amount equal to that which had been paid to the government for the land some years before. Time passed, and A. B. desired to recover the land. He then claimed that the sum which he had received for his share of the land more than 10 years previously was made in payment for the lease of the plot at so much per year, and that the lease having now expired, the land was being held by its possessor illegally. The issue went to court in Carriacou in 1944 in that form, but was dismissed by the District Commissioner with the observation that "if there is a bonafide title to the claim, and the claim is not merely fictitious, the magistrate's jurisdiction is ousted (Stone's Manual)." Later, the same issue was at stake in a case of trespass and assault. This time the presiding magistrate, having established that the cause of the dispute was a claim over land, apparently lent his authority to a settlement of this land claim out of court, under which the mortgagor recovered the share which he had mortgaged without repayment of the mortgage money, the mortgage being mistaken for lease. This settlement thus restored the initial subdivision. The receipt which records the disputed transfer of money makes no mention of any lease, but clearly states that the transaction is a mortgage; but whatever the illegality or injustice of the present settlement, the case illustrates vividly the strength of the folk convention that the initial situation of partnership is binding on the partners and their heirs, even under circumstances where the rights it protects have been surrendered.

The Actual Allocation: (b) Kinship

The second important relation which directed the actual distribution of allotments in a manner contrary to the formal intentions of the government and the record of allocation consists in kinship and marriage among the population receiving allotments. Of the 92 plots concerning which there is detailed information, only 11 were allocated to persons not directly linked by kinship or marriage to other allottees on the settlement. Of the remaining 81 allocations, 14 were made to persons linked by ties of marriage or kinship to one or another of 13 patrilineages which held the remaining 67 plots between them. One of these patrilineages received 11 plots at the official allocation, and held a partner's claim on yet another, while two or three other lineages numbered 5 allottees each among their members.

The significance of this lineage distribution of allotments for the later history of the settlement is shown by the fact that of the 24 effective sales made by the allottees or their heirs subsequent to the initial allocation, only 3 have been to strangers, including the Anglican Church, which purchased a chapel site by the cemetery. The remaining conveyances have taken place between persons involved in the original allocation, their descendants, or close kin. That is to say, the majority of secondary transfers on the settlement have involved reallocations of holdings between members of the principal land-holding lineages. In the event, it is not surprising to find that lineages favorably placed in the initial distribution have augmented their holdings in the area at the expense of families lacking wide local kinship connections.

3. ALIENATION AND SECONDARY TRANSFERS

Excluding the initial distribution of plots and the subsequent reallocations of forfeited holdings by the government, all cases involving sale of settlement land can be discussed as alienation producing secondary transfers. It was not possible to collect data of comparable detail on the contexts of these sales in all cases, though a good deal of information was gathered on this subject. In discussing these secondary transfers I shall therefore concentrate on the form and record of the sales, the quantities of land transferred, the relations of the parties, and similar matters concerning which coverage was complete.

Secondary transfers are classifiable in terms of the presence or absence of official records, conditions attached to the transfer, or restrictions limiting the range of participants.

Allotment records cover secondary transfers on 11 plots. Transfers not recorded officially affect 19 plots. Although in 2 cases, the government put up plots for sale on account of tax defaulting, there is no record of sale in the settlement files. The number of sales exceeds the number of plots involved whether or not the sales were recorded. Recorded sales on 11 plots number 16. Unrecorded sales on 19 plots amount to 22.

Of the recorded sales, as mentioned above, 3 are disguised registrations of partnership; 1 was a conditional gift of 24 perches to the holder's daughter's husband, and was revoked by the donor when the transferee married after the death of his wife. Only 2 recorded sales transferred undivided plots, and all the rest lacked both survey and diagrams of the areas transferred.

Of the 22 unrecorded sales, only 12 can be regarded as effective transfers to a person otherwise lacking a claim of some kind. In 2 of the remaining 10 cases, certain co-heirs redeemed mortgaged land to recover their inheritance. In 4 cases co-heirs conveyed land to one another. One case masks transfer under an alleged partnership. Another, in which a resident heiress disposed of almost all the holding under an alleged but invisible will, was later revoked as a sale without right by the court to which the issue was brought when certain co-heirs returned from overseas. In the two remaining cases lawyers sold part of an inheritance (plots 20 and 48) to the heiress's husband and sister's husband on account of unpaid debts. Only 24 of the total of 38 secondary alienations, recorded or otherwise, involved real or effective transfers of right; and only in 3 of these 24 cases have transfers been made to persons not already linked by ties of marriage or close kinship with other land holders on the settlement.

Sales are classified as restricted when the range of eligible purchasers is limited by the operation of some systematic principle, such as kinship preference, or by the reversionary rights of heirs under a partnership. A conditional sale is a transfer on a particular condition, for example, limitation of the purchaser's right of resale to the vendor and his heirs only. The purchaser under a conditional sale may or may not be drawn from a restricted range of persons. A *real* or *effective* transfer of rights in land takes place when the parties are not linked by other relations such as kinship, affinity, or partnership which entail claims to the land conveyed, either previously, or at the time of transfer, or in the future, under inheritance.

Real transfers of right are typically affected by the folk of Harvey

Vale through sales which are both unconditional and unrestricted. When external bodies, such as the government or lawyers acting with judicial sanction, initiate such transfers to recover tax or settle debts, there may be some deviation from folk practice. Under such circumstances it appears that kinship sentiments and claims normally lead kinsfolk to purchase the holding, or that the external agency selling the land prefers to deal with close kin of the defaulting individuals. In either case, what appears formally to be a real transfer of rights is simply a reallocation among a restricted group of kin.

Conditional sales are normally made to purchasers drawn from a restricted range. Normally the principles which define this range of eligible purchasers are kinship, marriage, affinity, or partnership. Of the total 38 secondary sales, 14 were simultaneously restricted and conditional, the condition in each case limiting the purchaser's power of alienation to the vendor and his heirs. Of these 14 conditional sales within a restricted range, 10 were purely private transactions, while the remainder proceeded by redemptions of mortgages which were only recorded because third parties were involved, in 2 of these 4 cases the third parties being lawyers. Thus, nearly half of the unrecorded transfers of land for money take place between close kin, and contain conditions which prohibit further alienation by the transferree to third parties. These characteristics of folk conveyance, its limiting conditions, restricted range of application, and absence of record, form a single body of custom. In these terms, land should not be sold except to close kin or others already bound by institutional ties to the seller, and it may only be resold by the purchaser to the former holder or his heirs. In such a context "sales" are arrangements in good faith which hardly require or permit formal recording.

Such conventions further affect the mode of partition for sale. In no case was secondary transfer preceded by a proper survey, and although rights really shifted between persons in approximately half the number of transfers, the range of such movement being usually restricted by such factors as kinship, the rights themselves being normally of the conditional character discussed above, there was as little point in surveying the land as in registering the transactions themselves. Moreover, the relatively high costs of assistance from Grenadian lawyers or surveyors, none being resident in Carriacou, must discourage their employment in such small-scale conveyances.

As practiced locally, mortgage differs from the conditional sale which prohibits alienation to third parties, principally in that the initiative for recovery under a mortgage rests with the initial holder. Most mortgages do not involve interest, and are hardly distinguishable from pledge. Sometimes, as mentioned above, conditional sales may be retrospectively interpreted by the vendor either as mortgage or lease.

Receipts pass for mortgage in much the same way as for sale. Of the 22 unrecorded conveyances, 3 were mortgages, the remainder sale. Of these 19 sales, 3 were handled by lawyers, 5 were effected with receipts, 2 involved reregistration of the plot for tax purposes, and 7 of the remainder were effected without any receipt. Concerning 4 transfers, nothing certain is known on this point, since all the principals concerned were absent from the island. In cases of unrecorded sale, prescriptive rights are not held to be a reasonable ground for the assertion of ownership.

Official records of sale for 9 plots mention their subdivision. The areas transferred were as follows: 1 acre each in 5 cases; 1 acre on two separate occasions for 2 plots; 1 acre and half an acre for 1 plot; and finally, 4 sales over a period of 27 years transferring a total of 3.25 acres to a purchaser whose father held a plot on the settlement, but who was not related to the vendor. In this last case, the vendor finally sold the last acre of her allotment to her sister's daughter's son without record.

Of the 19 plots affected by unrecorded sales, 1 was transferred directly as a unit, and another indirectly, when the brother of the childless deceased first holder redeemed the mortgage on it. In the remaining 17 sales, co-heirs transferred a quarter of an acre to one another in two cases, there were 5 transfers of half an acre, 7 of 1 acre, one of 1.75 acres, one of 2 acres, and one of 2.5 acres. Of the transfers involving a half acre and 1 acre, 3 and 5 respectively were made between close kin. The parties to transfers of relatively large areas are usually unrelated.

This record of the areas transferred gives a misleading impression of fragmentation by sale, unless it is supplemented by some information on relations of the parties to one another and to other landholders on the settlement. The simplest way to summarize and express the effect of these sales is to compare the actual allocation of plots made initially with the situation produced by these secondary transfers. In place of the 92 landholders by official allocation and partnership, there are now 100 landholders as a result of these 38 secondary transfers. Of the 8 persons who acquired settlement plots by secondary transfer, excluding the Anglican Church, only 2 are not descended from persons already holding plots on the settlement. It is thus clear that the secondary transfers reallocate rights in land mainly among the population already established in the settlement, and that the fragmentation of individual plots in this process will be substantially balanced by the aggregation of claims and holdings among the population concerned.

Apart from receipts, normally stamped and witnessed in a manner which is invalid at law, and excluding also the official record of secondary alienations, there is another method of seeking to record transfer. This involves reregistration of the area transferred on the tax roll by the transferee or his heirs in their own names. Such reregistration for tax payment is not legally acceptable evidence of a title to the land, but is regarded by the folk as intention to assert such title. Consequently, where sales of conditional or restricted character such as are made by kin for debt or tax are followed by reregistration of the area on the tax roll in the transferee's name, considerable hostility and suspicion is provoked among the former holders and their heirs, as such an act indicates that the possessor conceives his tenure as permanent and unconditional, and is prepared to assert his individual right at law. Such a right, which involves the power to alienate the land to strangers, naturally threatens the reversionary claims of the former holders, which are promptly asserted. Probably reluctance to provoke these reactions is sufficient explanation why only 2 of the 22 unrecorded sales were followed by reregistration on the tax roll.

4. THE SETTLEMENT AND ITS POPULATION

Population Growth

Forms of landholding, the areas which are involved, and the changes in either pattern develop through the processes by which rights in land are transmitted. These processes of transmission themselves reflect the size of the population in relation to land, its organization, and changes in either variable. It is therefore necessary to consider the demographic situation in detail in order to obtain a thorough understanding of the functions of any system of tenure, the forces which have formed it, and the principles by which it proceeds.

Land neither claims nor inherits people, but the contrary occurs; and the efficacy of one claim against another depends on the social recognition accorded to either. This social recognition in turn reflects cultural conventions about relationships to land in which such variables as sex, age, birth status, residence, relation to the former holder, mode of transfer, and residual rights of other kin of the former holder, are often simultaneously involved. That is to say, the status of any individual claim to land under certain systems of tenure depends directly on the number and type of other claims which are socially recognized.

I shall now consider the ways in which the process of transmission of land rights at Harvey Vale reflects the growth and organization of the population involved.

All members of the population classified in the following table have claims or rights by descent, marriage, or allocation, to portions of the

92 original plots and 8 secondary divisions about which detailed information was obtained. Including these 8 secondary purchases, there are 100 land holders who may for illustrative purposes be regarded as having had one mate each. As will be shown below, most of these initial holders and a fair proportion of their mates are now dead. For the moment we shall treat all these landholders and their mates as

TABLE 9

PERSONS WITH CLAIMS TO LAND AT HARVEY VALE IN NOVEMBER, 1953,
CLASSIFIED BY SEX, STATUS OF BIRTH, AND RESIDENCE

	Males	Females	Total
Present in Carriacou:			
Legitimate................	373	427	800
Illegitimate..............	116	141	257
Total..................	489	568	1,057
Absent from Carriacou:			
Legitimate................	228	191	419
Illegitimate..............	67	52	119
Total..................	295	243	538
Grand Total...........	784	811	1,595

having died. On such assumptions, the descendants of these 100 landholders and their mates now number nearly 1,600 persons, after a period of 50 years, or approximately two generations. All of these 1,600 persons have claims of some kind to settlement land. Some now hold portions in their own right, some are occupants under rights held by others, some have rights which they have not asserted in any form, others have direct claims in their own name. Still others have latent claims which will become rights under inheritance, while the remainder have indirect latent rights, normally on the basis of marriage or affinity. Given such rates of population growth on the one hand, and such distributions of claims and rights on the other, it is neither surprising that inheritance is the most important mode by which land rights are transmitted, nor that the norms and functions of inheritance should be extended to other processes, such as partnership and conveyance, in the nature of limiting conditions. Yet the overwhelming importance of inheritance rights to land among the folk is clearly a function of the social organization of their population and its high rates of increase. The distribution of inheritance is that aspect of the social organization which defines the rights and claims to land associated with relationships of differing kinds.

As will be shown, the population claiming land on the settlement frequently intermarry. There were also 40 absentees whose sex distribution could not be ascertained, and who are not included in the preceding table, although having claims on settlement land. Taking these facts into account, it may be said that the settlement population has been roughly doubling itself within each of the past two generations. Although this oversimplifies the situation, it probably does not overstate it. A rate of population increase such as this obviously will be of decisive importance in the modes of land distribution and tenure which are practiced. But before its impact can be assessed it is necessary to see in what ways it is limited.

In the first place, one-third of the population having claims to settlement land are absent from the island. Secondly, over one-fifth of the claimants are of illegitimate status. Only one-half of the claimants are both legitimate and resident in Carriacou. Of these 800 people, the majority are females. Of the 100 initial land holders, only 11 were women. Clearly, if Carriacou folk practice trusteeship on behalf of absentees with rights or claims, and combine this with a generalized denial of inheritance rights of illegitimate children to their father's land, they will halve the size of the problem of the distribution of rights in land which faces them as a consequence of their high rates of population increase.

Birth Status and Inheritance Claims

The status of illegitimacy is not always uniformly defined in Carriacou. The local terms distinguishing birth statuses are "lawful" and "unlawful." Lawful or legitimate issue are those born to parents bound by marriage. Under Grenadian law, the birth of these children may precede their parents' marriage by any period. The Carriacou description of these children as "lawful" refers not only to the fact that they were born according to the law of marriage, but also to their prima facie claims to inherit should their parents die intestate.

When an unmarried man lives with a woman who has children for him, he may distinguish these as his "lawful" heirs in contrast to those other children of his who are living away from him with their mothers. But the terms normally used to distinguish a man's resident and absent children are "inside" and "outside," the reference being to the home where the common father dwells. Only rarely will a man describe his "inside" children born out of wedlock as "lawful," and when he does so, the reference is to their priority over his other children in relation to inheritance. Since women normally retain control of both their legitimate and illegitimate children, they do not usually have occasion to distinguish the "inside" from the "outside" issue, and therefore use the terms "lawful" and "unlawful" for their offspring more consistently than men.

Sometimes a person reports his birth status, or that of others, to be legitimate, when no marriage took place between the parents. Such errors may be intended or accidental. Where the intention is to mislead, and land rights are under discussion, the reason is very often that there has been no testamentary disposition of the holding, and the persons reported as "lawful" would thus lack prima facie claims at law, though recognized as heirs under custom. In such circumstances, falsification of birth status is a device to support certain claims to land and can be used to discountenance others. Accidental misinformation on this subject occurs when the distinctions between "inside" and "outside" children are loosely equated with those between "lawful" and "unlawful."

To guard against these sources of error, genealogical data were collected from three different sets of persons about the great majority of the family lines which hold land on the settlement, and the correspondence of these genealogies was studied carefully. It therefore seems more likely that the relatively high legitimacy rate of the settlement population may be due to under-reporting of illegitimate claimants rather than to classification of the "unlawful" as "lawful-born." In such a case, the rate of population growth estimated above must be somewhat on the low side.

Of the 11 female allottees, 5 died unmarried. Of the 89 men who initially acquired land on the settlement, only 3 remained unwed, and an equal number were twice married. Thus, there is a much greater tendency for male land holders to marry than for females. Quite possibly, ownership of sufficient land to assure women of economic and social independence may reduce their inclinations to marry in Carriacou.

Married persons of either sex frequently have illegitimate offspring also; this is more common for males than females. Either party to a marriage may have had children by others previously, or may do so after the death of their spouse; but only males continue to have such children during marriage itself. Since most Carriacou men marry and also have illegitimate offspring, the inheritance rights of their children of these differing birth statuses clearly presents a problem. The way in which this problem is normally handled reflects the principal conditions of its context. These conditions involve a far higher reproduction rate within marriage than otherwise, the tendency of wives to survive their husbands, and the tendency toward female occupancy of land. Under these conditions the widow has a greater claim on her husband's estate than the mother of his illegitimate children, and, as she is already settled on the holding, can readily assert this claim. Moreover, widows have rights under intestate inheritance which effectively dispossess the children of their rivals. On the other hand, the mothers of these illegitimate children frequently control plots of their own, or have access to those of their kin. Exclusion of these illegitimate children from inheritance by their father's widow does not therefore produce as much hardship as may be expected.

Marriage and Widowhood

The high valuation of marriage within the native population of Carriacou is shown by the following analysis of the marital status of the total population of absent adults having claims on settlement land.

TABLE 10

Absent Adult Claimants, Classified by Sex and Marital Status, Harvey Vale, November, 1953

Sex	Marital status		Total
	Married	Single	
Males	71	129	200
Females	65	45	110
Total	136	174	310

Although the gross totals of single and married persons in the accompanying table seem to suggest casual attitudes toward marriage, closer study shows that this is not so. In the first place, the ratio of married persons among the absent female population is twice as high as that found among males. Since in every case except one these women were married to men from Carriacou, and typically to members of the settlement population, some 60 per cent of the female emigration from Carriacou is accounted for by the movement of wives abroad either with their husbands or to join them.

In the second place, two-thirds of the absent adult males are unmarried. The majority of these persons are at present overseas in order to earn sufficient money with which to build a home and rainwater tank, to purchase land, or otherwise make local investments enabling them either to marry or to maintain or establish a household. A goodly section of the remainder is unlikely to resettle in Carriacou. Emigration is therefore to some degree motivated among males by the cultural prerequisites for marriage, among females by the condition of marriage itself.

Of the 71 absent married males, 7 had left their wives and families in Carriacou, and 2 held plots on the settlement, but had left no immediate family in the area. Of the absent single males, 2 held plots in their own right on the settlement, and another 2 were widowed. Only one of the absent married women had wed a foreigner. This woman was married to a Grenadian living near Grenville, a town which is visited weekly by Carriacou boatmen. It seems that those Carriacou women emigrants who fall in love with foreigners while abroad normally prefer to have illegitimate children for their lovers rather than marry them. In such a case, the high ratio of single women among the female emigrant population indicates the high value which these women place on marriage to another native of Carriacou.

TABLE 11

MALE AND FEMALE LANDHOLDERS AT HARVEY VALE IN 1953,
CLASSIFIED BY SEX, SURVIVAL, MARITAL STATUS, AND
DEATH ORDER WITH RELATION TO THEIR SPOUSES

	Landholders		
	Male	Females	Total
1. *Living allottees:*			
Both spouses alive..............	8	—	8
Wives dead, husbands alive......	2	—	2
Husbands dead, wives alive......	—	2	2
Unmarried....................	2	—	2
Total living allottees.............	12	2	14
2. *Deceased allottees:*			
Husbands dead, wives alive......	20	—	20
Husbands dead, 2d wives alive...	2	—	2
Both spouses dead, wives first....	7	2	9
Both spouses dead, husbands first.	40	2	42
Unmarried....................	1	5	6
Total deceased allottees*..........	70	9	79
3. *Secondary purchasers*.............	7	—	7
Total landholders.................	89	11	100

* Includes one male deceased purchaser.

Marriage frequencies express the high value set upon marriage, but married persons, especially males, often have children born outside of marriage as well as within it. The differing birth statuses of these children are reflected in their differing positions with regard to inheritance. To a large degree the relative effectiveness with which a man's different sorts of children are able to press their inheritance claims depends on whether his wife survives him. Consequently the relative frequencies with which spouses of either sex survive one another affect the transmission of inheritance rights. Table 11 summarizes our data on this subject, and will be discussed below.

Emigration

Absence is relative, a product of distance and time. It was not possible to establish the duration of absence systematically and accurately for all emigrants during the survey. Some persons knew, some did not. Death had often removed those who were most knowledgeable about the emigrants. On the other hand, the location of these emigrants was positively known, and overlapping information obtained by separate genealogical inquiries showed a very high agreement of their reported distribution in the large number of cases where two or more local descent lines were intermarried.

The area which receives emigration considerably influences the migrant's prospects, and the chances of his return. Since these factors will in turn affect the distribution of land to which emigrants have claims or rights, especially with regard to security and continuity of tenure, it is necessary to examine the direction of emigration with care.

Two classes of emigrants can be usefully distinguished for present purposes, according to the types of claim on settlement land which they hold. "Principals" are persons of either sex who have a direct claim to all or some portion of particular plots. "Dependents" are persons with latent claims, whose parents hold direct claims but were still living at the time of this study. Spouses, or others, having claims based on affinity, are excluded from this classification, but female principals or dependents having claims in their own right are included. This distinction between principals and dependents does not refer to adult or minor status directly, but to the immediacy of claim and especially to the presence or absence of living parents, since most claims arise under inheritance. Thus, some principals may be minors, while many dependents are married adults.

Roughly two-thirds of the emigrants are concentrated in the nearby British colony of Trinidad, where opportunities for employment and land acquisition are very much higher than Carriacou provides. One-half of all emigrant principals live in Trinidad. Carriacou schooners visit Trinidad weekly, and the passage-fare is low, $10 B.W.I. ($5.80 U.S.) in 1953. Individual movement between Trinidad and Carriacou is therefore easy, but costs are relatively high when families move as units. The great majority of dependents in Trinidad are children of the principals living there. Of the total number of absent dependents, nearly 75 per cent are settled in Trinidad. Assuming on the basis of table 10 that about 60 per cent of the female principals in Trinidad are married, it would appear that at least half of the total of absent adult females have married Carriacou men and gone to live in Trinidad.

Aruba and Venezuela, which also attract considerable emigration, offer attractive employment opportunities but are less inviting for family migration and settlement than Trinidad, being farther away, offering little scope for land acquisition, and being under alien rule. These territories therefore attract few female principals from Carriacou, and a large proportion of the emigration to them involves

TABLE 12

DISTRIBUTION OF HARVEY VALE EMIGRANTS, CLASSIFIED IN STATUS OF CLAIM

Area	Principals			Dependents			Total principals and dependents
	Male	Female	Total	Male	Female	Total	
Trinidad	65	53	118	111	121	232	350
Aruba	15	9	24	21	14	35	59
Venezuela	24	6	30	24	8	32	62
U.S.A.	13	6	19	4	3	7	26
Grenada	2	10	12	5	8	13	25
Cuba	3	—	3	—	—	—	3
Panama	3	—	3	—	—	—	3
Columbia	2	—	2	—	—	—	2
St. Eustatius	1	—	1	—	—	—	1
Bahamas	—	1	1	—	—	—	1
Total	128	85	213	165	154	319	532*

* The whereabouts of 6 emigrants were uncertain or unknown.

single males, typically dependents. Most of these emigrants to Aruba and Venezuela later return to Carriacou where they settle, marry, and take up their inheritances. In this respect they differ from those who emigrate to Trinidad. Of the 6 absent male plot holders, 2 are married and live with their families in Trinidad, and of the remainder, 2 in Aruba, 1 in the United States, and 1 in Cuba, are unwed.

These data describe emigration patterns in which the numbers and ratios of women decline as a function of the cultural as well as spatial distance from Carriacou. They show how the probabilities that emigrant principals may control their land holdings from overseas or return to occupy these themselves correspond roughly with this distribution of women overseas. This means that males settled abroad with their wives in nearby Trinidad are more likely to delegate authority over their holdings in Carriacou than to reoccupy them themselves, while male emigrants to more distant areas are more likely to be single persons with dependent claims to land in the island, who will return and assert occupancy at some later time.

Migration contexts which produce such uncertainty about the emigrants' return will obviously have direct and intimate effects on the transmission of rights in land in the island, its distribution, and the security or permanency of its tenure for the emigrants, their kinsfolk, and co-heirs alike. On the one hand, the large number of absent principals makes more land available than would otherwise be the case, and facilitates its reallocation on inheritance informally and for indefinite periods in larger shares than those to which the co-heirs would otherwise be entitled. Emigration of landholders also provides opportunities for caretaker arrangements between kin and others with regard to land, which may postpone subdivisions due on inheritance and may take the forms of lease or rent. On the other hand, the chance that persons abroad may return to assert their claims rather suddenly denies such reallocations of their land in Carriacou any permanence or formal completeness. Likewise it denies occupants of such land that security of tenure which is essential if those attitudes basic to systems of individual right in land, restricted only by law, are to develop. Instead, landholding within this context of migration strengthens contrary trends toward trusteeship on a family basis, especially where inheritance is involved.

5. DIFFERENT CATEGORIES OF INHERITANCE

Of the 92 initial holdings 11 have not yet become subject to inheritance. If the 8 secondary divisions are grouped with these, the number of uninherited plots becomes 19. Of the remaining 81 plots, 37 have been inherited under wills through a total of 35 deaths, and 44 have been inherited without wills through a total of 38 deaths. Thus the frequency with which rights in land are transmitted by inheritance is more than twice that of sale. But since sales normally transfer rights to single persons only, while inheritance normally transfers rights to several people, the proportion of all transmissions which occur through inheritance is considerably higher than the figure above suggests.

Of the 35 cases of inheritance by testamentary disposition, 22 can be treated as unmixed or pure testacy, in the sense that there has been no intestate inheritance of these willed holdings. The remaining 13 cases of initial inheritance under will can be regarded as mixed or hybrid in character. These are cases in which intestate inheritance of rights initially devised under wills has since occurred, or, alternatively, cases in which formerly unwilled inheritance has since been devised under will. All 38 cases of unmixed intestacy involve no will, either initially or subsequently. For purposes of this classification, the validity of wills at law is immaterial. Even where the existence of a will is disputed, the inheritance in question has been excluded from the category of unmixed intestacy, and has been classified in terms of the preceding criteria.

A comparative breakdown of the settlement population according to the inheritance categories to which their claims belong is presented in table 13. In this breakdown those persons whose inheritance rights

TABLE 13

POPULATION HAVING CLAIMS TO LAND ON THE HARVEY VALE SETTLEMENT IN 1953, CLASSIFIED BY CATEGORY OF INHERITANCE, LEGITIMACY, AND LOCATION

	All claimants		Legitimate			Illegitimate				Plots in-volved
	In C'cou	Absent	In C'cou	Absent	Total	In C'cou	Absent	Total	Total	
(a) *No inheritance involved:*										
Males..................	61	38	53	32	85	8	6	14	99	
Females...............	61	31	49	29	78	12	2	14	92	
Total unaffected by inheritance...........	122	69	102	61	163	20	8	28	191	19
(b) *Unmixed testacy:*										
Males..................	159	47	111	32	143	48	15	63	206	
Females...............	181	51	128	40	168	53	11	64	232	
Claimants by unmixed testacy..............	340	98	239	72	311	101	26	127	438	23
(c) *Mixed testacy:*										
Males..................	90	53	68	33	101	22	20	42	143	
Females...............	114	41	92	30	122	22	11	33	155	
Claimants by mixed testacy..............	204	94	160	63	223	44	31	75	298	14
(d) *Unmixed intestacy:*										
Males..................	179	157	141	131	272	38	26	64	336	
Females..............	212	120	158	92	250	54	28	82	332	
Claimants by unmixed intestacy..............	391	277	299	223	522	92	54	146	668	44
Total:										
Males..................	489	295	373	228	601	116	67	183	784	
Females...............	568	243	427	191	618	141	52	193	811	
Grand Total..............	1,057	538	800	419	1,219	257	119	376	1,595	100

through their several kin and parents belong to different categories have been divided equally between the categories involved to avoid dual entry or inequalities of classification.

Some 12 per cent of the total population have claims on plots which have not been subject to inheritance since their initial allocation. Another 27 per cent have claims on plots inherited under unmixed testacy. About 19 per cent of the population are claimants to plots inherited under conditions of mixed testacy, while 44 per cent, or almost half the number with claims on inherited plots of all classes, inherit under unmixed intestacy. Those 37 per cent of all plots which have been transmitted by will involve some 46 per cent of the settlement population, and have an average for both categories of testate disposition of 20 persons per plot. Those 19 per cent of the plots not yet subject to inheritance account for 12 per cent of the total population, with an average of 10 claimants per plot. The 44 per cent of plots inherited under pure intestacy account for 44 per cent of the population, and average 15 claimants per plot.

The total population holding claims to inherited plots at the time of survey was 1404. Of these persons, only 32 per cent held claims based on conditions of unmixed testacy; 21 per cent held claims under conditions of testacy and intestacy together; while 47 per cent held their claims under conditions of unmixed intestacy. These ratios describe the extent to which deviation from the legal system of land inheritance has developed on the settlement in a period of 50 years. The deviation from legal norms is of the same order for inheritance as for sale, and in its content and development forms the body of the folk system of tenure. Since these data were gathered without selection from the settlement area, they provide a sample of case histories which are probably representative of Carriacou as a whole, with this exception—that all initial holdings on the settlement were based on recent legal title, and enjoyed official record.

Differences in the average number of claimants for plots of the various inheritance categories might seem to suggest that will-making is stimulated by numerous progeny. Such deduction from the averages would be inappropriate and erroneous. Similar deductions could equally be drawn from these averages to show that life-span of the holders, other things being equal, decreased in ratio to the numbers of their progeny. But other things are not equal in either case. Thus in six cases of mixed or hybrid testacy the wills concerned were made by widows of the initial land holders after they died intestate; and there are also cases of testamentary disposition effected by holders without surviving issue. Moreover, as noted above, there may well be some under-reporting of illegitimate claimants, intentionally or otherwise. This would seem to be the case with regard to the population descended from living landholders, since the ratio of illegitimate issue in this group is unusually low by comparison with other groups.

It therefore appears unlikely that inheritance with or without will can be explained in terms of the number of claimants involved; and a detailed examination of both processes and their conditions must therefore be made.

6. TESTAMENTARY DISPOSITION

I shall now inquire what factors are associated with testamentary disposition, in what ways, and to what extent, by a study of the contexts within which wills are made at Harvey Vale, and by an analysis of their contents.

Of the 11 female allottees 2 were still alive in 1953. Of the 9 deceased female allottees, 3 made wills themselves, 1 of them by asking her husband to dispose of her plot in his will. Of the 89 male allottees, 70 had died by the time of this survey, 32 of these having left a will,

38 intestate. The ratio of intestacy among female allottees is higher than among males.

Order of death of spouses is a variable with direct implications for will-making in many cases. Of the 3 testate females, 2 were survived by husbands. Of the 32 testate males, 1 was unmarried, 6 survived their wives, and the remaining 25 left widows behind them. Of these 25 widows, 2 were the allottees' second wives, and both they and their issue fared less happily under the will than the children of the first wives. Of the 38 intestate males, only 1 was unmarried at death, while none had been married twice.

It appears as a rule that men make wills when they survive their wives or have been twice married, but that wills are only made in 39 per cent of the cases in which the wife survives. Since the data in table 11 show that women survive their husbands in 4 out of 5 marriages, it follows that wills are made in half the number of marriages, but this includes all those cases in which widowers make wills. It appears that in Carriacou the presence of a healthy wife inhibits will-making on the part of her ailing spouse.

Actually, this calculation understates the extent to which men possessing hale spouses refrain from making wills. This understatement arises because in 6 of the cases of testacy, the will was made by the widow herself. If these 6 cases are subtracted, it appears that only 19 out of the 62 land holders whose wives survived them made wills, that is, less than 30 per cent.

The Contents of Wills

The conditions and contents of such wills as were made at the settlement are clearly worth study, if only because it seems unusual for men who die before their wives to make wills.

In 6 cases men made wills which set definite limits to the interests and powers of their widows with regard to the holding. In another 2 cases, certain legitimate issue were excluded from the inheritance; in 5 cases men allotted land by will to their illegitimate children; in 3 cases the wills recorded and sought to ratify partnership relations; in 4 cases the wills recorded sales of portions of the plot which the landholder had transacted during his lifetime; in 5 cases the wills recorded previous partitions of the land among resident heirs; and in 2 cases rights to land claimed under partnership were distributed by will. In 11 of these cases, 2 or more scattered holdings were involved, and the will sought to effect subdivision of these holdings severally among the heirs.

As regards the shares distributed by will, in 14 cases the land was divided unequally, and in 13 cases, equally. In 1 case the terms were known to be ambiguous, 1 will transmitted a holding intact, and the contents of 2 were not clearly ascertained. Daughters were excluded from the inheritance in 1 will, another excluded sons, and a third gave sons a portion double that of the daughters, somewhat in the Mohammadan fashion of inheritance.

Where there is no surviving issue, land may be transmitted by will. Where the holder has lawful issue, and makes a will, these are the typical heirs. Where some of the holder's lawful issue are to be excluded from the inheritance, or some of his unlawful issue are to be included, wills are required. Unless specially mentioned in his will, the claim of a man's illegitimate issue gives way in the inheritance to that of the legitimate. The position is different where women are the land holders.

In 3 cases, specially designated portions of certain plots were disposed of by will to the heir who undertook responsibility for the deceased's funeral expenses. In one case, the major share of a holding was transmitted to a nonlineal heir as reward for his care of the holder during the latter's decline. Frequently, holders may leave portions to their daughters' husbands, it being tacitly understood that such heirs will take care of the land and protect the interests of their issue by the testators' daughters in it, for future inheritance. This is obviously a device to strengthen the marriage and to preserve a portion of the holding for the testator's daughter's children. Apart from these special cases and others mentioned above, 3 illegitimate children received "house-spots" under as many wills.

From this review of the contents of the wills at Harvey Vale, it is easy to see what conditions are directly associated with the making of wills. The basic condition of will-making, and hence its function, is to record or to initiate departures from the folk system of land tenure, and especially from folk norms which govern the transmission of rights at inheritance. For this reason, the executor is typically a senior heir, or someone, such as the testator's brother, who exerts authority within the extended family and enjoys the testator's confidence.

The Administration of Wills

In order to exclude all marginal cases from the category of pure intestate inheritance, we have been using an extremely liberal definition of testacy. This definition has included the several cases of inheritance under wills which were made by widows who lacked the power to effect valid testaments. In several other cases, the wills actually made were invalid on various grounds, such as insufficient or unacceptable witness, improper delegation of the testamentary power, disposition of land not registered as the testator's property, and so forth.

In only 4 of these 35 cases of testamentary disposition were the wills registered, though this is required by law if the validity of a will is to be capable of assertion. Moreover, none of these 4 instances of registration was followed by the executor's demand for letters of administration, although such letters are essential to the execution of a will.

In 1 case, some heirs under a will alleged that it had been registered, while other heirs denied this. In 3 cases, none of the beneficiaries under wills was aware of their contents. In 4 cases, the contents of wills were disputed by co-heirs. In 3 cases, certain heirs had appropriated the wills themselves. In 2 cases, senior co-heirs disputed with one another which of them had been appointed executor under the will. In only 2 of the 6 cases in which widows made invalid wills for their husbands' land was the widow's power to make such a will disputed by any heirs. In 2 of the 15 cases now under discussion, the existence of wills was denied point-blank by certain claimants to the inheritance.

There are 17 cases in which some of the children of deceased landholders have been completely or partially expropriated from inheritance on the settlement. Of these, 7 follow directly on disagreement over the contents of wills or the modes of their execution. Another 2 derive from wills which transmit otherwise unrecorded claims in plots purchased under informal partnership, but which are now denied by the registered purchasers or their heirs. These data indicate an expropriation rate of 26 per cent for inheritance under wills as against 21 per cent under intestacy. Thus, as devices for eliminating or reducing uncertainty and dispute over inheritance, wills are of doubtful utility. Indeed, they provide a number of issues for dispute, such as their actuality, legality, location, authorship, and contents, which would not otherwise arise. But since wills are usually made to record or initiate deviations from custom, it is not surprising that they should frequently give rise to dispute. One rather extreme instance of this may be given to illustrate the variety of issues and factors involved.

A certain allottee, after nearly a lifetime of common-law wedlock, decided to marry his concubine. Several children had already blessed the union, but only one, a son, followed the marriage. The allottee was said to have made a will shortly before his death. His widow, having a life-interest in the land, remained in charge of the holding until she passed away. During this time the eldest son, who was executor under the alleged will, died overseas, and the last-born son collected title deeds to the plot from the administration as the "lawful heir" (entry in official files). This man later denied that his father had made a will, and is alleged by his siblings and their dependents to have appropriated and destroyed it. Asserting his parents' intestacy, the last-born son now claims and holds the entire estate as the only "lawful heir." Thus the last-born, "lawful" son has formally expropriated the children born before his parents' marriage and their descendants on grounds of "illegitimacy." Of course, under the Grenadian law, this distinction is invalid, since marriage, even if *in articulo mortis,* legitimizes all surviving children of the two parties. Nonetheless the position of this self-appointed "lawful heir" is strong and cannot be challenged at law by those expropriated, except for an expenditure out of all proportion to the possible benefit, and without certainty of success. This case also illustrates the importance which Carriacou people attach to difference of birth status in relation to inheritance of land from males, even though it carries this distinction to an invalid extreme.

The Execution of Wills

From the preceding it will be clear that the ways in which wills are executed may vary widely in different contexts. Certainly, only a fraction of the total number of wills even enter on the standard legal processes of administration and execution, while none proceed further. But even within these limits there is impressive variation.

Following on two deaths in 1953, execution of will was postponed as "too soon" after the testators' deaths. Under the Carriacou conventions, entombment of the deceased, which is normally a somewhat protracted and expensive process, should correctly precede division of the inheritance. The executor's absence overseas had postponed division in another 3 cases, and two executors had died abroad leaving wills unimplemented. In 5 cases of land held by widows under life interest, execution had been postponed until their deaths. In one case the terms of the will postponed execution until the testator's debts had been discharged. There were 7 cases in which absence of some heirs overseas has prevented execution, and another in which all heirs under the will are absent. Since the execution of wills is an informal process which normally lacks legal sanction, it depends for its validity and effect on the presence and consensus of all heirs and interested parties at the act. Hence absence of heirs delays execution.

In 4 cases of partial expropriation under wills certain of the terms were set aside in the execution. Subdivision of different holdings of the testator among his several heirs was involved in another 2 cases. In 3 of these 6 cases, it was alleged that the executor had carried out permanent subdivisions of the holdings concerned in the absence of certain co-heirs. In 2 of these 3 cases, it was also pointed out that the executors who subdivided these holdings were self-appointed and had acted without valid authority, the persons designated to execute these will having died overseas. There were 5 cases in which the heirs themselves had arranged informal and temporary divisions of holdings, pending due execution of wills. In 3 cases will were set aside, and the holdings concerned were sold to individual heirs, once by the government to enforce tax-payment, and twice by lawyers to realize debts. Thus, although the modes of execution do not conform to legal process, they are highly variable in themselves. There is, indeed, a very great difference between the will as a document and the distribution of rights to which it leads.

Deaths and the Trend Toward Intestacy

Of the 35 cases of willed inheritance, 22 were distinguished as instances of pure or unmixed testacy. This term covers all those cases in which there had been no intestate succession subsequent to the death of the initial testator. Thus dispositions by will which have been followed by death of childless heirs remain classifiable as instances of pure testacy in our terms, since no material alteration of the initial disposition is effected. But if heirs under will should die intestate and with living issue, then there are material alterations, and the combination of testate and intestate conditions of inheritance on the holding leads to its classification as a case of hybrid status or mixed testacy. Successive deaths alone do not account for the category of mixed testacy since, as mentioned above, this class includes 6 cases in which wills were made by widows after the deaths of their husbands intestate. But the progressive trend toward intestacy is so closely associated with the rate of decease among the heirs under will that some details of this death-rate are necessary.

At the time of survey, 16 of the 35 groups of heirs under wills had not been reduced by death; 7 by 1 death each, in 6 of these cases the testator's widow being the person to die, thereby abolishing her life interest in the holding but producing no material alteration in its disposition; 7 groups of heirs had lost 2 members each, subsequent to the testator's death; another 3 groups had lost 3 members each; one group had lost 5 heirs; and another had lost 7. Since the issue of heirs under will who die intestate themselves become heirs through their parents' deaths, the group of heirs to any holding, though suffering a decrease by the death of its members, normally increases in absolute size by the accession of their issue. Thus deaths among heirs under will do not as a rule connote reduction of claims on the inheritance. But they normally involve important changes in the status of the inheritance itself.

Most of the 13 cases of hybrid inheritance status or mixed testacy have developed through deaths of heirs intestate which involve material alterations in the inheritance subsequent to the testator's death. None of these heirs under will had himself made a testamentary disposition of his inherited portion. No clearer demonstration of the trend toward intestate succession, its strength, and the conditions in which it develops, is possible. These conclusions are fully borne out by a glance at the cases of unmixed testacy. In 22 of these 23 cases, no deaths occurred, subsequent to that of the initial testator, which involved material alterations in the disposition as laid down by the will. Of these 22 cases, the death of widows abolished their life interest in 6 cases, but led to no revision of the will; while in 16 cases there were no deaths involving heirs.

Wills record or initiate departures from folk custom, and seek to give these effect by copying the forms prescribed by law. But these forms are neither copied exactly nor followed with sufficient persistence for the wills concerned to possess legal validity. Even so, the innovations or ratifications which wills seek to enforce depend for their effectiveness on the agreement and stability of the groups to which they apply. A succession of deaths within this group progressively destroys the effectiveness of these normally invalid wills, and frustrates the departures from folk norms which they seek to promote. The conflict which wills arouse between interested parties is an expression of the conflict between formal law and the living law of Carriacou custom. Our data, besides documenting the forces and conditions that determine, develop, and maintain this living law, also show it to be an impressive adaptation of the people to their circumstances.

Consider the location of surviving heirs under will. Of first-generation heirs having direct claims under will, 44 males and 33 females were overseas at the time of this survey. Of second-generation heirs under will, 14 males and 13 females were also absent. Thus 58 male and 46 female heirs under these 35 wills were not resident in Carriacou in 1953, giving an average of 3 nonclaimants per will, with males in the majority. Of the 35 groups of heirs under will, only in 6 cases were all heirs present in Carriacou at the time of survey; and there is only one other group of heirs which does not include 2 or more absent heirs. These figures only relate to heirs actually designated by will.

The conditions that stimulate men to make wills also find expression in those invalid wills made by widows to dispose of their dead husbands' property. Generally widows making such wills after their husbands' deaths intestate are either concerned to prevent the expropriation of some of the children of the marriage by others, or to effect departures from the normal patterns of inheritance. Thus in one case, a widow willed some of her husband's land to her illegitimate offspring by a former lover, and there were two cases in which a widow's will sought to disinherit her husband's absent sons. If these migrants ever return, they are unlikely to accept such decisions without protesting.

7. INTESTATE SUCCESSION

Intestate succession occurs more frequently than its contrary at Harvey Vale and also affects a greater number of plots. Since it does not involve special arrangements of an individual character such as wills seek to enjoin, it usually follows the norms of folk custom with regard to inheritance of land. These norms can be stated simply.

Where a male landholder dies intestate leaving children of different birth status, the legitimate heirs have a right to inherit, while the illegitimate only have a claim of conditional character. Where there are no legitimate children of an intestate male, his illegitimate issue inherit without hindrance. Where the legitimate children are abroad, illegitimate children living in the island have a good chance of securing temporary occupation of part of their father's holding. The illegitimate children of intestate women inherit equally with the legitimate. During their lifetime, the widows of intestate landholders exercise complete control over their husbands' land, but may not alienate it.

Of the 38 cases of intestate succession occurring on the settlement, 2 or more holdings were inherited in 6 cases. Of these 38 cases, there has been undue appropriation of portions of the inheritance by some heirs at the expense of others in 8 instances. In 2 cases, the holder's widow has left her illegitimate offspring by an earlier mating in charge of the entire plot during her absence from the island. In 1 case, the son of an intestate allottee has rented out his father's holding during his absence overseas to an unrelated person; the rentier's two full sisters who live near the settlement have thus been denied access and occupancy; the rentier is alleged to have acted in this way on the grounds that as the only son in frequent contact with Carriacou he is responsible for maintaining the holding in its undivided state until other absent heirs return for its distribution. These cases are sufficient indication of the range of eligibility of claims to an intestate inheritance, and of the scope for interpretation and redefinition which the situation permits. To understand the processes and forms of intestate succession to land, it is therefore necessary to examine their demographic basis, the incidence of subsequent deaths among heirs, and their location. The conditions reviewed in this way are directly comparable with some of the data already discussed in relation to testamentary disposition.

In 16 of the 38 cases of initial intestacy, there have been no subsequent deaths within the families concerned. In 6 cases, 5 of these involving the allottee's widow, there has been 1 death each; in 4 cases there have been 2 deaths subsequent to that of the initial landholder;

in another 4 cases there have been 3, in 2 cases there have been 5 deaths, in one case 6, and in another 7. All these deaths have involved material alteration in the relation of the heirs to the inheritance. None has been preceded by preparation of a will.

Of the intestate initial allottees, 6 were women, whose illegitimate and legitimate children inherit equally. Of the intestate allottees of both sexes, 1 woman and 4 men left no surviving issue. Sixteen of the plots transmitted under intestacy were controlled by their holders' widows at the time of survey, and 3 of these widows were abroad, 2 with their entire families.

Excluding the illegitimate issue of intestate males, there were 53 male and 40 female heirs of the first generation living overseas in 1953, with inheritance claims on these 44 unwilled plots. There were also 36 male and 21 female heirs of the second generation, giving a total of 150 absent heirs, or 3.4 per plot, three-fifths of them being males. Excluding those 5 cases in which original holders died childless, in 3 of the remaining 33 cases no heir was absent from Carriacou at the time of survey, as against 5 cases in which no heir was in the island. As compared with the data relating to testate succession, there can be little doubt that migrancy of heirs is greater under intestacy.

Of the 534 legitimate descendants of testate landholders, 399, or 75 per cent, live in Carriacou. Of the 522 legitimate descendants of intestate landholders, 299, or 57 per cent, live in the island. It seems difficult to account for such marked differences in the emigration rates of these two inheritance groups, except in terms of the modes and conditions of these two forms of inheritance themselves.

Reregistration of portions of land inherited under conditions of intestacy would indicate assertion of intention to exercise rights individually. Such registration involves having the land in question placed under the name of its claimant on the roll which government compiles for purposes of tax assessment and collection. It amounts to a formal, though indirect, method of serving notice on other claimants to the portion that appropriation is proceeding. As such reregistration provides some measure of the tensions associated with inheritance with and without wills. Attempts at such reregistration have occurred on 2 of the 44 plots inherited under intestacy, as against 5 of the 37 plots inherited under will. These data suggest that the greater mobility of heirs under intestacy is linked with the greater security of tenure which this mode of inheritance provides, and its more permissive context.

The frequency with which women survive their husbands, and the rights of administration which these widows have, make it quite likely that subdivision of the estate among heirs will be preceded by the widow's administration. Hence the position of widows in intestate suc-

cession is of special interest. As has been shown, these women sometimes make wills when they wish to exercise influence over the subdivision after their death. Although these wills are technically invalid,
they may go unchallenged. Widows of intestate husbands who have
left issue of either birth status have no power of alienation or right
to rent the land without the heirs' consent. If neither the widow nor
her intestate husband has any lawful offspring, but both have illegitimate children, then the widow in charge of an intestate inheritance
may rent the land or leave her children in charge, but cannot sell it.
If the intestate holder has only left illegitimate children, and these
assert their claims, then the widow has no right to place the land in
charge of persons not related to its original holder, nor may she will
it away. Only if there are no surviving issue of the holder is she free
to will the land as she pleases, or, as happened in 3 cases of intestate
disposition, to sell some or all of it.

Land held in their own right by women who die intestate and
without issue is inherited by their "adopted" daughters, if any, or
failing them, by their mothers, their full sisters, or sisters' children.
Normally however, such women, unless they have an "adopted" daughter linked to them by ties of uterine kinship, will dispose of their
holdings while alive.

8. THE EFFECTS OF TESTATE AND INTESTATE SUCCESSION ON HOLDINGS

The relative effects of these two types of inheritance on the fragmentation of allotments is shown in table 14. In this table data on the
distribution and number of actual occupancies current in 1953 are
compared with the distribution possible, had all persons with direct
and incontrovertible claims under will or folk custom been holding
land on the settlement.

On an average, there are 2 occupancies to each holding inherited
under intestacy, while there are 3 occupancies per willed holding. For
both types of inheritance, the number of actual occupancies is only
half of those possible.

The 119 actual occupancies on these 38 willed holdings were distributed among 41 males and 78 females. The 89 occupancies under
intestacy were held by 27 males and 62 females. Thus there were in
1953 twice as many female occupants as males, while 50 years before
when the settlement was established there were 7 male allottees for
each female. This trend toward female predominance in occupancy is
partly an effect of higher rates of emigration among males, partly of
widowhood; but it must not be taken to indicate parallel disparity in
the areas controlled by the sexes. There are numerous cases in which a
resident male occupies a portion equal to and sometimes greater than

those of all his sisters together. Data on the size of the areas actually occupied in 1953 repay study.

TABLE 14

ACTUAL AND POSSIBLE OCCUPANCIES OF HOLDINGS INHERITED UNDER TESTACY AND INTESTACY AT HARVEY VALE IN 1953

Occupancies per holding	Intestate succession				Testate succession			
	Holdings		Occupancies		Holdings		Occupancies	
	Actual	Possible	Actual	Possible	Actual	Possible	Actual	Possible
1a (no issue)	4	4	4	4	—	—	—	—
1b (undivided)	17	5	17	5	3	—	3	—
1 Occupancy*	21	9	21	9	3	—	3	—
2 "	12	1	24	2	16	—	32	—
3 "	7	10	21	30	9	2	27	6
4 "	1	6	4	24	4	5	16	20
5 "	1	6	5	30	—	11	—	55
6 "	1	4	6	24	2	7	12	42
7 "	—	3	—	21	3	9	21	63
8 "	1	2	8	16	1	—	8	—
9 "	—	—	—	—	—	2	—	18
10 "	—	2	—	20	—	—	—	—
11 "	—	—	—	—	—	—	—	—
12 "	—	—	—	—	—	1	—	12
13 "	—	1	—	13				
14 plus	—	—	—	—	—	1	—	19
Totals	44	44	89	189	38	38	119	235

* Sum of 1a and 1b.

When tables 14 and 15 are studied together the principal features of the processes by which land is distributed and occupied become clear. These 82 inherited plots represent an area of approximately 200 acres, averaging about 2.5 acres each. The actual occupancies come to 208, or slightly less than half the number possible. The average area of these actual occupancies is thus about 1 acre. In the 50 years since the settlement was established, the size of occupancies on these plots has shrunk to two-fifths of the original. These data indicate the types of calculation which are necessary if holdings on a land settlement are to be maintained at something like their original level, by further allocations of surplus land.

Of these 208 occupancies, 16.4 per cent are less than a quarter of an acre in size, excluding house spots. Another 22.1 per cent are under half an acre, and a further 15 per cent under three-fourths of an acre, giving a total of 53.5 per cent of the actual occupancies. Only 22, or less than 11 per cent of the 208 occupancies in 1953, are as large as the original average-size plot of 2.5 acres. If this calculation

TABLE 15

ACTUAL OCCUPANCIES AT HARVEY VALE IN 1953 CLASSIFIED BY SIZE AND
MODE OF INHERITANCE

| | Occupancies under: | | |
Acreage	Intestate succession	Testate succession	Total
0 to ¼	5	29	34
¼ to ½	9	39	48
½ to ¾	24	7	31
¾ to 1	6	14	20
1 to 1½	21	15	36
1½ to 2	9	8	17
2 to 3	9	4	13
3 plus	6	3	9
Total	89	119	208

appears rather dismal, it is all the more necessary to keep in mind
that the number of actual occupancies is only half the immediately
possible total; and to remember that the number is as low as it is,
partly because of migrancy, which such inadequate holdings may
themselves stimulate, and partly because of the convention which
limits the inheritance rights of a man's illegitimate issue.

Of the occupancies on holdings inherited under will, 48 per cent are
half an acre or less in size, as compared with 15 per cent on holdings
inherited without will. Conversely, less than 6 per cent of the occupancies on willed holdings are 2 acres or more in size, as compared
with 17 per cent under intestacy. There can be no doubt from these
data that testamentary disposition has a far higher correlation with
the fragmentation of holdings by occupancies than does intestacy. Indeed, wills may well accelerate the atomization of plots. As shown
above, wills record or initiate departures from folk convention with
regard to land tenure and transmission, and in their formal aspects
present rich fields for chicanery and dispute. Stimuli of this type cannot fail to arouse strong reactions, and those of a defensive nature
include the occupation by unimportant heirs of the very small areas
devised to them to prevent their possible expropriation by the executor or major beneficiaries under the will. Intestacy neither presents
such formal grounds of tension, nor such opportunities for unequal
divisions among heirs to become permanent, since family consensus
is necessary before the division can be made. Hence, under intestacy
claimants entitled to microscopic shares such as a quarter of an acre
are more likely to look elsewhere than to press their claims.

The 119 occupants of willed holdings are 22 per cent of the total

legitimate issue of the original holders of these plots. The 89 occupants of plots held under intestacy are less than 17 per cent of the
legitimate claimants. Both these occupancy totals represent almost
exactly 30 per cent of the number of legitimate claimants under each
category who were in Carriacou at the time of survey.

Occupancy under rent or arrangements by which the occupant
"takes care" of the land are more common on holdings inherited without will than on willed holdings. Excluding rented house spots, 4 occupancies on unwilled holdings were held by rent, and 3 of these involved
undivided holdings; there were no such rentals on plots disposed of
by will. There were 6 occupancies involving "caretaker" arrangements on unwilled plots, 5 of these applying to undivided holdings,
as against 1 on plots transmitted by will. It is clear that intestate
disposition facilitates the retention of plots without division to a
greater degree than testacy.

Of the 6 living holders of plots by secondary purchase, who were
absent from Carriacou in 1953, 2 left their wives in charge, 2 their
mothers, 1 a sister, and 1 the father of his wife, who initiated and conducted the purchase in the holder's absence. None of these 6 absentees
had rented out his plot. Rental at Harvey Vale is therefore found only
on plots inherited without will.

9. THE AGGREGATION OF OCCUPANCIES

The number of occupancies on the settlement substantially exceeds the number of occupants. This is so because the fragmentation
of holdings by occupancy permits, and is accompanied by, individual
control of several occupancies. The processes and effects involved are
discussed here as aspects of aggregation. Aggregation applies to holdings by right or claim, as well as to the occupancy of such holdings.
As has been pointed out, the distribution of allotments on the settlement was itself accompanied by individual aggregation of holdings.
Inheritance and purchase have allowed this process to continue with
regard to holdings by right, in the same way that caretaker arrangements, rent, and the exercise of occupancy rights by dependent claimants on behalf of absent principals have permitted aggregation of
occupancies. Fragmentation of allotments and the dispersal of occupancy rights are therefore quite distinct, and the former entails nothing directly about the latter. A careful statement of the forms and
measures of aggregation with regard to occupancies and holdings is
thus essential to an accurate description and analysis of the present
distribution of land. Table 16 summarizes the distribution of these
multiple individual occupancies on the settlement in 1953. Table 17
completes the picture of these individual accumulations by showing

how they are distributed according to size and inheritance status of the holdings involved.

TABLE 16

MULTIPLE INDIVIDUAL OCCUPANCIES AT HARVEY VALE IN 1953, CLASSIFIED BY INHERITANCE STATUS OF THE HOLDINGS INVOLVED

Type of data	Holdings inherited		Total	Remarks
	Without wills	Under wills		
Allotments involved	32	16	48	—
Occupancies involved	39	33	72	
Occupants by sex:				
Male	7	5	12	
Female	10	7	17	Total = 29
Occupancies by occupant's sex:				
Number of male occupancies	16	17	33	
Number of female occupancies	23	16	39	
Area of male occupancies (acres)	22.50	23.75	46.25	Av. = 1.4 acres
Area of female occupancies (acres)	30.50	27.75	58.25	Av. = 1.5 acres
Area of all occupancies (acres)	53	51.50	104.50	Av. = 1.45 acres
The individual aggregates:				
Av. size of individual aggregate	3.125 acres	4.25 acres	—	Av. = 3.75 acres
No. of occupancies by right	21	20	41	
Area of occupancies by right	23.50 acres	25 acres	48.50 acres	
Occupancies held by rent	2	—	2	
Occupancies held as caretakers	10	10	20	
Occupancies held by dependent claims	6	3	9	
Multiple occupants without plots of their own:				
Males	2	2	4	
Females	1	—	1	

Table 16 describes the forms and effects of the processes by which individuals have accumulated occupancies at Harvey Vale. In every case the multiple occupancy includes one or more inherited plots or portions. The decisive significance of inheritance distributions for individual aggregation of holdings and occupancies is thus clear. The difference between the numbers of occupancies and occupants should be equally so. The 29 multiple occupants between them control 72 occupancies, with an average of 2.5 occupancies per person. Making allowance for these, there are only 165 individual occupancies on the 82 plots which have been subject to inheritance, as against 208 such areas. The reduction in size of areas occupied individually on these plots during the past 50 years is thus by half, and not by three-fifths as it would seem without taking these multiple holdings into account.

As regards the relation of these processes of individual accumulation to the two different modes of inheritance, in 1953 the 44 unwilled holdings were occupied by 66 individuals, whereas the 38 willed holdings were occupied by 98 individuals. On an average there were twice as many occupants per plot inherited under will as under intestacy. The fragmentation of holdings among occupants by will is thus twice as high as under intestacy.

TABLE 17

DISTRIBUTION OF INDIVIDUAL AGGREGATES ACCORDING TO SIZE AND
TYPE OF INHERITANCE INVOLVED AT HARVEY VALE IN 1953

Aggregates by Acres	Holdings inherited		Total
	Without wills	Under wills	
−1	2	1	3
1–2	3	2	5
2–3	5	1	6
3–4	2	—	2
4–5	3	4	7
5–6	—	1	1
6–7	1	1	2
7–8	—	1	1
8–9	1	1	2
Total	17	12	29

The areas controlled through individual aggregation of occupancies are relatively large. This means that the average size of occupancies held by other persons on the settlement may be substantially less than the average of all occupancies under inheritance, which was approximately 1 acre. The 104.5 acres controlled by the 29 multiple occupants include 6.5 acres off the settlement. Allowing for this, 98 of the 252 acres allotted at Harvey Vale were controlled by 29 persons in 1953. The remaining 154 acres were then distributed among 149 persons, averaging 1 acre each. But if plots not yet subject to inheritance are excluded, there are 135 other claimants occupying the remaining 102 acres of inherited land, giving about three-quarters of an acre per person. Either of these averages is low compared with that of 3.75

acres per individual with multiple occupancies. Their comparison indicates the measure and form of competition for control of land. Only 41 of the 72 portions controlled by multiple occupants are held by these individuals in their own right. Half as many again are occupied under caretaker arrangements, and the majority of the remainder under claims for future inheritance.

Of the individuals controlling multiple occupancies, 1 in 6 holds no land on the settlement in his own right. The total area controlled by the 29 multiple occupants is twice as large as that which this group holds in its own right. Of the 17 females with multiple occupancies, 10 are widows, who hold claims or rights to some of their fathers' plots as well as life interests in those of their husbands.

By far the most impressive feature of these multiple occupancies is the fact that all the individuals who control them are members of one or another of the 13 patrilineages which between them obtained 67 of the 81 initial allocations on the settlement. To some degree, as the proportion of widows among females who control multiple occupancies suggests, this accumulation of occupancies by the major lineages of the settlement has been facilitated by the intermarriage of its population. Yet this intermarriage should lead to the transfer of plots away from these lineages as well as toward them if transfer proceeded randomly, uninfluenced by structural factors. Similarly, under the prevailing norms of bilateral inheritance of land, it is reasonable to expect that transfers of control of land from these lineages would occur as frequently as transfers to them in all cases where lineage members and strangers had married. That this is patently not the case itself indicates the influences that prevent it.

Five of the multiple occupants lacking land in their own right are members of these prominent lineages. That this should be so indicates that the settlement population regards the exercise of interest by these lineages as providing a good measure of security in the tenure of land. These five lineage members controlling multiple occupancies, all of which belong to other persons, exercise occupancy rights as caretakers over land held by lesser lineages, affines, and unrelated persons alike. It therefore appears likely that landholders exercising their rights in association with the dominant families of the settlement enjoy greater assurance of peaceful tenure than they may otherwise expect, since the majority of contemporary holders lack legal title or proof of right. But at the same time these expectations and the system of social relations with which they harmonize guarantee that progressive accumulations of control of land by the principal lineages will take place. Moreover, because these lineage interests provide a stable basis for security of tenure, they operate to assist the displacement of legal forms by the folk conventions which define them.

10. CONCLUSION

I shall now summarize the more important findings of this paper as they relate specifically to Carriacou, and conclude with one or two more general observations.

1) After 50 years, over 60 per cent of the settlement land is now held under a system of customary tenure by persons whose titles are obscure and may well be invalid at law.

2) A substantially higher percentage of the transfers of rights to land on this settlement do not satisfy the conditions of legally valid transfer.

3) The processes by which customary tenure displaces the official legal system are cumulative and one-way.

4) The rate at which this displacement occurs is high on this settlement, and affects over 60 per cent of all occupancies after 50 years, or approximately two generations.

5) Unfamiliarity with legal forms and processes, coupled with their expensiveness and uncertainties, contributes to this progressive abandonment of legal tenure.

6) The rate and scale of population increase dominate the holding and occupancy of land on the settlement, and in quite specific ways.

7) Increasing pressure of population on land is mediated through a system of conventions, attitudes, and values which informs the customary system of tenure and gives it a different content and set of procedures from that of the law.

8) The conventions, attitudes, and values of this folk system are directly related to the social organization, and to the frequencies with which different types of circumstance or condition arise within the society.

9) This complex of folk attitudes reduces the number of effective claims under inheritance by conventions about legitimacy, marriage, widowhood, and especially absenteeism. It provides for a ranking of claims in terms of priorities, and also for the flexible adjustment of claims according to the circumstances involved. It therefore serves to organize the allocation of land rights in forms consistent with the social organization of the folk, and with the relative positions of claimants within that organization.

10) This complex of folk custom further restricts the tendency or power of landholders to alienate their land to folk not already on the settlement, and thereby inhibits the development of those attitudes toward alienation and conveyancing which are essential to the performance of legally valid sales, and to individualism of tenure.

11) Folk custom defines partnership in landholding as a relation which continues between the heirs of the original partners.

12) This customary system restricts the desire to make wills concerning land by removing the necessity or value of such dispositions, except where deviations from the folk norms of inheritance are at issue, or previous transactions are recorded. The innovations which wills seek to make normally involve departures from folk norms of intestate succession, while the facts which they record redefine the holder's claims to land.

13) The complex of folk attitudes to land inheritance further restricts action to record or execute such wills as have been made, thereby accelerating the return of testamentary dispositions to the norms of folk inheritance.

14) Inheritance under the law by will, and under custom without will, differ in their effects and functions, as well as in their form.

15) Inheritance under will seems to be more closely associated with greater tensions over land among heirs than inheritance under intestacy. These more severe tensions of willed disposition are expressed in lower degrees of migrancy of heirs and in higher degrees of fragmentation of the estates by occupancy than are to be found on those plots inherited without will.

16) Intestate succession stimulates no effort to formalize the inheritance at law, nor does it usually lead to permanent subdivisions of the holdings, since many of the heirs and claimants are typically absent, and such subdivision requires their consent. Instead it facilitates individual aggregation of control over land, but also enjoins the rotation of occupancies as circumstances require. Both these developments are only possible because the ownership of particular sections of the inherited land is imprecisely defined in the first place. Both these developments occur together and in association with the expansion of control over much of the area by its major kinship groups.

17) The extension of interest and control over land by these major kinship groups functions to stabilize the transmission and tenure of rights for all concerned, and in this way provides much the same advantages that are offered by the form and process of law, but without expense, and with more flexibility.

18) Intestacy, absenteeism, accumulation, and the exercise of supervisory functions by large kin groups all involve trusteeship norms and obligations which are opposed to the code of individual tenure as laid down in the legal system. These obligations and rights of trusteeship provide a realistic and flexible adaptation of the folk to their circumstances, especially to their conditions of high population increase and migrancy on the one hand, and low incomes and little land on the other. The adaptive values of the folk norms in these circumstances are greater than those offered by the law.

19) As a rule, married men in Carriacou are survived by their wives,

and the folk attitudes to marriage and widowhood tend to restrain will-making by men whose wives are alive. Together these conditions have a profound effect on the distribution of land occupancies, and also on the norms of folk tenure and inheritance. Together with the differing sex patterns of emigration, this high widowhood rate involves progressive elimination of males from actual occupancy of the majority of plots, although rights to such occupancy often continue to be traced through males. The widow's control of her late husband's plot normally starts with his intestacy, and concludes with her own. In other ways increase of female occupancy of land also promotes the increase of intestacy.

The transformation of land rights we have been discussing consists in a changeover from rights in things defined and sanctioned by law to rights or claims against persons, defined or sanctioned by custom. In the process the negative relations which constitute rights *in rem* have been replaced by the positive relations which constitute rights *in personam*. The changes in form of right are thus complex and important.

It will now be clear that the development and character of a system of customary tenure such as that just analyzed can only be understood in terms of its functions within the social context of the population which supports it. It should also be clear that detailed study of the *processes* by which rights in land have been transmitted within a population over a sufficient number of years alone can provide the data essential for understanding of its current *forms* of tenure, their development and their functions. In such a study, special attention must first be devoted to the demographic situation, then to those cultural conventions which define the range and relative priorities of claims, and finally to the relation between these two sets of variables.

In the light of such a study, problems of function and development dovetail, and give rise to conclusions of practical significance. For example, if the development and character of the system of customary tenure at Harvey Vale is only intelligible in terms of its social context, then so long as that social context retains its former character, the customary forms of tenure will continue to develop and flourish.

[11

Structure and Crisis in Grenada, 1950–1954

From 1950 to 1954, Grenada society was in a crisis. The structural bases of social order were challenged and shaken rudely. At one time the future of the society seemed rather obscure. The background, course, and implications of this crisis form the subject of this essay. Since this crisis was coextensive with Grenadian society, it provides excellent case material for the study of structural conflict and change, and may thus possess general significance. I shall accordingly describe the background of these events before relating and analyzing them.

1. CONTEXT

Habitat and Economy

Grenada is a hilly island of about 120 square miles, lying 12 degrees north and 61 degrees west, nearly 90 miles north of Trinidad and 70 miles southwest of St. Vincent. It is pear-shaped with a maximum length of 20 miles, and width of 12. The interior consists of mountains rising to 2,750 feet in the north. Geysers and crater lakes evidence former volcanic activity. Lavas in the interior soils give high fertility. Ash, turf, and agglomerates are found at the coast. The little level land is scattered in uneconomic parcels.

Northward, between St. Vincent and Grenada, lies a chain of tiny rocks and islets, known as the Grenadines. Of these, the largest, Carriacou, has an area of 13 square miles and a population of about 7,000. Carriacou is the northern limit of Grenada colony, and its largest dependency. Grenada and Carriacou differ sharply in economy and social structure, reflecting their differences of topography, climate, and history. The Carriacou island-spine is less than 1,000 feet. Rain

262

falls there between May and October and varies between 30 and 50 inches per annum. Grenada sometimes receives rain on 270 days in a year, and in the center of the island its average incidence is well over 100 inches. Even so, the southern tip of Grenada averages no more rain than Carriacou.

With this favorable climate and fertile soil, Grenada is well suited to agriculture, but the rugged terrain discourages large-scale cultivation. Slopes are too steep and conditions too variable for comparative assessments of cultivation costs and returns to be generally useful. With slave-labor, it is true that planters produced large crops of sugarcane between 1770 and 1830. The profitability of this enterprise is another question. Slavery was abolished in 1838 and imperial preferences on West Indian sugar were withdrawn between 1846 and 1854. The Grenadian sugar industry then declined rapidly, and by 1870 it had ceased to support the local economy. Sugar production virtually disappeared; and it was only after the island experienced a severe sugar shortage during the First World War that its government sought to revive the industry to supply the colony's needs. In consequence, the drier, low-lying southern area was put under cane-cultivation by a locally financed company which enjoyed government protection, and a factory was built at Woburn in 1935.

In 1946, of approximately 70,000 acres in Grenada, 8,500 were rain forest, 7,000 were pasture, 3,000 were waste, 11,000 were arable reserves, and 40,000 were under cultivation, according to the agricultural census.[1] An official estimate of crop-acreages in 1952–1953 gives the following figures: cocoa, 15,379 acres; nutmegs, 11,087 acres; coconuts, 4,638 acres; sugarcane, 1,800 acres; citrus, mainly limes, 1,200 acres; food crops, 7,200 acres; giving a total of about 41,000 acres under crops.[2] Despite attempts to replant cocoa during this period, the agricultural economy was fairly static. In 1952–1953 also, local livestock were estimated as 7,500 cattle, 6,000 horses, donkeys, or mules, about 9,000 sheep and goats, and 7,500 pigs.

Locally grown staple foods include maize; pigeon and other peas and legumes; tania, dasheen, and other eddoes; various types of yams; cassava; bluggoes and other varieties of plantain; pumpkins, okras, and other vegetables; breadfruit, avocado pear, and other tree crops, including the usual West Indian fruits: mango, guava, sapodilla, cherimoya, pawpaw, and so forth. Off-shore fishing, especially on the leeward side, supplies popular articles of diet; jacks, covally, snapper, grouper, rockhind, and kingfish being the main varieties.

The main Grenadian exports are cocoa, nutmegs, mace, copra, lime-oil, and cotton, of which only the last two items come from Carriacou. All cocoa and nutmeg crops are marketed locally; but export may be delayed by movements of price in the world market. Lacking reliable figures for the annual production of these and other crops, we may use annual export values to indicate their place in the local economy.

The significance of overseas price fluctuations is evident from table 18. In 1952 Grenada exported 54,000 cwt. of cocoa, as against 61,000

TABLE 18

VALUES OF EXPORT STAPLES, GRENADA, 1950–1953
(in millions of dollars, BWI)

Year	1 Cocoa	2 Nutmeg	3 Mace	4 Cotton	Total 1–4	Total of exports	1–4 as % of all exports
1950	$2.43	$3.22	$0.73	$0.12	$6.5	$7.02	92.6
1951	3.58	1.43	0.75	0.08	5.79	6.65	88.0
1952	3.54	1.54	0.78	0.11	6.01	6.80	88.0
1953	3.85	1.40	0.88	0.11	6.26	7.03	89.2

cwt. in 1953, but received an almost identical return. Nutmeg exports, being controlled by a producers' coöperative association, which purchases the entire local crop for sale abroad, reflects these overseas price changes even more clearly. In 1952 and 1953 nutmeg exports declined from 44,000 cwt. to 37,000 cwt., while exports of mace remained steady at 6,900 cwt. and 7,500 cwt.; but exports of nutmeg oil rose from 3,140 lbs. to 10,260 lbs. In both years the return from these nutmeg products was about $2.3 million (BWI).

Lime exports—juice and oil—realized $92,000 and $99,000 in 1952 and 1953, almost all deriving from Carriacou. In 1953 a modern factory began processing coconut oil for local use, and thus reduced the export trade in copra. In consequence, copra exports fell from 9,334 cwt. in 1952, valued at $153,000 BWI, to 2,715 cwt. valued at $40,000 the next year. Meanwhile the local factory produced 35,500 gallons of coconut oil, and raised the output of coconut meal from 170,000 lbs. to 340,000 lbs. Sugar production at the local factory rose from 1,600 tons in 1952 to 2,100 tons in the following year, but the output of rum remained level at 67,000 gallons. In comparison with cocoa and nutmeg, the other crops are clearly secondary. In 1950–1954 cultivation of cocoa and nutmeg for export provided the basis of the Grenadian economy.

Grenadians typically intercrop cocoa, nutmeg, and bluggoes or bananas. The bluggoes and bananas shade the growing cocoa and nutmeg plants. In between these trees tanias and other root crops may be grown so that the same field yields incomes in cash and kind. Besides nutmeg, Grenada also produces other spices such as vanilla and cloves. Grenadians justly describe their home as the "isle of spice."

According to the 1946 census, of the island's 69,000 acres, 4,000 were held by the Crown as a forest reserve; 40,000 acres were in 116 parcels of 100 acres or more by individuals or families who often held more than one parcel.[3] In addition, there were 4,800 plots of less than one acre each, 4,900 ranging between one and five acres, 1,200 holdings between five and twenty acres, and another 200 between 20 and 100 acres in size. This was much the same distribution as obtained in 1952–1953 when about 10,000 plots below 25 acres in size occupied a total of 18,600 acres, giving an average of 1.8 acres per plot, as compared with an average of 344 acres per "estate" of 100 acres or more. Clearly, land ownership is highly concentrated, despite its wide distribution, and access to land may be a problem.

Some implications of this pattern of land distribution are indicated in table 19, which relates data on government revenues and taxable private incomes to the gross domestic products for 1950–1953.

TABLE 19

NATIONAL, GOVERNMENT, AND PRIVATE INCOMES FOR GRENADA, 1950–1953
(in millions of dollars, BWI)

	1950		1951		1952		1953	
	$	Nos.	$	Nos.	$	Nos.	$	Nos.
Gross domestic product	13.524*	—	No data		15.0**	—	16.2**	—
Total government revenue	3.651	—	3.942	—	3.878	—	3.907	—
Gross taxable incomes	3.496	1,708	4.342	1,895	5.664	2,404	5.390	2,492
Company incomes	.653	61	.734	56	.716	56	.804	54
Private incomes	2.845	1,647	3.608	1,839	4.948	2,348	4.586	2,438
Private landed proprietors	.716	352	1.266	461	1.982	673	1.442	596
Total income tax levied	.378	—	.548	—	.671	—	.643	—

* Nora M. Siffleet, "National Income and National Accounts," *Social Economic Studies*, Vol. 1, No. 3, (1953), pp. 104–110.
** Personal communication from Dr. Carleen O'Loughlin, Institute of Social and Economic Research, U.C.W.I., Jamaica.

The occupational structure of Grenada society reflects this distribution of land rights and primary agricultural interests. Of a population estimated at some 83,000 in 1952–1953, the labor force was reckoned at 29,000, and of these about 8,500 were fully wage-employed. Of these 8,500, 5,600 worked in agriculture, the great majority on the 105 extant "estates"; another 500 prepared nutmegs for export, 1,400 found occasional employment on government public works, and about 1,000 were employed in commerce and trade.[4] However, this classification omits workers in domestic and other personal services, of whom 2,124 and 486 respectively were enumerated in the 1946 census, together with workers in the government numbering 486; "professions," 897; transport and communications, 641; construction, 3,348; factories and workshops, 3,980; fishing, forestry, and quarrying, 495. It also excludes peasants who undertake no wagework. Elsewhere, we learn that in 1952–1953 about 33,000 Grenadians lived on farms, about 19,000 of these being engaged in farm work, two-thirds of the latter as own-account or unpaid family workers. This occupational structure and distribution reflects the basic agricultural interests and land distribution outlined above.

History

From 1650 when the French colonized Grenada until 1674, when the French government assumed control, the island was held by the French West India Company, but made little progress. Under the French government, development was pursued with more vigor, and the immigrant population rose from 835 in 1700 to 13,900 in 1753, by which time the indigenous Carib Indians had been fully dispossessed, and local planters had switched from cultivating indigo to sugar with some coffee and cocoa. In 1762 the British under Rodney took the island, which remained in their hands after the Peace of Paris in 1763. In 1778, during the War of American Independence, a French fleet under d'Estaing took the island again, but the settlement of 1783 restored Grenada to the British, perhaps because its native French planters had begun to move to Trinidad, following an invitation by the Spanish governor of that island.

On resuming control, the British sought to increase sugar production by increasing the import of slaves, by new capital investments, and by making the capital, St. George's, a free port in 1787. French colonists in the island continued to enjoy civil and property rights, despite their Catholicism. After the Revolution of 1789 had begun in France, West Indian territories with French backgrounds were disturbed by new ideas which some men tried to translate into fact. First Haiti revolted, the slaves seizing independence. Then Victor Hugues established a revolutionary government in Guadeloupe from a base in Martinique. The British moved against these upheavals with limited success. In Haiti they suffered defeat. In 1794 they seized Martinique, Guadeloupe, and St. Lucia, but soon lost Guadeloupe.

In 1795 revolt broke out in Grenada, the leader being a native planter of mixed Negro-French descent, Julien Fedon. Fedon's lieutenants were also mixed-bloods, but they received some support from the blacks, most of whom were more at home with French culture and language, than with British. Under prevailing laws, civil and political rights held for Europeans only, so that free colored and black folk suffered severe disabilities. Fedon's revolt may thus have aimed at replacing white rulers by free colored and blacks. But the triumphant slave revolt in Haiti, and the revolutionary ideas of freedom and equality, could hardly avoid encouraging slave support.

The conspiracy was well organized. British colonists and officials were surprised and overrun. Their property was seized, their persons abused, their worst fears realized. Fifty-one Britons were held as hostages at Fedon's mountain camp. When this was attacked, forty-eight of them were killed. For the next fifteen months, Fedon ravaged Grenada, but did not manage to rule it. In June, 1796, his camp was overwhelmed by the British. Fedon himself escaped, and was not found. Of his accomplices thirty-eight were caught, tried, and executed, the state appropriating all their estates. All French proprietors who supported the revolt, and several others suspected of collusion, lost their property to the Crown. The civil liberties formerly enjoyed by French colonists were severely curtailed. Mixed-bloods continued to lack political rights and to suffer civil disabilities. Fedon's revolt thus had the effect of eliminating the French planter class as a distinctive social unit. Thereafter the planters were mainly British, as were the law and pattern of colonial government, and the established church was Anglican.

Fedon's revolt remains difficult to interpret because adequate records are lacking. That some free colored Grenadians of French culture hoped to improve their position by seizing control of the island for revolutionary France seems clear. Whether, if successful, this mulatto elite would, or could, have maintained slavery we cannot guess. That they received some slave support is certain; how much we do not know. The British however became alert to possible insurrections, and in 1802, 1806, and 1816 called out the island militia in unfulfilled expectations of slave revolt.

In 1808 the British prohibited the slave trade in their territories. By then there were 25,000 slaves in a total Grenadian population of 29,000. In 1832 the free black and colored elements were given civil rights, and Roman Catholics were also permitted to enter the Colonial Legislature. This Assembly exercised considerable power; it had 26 members elected by and from a roll of 136. In the two northern parishes 8 persons elected 6 from among themselves to the Assembly. In 1834, under British Imperial law, the first steps were taken to emancipate the slaves. The government of the United Kingdom undertook to compensate colonial slaveowners for their slaves, who were required to undergo a transitional period of six years' "apprenticeship" between full slavery and freedom. After a brief experience of this "apprenticeship," the interval was reduced to four years, and on August 1, 1838, the slaves became legally free.

The New Labor Pattern

Emancipation introduced a period of economic and political decline for Grenada. The colonial chronicle records:

The effect of freedom upon the African in Grenada seems to have been to fill him with a distaste for regular labour on the sugar estates for fixed

wages. The quantity of uncultivated land in the interior of the island, and
the ease with which it could be bought, rented, or, from his point of view,
squatted upon, caused the establishment almost immediately of numerous
"gardens" therein. . . . Cultivation of the mountain gardens by the labourers
led to the extension of cocoa planting, an industry better suited to their in-
dolent disposition than sugar-cane or coffee. . . . The metayer system was
introduced in 1848 on many estates, and to some extent proved a remedy, but
the very inferior cultivation given to the cane under this system prevented its
general development.[5]

The oligarchy of white planters and merchants continued to mo-
nopolize legislative functions and to oppose expatriate officials. Attempts were made to modernize the local economy, for example, by
creating a colonial bank; these efforts were costly failures. Most local
estates were owned by people in Britain who were in debt to merchants there. Unable to meet these charges, the owners progressively
abandoned their estates. Withdrawal of British imperial protection for
West Indian sugar between 1846 and 1854 accelerated this process. In
1856 Grenada contained forty-seven abandoned sugar estates, and
another nine on the eve of change.

Many of these did not entirely remain waste, as their mountain lands were
being cultivated in patches by the negroes in cocoa, coffee, and provisions.
In some cases this was upon the metayer system, modified for cocoa by the
further provision that in a certain number of years the proprietor resumed
possession of his land with full-bearing cocoa trees thereon, and gave the
labourer a fresh "garden" on another spot.[6]

The trend by which cocoa replaced sugar as the staple export and
nutmeg production began, is indicated by the figures in table 20.
By 1856, when cocoa exports had passed the million-pound mark, the
future of cocoa as the main Grenadian export was assured.

TABLE 20

COCOA AND SUGAR EXPORTS, 1846 AND 1881*
(in lbs.)

	Sugar	Cocoa	Nutmegs
1846..............	9,196,538	376,686	—
1881..............	2,038,712	5,864,090	c. 100,000

* See *Grenada Handbook and Directory, 1946*, p. 51.

Grenadian sugar planters did not give in to these changes without
a struggle. Their reaction to the Emancipation Act of 1838 was to
withhold finances from the colonial administration for several months.
They organized powerful, if unavailing, propaganda for West Indian

sugar preferences in Britain. They tried to improve local methods of cultivation and supported currency reforms which the ill-fated Colonial Bank attempted to introduce. They sought new supplies of labor to replace ex-slaves who had quit the estates, and legislated to secure indentured laborers, first from Madeira in 1846–1847, and later from India. About 2,500 indentured Indians came to Grenada between 1857 and 1863. These imports added new elements to a population which was already racially complex.

The process by which cocoa replaced sugarcane has special significance for Grenadian society. Unprofitable sugar estates passed at knock-down rates from absentee owners to local managers who lacked the capital or credit to develop them. The new owners put their estates under cocoa by letting out plots with certain rights of usage to ex-slaves on condition that the tenants planted cocoa and bluggoes thereon. The proprietor resumed control of a plot when its cocoa began bearing, but normally gave the tenant another on identical terms. On some estates the tenants received token payments per bearing tree when returning the plot, but estate practice probably varied in this respect among others.

In return for planting and tending the young cocoa, worker-tenants had rights to all bluggoes on their plot; to cultivate ground provisions therein; to live on the estate rent free; to occupy small gardens near their homes; to rent other plots farther afield at nominal rates; to tether stock on the estate; to use its noncommercial food crops such as avocado, mangoes, breadfruit, or akee (*Blighia sapida*); to take dead-wood as fuel; in some cases to take fallen coconuts for home use; and to build or repair their houses with estate timbers. Bluggoes or plantains were also sold to worker-tenants at nominal rates by the estate. The tenants had first claim on any paid estate work. The proprietor was expected to purchase manure from their stock for use on his fields. At Easter, Christmas, and Cropover[7] or Emancipation Day (August 1), they would enjoy a fête and dance at the estate's expense. The proprietor provided playing space and gear for such sports as cricket. Estate workers had rights to hunt small game such as manicou (a rodent) on the estate. On returning from his periodic visit to Britain, the proprietor was expected to bring gifts to his "people," individually, and as a group. He was also expected to provide them with credit when needed, to settle their internal disputes, to stand as godfather (*compère*) for their children, and generally to support and assist them.

These arrangements were of benefit not only to the workers. Wage rates were low, and wage employment was subsumed in the wider socioeconomic relation between "planter" and "people." The former had on his estate an adequate labor supply available as necessary. The latter enjoyed free sources of subsistence which cushioned their low wage and underemployment. It is thus not surprising that these ties linked successive generations of planters and people on most estates. On a proprietor's death, his property passed en bloc to his legitimate children, and was usually managed for the group by a senior son. The children of estate workers lived with their parents, identified themselves with the estate as a community, had most of their close kin there, and generally remained there after their parents' death. Often owners and workers were linked by some ties of "affinal" or ritual kinship. Owners and managers generally had children by girls born on the estates. Social factors which overlaid the economic nexus between owner and worker on these estates ramified widely indeed. These conditions defined and preserved estates as local communities, recruited primarily by descent, and having a clear internal structure which balanced differences of status by reciprocal obligations and rights. Management described the workers' customary perquisites as "privileges." Workers saw them as essential elements in a nexus which was paternalistic and social rather than economic.[8] Thus "perquisite" for planter was worker's prerequisite.

This mode of estate operation is significant in a number of ways. It enabled Grenadian planters to switch their production from sugar to cocoa with a minimum expenditure of capital. It increased the availability of land to the workers in two ways. First, it gave them usufruct of lands being put under cultivation for cocoa. Second, it encouraged the rental or sale of lands unsuited to this crop. Many persons holding their own plots by rental or purchase worked other plots on estates under the conditions just described. "Peasant" tenure of land accordingly implied either purchase, informal inheritance, rental, or usufruct. The "peasantry" were thus a rather heterogeneous social category, many of whom held no land in their own name, whether by tenancy or ownership, while others owned substantial portions and only represented a group by contradistinction with the elite in status, culture, color, and power. Finally, this mode of estate operation restructured relations between management and labor on the estates and reduced their cash elements substantially. To supplement inadequate wage-payments, the tenant-laborer received land rights and other perquisites. Instead of maintaining slaves or contracting independent free labor, estates included families which drew their own subsistence from it and were available for employment under customary, rather than contractual, norms. Instead of free workers or slaves, the rural labor force now consisted of "peasants," as the tenant-workers were called. Instead of employers or slaveowners, management consisted of elite patrons or planters. The bond between master and slave, or employer and laborer, had become a relationship between patron and client on the one hand, between planter and peasant on the other.

Population Growth

The continuity of this accommodation presumed continuing balances between population growth, labor demand, and land availability. Without discussing the composition of Grenada's population at this stage, I shall try to indicate the main relationships between its growth and the Grenadian economic context.

Grenadians are not infertile. Since the cholera epidemic of 1854, migration to Trinidad and South America has been the major form of population control. Situated outside the earthquake belt and rarely visited by hurricanes, the island escapes those periodic natural disasters which stimulate sharp increases in labor demand. Since 1900 population has constantly tended to outstrip local land resources and labor demands, since by then most properties had already been put under cocoa and nutmeg cultivation or tree crops that require limited work for harvest or maintenance. By 1914 the local government had also established some "land settlements" to meet rising demands for land. These settlements were subdivisions of old estates which had remained derelict for various reasons.

In 1861 the local population was about 32,000, increasing to 37,700 in 1871, and to 42,400 ten years later, at which date one-third of the 9,000 adult male Grenadians were said to own some land. Between 1881 and 1946 population rose from 42,400 to 72,400, many Grenadians being then settled in Trinidad, Curaçao, Aruba, or on Venezuelan oil fields, these being the areas to which the local surplus population has moved in search of work. A devastating hurricane in 1921, following on the end of the First World War, restored some economic buoyancy by increasing the need for labor to replant lost trees, especially nutmegs. By 1936 the new trees were bearing, and the fall in labor demand, coupled with the population increase and the prevailing low prices for Grenadian staples, were having their effect. In 1952–1953 the colony had a population of about 83,000, of whom about 76,000 lived in Grenada island itself, and the rest in Carriacou. The rate of natural increase was then 2.1 per cent per annum; and Trinidad, the principal objective of Grenadian emigrants, was seeking to limit this inflow.

Government and Constitutional History

Under the "representative" constitution introduced by the British in the eighteenth century, only propertied whites were eligible to enter or elect members of the legislature. An upper chamber, mainly nominated by the governor, functioned as an advisory executive council.

Blacks and browns lacked political rights. This constitution persisted until 1875 when the legislature agreed to a limited change; but by 1877 the new legislature asked the British government to assume responsibility for the colonial administration and thus abolished itself, perhaps because higher taxation and a more liberal franchise seemed to offer the only alternatives to Crown Colony rule. As a Crown Colony, the next Grenadian legislature contained equal numbers of nominated and official members, and the franchise was completely abolished.

In 1925 this constitution was modified to permit a margin of elective representation on the basis of restricted property franchise. In 1936 the number of elected legislators was brought equal to those nominated by the governor. The Executive Council then consisted of three officials, namely, the administrator directly responsible for the colony, the attorney general, and the treasurer, together with such other persons as the governor cared to appoint. Under this constitution, the power to propose bills and ordinances was vested in the government. Elected members were free to criticize such proposals, but the government majority ensured legislative passage. In the general election of May, 1944, the last held under this constitution, 4,005 of about 27,000 adults in the colony were entitled by property qualifications to vote.

An intriguing dimension of Grenada's history is its changing "federal" involvements. These began in 1833 when the colony was included in a general government of the British Windward Islands, which then embraced St. Vincent, Tobago, and Barbados, the last being the seat of government. Under this arrangement Grenada was administered by a resident lieutenant-governor, responsible to the governor of the Windward Islands in Barbados. In 1838 St. Lucia joined the group. In 1882 Barbados was separated from the unit, and Dominica was brought in. Proposals for establishing a common council and administration were mooted without effect. In 1888 Tobago was transferred from the Windwards to the colony of Trinidad. In 1897 a royal commission suggested, without effect, that the Windwards should be federated with Barbados. By 1905 the Colonial Office was pursuing the more limited objective of uniting Grenada and St. Vincent in a single colony. This project also failed to mature. This record shows that under Crown Colony rule the British government was concerned to rationalize the administrations of these island-territories to reduce their expense and perhaps to increase the range and efficiency of their services. This program failed for various reasons, among them the fact that the islanders involved had no positive means of expressing their political interests.

With reintroduction of elective franchises in the British West Indies, a wider basis for federal associations became possible; and in 1946 representatives from the various British Caribbean units met under the leadership of Mr. Creech Jones, then colonial secretary, Britain, and formed a standing committee on closer association of the British West Indies. West Indian federation was in the air; and Grenada, represented by a long-standing federalist, the late T. A. Marryshow, gave its support to the scheme, the more readily perhaps because it hoped to provide the capital site. However, although negotiations on federation with other governments proceeded throughout the period under review, they had little immediate significance for developments in Grenada, except in stimulating those constitutional reforms, necessary if Grenada was to become part of an independent West Indian Federation.

Following on a decision of the island legislature in 1950, the colonial constitution was changed by an imperial order in council of August 1, 1951, which introduced universal suffrage and authorized new elections. These were held on October 10, 1951, when 69 per cent of the 34,133 eligible voters went to the polls with the results related below.

Under the constitution of 1951, the Legislative Council had as president the administrator in charge of Grenada, and contained two other ex officio members, the attorney general and the treasurer, besides three nominated and eight elected members. As president the administrator had a casting but no original vote. A deputy president was elected by council members to act in the administrator's absence. On matters of finance, the council constituted a standing committee, in which only unofficial members had votes. This committee discussed all expenditures which required approval by the council. The council could pass laws, known as ordinances, which were forwarded by the administrator to the governor of the Windward Islands, and by the latter to the Secretary of State for the Colonies in London who could suggest changes before they received royal assent. Changes of a constitutional nature required approval by the British Parliament, which also exercised a general supervision of local affairs through members' questions, motions, and other means.

The Windward Islands group continued to have a common governor, whose headquarters was Grenada, and whose office derived from letters patent. In 1950–1954, the group contained St. Lucia, St. Vincent, Grenada, and Dominica, each colony paying an equal share of the expenses of their common governor and officials. Each colony had a resident administrator, responsible to the governor for routine administration. The governor of the Windwards is forbidden to approve laws on racial discrimination, tariffs, currency, divorce, or imperial troops, nor may he make treaties. When in Grenada, he presides over the island's executive council, which was also established by letters patent. In the governor's absence the administrator of Grenada discharges this role. In 1952–1954 the Executive Council included, besides the governor and administrator, the attorney-general and treasurer, one other official, one nominated member of the Legislative Council, and three elected members chosen by the Legislative Council.

Under the Royal Instructions, the Governor or the Administrator, as the case may be, is normally required to consult his Executive Council in the exercise of his authority, but he may act in opposition to the advice tendered to him by the Members of the Council, in which case the Governor is required to report the matter to the Secretary of State [for the Colonies] by the first convenient opportunity, with the reasons for his action.[9]

In 1952–1953 the Grenada government contained the following departments: Administration, Agriculture, Audit, Education, Electricity and Telephones, Labour, Legal, Medical, Police, Post Office, Prisons, Public Works (including Road and Water authorities), and Treasury (including Customs and Income Tax). A number of statutory boards and committees assisted these departments. The colony, including Carriacou, was divided into six parishes, each having its own local government. Except in Carriacou, all parochial administrations were half elected, half nominated. Usually the elected legislator also sat on the Parochial Council.

Beside local legislation, the colonial courts applied English common law. The colony was divided into three magisterial districts, each with its own court. In addition, a local supreme court sat at St. George's and exercised original, summary, appellate, and criminal jurisdictions. From the Supreme Court appeal lay either to the West Indian Court of Appeal or to the Court of Appeal of the Windward and Leeward Islands. The latter court met under the presidency of the Grenadian chief justice, who was also an ex-officio member of the West Indian Court of Appeal. Magistrates' courts had original and summary jurisdiction in minor civil and criminal issues which arose in their districts. Appeal from these courts lay through the local supreme court. The most important limitation of these lower courts was their inability to settle claims for land in excess of £20 ($96 BWI, or $56.00 U.S.).[10]

Education was avaliable in local primary and secondary schools. The government maintained most of the primary schools and subsidized others controlled by various denominations. Education in the primary schools was free. In addition, the government subsidized four denominationally controlled secondary schools and financed its own Boys' Secondary School. These schools charged fees but also received pupils on scholarships. In 1953 the local secondary schools contained 555 boys and 626 girls compared with 9,592 boys and 8,904 girls enrolled in the primary schools. The island provided one university scholarship every two years, but during 1953 there was no previous holder of this scholarship on the Island. There were not many open scholarships to the secondary schools. Children successful in the Cambridge School Certificate examination held locally each year thereby qualified for recruitment into the local civil service. Many became schoolteachers themsleves. The Public Service Commission selected applicants on interview, and also had power to hear complaints from civil servants.

Parochial councils administering local government have powers to levy town and water rates, market and slaughterhouse dues, cemetery fees, pound fees and jetty dues. They may also enact certain bylaws under the Ordinance of 1886 which first established them. For staff, these councils each have a salaried warden assisted by some clerks and bailiffs called overland runners. Councils prepare budgets of revenue and expenditure, but are often poorly informed about their exact financial position. A committee appointed in 1947 to examine and recommend improvements in local government found that whereas the St. George's Parish Council had an average annual revenue of £9,500 ($26,600 U.S.) and the St. Andrew's Parish Council averaged £1,600 ($4,500 U.S.), the other councils had on an average about £500 ($1,400 U.S.) per year each. With such minute resources these councils could scarcely pay their employees' wages, and the 1947 Committee accordingly recommended various changes designed to strengthen their finances and increase their scope of action by transferring certain functions to them from the central government. It also recommended establishment of a local government board to supervise and coördinate the action of these parish councils. The Committee found that most functions normally discharged by local government bodies were exercised by the central government in St. George's, which is not surprising since Grenada is only 120 square miles. It noted that the local government of Carriacou was vested in the district officer as chairman of a wholly nominated board which lacked ability, power, and funds. The Committee was urged by members of the St. George's District Board to recommend that the capital should be made a borough and be separated administratively from the rest of the Parish of St. George. The need for coördination was not as strong as the pattern of separatism; and by 1952–1953 it was apparent that the recommendations of the 1947 Committee had been decently shelved.[11]

We have seen that Grenada government revenues averaged $3.9 million (BWI) during the years 1951–1953, and that this sum represented about one-quarter of the annual value of the gross domestic product. Half of this annual revenue came from customs duties, and another 10 per cent from excise and licenses. Income tax supplied about 10 per cent; and on an average Grenada received about $280,-000 (BWI) per annum from Great Britain under various colonial development and welfare schemes. Taxes on income, land, or heritable estates were exceedingly light. With these tax policies the government restricted its expenditure to avoid the need to solicit grants from Britain which would involve British Treasury control.

The Social Structure

Of 72,000 persons who lived in Grenada in 1946, 630 (0.9 per cent) were white, 3,500 (4.8 per cent) were East Indian, and the remainder were black (73.4 per cent) or colored (20.9 per cent). There was little change in racial composition by 1953, except that the island then contained two Chinese, both recent immigrants. In these classifications descendants of Maltese and Portuguese immigrants from Madeira are classified by phenotype as white or colored. Most whites are British by origin, expatriate officials and their families forming an important segment of this group. So do the Roman and Anglican priests, all of whom in 1952–1953 were recruited from abroad. Excluding these expatriate officials, Grenada's white colony consists of planters, few of whom are recent immigrants, and a handful of Syrians. The white planters include three or four families of French descent. Many members of the planter class engage in commerce, some in government also. These planter families are usually linked by kinship and affinity with one another and with similar groups in nearby islands.

Apart from the whites, colored, and Negroes, East Indians are the only important group. Being small in number, they accommodate themselves to the Creole society of white, colored, and black as best they can. Some Indians have achieved prominence through wealth, typically gained by produce dealing and usury, followed by investments in land. However, the great majority who lack wealth form an ethnic segment of the Grenadian lower or "peasant" class. Such Indians rarely mate with Negroes, and differentiate themselves by stressing their Indian cultural heritage. With few exceptions, Grenadians of colored and Negro descent are the issue of slaves. East Indians in Grenada are descended from indentured laborers, who were brought to Grenada between 1857 and 1865. Both Negroes and Indians accordingly share a history of economic and political subordination.

Data gathered in 1953 on Grenadian stratification show a basic division between a Western-oriented elite which contains less than 7 per cent of the people, and the rest, among whom rural traditionalism and African orientations prevail.[12] On a status scale ranging between 0.18 for the highest and 1.00 for the lowest status, folk statuses fell below 0.87 while elite status spread out above this. Correlations between social status, pigmentation, association, and family are extremely high, First-degree kinsmen, especially agnates, share almost identical social status. Occupation and educational achievement are ambiguous criteria for placement. Family groups of approximately equal status and color tend to intermarry. Members of the highest, richest, smallest, and whitest stratum, most of whom own land, were almost all schooled in Britain, as were their fathers before and their legitimate children after them. Each stratum tended to form an exclusive field for informal association as shown by clique, mating, and club behavior.

Certain significant subdivisions within the elite section are quite clear. The small, near-white planter group at the apex of the hierarchy, took little part in commerce and none in the official life of the government or the church. The larger brown "upper-middle classes" next in rank dominated Grenadian commerce, official councils and committees, certain clubs and other organizations. In none of these formal or informal groupings did any members of the lower levels of the elite take part.

Grenada's professionals were either expatriates—for example, administrators, priests and doctors—or were recruited from the local upper classes. Few of the well-to-do people who dominated the economic and administrative interests of the colony could be classified as dark. In the annual Carnival at Mardi Gras people of different social status took part in separate entertainments or occupied sharply differentiated positions in the same situation. The island beauty contest catered to the brown elite. Carnival "jump-up" and steel band contests, attended by masked dancers, catered to the folk. Between these two sections, social mobility could scarcely occur. Most island scholarships were won by boys of elite background, generally from its lower levels. In 1952–1953 none of these island scholars remained on the island. Dissident members of the propertied elite were occasionally exported by their kin, usually to Trinidad. Marked upward mobility in 1953 was represented by five men only, of whom four were East Indians whose produce-dealing profits had been invested in land, while the fifth and wealthiest Grenadian was a black ex-policeman who, if literate, was still quite unrepentant, and who is said to have made his millions from gambling in Chicago. This gentleman was regarded by all as a social conundrum, and by his actions he indicated that he shared this view.

To complicate and underpin this rigid stratification, there were important differences of culture and institutional practice between the various social sections. Law prohibited both the typical Grenadian folk cults of Shango and "Shouting" Baptism. The official creed of the dominant strata was Anglican; that of the folk, Roman Catholic.

As regards mating and family, the sections differed sharply, marriages being as rare among the folk as they were normal among the elite under laws which penalized property inheritance by bastards. While the folk lacked political rights until 1951, the elite had monopolized all locally available political interests before and under Crown Colony rule. While the folk knew only the Foresters and Friendly Society movements, the elite had long been organized in a plethora of associations, utilitarian, economic, occupational, ritual, social, and so forth. While all the elite had a background of secondary education, were literate, and spoke correct English, few folk had got beyond primary school, a great many were illiterate, and the French Creole patois was still the dialect they used among themselves. While the elite held property under legal title, most folk did not. While the elite used banks, the folk preferred *susu* associations for thrift and credit.[13] While the elite hired labor, the folk worked in coöperative groups of various types known as *maroon* and *jamboni*. Folk wakes, nine-nights, and All Souls rituals were quite foreign to the elite, many of whom could not understand the Creole French patois spoken by the folk. In short, throughout all ranges of culture the differences between elite and folk matched their status separation.

Among the elite there were also important differences of culture and status between the handful of whites and near-whites who, having been schooled in Britain, found the Creole culture somewhat strange, and the colored majority who knew of little beyond Grenada and Trinidad. British officials also tended to form a separate group. Their structural position led them to differentiate themselves from the near-white Creole stratum, while maintaining good working relations with its key members. Clearly, the finely woven network of status, color, property, kinship, political, and economic interests which characterized this elite, limited their room for adjustment to new situations and events. Leading elite personages held numerous roles in business, clubs, government councils and committees, special agencies, occupational associations, the church, and family and lineage units. Such personal networks were difficult to coördinate smoothly, even in stationary conditions. It was an even more difficult task to adjust them smoothly to new structural conditions.

Elite functions in government, law, medicine, commerce, and education were concentrated in the brown stratum. Leadership in culture and style was combined with the economic dominance of the small, near-white "upper class." Subordinate technical and executive roles were dispersed among the larger lower strata of the elite section, very few of whom had moved into these positions from folk backgrounds through the secondary school system. With a multiplicity of official and quasi-official leadership roles to be distributed among a small number of interested elite males, many held role-clusters which represented interlocking or competing interests. Moreover, being recruited mainly by descent and organized in cliques and other informal associations, the elite, especially at its upper levels, was subdivided and contraposed by principles of kinship, marriage, interest, color, and clique. The net result was a high degree of structural immobility, since its balanced distribution of group memberships and cleavages represented a delicate equilibrium which could not easily promote or accommodate major changes. The elite preoccupied themselves with maintaining their own internal equilibrium as a closed unit having a fixed position in the Grenadian society. Faced with a crisis, they could only act uniformly by adopting a negative, exclusive posture.

In 1952 some 15,000 Grenadians, or 18 per cent of the population, lived in townships, half of these in St. George's, the capital, and one-sixth in Gouyave, the next largest town. Gouyave, like other country towns, was a port and fishing village which served a farming population and had a small weekly market. Most of Grenada's elite lived in or near St. George's, the planters being settled on their estates. As an electoral district, St. George's was dominated by the late T. A. Marryshow, whose political interests centered on federation and constitutional reform rather than on industrial or economic change. Under the restrictive franchise which held from 1925 to 1951, Grenada had only one political party, the Grenada Labour Party. This was established at Gouyave in 1929 and by 1946 had a membership of 300, having also been registered as the General Workers' Union. By then, some St. George's wage workers were also organized in the Grenada Workers' Union. Until 1950 no rural workers were unionized. Thus the urban population was industrially more diverse and better organized than rural folk.

In the country, social differentiation was simple. A handful of planters ran the estates, each with its own resident laborers. Casual workers were recruited as required from the "peasantry" on the estate margins. Many "peasants" depended on wage labor on or off the estates. Others occasionally hired help. Laborers living on estates were expected to take wagework when it was offered. Wage rates were low, but the "privileges" of resident workers and the ill-defined obligations of their planter patrons prevented the situation from becoming intolerable.

In 1950 the planters had an intermittently functioning agricultural association, the members of which normally convened at the St. George's Club. Merchants were organized in the Grenada Chamber of Commerce, which represented the dominant interests of the urban brown elite. Elementary schoolteachers had their own union to pursue their interests, and there were also a number of citizens' associations, peasants' and industrial clubs, friendly societies, Foresters, and Odd-fellows. Formal associations subserved functions of status placement rather than political or economic interests for marginal members of the elite. For the small, economically dominant groups, the bureaucracy and the Legislature, the Chamber of Commerce and the planters' association, were the main units expressing economic and political interests. Club life was formally distinct, except among planters.

2. CRISIS

1938 to 1950

In 1937 and 1938 there were riots and disturbances in Barbados, Trinidad, Jamaica, British Guiana, St. Kitts, and other British West Indian territories: but not in Grenada.

The Acting Governor of the Windwards, warned by these upheavals, appointed a local commission "to enquire into the economic condition of the various classes of wage-earners in Grenada with special reference to the agricultural industry, and to obtain recommendations." The commission consisted of native Grenadians, mainly members of the brown urban elite, with commercial and professional backgrounds. Its report, tabled in the legislature in 1938, recommended small wage increases, further land settlement, the establishment of a labor department, the replacement of labor "privileges" and perquisites by a fixed monetary wage, and the conversion of patron-client relations on estates into impersonal market transactions. On a more general level, the report protested the high cost of living and recommended provision of credit facilities to workers, but concluded that estates could not pay higher wages, because of poor overseas prices for export crops.[14]

The report paints a picture of economic distress. During the world depression, prices for Grenadian staples fell and remained low. Planters became indebted, and tried to keep their labor costs as low as they could. Meanwhile the price of imported food, clothing, and other products rose sharply. Population continued to increase, while migration outlets contracted. When the hurricane damage of 1921 had been repaired, local employment, especially in agriculture, declined. Low wages and wide unemployment probably underlay the upheavals of 1937–1938 in other British West Indian colonies. That Grenada escaped such disturbance may well have been due to its social organization, which simultaneously restricted the scope for mass action by workers, and bound planters and peasants together in solidary associations within the framework of estate-communities.

In recommending the conversion of these relations into impersonal cash transactions, the Commission undoubtedly expressed the wishes of some planters who regarded the workers' perquisites as onerous; but the Commission also expressed its own urban, commercial ethos in this proposal. However, this change-over from a predominantly social and personal bond to a strictly economic and impersonal one could neither proceed on all estates uniformly, nor without breaching relations between planters and people. Land rights were central to workers' "privileges," and included customary access as well as tenancy. Following on the 1938 Commission of Enquiry, in 1939 the government passed a Tenants' Compensation Ordinance which provided a legal basis and formula for settling these issues. Under this ordinance, a worker or tenant could claim compensation from his employer or landlord for improvements made on an occupied plot. Some planters honored the ordinance by paying compensation to workers for trees they had brought to maturity. In return, they would charge rents for garden land, and the price of the bluggoes traditionally sold to resident workers increased on most estates. Changes in these features of relations between planter and worker tended to promote uncertainty and change in other aspects, especially in a context of rising living costs during and after the Second World War.

At this point the start of a new world war relieved the strain on the Grenadian economy. Migration flowed fast to Trinidad, Venezuela, and the Dutch islands of Curaçao and Aruba. Wages began to rise and planters began to charge workers in money for "privileges" formerly free.

The Second World War created favorable and expanding markets for Grenadian staples. Cocoa and nutmeg prices rose, and with the fall of Indonesia in 1943, Grenada enjoyed a virtual monopoly of the Allied nutmeg market. To maximize this advantage, the government established a statutory coöperative association with the support of the nutmeg growers, and empowered this body to handle all future nutmeg exports. The association thus became one of the biggest employers of labor in the island, and an important funnel for disbursements.

As the price of local staples rose, and the content of the traditional "privileges" declined, farm workers began to look for some amelioration of their lot. The 1938 Commission had recommended a statutory minimum wage of 1s. 3d. per day (30 cents BWI; 18 cents U.S.) per able-bodied man, 1s. per day (24 cents BWI; 14 cents U.S.) per woman, which increased current rates by 3d. per day. Under traditional arrangements, road work, the main alternative to farm labor for rural folk, was paid at the prevailing agricultural rate. The government established this minimum wage in 1939, and set up a cost of living index with a base value of 100. By January 1946 this index

stood at 184; in January 1947 it was 190; in January 1948 it was 210.
In 1949 the government increased the statutory minimum wage to 78
cents and 66 cents BWI (47 cents and 40 cents U.S.) per day for men
and women respectively; in January 1950 the cost of living index was
220.

Favorable prices for cocoa and nutmeg had enabled many planters
to clear off their debts. Estates became worthwhile investments, and
so began to change hands. Land values rose and speculative interests
emerged. Tourism was being planned, and after 1945 some wealthy
folk abroad sought to purchase land in Grenada. Some local Indian
entrepreneurs also began to speculate on land. Often the new proprietors were unaware of the traditional obligations of Grenadian
estate owners. Finding their properties encumbered by people with
customary rights, they sought to reduce these commitments as far as
possible. Thus transfers of property involved further role redefinitions
which introduced further uncertainties into the relation between
planter and peasant-worker. No unions at this time addressed their
efforts to the estate workers.

In 1946 the rising cost of living stimulated the longshoremen at
St. George's to seek trade union organization. The Grenada Workers'
Union, registered that year, sought also to enroll clerical and shop
workers in St. George's, but took no direct interest in agricultural
workers, who at this time depended entirely on movements of the
government statutory minimum rates for any wage increases. In asso-
ciation with the General Workers' Union of Gouyave, the Grenada
Workers' Union of St. George's formed the Grenada Trade Union
Council (GTUC), which, in 1950, for the first time, attempted to
negotiate wage increases for estate workers after the government had
once again raised the statutory minimum wage to 82 cents and 68 cents
BWI per day for men and women respectively. In negotiating with the
GTUC, the planters were represented by the Grenada Agricultural
Employers' Society whose membership was the same as that of the
Agricultural Association. By their resulting agreement, the "statutory"
wage was linked to changes in the local price of cocoa, and was to be
adjusted quarterly thereafter. As the upward movement of cocoa
prices had not yet reached its peak, the next quarter therefore brought
a further increase of 12 cents per day to workers of both sexes, bringing the rural wage rates to 94 cents and 80 cents BWI (55 cents and
48 cents U.S.) per day respectively for men and women.

1950

Early in 1950, one of the larger estates was sold to a British
buyer. This holding had belonged to a leading local family for some
decades. During that time it had supported many people who lived

and worked on it. The sale was made through an agent. Although the contract transferred the estate "free of encumbrances," it seems that the vendor, who was blind, did not take these customary tenancies into account in setting the price. The purchaser on arrival found the people living on his estate. They disliked him as the new master, and may have resented the sale. They asserted their rights and privileges. The new owner decided to evict them, as he was quite entitled to do under the contract of sale. The people needed help and advice from someone literate and sympathetic. Mr. Eric M. Gairy, a young Grenadian ex-teacher who had recently been deported from Aruba for labor agitation, came forward as their spokesman. A Negro of peasant stock, Mr. Gairy was by background and experience well suited to the role. His intervention was a complete success. He claimed full cash compensation under the Tenants' Compensation Ordinance for the persons evicted. Because the purchaser denied his liability under the contract, the agent had to extract compensation from the former owner. It is said that the compensation paid approached £3,000. The vendor felt the agent had betrayed him, the workers, that seller and purchaser alike had dealt with them unfairly. As their successful spokesman, Gairy became the Galahad of the workers and peasants in this part of the island.

Economic and social conditions were ripe for labor agitation. Earlier that year, the government had again increased the statutory minimum wage in agriculture by 4 cents BWI or 2d. per day. The civil service was demanding 100 per cent increases in their current cost-of-living allowances; in St. George's the Grenada Workers' Union was seeking employers with whom they could negotiate wage increases for clerks and shop assistants; stevedores were negotiating increases with the shipping agents who were also the major export-import firms; and the GTUC with a combined membership of 5,000 was negotiating increases for farm workers based on local cocoa prices. At Grenville, a leaderless strike of 240 nutmeg-crackers produced intimidation and involved the police.

In July, 1950, Gairy registered a new trade union, the Grenada Manual and Mental Workers' Union (GMMWU), with himself as president-general. Within a month, he addressed demands for a 50 per cent wage increase to the Grenada Sugar Factory Ltd., whose plant and estates lay near the scene of his recent triumph. After letters were exchanged, Gairy called out the sugar workers, 496 in all, on August 24. The next day another 430 workers on eleven estates in the parish struck in sympathy. Being unable to agree, the sugar company and Gairy referred their dispute to arbitration in September, by which time Gairy had also addressed demands for a wage increase of 20 per cent for all estate workers to the Grenada Agricultural Employers'

Society. The Society promptly concluded negotiations with the GTUC on September 27, and informed Gairy that this matter had already been settled with another union.

A retired chief justice who lived on the island was the natural chairman for the tribunal appointed to arbitrate the sugar dispute. The company claimed it could afford no wage increase unless the government agreed either to increase its subsidy or to raise the price of sugar by one cent per pound. The union objected to both these alternatives on grounds that its supporters paid most of the local taxes and ate most of the local sugar. The tribunal tried to satisfy both parties, awarding wage increases of 25 per cent, or half its demand, to the union, while authorizing the company to raise the price of sugar by one cent per pound. In addition, on Gairy's demand, the company agreed to grant double pay for work done on holidays, and to give all who worked more than 200 days each year seven days' paid leave.

Within three months of its establishment, the GMMWU had a membership of 2,070. Its success and expansion may have encouraged shipping agents in St. George's to come to terms with the stevedores, as the Agricultural Employers' Society had already done with the GTUC. The government undertook to investigate civil servants' wage claims through a commissioner. Mr. Gairy busied himself with expansion.

The literary exchange with the Agricultural Employers did not satisfy him. In October, 1950, after concluding their agreement with the GTUC, the Agricultural Employers received a further demand for a 46.5 per cent increase on the minimum wage from the now-triumphant Gairy. The new demand represented a 26.5 per cent increase on Gairy's previous claim. It also asked for various ancillary benefits. Gairy would not let the GTUC outbid him. In the following month the Agricultural Employers announced their willingness to give seven days' paid leave per annum to all who worked 200 days per year or more. As Grenadian nutmeg and cocoa estates usually offered work four days a week on an average, this announcement was mainly formal and did not impress Gairy, who continued to fulminate at various public meetings. Meanwhile local cocoa prices began to fall, and the daily rates for farm work under the planters' agreement with the GTUC were consequently reduced from 94 cents per man-day to 91 cents, and from 78 cents per woman to 76. On discovering this in December, 1950, the GTUC requested the Employers' Society to let the current wage rates stand, rather than reduce them, arguing that "any fall in the wages of the workers might lead to other disturbances." The Society replied on January 17, 1951, that it could not agree to changing the terms of the agreement because "the first change of the rate of bonus has had responsible agreement." [15]

1951

Gairy had received no reply from the planters to his last demand, which asked for wages of $1.20 BWI per man-day (5s.) and $1.00 (4s. 2d.) per day for women.

On January 29, Gairy visited the estate for whose evicted workers he had secured compensation in the previous year. While Gairy was talking with them, the owner interrupted him, and consequently work ceased there. The Labour Officer sought to mediate, but Gairy demanded his 46 per cent increase. The owner said he was bound by the agreement made between the GTUC and Agricultural Employers' Society. The next day the workers on the adjoining estate went on strike. Two weeks later, workers on another estate nearby went on strike. At this stage the Agricultural Employers' Society, realizing that the estates were striking one by one, called a meeting, and reaffirmed loyalty to their agreement with the GTUC. The following week, the Labour Officer delivered three broadcasts on unionism. On February 18, "the heads of the four leading denominations issued a joint appeal to their congregations in an attempt to prevent the island-wide strike which was due to commence the following day." [16] On February 19, Gairy called the first island-wide strike in Grenada's history. This strike lasted for a month, and ended with the complete victory of the GMMWU, although its leader was taken in custody and removed to Carriacou soon after the strike began.

The strike was marked by "acts of intimidation, violence, larceny, arson." An official report by the Labour Department says:

. . . for one month, commencing 19th February 1951, Grenada experienced a strike of agricultural and road workers which caused an upheaval such as has not been known within living memory. Workers who showed a disinclination to go on strike were intimidated and beaten by their co-workers, by the unemployed and by the unemployables; estates were looted in broad daylight, while Management stood by unable to interfere; valuable produce trees were deliberately damaged; estate buildings, medical health centres, schools, and privately owned residences were burnt; rioting and bloodshed occurred; the small police force appeared totally inadequate to deal with the situation, and it became necessary to seek police assistance from . . . St. Lucia and Trinidad. Units of the British Navy were hastily summoned, and a small garrison of British troops were stationed here for months afterwards.[16]

The police superintendent who brought this chaos to order was a retired British brigadier hastily recruited from Barbados. His report mentions

. . . houses burnt down at night, widespread looting of cocoa and nutmeg plantations by day . . . damage and loss . . . about £45,000. No deaths were caused by the rioters, but the Police shot four and wounded five before the disturbances were quelled. The Administrator in his Budget Speech in December remarked that "it has been suggested that the employers of labour did not understand and were not ready to accept . . . Trade Unionism . . . that members and followers of the Union . . . were ignorant and untrained in the weapon . . . placed suddenly in their hands. . . . As there had been no rioting or looting in the island for 156 years, the events of this spring have left a sense of fear . . . which still persists." [18]

The events of this critical month reveal a social breakdown. Grenadians who believed that the disturbances in other British Caribbean territories "could never happen here" were excited participants. Planters demanded weapons, wore bowie knives, and barricaded their homesteads. One shot at people approaching his house. Others abused the Governor to his face. Workers found profitable markets for looted produce in local dealers. On several estates workers quarreled with one another over ownership of cocoa and nutmeg trees each claimed his ancestors had planted. In one case workers subdivided an estate informally among themselves. Roadblocks isolated the capital where most of the elite lived, kept its markets empty, and produced food shortages there. Lucky agents did an excellent business in fire insurance and firearms. So did Gairy when universal suffrage was introduced and a general election was held in October of that year. Having set up the Grenada United Labour Party (GULP) with himself as perpetual head, Gairy appealed for votes to the newly enfranchised strata, many of whom already supported his union.

Soon after the government had learned that the planters were willing to negotiate with the union, the police restored order, and the strike came to an end on March 19 when the GMMWU and the Grenada Agricultural Employers' Society came to terms. Under their agreement, agricultural wages were raised to $1.20 BWI (70 cents U.S.) for men, and $1.00 BWI (38 cents U.S.) per day for women, as Gairy demanded. In addition, all who worked 200 days in a year were entitled to seven days' paid leave; and a reference board was set up to settle differences between employers and the union, and to interpret these settlement terms. For the rest of the year the board was occupied with the problem of defining an "eight-hour day"; the planters claimed that this meant eight hours' work, whereas the union held that it included time for lunch.

On October 10 the first general election was held having universal suffrage as its basis. Eligible voters numbered 34,133, that is, more than eight times the number previously eligible. Sixty-nine per cent of those eligible voted, and of the ballots cast, 20,622 or 88 per cent were accepted, 2,235 being Carriacou votes which Gairy's GULP did not contest. Excluding the Carriacou votes, there remained 18,387 ballots of which 13,162 or 71 per cent were for GULP candidates.

Several rival candidates lost their deposit. In Grenada itself, only T. A. Marryshow in St. George's withstood the GULP attack. This political eruption of the formerly disenfranchised social section provided Grenadian elite with a major shock, especially in the current industrial context. With this election victory, Gairy, already the dominant force in Grenada industrial affairs, seemed to have won political control of the island also. With the legislative power now at his disposal it seemed that Gairy could initiate such policies as he wished, in and beyond the industrial field.

Other gains were also made by workers in 1951. Road workers received the wage increases granted on farms. Skilled men in the Public Works Department received a 33.3 per cent wage rise. Civil servants first received an interim 33.3 per cent increase in the cost of living allowance which was backdated to January, 1951, and got their full demands later in the year. Other government employees, such as the prison staff or the sanitary inspectors received substantial increases. The longshoremen demanded a 50 per cent increase from the shipping agents. Only the shop assistants had difficulty in finding a group of employers with whom to negotiate. Remembering the experiences of the sugar company, the agricultural employers and the shipping agents (many of whom also belonged to it), the Chamber of Commerce declared its inability to represent the urban merchants. Some of the merchants undertook to negotiate individually with the Grenada Workers' Union only when the Labour Officer advised them that the alternative was another strike. Even then, twelve employers who decided to negotiate together did so as individuals; and after having reached a settlement that increased wages, only six of them ratified this when approached later by the union individually.

1952–1953

The year 1952 marked an uneasy calm after the recent storm. Relations between master and man, planter and peasant, government and people, were tense, opaque, and confused. The "man" often seemed the master, the people seemed to be the government. "Peasant" had struck against planter.

Since the shop assistants in St. George's could not secure satisfaction from their employers, the Governor, on the recommendation of the newly elected Legislature, made an order raising their minimum wage, and providing such other benefits as Gairy usually demanded. Soon after, the longshoremen won most of their claims from an arbitration tribunal which heard their dispute with the shipping agents. The government appointed a commissioner to investigate civil service salaries and to make recommendations. On behalf of the Windward Islands as a whole, the Governor also imported a British trade unionist as Labour Adviser. The Grenada Sugar Factory freely raised the wages of its daily workers to levels current on cocoa and nutmeg estates. The local cigarette factory freely gave its workers a 25 per cent wage increase. Some employers were adjusting to the new conditions. However, the planters were adamant, and so remained Gairy's main target.

Toward the end of 1952, Gairy made further demands on the "agricultural employers," who replied with a memorandum that they could not afford higher wages. The dispute, being unresolved and threatening to end in a strike, was referred to arbitration. Meanwhile Gairy harassed the planters by a series of work stoppages on individual estates, challenging their right to appoint and dismiss employees, and similar matters. A few houses were set on fire at night, and the circulation of firearms increased by theft, purchase, and crude manufacture. Many people simultaneously compared Gairy with Fedon, and his union with the Mau Mau.

The colonial government took precautionary measures to cope with any repetition of the preceding disorder. It held that "the attraction of valuable loot, namely cocoa and nutmeg from the plantations, which found a ready sale, prolonged the strike" [19] of February-March, 1951. Official statistics certainly show a sharp rise in the rate of reported praedial larceny during these months. Farm workers on strike, lacking financial support from their union, sought to supply their needs by selling estate crops. Produce dealers found this trade profitable. Clearly, the great bulk of the 1951 crops were exported as usual, but that year they moved from field to boat along unorthodox channels. With this experience in mind, the government passed a special ordinance which enabled the Executive Council to prohibit the sale of produce in any further emergencies. Heavy penalties were attached to the possession, receiving, purchase, or sale of stolen goods at such times. Enforcement of this law was carefully planned. The large-scale looting of 1951 was not likely to be repeated.

The government also strengthened the local police. A volunteer constabulary, 200 strong, was trained as militia. British frigates cruised about nearby. The retired brigadier improved police efficiency and morale. The new Labour Adviser sought to examine trade union accounts. Besides advising leaders on union techniques, he addressed several meetings of workers about trade union democracy, organization, and methods. The government distributed a weekly newsletter written in dialect to inform the people about its plans and local developments. Legislation modernizing the local labour laws was passed. The government seemed to have defined its role as that of a neutral referee, responsible for law and order.

The planters regrouped themselves into a Grenada Agriculturists'

Union which replaced the old Agricultural Association and Agricultural Employers' Society. On its registration in 1952 as a trade union, the new body had 89 members, almost all of whom owned more than one hundred acres. One planter thoughtfully established a company union for the workers on his estate, and negotiated with them privately thereafter. The Labour Adviser secured accounts from the two older unions in the GTUC, but failed with the GMMWU. In an attempt to pour oil on troubled waters, he devised a cocktail party to which planters, officials, and union leaders were invited. The officials came dutifully. So did some planters, after persuasion. The union leaders turned up in strength. The party was held in a room large enough to accommodate two widely separate groups, one consisting of planters and officials, the other of union leaders. One planter who was present informed the writer that when he "frisked" his peers, they all had weapons on them. The Labour Adviser became a social outcast after this incident and was happy to leave in late 1953.

In 1952 Gairy was at the height of his power as an industrial and political leader. He then sought to convert this power into high social status. This was rather too much for the Grenadian elite, not only the planters, but also the urban brown "upper middle class." This effort with its implicit assumption of equality, was curtly rejected. For this reason, among others, the Labour Adviser who brought unionists and planters together socially did so at the cost of his own social status.

Defeated in his bid for social recognition by the elite, and filled with the sense of his power, Gairy openly flouted the colonial administration and its law. He refused to render his union's accounts as obliged to do under the Trade Union Registration Ordinance. He did not renew his driving license despite several warnings. In late 1952 the government quietly set out to show Mr. Gairy that he was not above the law. A court order prohibited him from driving in Grenada for twelve months. Gairy hired a chauffeur. But on each occasion thereafter that he flouted Grenada law, the government took legal action against him, usually with success.

These events may well have marked the turning point of the local crisis. They were all clearly noneconomic. Having defeated the sugar company, the GTUC, and—most resoundingly—the planters and their friends in strikes and at the polls, Gairy had sought recognition as their equal and met with flat rejection. At bottom, Gairy's desire for social status was partly structural and partly personal. Being accepted as an equal by the elite would furnish the most signal declaration of his total success and of the elite's defeat. Precisely for this reason the elite excluded him from their associations. Moreover, Gairy often reminded Grenadians that he was unique. This society had never known a general strike, nor a popular vote, nor a successful labor leader.

Given its ascriptive basis for status placement, there was really little chance that Gairy's impressive achievements as an agitator and leader of strikes would be rewarded by the elite with their social acceptance. Yet, granted his power and sense of his own importance, it was also unlikely that Gairy should tamely accept rejection by the elite. Frustrated by social barriers, he accordingly flouted the law, thereby implicitly asserting his status as that of one above the law. But when the government quietly enforced its law in a series of legal actions, Gairy found himself alone as the sole defendant, cut off from his following if he chose to go to court, but fined if he refused. Planters also learned this lesson and sued Gairy personally, as occasion offered. These legal actions expressed the government's confidence that it had adequate reserves of force, that Gairy's support was declining, and that the impersonal enforcement of law was an effective and necessary safeguard against more disorder.

In late 1952 Gairy made further demands on the Grenada Agriculturists' Union, threatening another island strike if these were not conceded. These demands were indefinite and imprecise. They specified no objectives or conditions of settlement. Gairy also published several articles in the local paper claiming "astral" influence, and hinting that he had supernatural support. On the eve of the promised strike, he asserted in a public meeting that God would send down a sign of favor for all to see. That night there was a downpour, heavy, even by Grenadian standards. The road between St. George's and Gouyave was blocked by fallen rock, which many regarded as a sign of divine support. Some "middle-class" folk suspected that the power which moved the rock was magical (Obeah) rather than divine. The Public Works Department tackled this roadblock with unusual energy, but took a fortnight to remove it. With Gairy's divine sign blocking the road, and a wave of awe sweeping Grenada, police took up protective positions, and the government appointed yet another arbitration tribunal to investigate and resolve the dispute. These actions may have forestalled resumption of the conflict halted in March, 1951.

The tribunal appointed to arbitrate the dispute reported in mid-1953. Since Gairy had made no specific demands, the nature and scope of the dispute was uncertain. Probably Gairy really wanted some admission by the planters of "total surrender" to him and his forces. An obvious expression of this would have been for the elite to admit him to their clubs and homes. It is significant that Gairy first made these pointed threats and vague demands after he was socially rejected by the elite.

Since the union had addressed these demands to the Grenada Sugar Factory also, its claims on the factory and the planters were taken together. Lacking clear ideas of the issues in dispute, the three members of the arbitration tribunal failed to agree on remedial action, inevitably perhaps because one represented the union, another the planters. Accordingly the chairman alone made the award, as required under the Trade Disputes (Arbitration and Enquiry) Ordinance in such a case. This award rejected GMMWU claims for higher wages, but provided paid holidays for those who had worked 150 or more days per year.

Gairy's reaction was to reject this award on the ground that the arbitrators had failed to agree. This position threatened the entire procedure of arbitration, which had proven itself the only method of peacefully settling local trade disputes. But if arbitration procedures were discredited, the government would have to regulate and enforce industrial order by positive measures. In that event disorder was probable because Gairy's party was strong in the Legislature, and could enforce its will there or repudiate those government policies it disliked. To resolve this impasse, the reference board originally set up under the agreement of March, 1951, was reconstituted. It met five times in 1953 and sought to find agreement on methods of resolving trade disputes. The board rejected Gairy's requests that planters should deduct union dues from workers' pay, and that he and his assistants should have free access to all estates. The board also heard protests against dismissals of certain workers.

Gairy's main reaction to the tribunal's award was an island-wide campaign to promote a general strike. In the northern parishes he called a series of impromptu stoppages on individual estates in May and June, ostensibly in protest against "victimization" of workers laid off. Most of these preliminary strikes took place on estates recently acquired by Mr. Nyack, a wealthy Indian. The estate people were sharply opposed to Nyack, his proprietorship, and his methods. It is said that on his first visit to one of these estates, the resident workers forced the new owner to withdraw. The other estates on which Gairy called midsummer strikes belonged to another outstanding mobile, the wealthy black ex-policeman.

During his island-wide campaign, Gairy made a habit of indulging in Philippic invective against recalcitrant planters and merchants. He also sought support from the folk by bringing cultists to address his meetings as chaplains, and by promising to hold a Shango sacrifice at a traditional site. To mollify Christians, he held a Grand Mass in a rural Catholic Church which his supporters from other parishes attended, traveling by bus. By such actions Gairy sought to convince supporters of his mystical power, but revealed his own weakness.

In 1953 the planters treated union demands and threats more seriously than they had in 1951. Some planters indeed refused to discuss anything with the union, denying the latter's claim to coördinate status. Others produced returns form 21 estates to show that operating costs left owners marginal profits. Meanwhile, the waterfront workers formed a union under their own direction, and negotiated further wage increases and improved conditions. The local tourist hotel toward which Gairy had directed threats offered its workers increases above the level of his demands under new arrangements. Government legislation forbade stoppages in "essential services" such as water, sanitation, medicine, and communications. Official committees in these departments invited workers to submit their grievances. The sources of Gairy's support were thus reduced.

On November 26, 1953, Gairy called his second island strike of farm workers, except for sugar workers as they were then unemployed, waiting for the crop to begin.

No demands were made on the employers, nor was a request received for consideration by the Reference Board of any issues in dispute. About one-third of the estimated 6,000 agricultural workers stopped work—many of them because of the fear of arson, violence or intimidation—but by the week preceding Christmas, the vast majority were back at work or had been replaced by the unemployed, except in the parishes of St. John's and St. Mark's where the majority of workers remained on strike. There was the usual crop of incidents—arson, stone-throwing at night, intimidation—but this was on a vastly reduced scale. . . . Larceny of licensable produce—cocoa, nutmegs, coconuts . . . was effectively checked by the prompt introduction of legislation prohibiting the sale or transfer of such produce without a permit.[20]

1954

After the Christmas holidays, Gairy made a final effort to get his dwindling strike under way. On New Year's Day, 1954, he called out the sugar workers who were now wanted for harvest.

At the same time the Union renewed its efforts to obtain the support of those agricultural workers who had previously shown an unwillingness to associate themselves with strike action. The response was a little better than previously, as about 50 per cent of the labour force did not turn out to work. By the end of January 1954 there was however a gradual . . . return to work which became complete by the end of February. . . . On 26th April 1954, two months after . . . at a time when relations between the employers and the workers' Unions were strained, the Employers' Union announced a voluntary increase of 24 cents to men and 20 cents to women on the basic daily rate [bringing this] . . . to $1.44 [5/8d or 82 cents U.S.] and $1.20 [4/8d or 72 cents U.S.] for men and women respectively. In addition . . . the Employers' Union announced that the customary perquisites enjoyed by their workers would be continued so as to augment the daily wage rates.[21]

This action effectively undercut Gairy's agitation and brought the crisis to an end. It resolved the social conflict between planters and workers by an undertaking which restored the traditional pattern of relations with its old privileges, obligations, and loyalties, and which also granted wage increases freely. Although Gairy might claim these awards as the fruit of his efforts, the workers knew otherwise. His second island-wide strike had been as critical a failure as the first had been a critical success. Whereas the first strike followed a specific demand to which there had been no reply, the reverse was the case with the second. The first strike, like Fedon's uprising, caught the government and the planters unawares, the second did not. Whereas the first strike represented an abrupt structural change, the second established a new equilibrium. Nonetheless the second strike may have been quite as important as the first in forcing the planters to recognize that labor had both grievances and power, and that unless these grievances were satisfied, Gairy's agitation would flourish. By first defeating Gairy's second strike, and then trying to meet the grievances of their workers, the planters simultaneously achieved several objectives, reestablishing direct relations with their people while denying Gairy and his union coördinate status. These objectives were political rather than economic; but then the crisis was also political in nature, though economic in form. In Grenada during these years the issue at stake was nothing less than the continuity or modification of the social structure of which the planters were the guardians, leaders, and chief beneficiaries. In essence the conflict became a struggle between Gairy and the planters for the workers' loyalty, the government being primarily concerned with the preservation of law and order. The planters' decisions of April 26, 1954, marked the end of the Grenadian crisis, and Gairy lost his disruptive potential.

3. ANALYSIS

These data reward study from several points of view. They raise questions about the "causes" or determinants of the crisis, about the factors which regulated its form, about the nature of Grenada society, and about the relation between government and structural change. These questions and their answers are closely related; but it is useful to consider them separately.

The Problem of Cause

In the summer of 1952, when Gairy's power was at its height, Professor Simon Rottenberg, an American labor economist, visited Grenada to investigate its labor troubles. Rottenberg spent only six weeks in Grenada, but wrote a revealing report. He summarized the essentials of the conflict clearly, and showed how its components reinforced one another to produce the impasse of 1952; but his "explanation" of the crisis was mistaken. Rottenberg conceived this crisis as illustrating "Labour Relations in an Undeveloped Economy," and thus directed attention to levels of economic development as determinants of relations between employer and employee. His conclusion that "the economic forces which define the strategic positions and capacities of the parties in labour relations in Grenada move in opposite directions" [22] reveals the framework of economic determinism which underlies his analysis. So does the title of his paper, and various statements in the text, although his own data indicate otherwise. Thus, discussing the planters, Rottenberg admits that " 'getting out production at low cost' which is the first principle of entrepreneurial conduct in the developed countries here becomes submerged by the principle of preserving a customary social fabric." Of the workers he observes that many grievances which

> . . . evoke more emotional response than insufficiency of the daily wage rate . . . are not capable of adjustment by the ordinary process of collective bargaining. . . . The membership pattern of the union [includes people] . . . who are exclusively engaged in "own account work." . . . Disputes are enormously varied. . . . The union's grievance book is filled with them. There are complaints about cows doing damage to gardens; unjust accusations of thefts of coconuts; the cutting into land by road builders; the failure to compensate for damages suffered by collision with vehicles; attacks by dogs and the like. . . . There is a real question whether the union can operate . . . in a community in which disputes which have no relevance to job relationship are so important, and in which the difference between the wage worker and the self-employed peasant is a purely formal one.[23]

Clearly, neither the planters nor the peasant workers regarded the conflict as primarily economic, and some hardly saw this aspect at all. It is equally clear that the movement which Gairy promoted and led, despite its registration as a union, differed radically from trade unions such as the Grenada Workers Union or its British and American models.

By contrasting "developed" and "undeveloped" economies, Rottenberg implies corresponding modalities of labor relations, that Grenadian labor patterns and the Grenadian crisis are characteristic of "undeveloped" economy, and that both these latter are fully explained thereby. However such explanation fails to reveal why the crisis occurred when it did, or why it took a noneconomic form. It suggests also that similar patterns and crises should be found in other undeveloped economies, their irrationality increasing presumably in proportion with the degree of underdevelopment. Comparative data show quite clearly that this is not the case. Carriacou, itself part of the colony of Grenada, was completely unaffected by the events of 1950–1954, despite Gairy's presence in that dependency during the strike of

1951. Compared with Grenada, Carriacou represents a far lower level of development; the two islands have almost identical population densities—530 persons per square mile in 1953—but quite dissimilar modes of labor relation. Granting that Grenada and Carriacou are distinct societies, if the Grenadian upheaval is "explained" by the level of economic development, Carriacou should have had an even greater disturbance. On this principle, we have also to ask why the crisis occurred in 1951 rather than some other point in local history. "Explanations" as vague as this are scarcely worth the name.

Taking official estimates of the Grenadian agricultural labor force in 1950–1954 at about 6,000 persons, roughly divided between the sexes, then in 1950—if these worked an average of 150 days per annum for wages below $1.00 (BWI) per day—the labor cost of estate operations would approximate $800,000 (BWI) and would fall just under one million in 1951 (when rates had been raised to $1.20 and $1.00 per day for men and women respectively). Against these costs, we may set the annual values of exported staples and the taxable incomes of landed proprietors, which are presented in tables 18 and 19 above. These figures show that in 1951 the planters could well have afforded to raise wages freely without a strike. Some planters freely admitted that they could afford higher rates than the union had asked for. When asked in this case why they did not grant these increases, they replied, "What right have these people to strike? For generations, the workers have enjoyed the privileges of our estates; what right have they got to strike?" Thus for the planters the "privileges" of labor did not include the right to demand wage increases or to go on strike. For generations estate workers had been conceived of as a peasantry; but this status was hardly consistent with strikes and unionism among them. It is clear that such factors and categories express structural relations, which are social and political, rather than economic, in nature and form.

That economic factors helped to cause this crisis cannot be doubted. Increases in the price of local staples and in the local cost of living had led to regular increases in the statutory minimum wage. This statutory wage had been instituted by the government in 1938, there being no other institutional means of action in this field, apart from the planters' association. Underlying the situation of 1950 and contributing to its tension was the reduction of workers' privileges which had been proceeding since 1939, with corresponding reductions of solidarity between planters and workers. To discriminate between the economic and social aspects of this process is not simple. As planters progressively reduced their obligations to the people, so loyalties declined. Conversion of traditional master-man relations into more limited and economic ones was then marked by simultaneous deteriorations in the workers' position and in their relations with management. When estates once more began to change hands, the workers, uncertain of their rights and position, resented and feared these sales. Some felt that their old masters had betrayed them, that they had been transferred together with the property, and sought to assert their customary rights defiantly. Estate transfers accordingly created difficulties for British, Indian, and black Grenadian purchasers alike. Gairy achieved his first success in precisely this situation. Clearly, the workers' resentment and insecurity reflected social rather than economic factors. Equally clear, the reduction of estate privileges was accelerated by the economic depression of the 1930's and owed its intense effect to population growth and restricted emigration. In such a situation, underemployment continued to increase, while the "privileges" which formerly made life tolerable for the worker declined in incidence and scope.

The Problem of Form

Our second question is rather more refined, but really deals with similar issues. Given that a crisis did in fact occur, an accurate "causal" analysis should show how this came to take the form it did, rather than some other.

To resolve this problem, we must first distinguish the two senses in which we can say that the crisis exhibited form. First, at any moment after it began, the conflict expressed a clear opposition between planters and elite on the one hand, estate workers and most of the black "lower-class" on the other. The government remained officially neutral and apart from this contraposition, the workers' leaders being strong in the legislature while the elite provided leading bureaucrats. In preserving neutrality, the government enforced the law and, after the initial outbreak of February, 1951, prevented further disorders. The government also provided planters and workers with institutional means for settling their differences, and refused to take either side in these disputes, while advocating collective bargaining.

It is easy to see why the crisis formally contraposed farm workers as representatives of the folk, and planters as representatives of the elite. Without this extensive contraposition, the conflict would not have been societally inclusive. Conflict and crisis alike consisted in this general contraposition. Until the crisis, contraposition was not overt; but the years which led to the breakdown saw a latent contraposition gradually manifest itself. Until then, relations between planter and people had been marked by reciprocal solidarities rather than contraposition. As planters and workers grew estranged and loyalties were reduced, elite and folk polarized correspondingly, simply because the planters and farm workers were the basic elements in their respective social sections. Without this polarization there could have been no crisis; but once polarization had occurred between peasant and planter, it became coextensive with Grenada society.

The second sense in which the crisis exhibited form is explicitly diachronic. It consists in a set of events which had a clear beginning, middle and end. An adequate analysis should therefore show how these events occurred in this form and order. We can distinguish the following ten phases of this sequence: (1) Leaderless strikes and limited wage negotiations accompanied a rising cost of living and periodic increase by the government in the statutory minimum wage for nonunionized and disunited farm workers. This was the situation immediately before the breakdown. (2) Gairy secured full compensation for resident workers evicted from an estate which had been recently transferred. (3) Gairy, having registered a trade union, called the first successful strike in Grenada's history against the local sugar company, an "impersonal" corporation. This strike was supported by workers on estates which were owned and managed personally in the traditional style. (4) Gairy, having been ignored by the planters, launched a general strike which was marked by violence and complete success. Although the object of the strike was to secure higher wages for the planters' employees, it involved the entire population, who aligned themselves on one side or the other in the conflict. (5) Gairy's movement won six of the eight seats when elections were held shortly after the conflict on the basis of universal suffrage for the first time in local history. (6) The planters formed themselves into an agriculturists' union to deal with this movement. (7) Gairy demanded personal recognition from the elite as their status equal, but was curtly rejected. (8) Gairy threatened another island-wide strike without making specific demands, and the government intervened to appoint a tribunal. (9) Following this tribunal's report, Gairy launched a campaign against its award, leading to a second island-wide strike, which failed completely. This strike was not marked by looting or violence. (10) Shortly after this strike had collapsed, the planters awarded their workers significant wage increases, and undertook to reëstablish all traditional privileges.

Once the sequence of events that formed the crisis has been itemized, the structure of its development becomes quite clear. Crisis was possible after privileges had been reduced, since this weakened the bonds between planters and people severely. Gairy emerged as a leader in this context, precisely because he spoke for workers who had been denied their customary rights. His first strike was against the sugar company, on whose plantations these rights and relations did not exist. This strike was freely supported by workers on cocoa and nutmeg estates, whose loyalty to their masters had been lost. The planters, by rescinding privileges, had redefined themselves as employers rather than patrons. As such, they invited demands and complaints from their workers. When these were forcefully made, the planters, in their pride, overconfidence, and astonishment, decided to ignore them. The result was a breakdown in communications between planters and people which completed the process of polarization and found expression in the violent upheaval of February to March, 1951, during which Grenadian society was clearly split by the conflict between folk and elite. Following his victory in this strike, Gairy was equally victorious at the polls. He accordingly demanded social recognition from the elite. Had they accepted him, it would have symbolized admission of total defeat. The elite accordingly rejected Gairy completely. In return, he threatened and finally called an island-wide strike which had no specific industrial objectives, and which failed to enlist the necessary support for precisely this reason. The planters, having learned their lesson, followed up their success by increasing their workers' wages and restoring the traditional privileges. In this way they simultaneously reëstablished direct and solidary relations with their people on the traditional basis of estate communities, and exhibited Gairy to the people as a troublesome agitator, pursuing purely personal goals at Grenada's expense. The crisis accordingly concluded by depriving Gairy of his chief industrial support, while leaving him unchallenged at the polls.

In truth, Gairy's demand for social equality was the turning point of the entire crisis. Undoubtedly the demand was motivated by personal factors, but it is intelligible only in context. Wittingly or not, by this demand Gairy revealed the real character of his leadership. As we have seen, his was not a normal trade union; his party, the GULP, was so only in name; both union and party were products of a social movement seeking structural change. Of this movement Gairy was leader and symbol; and his electoral and industrial victories, universal suffrage, and unionism were expressions of structural change; but in his view such changes could only be final and irrevocable if distinctions between elite and folk were swept away. Accordingly, Gairy needed recognition by his enemies as their equal or superior. Accordingly, he was rejected, not only by the elite, but also by some of his own followers, who interpreted these desires for high personal status as involving disassociation from themselves. The workers may have failed to see the wider symbolic significance and structural logic behind Gairy's behavior; but their instinct was probably sound.

Only if the elite had accepted Gairy and his associates as their equals, could we say that the former Grenadian social structure had sharply changed. However, although Gairy's movement drew its force from demands for structural change, the change that the workers wanted was the restoration of traditional relations between planter and people, rather than the liquidation of these social differences. Thus Gairy misconceived the movement of which he was head.

The structural logic that regulated this sequence is quite clear. Once the nature and distribution of "privileges" had become uncertain, the roles and relations of planter and "peasant" became correspondingly ambiguous. These changes found expression in corresponding status redefinitions, planters tending more and more to have the status of employers, "people" tending more and more to occupy the status of laborers. The processes by which these incomplete status redefinitions developed increased the cleavage between these strata and generalized it as a common background of frustrations and dissatisfactions among workers whose expectations had been disappointed. In this context Gairy's leadership gave the workers a single focus around which they could unite against the "agricultural employers." The uncertainty of many workers about the correctness of such action divided their loyalties and fostered ambivalence, with the result that violence was the most distinctive feature of their first strike. This violence initially took the form of intimidation, those workers who most actively supported the strike using force against others who opposed such behavior. Only later was violence directed at planters and their homes, and even then only after Gairy's removal to custody in Carriacou when hostility against the colonial government also led to the destruction of schools, clinics, and other installations. Although successful, such intimidation did not resolve the workers' conflict of loyalties, and Gairy's strength in the industrial field thereafter depended on combining a propaganda of success with intimidation of dissidents. Clearly, intimidation would only succeed so long as Gairy's record of successful strike action won him the free support of most workers. When this record was broken, belief in his leadership failed also, and in 1953–1954 intimidation did not stop workers' returning to work. These conflicting loyalties and the ambivalence among the workers made it easier for the planters to recapture their allegiance by policies which expressed their responsibility, individually, and as a group. The planters' new policies reversed earlier trends, and once more established planters as patrons, rather than employers. The crisis accordingly concluded with the substantial restoration of the traditional status of peasants and planters linked by reciprocal roles in solidary relations based on estate-communities. In effect the basic features of the social structure were strengthened and preserved.

The preceding analysis also explains why Gairy made no specific demands in 1953 before calling his second strike. This was a strike in name only. Not only did it lack a specific objective, but it also included a "fishermen's" strike, although almost all these strikers worked

on their own account, receiving set shares of the catch in their boats.
Many Grenadians who had been puzzled by the "peasants'" strike of
1951 were also mystified by this fishermen's strike; and under these
conditions some asked if these men were striking against the fish. In
fact, these men were not really on strike at all, nor could they be,
since they lacked employers against whom to strike. What the fishermen had done was to declare solidarity with the "striking" farm-
workers and to take common political action for objectives that were
neither clearly realized nor capable of full expression in trade union
demands. For this reason Gairy set no specific targets for this second
strike; and perhaps, this strike would not have occurred had the elite
accepted him in their clubs, thereby admitting their total defeat and
abandonment of the old status structure under pressures for structural
change. In fact, as we have seen, Gairy misconceived the people's goals
—goals that stressed the restoration of traditional symbiotic relations
with certain adjustments, rather than their elimination in favor of new
ones. While Gairy sought radical change, the mass of his followers
wanted structural restoration. In consequence, leader and followers
marched out of step; loyalties were confused, ambiguous, and conditional; inconsistency and intimidation prevailed.

The Politics of Change

Grenada society was founded on slavery. During this period
white planters monopolized legislative powers. In 1838 the slaves were
freed, but they were not enfranchised. During the next forty years, new
relations between planters and people replaced the old relations of
planters and slaves. By this transition the planter's slaves became his
people, living on his estate, enjoying customary rights, and supplying
the labor he needed. Simultaneously, Grenadian production switched
from sugar to cocoa and nutmeg. With these modifications estates persisted as the basis of local organization. Many ex-slaves acquired land
from or between estates; some worked on estates as casual laborers,
others recruited labor from their neighbors. The free society that
emerged was built up on two major social formations—planters and
peasant-workers—just as the unfree society had been based on relations between planter and slave. Until new political relations between
planter and people were firmly established, the old governmental organization in which planters were dominant and the people lacked
constitutional rights persisted. This transition ended when solidary
ties had developed, and planters were then content to surrender their
constitutional rights to the Crown, which became fully responsible for
the colonial administration, the franchise being abolished. Under this
Crown Colony system, planter interests remained politically dominant.
The new relations between planter and people, expressed in "privi-

leges" and obligations of a symbiotic character, provided the new society with its basic political bonds. For this reason, planters no longer needed legislative power once they had established these new relations. The colonial government, accordingly, had purely routine functions, such as the administration of law, communications, revenue, health, and education. There was no garrison and no need for one. At this time the native political system consisted of two major sections, the Creole elite and folk, each based on a major social formation, the planters and worker-peasants, relations between which were territorially distributed through a network of individually controlled estate communities. Accordingly, planters and peasants were never contraposed as categories or groups; instead they were bound together in solidary relations as members of discrete communities.

As "privileges" were reduced and revoked, the consensus which underlay this political system diminished accordingly. Polarization proceeded apace until planter and peasant were contraposed. This situation generated a conflict which called for united action under a leader. In this context, Gairy emerged.

Meanwhile, the British had introduced constitutional reforms and liberalized the franchise. Gairy won a sweeping victory at the polls, yet his triumph was empty. It is worth asking why, having acquired this legislative power, Gairy failed to promote the structural changes he wanted by these means. This question raises the problem of the nature of Gairy's leadership, and of the crisis itself.

Gairy saw himself as an uncompromising charismatic leader to whom all workers owed devotion and unswerving obedience. But he did not succeed in winning the workers' loyalty fully. Intimidation was constantly necessary to ensure a solid front. Leadership which depends on such methods lacks the true charisma Gairy claimed.

Gairy was also mistaken about the people's desires. His demand for social equality unconsciously expressed his conception of structural change as well as his personal status interests. Under universal suffrage legislative position did not carry this social equality, but could perhaps be converted into acceptance. In fact, the people wanted to resume the old solidary relations between themselves and the planters, which were characterized by a symbiotic adjustment of needs and resources.

This does not mean that peasants and planters had much in common besides their symbiosis; but the workers were familiar with this relation. They looked back to the days when it had assured them their subsistence; and they longed to restore this traditional pattern in good working order, rather than risk the unknown with Gairy.

Gairy's misunderstanding of the movement he led helped him to misunderstand his own position as leader. In one view, his social acceptance by the elite would express his personal triumph in changing the social structure. To many followers, this indicated Gairy's unfitness for leadership, since the desire for higher status was interpreted as rejection of low-status folk.

However, Gairy was not unperceptive. His union and party were both one-man shows, of necessity. It is hardly useful to criticize him on these grounds; he led neither a normal trade union nor political party, but a social movement with inchoate goals and organization, which required these two modes of action. In establishing these organs, Gairy adapted positively to his situation.

This brings us to the problematic relation between government and structural change. We have seen that until 1950, the government's functions were mainly those of routine administration within limits set by restricted budgets. Grenada society is clearly too small to form a viable independent unit. It depends on Britain for institutional forms, skilled personnel, markets, and financial assistance. In return the island has lost decisive power over policies for radical change within it. Accordingly, the administration was less significant than the political relations of planter and worker, the breakdown of which produced this crisis. The government's role in this conflict was nonetheless crucial, since the course of events raised many policy issues in urgent terms. But as legislative power was inadequate to deal with issues of this form and scope, it could not resolve the struggle.

Under traditional conditions the political aspect of Grenada society consisted of relations between elite and folk, with planter-peasant solidarities as the pivot. With the gradual breakdown of these traditional relations, a crisis that was structural in base and political in form developed. This crisis resolved itself into confused upheavals, the source and focus of which was structural continuity or change. Such change had already taken place to some degree in the political breakdown that set off the social disturbance. Grenadians were sharply divided on how to explain or resolve this crisis.

The responsible British officials saw that Grenadians would have to settle these problems themselves, and decided that the government should remain strictly neutral throughout the conflict, committed merely to maintain law and order. This policy deprived Gairy of the overwhelming popular support that militant leaders usually enjoy when "persecuted" by a hostile colonial government concerned to protect the status quo. It also deprived the planters of official protection, and forced them, first to rethink their position, then to negotiate with the workers' trade union, and finally to reëstablish the old structural patterns in which there was neither scope nor need for a militant workers' union. The government's neutral policy was quite as successful as it was difficult to maintain.

It is revealing that both Gairy and the Governor recognized that the constitutional changes and GULP electoral triumph of 1951 hardly affected the crisis under way, or the actual balance of power between the conflicting parties. The political struggle which had already been joined for the future of Grenadian society ended as it began, on the estates and the roads quite outside the legislative chamber.

Shortly after its end, Hurricane Janet devastated Grenada. The British government gave the island £2,000,000 for rehabilitation, and loaned it another £1,500,000 on easy terms. Like other Caribbean natural disasters, the hurricane was a blessing in disguise. It created substantial increases in labor demand. It made replanting necessary; and planters, having already reëstablished traditional relations with their people, were accordingly free to restore the full complement of workers' privileges and to replant by traditional methods if they so wished.

We may summarize this analysis as follows: social structure constitutes the primary system of political relations and goals. Legislative constitutions and bureaucratic forms are quite secondary. Structural change always involves political action, within or beyond constitutional frameworks. Its causes and conditions are complex and hard to unravel. Action oriented toward such change takes various forms, of which explicitly political action within a constitutional framework is perhaps less common, the more basic the changes involved. Desire for structural change may thus generate movements which seek to institutionalize new relations; but the conflicts which these produce often end inconclusively, despite violence, when certain modifications of the old social structure have been made.

[12

Short-range Prospects in the British Caribbean

Projections

Prediction is not the favorite pastime of social scientists. It can be a risky business, even for journalists. When unavoidable, one favorite solution is to develop oracular statements, cryptic or general enough to rule out disproof. An alternative evasion is to set up a chain of dichotomous contingencies without indicating their relative probability.[1]

Projections and predictions differ sharply. Predictions are verifiable, specific statements about future events. Projections indicate trends of development, their conditions, directions, and strength. A rigorously formulated projection may permit predictive tests in certain areas. Where feasible this is of value. But it is neither a necessary nor a sufficient feature of useful projections. A good projection sets out the implications of present trends for future developments, and thus presumes understanding of relations between the present and past. All projections presume some continuities in the field at certain levels; and these continuities are certainly more evident in history than speculation. A reasoned projection accordingly rests on detailed knowledge of given historical fields, on analysis of their current structure and trends, and on certain assumptions or conclusions about their external contexts. In addition, a systematic projection presumes integration of two quite distinct types of theory, one dealing with the nature of the units in question, the other with continuity or change. Unless these two streams of theory are integrated in it, there is little to differentiate the projection from ad hoc guesswork.

It happens that I have been gradually developing two relevant bodies of theory which can provide the basis for reasoned projections

304

about British Caribbean probabilities in the near future. One of these theories applies a framework of social and cultural pluralism to the study of Caribbean societies.[2] The other deals with processes of structural maintenance or change.[3] By combining relevant ideas in these two theories, and applying these to the Caribbean future, it is possible to avoid ad hoc guessing, to test these general conceptions, and to explain both the present and the future which springs from it. To merit scientific consideration, projections must be grounded on formal theory as well as on empirical knowledge of the relevant field.

Population

The British Caribbean consists of twelve dependent territories, two of which, British Honduras and British Guiana, differ in their mainland situation; large empty interiors; low overall population densities; and aloofness from the Federation which the ten island-units formed. Such differences of size, position, population, and relations to the Federation require attention.[4] Important differences of racial composition, cultural structure and economic level are also present.

The principal features shared by these units include colonial status, economic dependence, dependence on British institutional models, histories of slavery, monoculture, frequent transfers between European powers in the seventeenth and eighteenth centuries, racial and cultural heterogeneity, and malintegration and social pluralism. Today, except in Dominica, Guiana, and Honduras, population densities are overly high in most units. Since 1955 several thousand West Indians have migrated to Britain, mainly from Jamaica, Barbados, the Windward and Leeward Islands. Although population problems are acute, population policy is almost absent. Only Barbados presently has an officially sponsored program of birth control. For most of the other units, population policy is uncontrolled emigration. Trinidad prohibits West Indian immigration for political and economic reasons. The future of these Caribbean societies is thus closely related to their demographic conditions and development. West Indian migrants are not welcome in most countries of the world. Only Britain has recently accepted them in large numbers, and for various reasons. How long this will continue is not quite clear; but West Indian leaders are rightly worried at the prospect that Britain may stop this migration when the West Indies obtain independence.

External Relations

These British Caribbean colonies are dependent units. They are so weak and poor that their influence on developments elsewhere is

negligible. By the same token, they are easily affected by policies in
the metropolitan countries with which they have close relations. These
units are chiefly significant to foreigners because of their geopolitical
situation and problematic social stability.

I cannot consider the global context of West Indian societies at
length here. West Indian units must adapt themselves to this context
as best they can. There is little they can do to influence its development. Nonetheless, as this context provides the background for our
projection, its implications should be defined.

I assume that the cold war continues in the near future, and that
during the next two or three years with which this essay deals, the
world remains uneasily in the indeterminate status quo based on shifting distributions of global pressures and power. I assume that a nuclear
war would rob the immediate future, and any projections, of meaning.
West Indian contributions to this global struggle depend entirely on
West Indian stability. A reasonably stable British Caribbean represents
a stable sector of the global arena, small and poor no doubt, but not
entirely unimportant. A West Indies in turmoil provides opportunities
for political exploitation revolutionaries would be silly to miss. I
assume that both the Anglo-American and Sino-Soviet blocs share this
assessment, and that these considerations give Dr. Castro's Cuba her
present importance. I cannot imagine that any Communist forces
would attempt to invade the British Caribbean units; but it is possible that such forces would assist a popular revolt in these units, if
properly invited.

I assume that Britain is anxious to give these colonies independence,
and that her main concern is to create conditions that promote their
stability and economic growth. It is clear now that Britons wish to
control West Indian immigration. Britain can hardly do so before the
West Indies become independent. It is thus probable that the inflow
will be restricted shortly afterward, perhaps on a basis subject to
periodic revision. Such restrictions on emigration will increase economic distress and social malaise in some West Indian units, unless
compensations are found. The Trinidadian premier, Dr. Eric Williams,
has already announced that revolution would break out within twenty-
four hours of British action to stop this immigration.[5] Dr. Williams
did not say where, how, or why this "revolution" would take place,
and his statement expresses anxiety rather than analysis. This anxiety
undoubtedly rests on hard demographic and economic facts, but the
significance of these facts depends on certain social and cultural conditions which also require study. If there is a West Indian revolution
within twenty-four hours of British action to stop West Indian immigration, it would clearly be owing to West Indian social and economic conditions rather than to British migration laws.

It is already clear that the central theme of our projection is the question of stability or change. For this reason, I shall only discuss the present situation, its immediate antecedents and immediate future. West Indian stability is not identical with persistence of the status quo. The West Indian status quo is now future-oriented, at least formally. The West Indies Federation should become independent on May 31, 1962. British Guiana and British Honduras remain outside this grouping, but expect further increases of self-government shortly. All units in the Federation will receive full powers of internal self-government before the date of federal independence. However, the West Indian present is bound as fully to its past as to the future. Pursuit of present goals presumes continuity of the social movements and trends that established and support them. Continued operation of these social forces at present levels of strength itself presumes continuity of the basic societal processes from which they derive. Thus if the West Indian present is a moving equilibrium oriented to certain goals and problems, maintenance of this status quo is equivalent to continued pursuit of present goals and continuity of present trends. The maintenance of such conditions itself presupposes continuity in the basic processes and forms of West Indian social life. Accordingly the maintenance of present trends and directions expresses West Indian stability and implies maintenance of the social structure.

Creole Society

West Indian society is Creole society, with certain variations. Creoles are natives of the region, other than Amerindians, Chinese, East Indians, and some occupationally specialized minorities, such as Lebanese or Jews. These exclusions define Creoles as native West Indians of European, African, or mixed descent. The creole society and culture accordingly derives from Europe and Africa. Expressed in terms of color, Creoles form a trinity of black, white, and brown. Despite obvious debts to Europe and Africa, the Creole society and culture are distinctive local products, part amalgam, and part mixture of discordant and incompatible elements. The Creole milieu provides a classic example of social and cultural pluralism in its extreme form; the plural society. Historically based on European control of African slaves, the current social order reflects these antecedents. As David Lowenthal says:

Many coloured people are as wealthy as some whites; many black people hold high political office; social mobility is probably increasing in most of the islands. Nevertheless, it is still true that black folk in The West Indies are generally the poorest and have the lowest status; the small, but increasingly important, middle class is chiefly composed of coloured people and special minorities; while the upper class—with the most money, the highest status, and the greatest power—is chiefly confined to a small group of whites and near-whites. Racial composition and social situations vary from island to island; there are many "poor whites" in Barbados who are not considered upper class, while in Grenada and Dominica, where whites are few, the local élite is predominantly light-coloured. But these are minor variations within the general social alignment of classes. As in post-revolutionary Haiti, so in The West Indies. . . . Every rich Negro is a mulatto, every poor mulatto is a Negro.[6]

Creole status hierarchies are conceived and expressed in terms of color. General stereotypes equate high status and light pigment, low status and dark pigment, medium status and medium pigment. In addition each color-class exhibits cultural peculiarities and distinctness to itself as well as others. These social and cultural differences include language skills and habits, literacy, education, occupation, property forms, employment patterns, saving institutions, mating, family, and kinship practice, local groupings and other associations, religion, magic, ritual and belief, customs, norms, and ideologies and values of the most trivial or important kinds. These cleavages of culture between high-status "whites," mid-status "browns," and low-status "blacks" ramify throughout all phases and aspects of intersectional relations and activities in the West Indies, and underlie the discontinuities between these social sections noted by Leonard Broom.[7] The resulting combination of economic, behavioral, cultural, and color differentiation reduces social cohesion and intersectional mobility in Creole society to a minimum.

The Analytic Frame

Pressures for change which seek to redistribute social values focus directly on the positions and relations of the social sections that are the principal components of this social structure. Accordingly structural changes involve changes of sectional relations and cannot develop except under conditions of maximum strain and instability in which the continuity of the social system as a unit is clearly at stake. The Grenadian crisis of 1951–1954 which I have described elsewhere illustrates the general pattern of West Indian movements for change.[8] As has also been shown, structural changes in Creole society are changes of status structure, and thus involve changes of intersectional relations.[9] Yet other studies show that basic changes in the status of government and society proceed together with changes of status structure. Changes in the status of a society involve changes in its external relations, and these may find expression in changes of governmental regime. Changes in the status structure of a given society proceed by political action which redistributes social values and redefines the composition or inter-relations of status groups. Typically these processes also involve changes in governmental system and ideology.[10]

These principles provide the theoretical basis for our projection. Their implications are quite clear. They indicate that structural variations of Creole society will reflect differing racial and cultural ratios and composition. They show that recent constitutional advances, negotiations for independence, nationalist ideologies, and stress on federation and economic development reflect and accompany certain changes of status structure in these Creole societies, and of their statuses as separate units also. Careful study of these governmental changes indicates the changes of social structure which underlie and promote them. We should therefore focus attention on those conditions that must prevail if current movements for independence, national status, and economic development are to maintain their strength. Our theories must explain the selection and pursuit of these targets, their distribution and differences in different Creole societies, their appeal, support, and opposition. The essential basis for projections about British Caribbean developments accordingly integrates the theories of pluralism and structural change, so that current trends in these Creole pluralities may be evaluated and understood.

Territorial Differences

There are marked structural differences between British Honduras, British Guiana, and Trinidad, and between these units and all others. Trinidad and British Guiana contain large East Indian populations. In British Guiana, East Indians have a population majority and support Dr. Cheddi Jagan, the present premier, who is also East Indian. In Trinidad, East Indians represent approximately 40 per cent of the population, and the Creole premier, Dr. Eric Williams, seeks to keep race and politics apart.[11] British Guiana under Dr. Jagan has kept aloof from the West Indies Federation, and has established friendly relations with Castro's government in Cuba. Under Williams, Trinidad is the foremost advocate of a strong centralized federation, charged with power and responsibilities for regional development. Williams has used every chance to promote a vigorous national sentiment in Trinidad, and on occasion has generalized this Trinidadian nationalism throughout the Federation, for example in his dispute with the United States over Chaguaramas, the site of the future federal capital. While Jagan's program for the economic development of Guiana places primary emphases on the peasants,[12] most of whom are Indian, Williams' economic program for Trinidad stresses industrialization and restricts Creole immigration.

These differing orientations of Guiana and Trinidad reflect their differences of structure. Trinidad with its Creole majority and premier is explicitly Creole in culture and orientations.[13] Guiana with its Indian majority and premier lacks this commitment to Creole culture or values.[14] Many Indians in Trinidad as well as in British Guiana are weakly acculturated to Creole norms;[15] but their number is larger in Guiana, where they are free to choose other goals. The prevalent ideology in British Guiana is socialist; in Trinidad, Williams emphasizes nationalism, federation, and economic development. By these means, Wiliams hopes to replace racial divisions with national identity, defined by contradistinction with other national units. Such an ideology might encourage the creolization of enough Indians in Trinidad to preserve the unit's Creole orientation, despite the Indians' superior fertility. Jagan and the Indians of British Guiana need no such creed, and may well regard it as regressive for Guiana.

The position and society of British Honduras are structurally unique. This territory straddles the boundary of two quite different worlds, the Negro-white Creole and the Spanish-Indian mestizo culture-areas.[16] This cleavage divides Hondurans culturally, linguistically, and by race. In consequence Hondurans hold conflicting loyalties and orientations. Many wish to quit the British Commonwealth and the Creole cultural province for Guatemala and the Central American mestizo field. Others wish to remain Creole and British. As Honduran autonomy increases, this cleavage will tend to deepen, and some choice between association with the West Indies or with Guatemala will have to be faced. The final decision may then be determined by the balance of forces within Honduras.

Apart from Trinidad, Honduras, and British Guiana, all other British Caribbean units have a similar basic structure.[17] They lack important East Indian enclaves and the basic Indian-Creole cleavage. None face the problem of choice between Creole and mestizo ways of life. All either have or will shortly enjoy internal autonomy. Excluding Barbuda and Dominica, all these units are overpopulated. All are undercapitalized and have considerable unemployment and underemployment. All are too small and weak to compete successfully in the world market. All depend on preferential treatment in British and other Commonwealth markets. The racial composition of all these societies is essentially the same—white, brown, and black accounting for the overwhelming majority of their people. All display the Creole social structure in its simplest, purest form. In all, the handful of whites have highest status, wealth, and power. In all, four-fifths of the people are black, poor, ill-educated, and of low status, the majority of the remainder being colored, of middling wealth, skill, status, and cultural allegiance.

These structural uniformities are found together with significant differences of size and position. Jamaica is several hundred miles removed from her nearest federal partner, but only 90 miles from Cuba. With an area of 4,400 square miles, a population of 1.6 million, and gross domestic product estimated at about £230 million,[18] Jamaica could perhaps form a viable independent unit. This is one aspect of the choice Jamaicans will have to make in their referendum on federal membership. Of the other islands, excluding Trinidad, only Barbados could conceivably stand on its own. Several Windward and Leeward Islands already depend on grants from the British or federal treasuries. These units already share certain services, and have long histories of mutually unsatisfactory association. Thus, of these nine islands, only Barbados and Jamaica enjoy sufficient independence of action to permit internal movements for change.

In Jamaica, programs of economic development stress tourism, industrialization, and increased farm production as the major means of prosperity and progress. In Jamaica, the ideology of nationalism dates back to 1939, when Norman Manley founded his People's National Party. Progress is now defined as prosperity,[19] and nationalism as racial harmony in an integrated ideology which receives strenuous elite support.

In Barbados, the fantastic population density restricts the scope for social reform most severely. Barbadian population density stands now at approximately 1,400 per square mile, and is still rising. In addition Barbadians have a history of stable sectional symbiosis. Ideologies, national or socialist, are difficult to implant or nourish in these conditions. Their absence perpetuates parochialism and traditionalistic orientations. Sugar and emigration together barely keep the Barbadian economy afloat. Since Trinidad began to restrict West Indian immigration, Barbadians have been moving to Britain. Without freedom of movement within the Federation, Barbados may withdraw. An independent Barbados could perhaps maintain its present population at current levels of living by extracting special concessions from Britain, by importing capital, by increasing its tourist trade, and by exporting surplus Barbadians to new areas if Britain excludes them. There is no obvious gain for Barbados within a federation which does not furnish either of these conditions. As a colony with full internal self-government, Barbados may in many respects be better off alone.

For the Windwards and Leewards, dependence on some larger unit is the only feasible prospect. Their withdrawal from federation would rob this body of its connecting links and major objective. Failing freedom of migration to Trinidad, or federal funds to finance local development, some of these units are now rethinking the value of federation for them. Recognizing this, Great Britain has promised interim economic aid to these islands, and to study the future needs of their economies. There are signs that the United States may also offer help.

The West Indies Federation

The future of this Federation is now obscure at two levels. It is not clear whether the Federation will hold together until independence on May 31, 1962, or how many units will elect to remain in it. Assuming that the Federation persists with all or most of its present members and receives independence as currently planned, it is also not clear how the newly independent state will meet its pressing problems. These two sets of difficulties are best discussed separately.

As of 1961 the federal government maintains, along with its personnel in temporary headquarters at Port of Spain, Trinidad, one battalion of the West India Regiment, a shipping service between the islands, responsibility for British West Indian Airways, the University College of the West Indies, and certain minor agencies. Under its present constitution, federal funds and powers are strictly limited, and the small populations of the Windwards and Leewards are over-represented in the Legislature, while the peoples of Trinidad and Jamaica who supply 85 per cent of federal population and funds do not have proportionate representation. There is yet no permanent capital, no customs union, no freedom of entry to Trinidad, no regional development plan, or federal power of taxation.

In anticipation of federal independence, all member-units will receive internal self-government, and a new federal constitution will provide for legislative representation on a basis corresponding with population size. The Federation will in the future be financed from customs duties, and over the following nine years, it is planned that a customs union throughout the federal area will be established. In step with the establishment of this customs union, restrictions on free movement of persons between the territories may be removed. Federal responsibilities will increase at the same rate. The West India regiment is to have two battalions. The federal government will represent all its units in the United Nations, the British Commonwealth and external relations generally. Each unit will control its own income tax and industrial development separately. Each unit will be able to veto further proposals for constitutional change. These are the legal blueprints and bureaucratic programs of federation. The problems for which this machinery has been designed are scarcely indicated there.

The persistence of federation presumes ratification of these arrangements by each member-unit separately. Hardly any of the units are fully satisfied with the present federal blueprint. Barbados demands freedom of entry to Trinidad at once, and some smaller islands support this. Trinidad refuses to permit this movement until the customs union is fully established nine years hence. Trinidad advocates a strong federal center equipped to integrate the unit-economies and to promote development on a regional basis. Trinidad has also threatened to quit the Federation if Jamaica withdraws. Trinidad contains the site of the future federal capital, and leads in the promotion of "West Indian nationalism." The Windward and Leeward islands have looked to Trinidad for ideas, migration opportunities, and funds for local investment. Their present disappointment at Trinidadian policies is expressed in demands for freedom of entry backed by threats of secession. Jamaica has compelled the other units to grant all her chief demands. These include Jamaican control over local industrial development and taxation, coupled with representation in proportion to population, and safeguards against further constitutional change. Nonetheless, Jamaican membership in the Federation remains uncertain. A referendum on this question will be held when Jamaicans will decide whether to continue in the Federation or to withdraw. If Jamaica withdraws after an antifederal majority vote, Trinidad may wish to do likewise, unless important new resources become available to the Federation.

It is idle to speculate about current threats of withdrawal from the Federation. The association will collapse only if Trinidad or most of the small islands leave it. A West Indian federation is quite viable without Barbados or Jamaica. Moreover, if Jamaica secedes, British Guiana may decide to join the Federation. If the small islands withdraw as a group, or if Trinidad secedes, the federal form and idea will lose its value. However, it is unlikely that the small islands will agree to withdraw as a group. There are obvious advantages in their federal membership, if foreign aid is funneled through the federal government. Thus even if Jamaica secedes after her referendum, the Federation may persist, provided its dominant member, Trinidad, can secure the additional help she will need to meet her new responsibilities. The United Kingdom, the United States, and the United Nations will certainly assist an independent West Indies federation, whatever its membership; and British Guiana might be willing to enter if Jamaica withdraws. It is thus possible that the Federation can survive, with or without Jamaican participation.

The problems that will face an independent West Indies federation, whatever its composition, are severe but manageable.[20] Overpopulation, undercapitalization, and unemployment are obvious economic ills. But members of an independent West Indies federation may enjoy rights of free entry into the United States similar to those of other free nations in the New World. Important increases in West

Indian migration to America should reduce the movement to Britain together with British anxieties about this influx, and strains in the West Indian economy. Foreign aid has already been offered the new state, and this might include the skills and resources to promote economic development. In such conditions unemployment rates should fall. Policies to control population may then develop. Although the West Indian economy would still face difficulties even under such favorable conditions, it would then provide a firmer basis for the social order, and might promote social change and stability together. Thus the most important factor in the immediate future of the West Indies is undoubtedly opportunities for increased emigration.

British Guiana holds a unique position. Its present government has Marxist orientations, friendly relations with Cuba, mass support from Guianese Indians, and dislike of the West Indies Federation as presently constituted. However, an independent federation may attract Guiana, especially if Jamaica withdraws and the Indian and Creole populations become more nearly equal. One advantage of federation in such conditions to Jagan might lie in the strategy of political expansion. In the event of Guianese independence, the Caribbean would have governments sympathetic to Marxism at either end. Recognizing this, Britain may seek to delay or otherwise limit Guianese independence. Guiana's entry into the West Indies Federation provides the most promising solution of this problem, if Jagan can be made to agree.

The Position of Jamaica

In various ways Jamaica holds the key to developments in the British Caribbean in the immediate future. It is in Jamaica also that the general question of structural maintenance or change is most immediate and critical. Analysis of Jamaica's situation may thus throw light on the basic forces and tendencies of Caribbean social structure. This unit has certain advantages of size, situation, and structural simplicity which together explain its relatively rapid political development. Issues which remain obscure in other parts of the Caribbean emerge clearly in Jamaica. There is no Indian-Creole or Creole-mestizo cleavage to override or conceal them.

Jamaican society is a hierarchy of three social sections differentiated by color, culture, status, and interest.[21] Of these, the minute white upper section represents about one per cent of the population, the black lower section includes four-fifths, and the brown middle section, the remainder. Until 1938 whites monopolized decisive power in Jamaican political and economic affairs. In 1938 the blacks protested against social and economic conditions; their protest was canalized and organized by members of the brown middle section, who differed from the blacks in color, values, norms, aspirations, education, beliefs, associations, wealth, status, and occasionally language. Two men became outstanding leaders, Bustamante in the trade-union field, and Norman Manley in political party and constitutional development.[22] Of these men, Bustamante first championed the cause of the workers and of the black lower section generally. The devotion he aroused was intense, and for years his leadership was secure. Manley advocated responsible government based on universal suffrage, socialism based on nationalization of property aggregates, and nationalism based on the need to weld the three Creole sections into a solidary unit which could claim independent status. The introduction of universal suffrage and a more liberal constitution in 1944 was largely due to Manley's demands; but in this and the succeeding election of 1949, Jamaicans rejected Manley's socialist program and elected Bustamante's candidates.

In these years Manley's socialism represented an explicit program of structural change aimed at redistributing social values and changing intersectional relations. The two upper sections were accordingly alienated. The large lower section supported Bustamante, whose championship in 1938 they never forgot. Among the factors which frustrated Manley's efforts were certain differences of orientation which communications could not bridge. Manley's program of reform was conceived in terms of economic means and objectives. Bustamante offered no program for reform. He represented social protest in and against conditions as they were. The majority of the lower section were accustomed to thinking about their position in fatalistic racial and magico-religious terms,[23] and did not respond to Manley's rationalistic economic program or to his advocacy of nationalism and constitutional reforms. Bustamante's charisma and bread-and-butter union leadership suited them better.

By 1955, when Manley finally won power, social reform and social protest had both ceased to motivate Jamaican politicians. Manley proclaimed new goals of economic development, constitutional reform, and federation. His early programs of socialism and structural change were thoroughly abandoned.[24] Manley's adoption of economic development instead of socialism was forced on him in two defeats by an electorate opposed to structural change. Like his rival Bustamante, Manley's capacities for political action and social reform were limited and defined by the structure of his situation as a Jamaican leader. Like Bustamante, Manley has accommodated himself to his situation in perfect good faith. But this situation has permitted the middle section to appropriate the powers and positions of that above without any corresponding changes in the position or prospects of the black section, despite unionism and universal suffrage. Members of the middle section manage the political parties and trade unions alike. Other members of this section staff and manage the expanded bureaucracy, and some have also moved into new economic positions under development schemes. Well-paid unionized workers enter the lower fringes of the middle section, just as leaders of this section moved into positions formerly monopolized by whites.

Since 1955, Manley's government has concentrated its energies on promoting internal autonomy, tourism, industrialization, and agricultural improvement. It has done important work in negotiating favorable terms of trade, in road-building, airport improvement, improving technical education, and in modernizing and expanding the bureaucratic machinery to match Jamaica's economic growth. For the lower section, piped water and local health centers are becoming available. In 1957 the government introduced a ten-year program to provide 16,000 scholarships to secondary schools. Half of these scholarships are annually won by pupils of fee-paying schools, very few of whom may belong to the lower section. After a grant from the British government was exhausted, low-cost housing programs came to a virtual halt. Unemployment may have increased during this period, owing to recent technological changes, population increase, and the failure of industrialization or tourism to provide sufficient jobs. Manley's nationalist ideology, constitutional reforms, and advocacy of federation have meant progressively less to the Jamaican lower section, whose hopes of change under his leadership or Bustamante's have been disappointed. Since 1955, over 100,000 Jamaicans have moved to Britain, the overwhelming majority being of very low status.

As disaffection increased among the lower section, so did their demands for emigration to Africa. In 1959 and 1960 this movement produced increasing unrest. A conspiracy to overthrow the government by violence was unearthed. Further violent encounters were followed by an investigation.[25] In March 1961 the Jamaican government despatched a mission to certain African countries to explore opportunities for Jamaican immigration. Most members of this mission were advocates of emigration to Africa. The strength of this demand reflects the measure of disaffection current in the lower section.

When Jamaica holds its federal referendum, this disaffection of the lower section will decide the issue. Jamaicans have little understanding of or interest in the Federation. Independence and national status are at best ambiguous concepts in these conditions. Since Manley has now won federal concessions on all important Jamaican interests, there should be a heavy vote in favor of federation, if this is indeed the issue on which Jamaicans will vote. In fact, the maintenance or change of Jamaican society and of its present government and regime are the issues really at stake in this referendum. Its unresolved problems of 1937–1938 confront Jamaica in 1961–1962.

The current emigration and desire of low-status blacks to quit Jamaica recall the exodus of ex-slaves from plantations to the hilly interior immediately after Emancipation.[26] The disaffection which prompts this current withdrawal may also prompt revolt. This disaffection is concentrated in the lower section whose frustration equals their disillusion with the governments of Manley and Bustamante. From 1938 to 1944, expectations of structural change were widely encouraged. Manley's radical socialism expressed this systematically. Changes indeed took place. Power and responsibility were progressively transferred from the upper to the middle section. As this proceeded, the status of Jamaican society and its government were also redefined by federal involvements, increased local autonomy, and bureaucratic expansion. Goals of social reform and structural change were replaced by programs of economic development which represented a compromise of interests between the politically expansive middle section and the economically dominant upper one.

After some years the limitations of this program are painfully evident in mass unemployment, slums, demands for withdrawal, and violent black racism. The rural and urban proletariats of the black lower section are naturally the most disaffected elements, but many peasants are also alienated after years of frustrated expectations. Such people see the upper sections enjoying higher standards of living and the benefits of recent development, while their own position changes little. Accordingly they regard the current government, its members, regime, and ideology, as alien or inimical to their interests. Current policy is interpreted as an instrument for pursuit of interests of the white and colored sections. The elite ideology of nationalism is challenged by a black racist ideology of the lower section, and elite programs of federation and economic development compete with threats of revolt and demands for withdrawal to Africa. The current predominance of the middle section in the political parties, trade unions, and bureaucracies is questioned and challenged by the black. The present parliamentary regime is discredited by comparison with one-party systems such as Cuba's which seek to promote social reform. Thus the maintenance or change of current intersectional relations underlies questions of federal participation. A vote to remain in the Federation involves a permanent change in the status of Jamaican society and its government alike; it also completes the appropriation of local power by the middle section, and thus concludes those changes of intersectional relations which have been pursued actively since 1938–1939. A vote to withdraw from the Federation reverses these recent trends and repudiates the ideologies of economic development and Creole nationalism which legitimate them. It implicitly rejects the current structure of intersectional relations, and sets new directions of change. It opens the way to further structural revisions during which the sections as presently constituted and related may undergo change, along with the status and format of the governmental regime. The implications of an antifederal majority in Jamaica's referendum are far-reaching, for other British Caribbean societies as well as Jamaica.

We can only understand the current disaffection in Jamaica if we recognize how its pluralism has regulated Jamaican social and political development. The same principles which "explain" Jamaica's current situation enable us to perceive the conditions and outlines of its future development. Seen in perspective, the forthcoming referendum on federation is far less significant than the balance of forces for the continuity or reversal of recent trends its results will represent. Jamaica is currently divided between those whose loyalties lie toward the current governmental regime, the two-party system, the ideology of national development, and the current social structure, and others who reject these values and dream of withdrawal, change, or revolt. Those who support current programs generally oppose important modifications of the social structure which may reduce their social status or prospects of social mobility. However, since members of the black social section have little prospect of social reform or social mobility, they are forced to choose between withdrawal, resignation, or revolt. The longer present trends and policies continue, the larger will be the number of black Jamaicans who choose withdrawal or revolt. Accordingly, the maintenance of current social trends and the current plural structure depends on the export of black Jamaicans to Britain, America, or Africa, where many wish to go. Failing an African emigration, violence is likely, and could lead to structural breakdown if not to radical change. To win his referendum, Manley must convince the black lower section that he is genuinely in favor of emigration to Africa and can promote it, given the chance. To preserve current adjustments after this referendum, further opportunities for emigration are essential.

Conclusion

Analysis of Jamaica's situation throws light on the general dynamics of Creole society, and so on British Caribbean prospects and problems in the immediate future. The motive forces of Jamaican developments are its sectional interests and conflicts. The current Jamaican dilemma is a conflict of sectional goals and orientations. The dominant upper sections espouse economic development, the status quo, the parliamentary system, and the West Indies Federation.

The black lower section in its disaffection demands withdrawal from Jamaican society, supports Bustamante's opposition to federation, proclaims black racism, or resigns itself to the status quo. The federal referendum cannot itself resolve these differences, but will merely express them. The results of this referendum will probably reflect various contingencies. If Manley dies, or if other federal units secede, the referendum may be postponed, perhaps indefinitely. The sectional contraposition will continue whether or not the referendum is held, until such time as social mobility and cultural change eliminate the current exclusive sociocultural sections and establish some other system of stratification.

In Trinidad, differences within the Creole section comparable to those in Jamaica lose their structural primacy and dynamism in face of the overriding division between Creoles and Indians. This racial contraposition is central to future developments in Trinidadian society. In British Guiana where the Indian majority is sure, the Creole segment has limited effect, but indirectly this explains Guianese aloofness from federation and explicit support for socialism. In Barbados the basic division is that between whites and nonwhites; colored Barbadians with black support can win political positions formerly reserved for whites; but the Barbadian economic and demographic situation rules out drastic programs of internal change. Such programs are also impracticable in the smaller islands with their heavily dependent economies. Nonetheless, an upheaval in Jamaica may be followed by upheavals in these units, perhaps in St. Lucia and St. Kitts, first of all.

I conclude that at present the West Indian future is rather problematic. The present federal organization and social order rest on insecure foundations. To enhance stability at either level, emigration, population control, education, and economic development are all required. Without sharp increases in current rates of social mobility, migration, and education, social breakdown is probable in the immediate future—but not inevitable.

It remains to show how this projection derives from the theories of structural change and Creole pluralism mentioned above. Although pervasively pluralistic, the British Caribbean colonies vary in sectional composition and structure, in situation, complexity, and scale. While all share a preoccupation with problems of political stability or change, consequent on withdrawal of the system of Crown Colony rule from this region, their differing responses to the common challenge of autonomy express their differing situations and social constitutions. In the political developments that have followed withdrawal of Crown Colony rule, changes of governmental form, status, and ideology have been functionally interdependent with changes in the structure and status of the units themselves. Although analytically separable, neither of these two levels or aspects of change can be understood in isolation.

In these processes of political development, the conditions of social structure provide the regulating forces for each unit separately. Common or convergent developments within this group of societies correspond initially to their communities of structure and situation. Thus neither British Guiana nor British Honduras have espoused federation. while Trinidad, with its fast-dwindling Creole majority, championed it keenly.

The structural features which affect these processes of political development most directly and profoundly are the networks of relations between the culturally differentiated social sections. This system of relations has political primacy for two reasons. First, the social sections are sharply distinguished in status as well as culture. They constitute separate status-units. Second, the network of intersectional relations corresponds to the status structure of the colonial society and thus to its political order. Intersectional relations are ipso facto political relations and serve to regulate and express maintenance or change of the colonial status structure which they subsume. Moreover, since sectional norms, interests, and institutions are sharply divergent and often conflict, the balance of sectional forces will regulate the course of political development. Convergence of intersectional interests is thus the measure and condition of social stability. Changes in the relative position or power of these social sections constitute changes in the colonial social structure, and are mediated through changes of intersectional relations which are typically accompanied by changes of governmental form, status, program, and ideology. Often these processes of structural revision involve changes in the status of the society as a unit also.

Data supporting this generalization are readily available. In this region the Crown Colony governments maintained and expressed a quite specific mode of intersectional relations, represented a unique governmental form, and entailed a specific international status for these societies. The upheavals of 1937–1938 that led to abandonment of this system and status themselves involved and expressed signal changes in traditional patterns of intersectional relations. In the following years, as power was transferred from London, the form and status of these Caribbean governments continued to change, and so did certain sectors of their intersectional networks. The historically dominant upper section lost political power to that immediately below. These two upper sections developed a symbiotic association. Together they promoted the development of federal government and ideology, a process which itself involved further changes in the form and status of these colonial governments and societies. Thus continuation of recent trends presupposes persistence of the new intersectional accommodations and may serve to consolidate them further. Reversal of recent trends accordingly presupposes rejection of current intersectional relations, and might signify further changes in the distribution of sectional power, the nature and form of intersectional relations, and the structure of social status. Expressing and mediating these structural changes, we will find other changes in the form, status, and ideology of government, and perhaps in the status of the society as a unit. The West Indian case illustrates the proposition that *changes in the status structure of a given society proceed by political action which redefines the form, status, and ideology of its government, and often the status of the society also.*

Notes

Preface

1 J. S. Furnivall, "Some Problems of Tropical Economy" in R. Hinden, ed., *Fabian Colonial Essays* (London: Allen & Unwin, 1945), pp. 167–171, and *Colonial Policy and Practice* (London: Cambridge University Press, 1948), pp. 303–312.

2 H. S. Morris, "Indians in East Africa: A Study in a Plural Society," *British Journal of Sociology,* Vol. 7 (1946), pp. 194–211, and "The Plural Society," *Man,* Vol. 57 (1957), pp. 124–125; Vera Rubin, "Discussion" in Vera Rubin, ed., *Social and Cultural Pluralism in the Caribbean,* Annals of The New York Academy of Sciences, Vol. 83, Art. 5 (1960), pp. 780–785; R. T. Smith, "Review of 'Social and Cultural Pluralism in the Caribbean,'" *American Anthropologist,* Vol. 63 (1961), pp. 155–157; E. P. Skinner, "Group Dynamics and Social Stratification in British Guiana" in Rubin, ed., *op. cit.,* pp. 904–912, and "Discussion," pp. 912 ff.; Daniel J. Crowley, "Cultural Assimilation in a Multi-racial Society" in Rubin, ed., *op. cit.,* pp. 850–854; Burton Benedict, "Stratification in Plural Societies," *American Anthropologist,* Vol. 64 (1962), pp. 1235–1246; J. D. Speckmann, "The Indian Group in the Segmented Society of Surinam," *Caribbean Studies* (Puerto Rico), Vol. 3, No. 1 (1963), pp. 3–17; Gordon K. Lewis, "Review of Eric Williams, 'History of the People of Trinidad and Tobago,'" *Caribbean Studies,* Vol. 3, No. 1 (1963), pp. 100–105.

3 Lloyd Braithwaite, "Social Stratification and Cultural Pluralism" in Vera Rubin, ed., *op. cit.,* pp. 819.

4 Furnivall, *Colonial Policy,* p. 308.

5 *Ibid.,* p. 310.

6 Braithwaite, *op. cit.,* p. 822.

7 Talcott Parsons, "A Revised Analytical Approach to the Theory of Social Stratification" in R. Bendix and S. M. Lipset, *Class, Status and Power: A Reader in Social Stratification* (Glencoe, Ill.: Free Press, 1953), p. 93; see also Parsons and E. A. Shils, *Toward a General Theory of Action* (Cambridge, Mass.: Harvard University Press, 1951), p. 24:

"One of the most important functional imperatives of the maintenance of social systems is that the value orientations of the different actors in the same social system must be integrated in some measure in a *common* system . . . the sharing of value orientations is especially crucial, although consensus with respect to systems of ideas and expressive symbols are also very important determinants of stability in the social system";

see also *Ibid.,* pp. 55, 165, 172, 176–177.

8 Kingsley Davis and Wilbert E. Moore, "Some Principles of Stratification," *American Sociological Review,* Vol. 10 (1945), pp. 244.

9 Talcott Parsons, *The Social System* (London: Tavistock Publications Ltd., 1952), p. 42; see also pp. 118, 251, 273.

10 D. F. Aberle, A. K. Cohen, A. K. Davis, M. J. Levy, Jr., and F. X. Sutton, "The Functional Pre-requisites of a Society," *Ethics,* Vol. 60 (1950), p. 106.

11 *Ibid.,* p. 103. These writers recognize four conditions which may terminate "the existence of a society," namely, the biological extinction or dispersion of the members, the apathy of the members, the war of all against all, and the absorption of the society by another larger society. On apathy, see Furnivall's comment, note 4, above. On the conquest and absorption of one society by another, the writers would not say "that the society thus absorbed had never *been* a society, but that in a *new* situation it showed a relative inadequacy of one of its functional prerequisites that resulted in its absorption" (*ibid.,* p. 104, n. 8; their italics). This statement implies two points of interest: (1) The Theory as it stands fails to distinguish absolute and relative "functional prerequisites," or their adequacies. (2) It fails to deal with the situation of the plural society in which one or more units have been absorbed by another. On this we are merely told "that the rank order must be legitimized and accepted by most of the members—at least by the important ones—of a society, if stability is to be attained. . . . Coercive sanctions and initiative must be vested in specified status positions" (*ibid.,* p. 106). This passage neatly describes the condition of social pluralism in which the rank order is maintained by a dominant minority which controls coercive sanctions. Here, legitimation is regarded by these writers as adequate provided the dominant minority accepts it. In this case, the common value system will be the property of the ruling group, and we cannot claim that the social order depends on its general acceptance. The common value system of the ruling group in a plural society is not commonly shared by the subordinates.

12 *Ibid.,* p. 103.

13 Max Weber, *The Theory of Social and Economic Organization,* trans. by A. R. Henderson and Talcott Parsons (London: William Hodge & Co. Ltd., 1947), p. 298.

14 Emile Durkheim, *Professional Ethics and Civic Morals,* trans. by Cornelia Brookfield (London: Routledge & Kegan Paul, 1957), p. 61.

15 Benedict, *op. cit.,* p. 1237.

16 Furnivall, *Colonial Policy,* p. 307.

17 *Ibid.,* p. 307.

18 Braithwaite, *op. cit.,* p. 820.

19 *Ibid.,* p. 822.

20 *Ibid.,* p. 819.

21 D. F. Aberle *et al., op. cit.,* p. 104.

22 R. T. Smith, "British Guiana," *Sunday Guardian of Trinidad,* The West Indies Federation Supplement, April 20, 1958, pp. 25–29; R. T. Smith, *British Guiana* (London: Oxford University Press, 1962), p. 143:
    "The present trend of unification around commitment to a set of common values and co-operative behaviour will continue ever more securely the perfectly acceptable variety of religion and cultural tradition. This

trend is not something that is just starting, but something that is already well advanced";

see also pp. 99, 136, 198, 203; see also Skinner, in Rubin, *op cit.*, pp. 904–912, and the recent paper by Leo A. Despres, "The Implications of Nationalist Policies in British Guiana for the Development of Cultural Theory," *American Anthropologist,* Vol. 66, (1964), pp. 1051–1077.

[23] Clarence Senior and D. R. Manley, *Report on Jamaican Migration to Great Britain* (Kingston, Jamaica: Government Printer, 1955); W. F. Maunder, "The New Jamaican Migration," *Social and Economic Studies,* Vol. 4, No. 1 (Jamaica: University College of the West Indies, 1955); M. G. Smith, Roy Augier and R. Nettleford, *The Ras Tafari Movement in Kingston, Jamaica* (Jamaica: UCWI, 1960), p. 16.

[24] Edith Clarke, "Land Tenure and the Family in Four Communities in Jamaica," *Social and Economic Studies,* Vol. 1, No. 4 (Trinidad: 1953).

[25] See Braithwaite, "Progress Towards Federation, 1938–1956," *Social and Economic Studies,* Vol. 6, No. 2 (1957), pp. 133–184; David Lowenthal, ed., *The West Indies Federation: Perspectives on a New Nation* (New York: Columbia University Press, 1961); R. T. Smith, "British Guiana," *Sunday Guardian of Trinidad,* April 20, 1958, and *British Guiana;* Skinner, *op. cit.*

Compare with essays 1, 4, and 12, in this volume. An unpublished paper, "Politics and Society in Jamaica" (1956), anticipated the social unrest of 1960–1961 by an analysis of governmental policies in terms of the integrative needs of this plural society.

[26] M. G. Smith, *Stratification in Grenada* (Berkeley and Los Angeles: University of California Press, 1965).

1: West Indian Culture

[1] Alfred G. Mayer, "Historical Notes on Ideological Aspects of the Concept of Culture in Germany and Russia" in A. L. Kroeber and Clyde Kluckhohn, *Culture: A Critical Review of Concepts and Definitions* (Cambridge, Mass.: Peabody Museum Papers, Vol. 47, No. 1, 1952).

[2] Sir E. B. Taylor, *Primitive Culture* (1871), Vol. I (New York: Harpers, 1958).

[3] A. L. Kroeber and Clyde Kluckhohn, *op. cit.,* p. 157.

[4] John H. Pilgrim, "West Indian Digest," *The Sunday Gleaner* (Kingston, Jamaica), June 5, 1960, p. 7.

[5] *Ibid.*

[6] S. F. Nadel, *The Foundations of Social Anthropology* (London: Cohen & West, 1951), pp. 79–80.

[7] Lambros Comitas, "Metropolitan Influences in the Caribbean: The West Indies," in Vera Rubin, *Social and Cultural Pluralism in the Caribbean,* Annals of The New York Academy of Sciences, Vol. 83, Art. 5 (1960), pp. 809–815.

[8] M. J. Herskovits, *The Myth of the Negro Past* (New York: Harpers, 1941); M. J. and F. S. Herskovits, *Trinidad Village* (New York: Knopf, 1947).

[9] W. R. Bascom, "The Esusu: A Credit Institution among the Yoruba,"

Journal of the Royal Anthropological Institute, Vol. 72 (London, 1952), pp. 63–70.

10 Margaret Katzin, "The Jamaican Country Higgler," *Social and Economic Studies,* Vol. 8, No. 4 (Jamaica: University College of the West Indies, 1959).

11 Raymond T. Smith, *The Negro Family in British Guiana* (London: Routledge & Kegan Paul, 1956).

12 Morton Fried, "The Chinese in British Guiana," *Social and Economic Studies,* Vol. 5, No. 1 (1956), pp. 54–73.

2: Ethnic and Cultural Pluralism in the British Caribbean

For further reading, consult: George Cumper, *The Social Structure of Jamaica* (Jamaica: Extra-Mural Department, University College of the West Indies, n.d.), and *The Social Structure of the British Caribbean (excluding Jamaica)* (Jamaica: Extra-Mural Department, UCWL, n.d.); M. J. Herskovits, *The Myth of the Negro Past* (New York: Harpers, 1941), M. J. and F. S. Herskovits, *Trinidad Village* (New York: Knopf, 1947); J. H. Parry and P. M. Sherlock, *A Short History of the West Indies* (London: Macmillan, 1956). Mary Proudfoot, *Britain and the U.S.A. in the Caribbean* (London: Praeger, 1954). Eric Williams, *The Negro in the Caribbean* (Manchester: Panaf Ltd., 1946).

3: A Framework for Caribbean Studies

1 T. Lynn Smith and A. Marchant, eds., *Brazil: Portrait of Half a Continent* (New York: Dryden Press, 1951).

2 Martha W. Beckwith, *Jamaica Anansi Stories,* Memoir of the American Folklore Society, XVII, New York (1924); and *Black Roadways: A Study of Jamaica Folk Life* (Chapel Hill: University of North Carolina Press, 1929).

3 N. N. Puckett, *Folk Beliefs of the Southern Negro* (Chapel Hill: University of North Carolina Press, 1926).

4 Artur Ramos, *The Negro in Brazil,* trans. by Richard Pattee (Washington, D.C.: Associated Publishers, Inc., 1939); M. J. Herskovits, "The Negro in the New World: The Statement of a Problem," *American Anthropologist,* Vol. 32 (1930), pp. 145–155, *Life in a Haitian Valley* (New York: Knopf, 1937), and *The Myth of the Negro Past* (New York: Harper & Bros., 1941).

5 M. J. and F. S. Herskovits, *Rebel Destiny: Among the Bush Negroes of Dutch Guiana* (New York: McGraw-Hill, 1934), and *Suriname Folklore,* Columbia Contributions to Anthropology, XXVII (New York, 1937).

6 Robert Redfield, "The Folk Society and Culture," *American Journal of Sociology,* XLV (1940), 731–742; *The Folk Culture of Yucatan* (Chicago: University of Chicago Press, 1941), "The Folk Society," *American Journal of Sociology,* LII (1947), 293–308, and "The Natural History of the Folk Society," *Social Forces,* XXXI (1953), 224–228.

7 W. L. Warner, B. H. Junker, and W. A. Adams, *Color and Human Nature* (Washington, D.C.: American Council on Education, 1941); A. Davis, B. E. Gardner, and M. R. Gardner, *Deep South* (Chicago: University of Chicago

Press, 1941); M. C. Hill and H. R. MacCall, "Social Stratification in a Georgia Town," *American Sociological Review,* XV (1950), 721–729; Franklin Frazier, *The Negro Family in the United States* (Chicago: University of Chicago Press, 1939); T. S. Simey, *Welfare and Planning in the West Indies* (London: Oxford, 1946); B. Matthews, *The Crisis in the West Indian Family* (Trinidad: University of West Indies Press, 1953).

8 John Dollard, *Caste and Class in a Southern Town* (New Haven: Yale University Press, 1937); Dollard *et al., Frustration and Aggression* (New Haven: Yale University Press, 1939).

9 Hortense Powdermaker, *After Freedom: A Cultural Study of the Deep South* (New York: Viking Press, 1939); "The Channeling of Negro Aggression by the Cultural Process," *American Journal of Sociology,* XLVIII (1943), 750–758.

10 A. A. Campbell, "St. Thomas Negroes: A Study of Personality and Culture," *Psychological Monographs,* Vol. LV, No. 5 (1943), Illinois; Simey, 1946, *op. cit.;* C. V. D. Hadley, "Personality Patterns and Aggression in the British West Indies," *Human Relations,* Vol. II, No. 4 (1949), pp. 349–362; G. J. Kruijer, "St. Martin's and St. Eustatius Negroes as Compared with Those of St. Thomas," *West-Indische Gids,* XXXIV (Amsterdam, 1953), 225–237; Yehudi Cohen, "A Study of Interpersonal Relations in a Jamaican Community" (unpublished Ph.D. dissertation, Yale University, 1953), and "The Social Organization of a Selected Community in Jamaica," *Social and Economic Studies,* Vol. 2, No. 4 (1954), pp. 104–137; Rhoda Metraux, "Some Aspects of Hierarchical Structure in Haiti" in Sol Tax, ed., *Acculturation in the Americas* (Chicago: University of Chicago Press, 1952), pp. 185–194; Madeline Kerr, *Personality and Conflict in Jamaica* (Liverpool: Liverpool University Press, 1952).

11 W. M. Macmillan, *Warning from the West Indies* (London: Faber, 1936); Lord Olivier, *Jamaica, the Blessed Island* (London: Faber, 1936); Paul Blanshard, *Democracy and Empire in the Caribbean* (New York: Macmillan & Co., 1947); Simey, *op. cit.*

12 W. R. Bascom, "Acculturation among the Gullah Negroes," *American Anthropologist,* Vol. 43 (1941), pp. 43–50, "The Esusu: A Credit Institution among the Yoruba," *Journal of the Royal Anthropological Institute,* LXXII (London: 1952), 53–70, and "Two Forms of Afro-Cuban Divination" in Sol Tax, ed., *op. cit.,* pp. 169–179; Andrew T. Carr, "A Rada Community in Trinidad," *Caribbean Quarterly,* Vol. 3, No. 1 (Trinidad: 1953), pp. 35–54; O. D. Eduardo, "The Negro in Northern Brazil: A Study in Acculturation," *Memoirs of the American Ethnological Society,* XV (New York: 1948); Andrew Pearse, "Aspects of Change in Caribbean Folk Music," *UNESCO International Folk Music Journal,* VII (1955), 29–36; George E. Simpson, "The Vodun Service in Northern Haiti," *American Anthropologist,* Vol. 42 (1940), pp. 236–254, "Haitian Magic," *Social Forces,* Vol. 19 (1940), pp. 95–100, "Sexual and Familial Institutions in Northern Haiti," *American Anthropologist,* Vol. 44 (1942), pp. 655–674, "Four Vodun Ceremonies," *Journal of American Folklore,* Vol. 59 (1946), pp. 154–167, "Acculturation in Northern Haiti," *Journal of American Folklore,* Vol. 64 (1951), pp. 397–403, and "Discussion of Dr. Price-Mars' Paper" in Sol Tax, ed., *op. cit.;* D. M. Taylor, "The Black

Caribs of British Honduras," *Viking Fund Publications in Anthropology,* No. 17 (New York, 1951); Emilio Willems, "Race Attitudes in Brazil," *American Journal of Sociology,* LIV (Chicago, 1949), 402–408, "Caboclo Cultures of Southern Brazil" in Sol Tax, ed., *op. cit.,* pp. 231–243; see also M. J. Herskovits, *Acculturation, A Study of Culture Contact* (New York: J. J. Augustin, 1938), *Dahomey* 2 vols. (New York: J. J. Augustin, 1938), *Man and His Works* (New York: Knopf, 1948), "The Contribution of Afro-American Studies to Africanist Research," *American Anthropologist,* Vol. 50 (1948), pp. 1–10, "Introduction" in Sol Tax, ed., *op. cit.,* "Some Psychological Implications of Afro-American Studies" in Sol Tax, ed., *op. cit.,* and M. J. and F. S. Herskovits, *Trinidad Village* (New York: Knopf, 1947).

[13] M. J. Herskovits, *The Myth of the Negro Past,* and "Problem, Method and Theory in Afro-American Studies," *Phylon,* Vol. 7 (1946), pp. 337–354.

[14] *Ibid.,* p. 352.

[15] *Ibid.,* p. 352.

[16] Meyer Fortes, *The Web of Kinship Among the Tallensi* (London: Oxford University Press, 1949), p. 346.

[17] Daryll Forde, "Introduction" in Daryll Forde, ed., *African Worlds* (London: Oxford University Press, 1954), p. xvii.

[18] Meyer Fortes and E. E. Evans-Pritchard, "Introduction" in Fortes and Evans-Pritchard, eds., *African Political Systems* (London: Oxford University Press, 1940), p. 17.

[19] M. J. Herskovits, *The Myth of the Negro Past.*

[20] *Ibid.,* p. 18.

[21] M. J. Herskovits, "Problem, Method and Theory in Afro-American Studies," p. 348.

[22] S. F. Nadel, *Nupe Religion* (London: Oxford University Press, 1954).

[23] M. J. Herskovits, *Life in a Haitian Valley, Dahomey, The Myth of the Negro Past,* pp. 169 ff.; Bascom, "The Esusu: A Credit Institution Among the Yoruba," "Two Forms of Afro-Cuban Divination."

[24] Frazier, *The Negro Family in the United States,* "Theoretical Structure of Sociology and Sociological Research," *British Journal of Sociology,* Vol. 4 (1953), pp. 293–313; Fernando Henriques, "West Indian Family Organization," *Caribbean Quarterly,* Vol. 2, No. 1 (1952), p. 24, Letter to the Editor, *Caribbean Quarterly,* Vol. 2, No. 3 (1953), p. 56, review of *Personality and Conflict in Jamaica* by Kerr in *Caribbean Quarterly,* Vol. 3, No. 1 (1953), pp. 61–62; Simey, *op. cit.;* Matthews, *op. cit.;* cf. also M. J. Herskovits, "Some Psychological Implications of Afro-American Studies," in Sol Tax, ed., *op. cit.,* and Letter to the Editor, *Caribbean Quarterly,* Vol. 2, No. 2 (1952), pp. 44–45.

[25] L. P. Mair, "African Marriage and Social Change" in Arthur Phillips, ed., *Survey of African Marriage and Family Life* (London: Oxford University Press, 1953), pp. 1–171, especially pp. 28–45.

[26] Mary F. Smith, *Baba of Karo: A Woman of the Moslem Hausa* (London: Faber, 1954); M. G. Smith, "Slavery and Emancipation in Two Societies," essay 6 of this volume, originally published in *Social and Economic Studies,* Vol. 3 (1954), pp. 240–290.

[27] Matthews, *op. cit.,* p. 13.

[28] M. J. Herskovits, *The Myth of the Negro Past,* pp. 110–142.

[29] J. G. Leyburn, *The Haitian People* (New Haven: Yale University Press, 1941), pp. 46–50, 86; D. Pierson, *Negroes in Brazil* (Chicago: University of Chicago Press, 1942).

[30] D. G. H. Hall, "Jamaican Economic Development, 1840–65" (unpublished Ph.D. dissertation, London University, 1954).

[31] Pearse, *op. cit.*

[32] Leyburn, *op. cit.,* pp. 46–50, 86.

[33] M. J. Herskovits, "Problem, Method and Theory in Afro-American Studies," p. 351.

[34] *Ibid.,* p. 351.

[35] Maya Deren, *Divine Horsemen: The Living Gods of Haiti* (London: Thames & Hudson, 1953), pp. 61–71, 82–85, 270–286.

[36] Pearse, *op. cit.*

[37] Redfield, "The Folk Society and Culture," *The Folk Culture of Yucatan,* "The Folk Society," "The Natural History of the Folk Society."

[38] Redfield, R. Lindon and M. J. Herskovits, "Memorandum for the Study of Acculturation," *American Anthropologist,* Vol. 38 (1936), pp. 149–152.

[39] Sol Tax, "Culture and Civilization in Guatemalan Societies," *Scientific Monthly,* Vol. 48 (1939), pp. 463–467.

[40] Julian Steward, *Area Research: Theory and Process,* Social Science Research Council Bulletin 63 (New York, 1950), p. 106 ff.

[41] M. J. Herskovits, *Man and His Works,* p. 606.

[42] Bascom, "Urbanization among the Yoruba," *American Journal of Sociology,* LX (1955), 446–454.

[43] M. G. Smith, *The Economy of Hausa Communities in Zaria Province,* Colonial Research Publications, No. 16 (London: H.M.S.O., 1955).

[44] Steward, *op. cit.,* p. 20; G. M. Foster, "What Is Folk Culture?" *American Anthropologist,* 55 (1953) pp. 159–173; C. M. Arensberg, "The Community Study Method," *American Journal of Sociology,* LX (1954), 109–124.

[45] Marion J. Levy, Jr., *The Structure of Society* (Princeton, N.J.: Princeton University Press, 1952).

[46] Beckwith, *op. cit.;* Cohen, "Interpersonal Relations in a Jamaican Community," "Social Organization of a Selected Community"; Edith Clarke, "Land Tenure and the Family in Four Communities in Jamaica," *Social and Economic Studies,* Vol. 1, No. 4 (1953), pp. 81–117; M. J. Herskovits, *The Myth of the Negro Past,* and M. J. and F. S. Herskovits, *Trinidad Village;* Kerr, *op. cit.;* Matthews, *op. cit.;* R. T. Smith, "Family Organization in British Guiana," *Social and Economic Studies,* Vol. 1, No. 1 (1953), pp. 87–112; Taylor, *op. cit.*

[47] Hadley, *op. cit.;* Macmillan, *op. cit.*

[48] "Editorial Note," *Caribbean Quarterly,* Vol. 3, No. 1 (1953), p. 3; see also: Frank Mayhew, "My Life," *Caribbean Quarterly,* Vol. 3, No. 1 (1953), pp. 13–23; L. Broom, "Urban Research in the Caribbean," *Social and Economic Studies,* Vol. 1, No. 1 (1953), pp. 113–119.

[49] Lloyd Braithwaite, "Social Stratification in Trinidad," *Social and Economic Studies,* Vol. 2, No. 2 (1953), pp. 5–175, "The Problem of Cultural Integration in Trinidad," *Social and Economic Studies,* Vol. 3, No. 1 (1954), pp.

82–96; Henriques, "Colour Values in Jamaican Society," *British Journal of Sociology*, Vol. 2 (1951), pp. 115–121, and *Family and Colour in Jamaica* (London: Eyre & Spottiswoode, 1953).

⁵⁰ Henriques, Letter to the Editor, *Caribbean Quarterly*, Vol. 2, No. 3 (1953), p. 56.

⁵¹ Simpson, "Haiti's Social Structure," *American Sociological Review*, Vol. VI (1941), pp. 640–649, "Acculturation in Northern Haiti," Discussion of Dr. Price-Mars' Paper," M. J. Herskovits, *Life in a Haitian Valley;* Leyburn, *op. cit.;* John Lobb, "Caste and Class in Haiti," *American Journal of Sociology,* XLVI (1940), 23–34.

⁵² Pierson, *op. cit.;* Eduardo, *op. cit.;* Smith and Marchant, eds., *op. cit.;* Davis *et al., op. cit.;* Dollard, *op. cit.;* Powdermaker, *op. cit.;* Puckett, *op. cit.;* R. Park, *Race and Culture* (Glencoe, Ill.: Free Press, 1950); E. C. and H. M. Hughes, *Where Peoples Meet* (Glencoe, Ill.: Free Press, 1952); C. Wagley, "The Folk Culture of the Brazilian Amazon" in Sol Tax, ed., *op. cit.;* also Wagley, ed., "Race and Class in Rural Brazil" UNESCO (1953).

⁵³ Redfield, *The Folk Culture of Yucatan;* J. Gillin, "Mestizo America" in Ralph Linton, ed., *Most of the World* (New York: Columbia University Press, 1948), pp. 156–211, *The Culture of Security in San Carlos* Publication No. 16 (New Orleans: Middle American Research Institute, 1951), "Modern Cultural Development and Synthesis in Latin America" in Sol Tax, ed., *op. cit.;* M. M. Tumin, *Caste in a Peasant Society* (Princeton, N.J.: Princeton University Press, 1952); Wagley, *Economics of a Guatemalan Village,* Memoir of the American Anthropological Association, No. 58 (Menasha, Wis.: 1941), and *Social and Religious Life of a Guatemalan Village,* Memoir of the American Anthropological Association, No. 71 (Menasha, Wis.: 1949).

⁵⁴ J. Steward and R. Manners, "The Cultural Study of Contemporary Societies: Puerto Rico," *American Journal of Sociology,* LIX (1953), 123–130.

⁵⁵ Sidney W. Mintz, "The Folk-Urban Continuum and the Rural Proletarian Community," *American Journal of Sociology,* LIX (1953), 136–143, "The Culture-History of a Puerto Rican Sugarcane Plantation, 1876–1949," *Hispanic-American Historical Review* (1953), pp. 224–251.

⁵⁶ Clarke, *op. cit.*

⁵⁷ Leyburn, *op. cit.;* Lowry Nelson, *Rural Cuba* (Minneapolis: University of Minnesota Press, 1950).

⁵⁸ Steward, *Area Research: Theory and Process,* p. 116, 140–143; see also Mintz, "On Redfield and Foster," *American Anthropologist,* Vol. 56 (1954), pp. 87–92.

⁵⁹ G. E. Cumper, "A Modern Jamaican Sugar Estate," *Social and Economic Studies,* Vol. 3, No. 2 (1954), pp. 119–160.

⁶⁰ Dollard, *Caste and Class in a Southern Town;* Powdermaker, *After Freedom,* "The Channelling of Negro Aggression"; Campbell, *op. cit.;* Kerr, *op. cit.;* Cohen, "Interpersonal Relations in a Jamaican Community," "The Social Organization of a Selected Community"; Metraux, *op. cit.;* Kruijer, *op. cit.;* Hadley, *op. cit.;* Simey, *op. cit.;* Braithwaite, "Social Stratification in Trinidad."

⁶¹ Warner, Junker, and Adams, *op. cit.*

[62] Henriques, review of *Personality and Conflict in Jamaica* by Kerr; Frazier, "Theoretical Structure of Sociology and Sociological Research," p. 172.

[63] Cohen, "Interpersonal Relations in a Jamaican Community."

[64] Simey, *op. cit.*, pp. 90–105, especially p. 99; Hadley, *op. cit.*

[65] C. Llewellyn Gross, "The Use of Class Concepts in Sociological Research," *American Journal of Sociology*, Vol. 54 (1949), pp. 409–421.

[66] Simey, *op. cit.*, p. 96.

[67] Powdermaker, *After Freedom*, p. 334.

[68] Kerr, *op. cit.*, pp. 165–174.

[69] Campbell, *op. cit.*

[70] Ralph L. Beals, "Acculturation" in A. L. Kroeber, ed., *Anthropology Today* (Chicago: University of Chicago Press, 1953), pp. 621–641, and "Social Stratification in Latin America," *American Journal of Sociology*, LVIII (1953), 327–339; R. Bendix and S. M. Lipset, eds., *Class, Status and Power: A Reader in Social Stratification* (Glencoe, Ill.: Free Press, 1953); Blanshard, *op. cit.*; Braithwaite, "Social Stratification in Trinidad"; Broom, "The Social Differentiation of Jamaica," *American Sociological Review*, XIX, pp. 115–123; Richard Centers, *The Psychology of Social Classes* (Princeton, N.J.: Princeton University Press, 1949); Davis, Gardner, and Gardner, *op. cit.*; Walter Goldschmidt, "Social Class in America: A Critical Review," *American Anthropologist*, Vol. 52 (1950), pp. 468–482; Maxine Gordon, "Cultural Aspects of Puerto Rico's Race Problem," *American Sociological Review*, XV (1950), 382–391; Gross, *op. cit.*; Henriques, *Family and Colour in Jamaica*; Hill and MacCall, *op. cit.*; E. C. and H. M. Hughes, *Where Peoples Meet* (Glencoe, Ill.: Free Press, 1952); Levy, *op. cit.*; H. W. Pfautz, "The Current Literature on Social Stratification: Critique and Bibliography," *American Journal of Sociology*, LVIII (1953), pp. 391–418; Park, *op. cit.*; W. L. Warner, M. Meeker, K. Eells, *Social Class in America* (Chicago: Research Associates, Ltd., 1949).

[71] Levy, *op. cit.*, p. 164 ff.; Talcott Parsons, "A Revised Analytical Approach to the Theory of Social Stratification," in Bendix and Lipset, eds., *op. cit.*, p. 93.

[72] Bendix and Lipset, *op. cit.*

[73] Parsons, *op. cit.*, p. 110, his italics.

[74] Warner, Meeker, and Eells, *op. cit.*

[75] O. Klineberg, ed., *Characteristics of the American Negro* (New York: Harper & Bros., 1944); Gunnar Myrdal, *An American Dilemma* (New York: Harper & Bros., 1944).

[76] Pierson, *op. cit.*

[77] Beals, "Social Stratification in Latin America," p. 339.

[78] Gillin, *op. cit.*, *The Culture of Security in San Carlos*; Tumin, *op. cit.*

[79] Beals, "Social Stratification in Latin America," p. 338.

[80] Warner, Junker, and Adams, *op. cit.*

[81] See works cited by Campbell, *op. cit.*; Gordon, *op. cit.*; Hadley, *op. cit.*; Kruijer, *op. cit.*; Cohen, "Interpersonal Relations in a Jamaican Community," "The Social Organization of a Selected Community"; Matthews, *op. cit.*; Clarke, *op. cit.*; Pearse, "Aspects of Change in Caribbean Folk Music," "West

Indian Themes," *Caribbean Quarterly*, Vol. 2, No. 2 (1952), pp. 12–23; also E. B. Reuter, "Culture Contacts in Puerto Rico," *American Journal of Sociology*, LII (1946), 91–101.

82 See works cited by Redfield, *The Folk Culture of Yucatan;* Gillin, "Mestizo America" in Ralph Linton, ed., *Most of the World* (New York: Columbia, 1948), pp. 156–211. *The Culture of Security in San Carlos,* "Modern Cultural Development and Synthesis in Latin America"; Wagley, *Economics of a Guatemalan Village, Social and Religious Life of a Guatemalan Village.*

83 Blanshard, *op. cit.;* Mary Proudfoot, *Britain and the U.S.A. in the* Caribbean (London: Praeger, 1954); Simey, *op. cit.;* Macmillan, *op. cit.*

84 Olivier, *op. cit.*

85 Braithwaite, "Social Stratification in Trinidad"; Henriques, *Family and Colour in Jamaica;* Broom, "The Social Differentiation of Jamaica."

86 Henriques, *Family and Colour in Jamaica*, pp. 105, 161.

87 Braithwaite, "Social Stratification in Trinidad," pp. 102–103, also p. 75.

88 Henriques, *Family and Colour in Jamaica*, p. 41.

89 Braithwaite, "Social Stratification in Trinidad," pp. 52–53.

90 *Ibid.*, p. 170.

91 Henriques, review of *Personality and Conflict in Jamaica*, p. 62, and *Family and Colour in Jamaica*, p. 172.

92 *Ibid.*, p. 172.

93 M. J. Herskovits, "Problem, Method and Theory in Afro-American Studies," p. 350.

94 Henriques, *Family and Colour in Jamaica*, p. 160.

95 Broom, "The Sociological Differentiation of Jamaica," p. 119.

96 Braithwaite, "Social Stratification of Trinidad," pp. 47, 156.

97 Henriques, *Family and Colour in Jamaica*, p. 42.

98 *Ibid.*, p. 52.

99 *Ibid.*, p. 168.

100 Mary F. Smith, *Baba of Karo;* M. G. Smith, "Slavery and Emancipation in Two Societies."

101 Powdermaker, *After Freedom!*, p. 354.

102 Broom, "The Social Differentiation of Jamaica," p. 117.

103 See works cited above by Beckwith, Blanshard, Campbell, Carr, Clarke, Deren, Gillin, Hadley, Kerr, Leyburn, Lobb, Macmillan, Pearse, Mayhew, Matthews, Pierson, Puckett, Simpson, Willems, Wagley.

104 Beals, "Social Stratification in Latin America"; R. A. J. van Lier, *The Development and Nature of Society in the West Indies* (Amsterdam: Royal Institute for the Indies, 1950).

4: Social and Cultural Pluralism

1 J. S. Furnivall, *Colonial Policy and Practice* (London: Cambridge University Press, 1948), p. 304.

2 Sir E. B. Tylor, *Primitive Culture* (New York: Harper, 1958), p. 1.

3 Marion Levy, Jr., *The Structure of Society* (Princeton, N.J.: Princeton University Press, 1952), p. 113.

[4] A. R. Radcliffe-Brown, *Structure and Function in Primitive Society* (London: Cohen & West, 1950), p. 193.

[5] *Ibid.*, p. 194.

[6] Meyer Fortes, "The Structure of Unilineal Descent Groups," *American Anthropologist*, Vol. 55 (1953), p. 36.

[7] Raymond Firth, *Elements of Social Organization* (London: Watts, 1951), p. 28.

[8] S. F. Nadel, *The Foundations of Social Anthropology* (London: Cohen & West, 1951), p. 187.

[9] *Ibid.*, p. 188.

[10] Firth, *op. cit.*, p. 27.

[11] David Bidney, *Theoretical Anthropology* (New York: Columbia University Press, 1955).

[12] Nadel, *op. cit.*, pp. 79–80.

[13] *Ibid.*, p. 108.

[14] B. Malinowski, *A Scientific Theory of Culture, and Other Essays* (Chapel Hill: University of North Carolina Press, 1944), p. 52–53.

[15] Nadel, *op. cit.*, p. 120.

[16] R. Linton, *The Study of Man* (New York: Appleton Century Co., 1936), chapter 16.

[17] R. A. J. van Lier, *The Nature and Development of Society in the West Indies* (Amsterdam: Institute for the Indies, 1950).

[18] M. G. Smith, "The Hausa System of Social Status," *Africa*, Vol. 29, No. 3 (1959).

[19] Lloyd Braithwaite, "Social Stratification in Trinidad," *Social and Economic Studies*, Vol. 2, No. 2 (1952), pp. 3–175.

[20] Raymond T. Smith, *The Negro Family in British Guiana* (London: Routledge & Kegan Paul, 1956).

[21] Robert Redfield, *The Transformation of Primitive Society* (Ithaca, N.Y.: Cornell University Press, 1954).

[22] S. Rottenberg, "Labor Relations in an Underdeveloped Economy," *Caribbean Quarterly*, Vol. 4, No. 1 (1955).

[23] Furnivall, *op. cit.*, p. 305.

[24] M. M. Tumin, *Caste in a Peasant Society* (Princeton, N.J.: Princeton University Press, 1952).

[25] Lord Olivier, *Jamaica, the Blessed Island* (London: Faber, 1936).

[26] INCIDI, *Ethnic and Cultural Pluralism in Inter-tropical Countries* (Brussels: Proceedings of 30th Conference of Institute for the Study of Differing Civilizations, 1957).

5: Some Aspects of the Social Structure in The British Caribbean about 1820

[1] John Stewart, *A View of the Past and Present State of the Island of Jamaica* (Edinburgh: Oliver & Boyd; London: Whittaker, 1823), pp. 35–36.

[2] Rev. R. Bickell, *The West Indies As They Are* (London: Hatchard, 1825), pp. 84–86.

[3] Stewart, *op. cit.*, p. 161.

4 Mrs. Carmichael, *Domestic Manners and Social Conditions of the White, Coloured and Negro Populations of the West Indies* (2 vols.; London: Whittaker, 1833), Vol. I, p. 59.

5 M. G. Lewis, *Journal of a West India Proprietor* (London: John Murray, 1845), p. 113.

6 These Deficiency Acts were laws intended to maintain a fixed ratio on plantations between whites and nonwhites.

7 Stewart, *op. cit.,* p. 249.

8 M. G. Lewis, *op. cit.,* p. 111.

9 *Ibid.,* p. 184.

10 *Ibid.,* p. 182.

11 Mrs. Carmichael, *op. cit.,* Vol. II, p. 219.

12 *Ibid.,* Vol. II, p. 231.

13 Stewart, *op. cit.,* p. 113.

14 Mrs. Carmichael, *op. cit.,* Vol. I, p. 63.

15 *Ibid.,* Vol. II, pp. 260–261.

16 *Ibid.,* Vol. I, p. 96.

17 *Ibid.,* Vol. I, pp. 60–61.

18 Sir William Young, *The West India Commonplace Book* (London: Phillips, 1807), p. 50, see also pp. 46–47.

19 *Ibid.,* p. 52.

20 Lewis, *op. cit.,* p. 151.

6: Slavery and Emancipation in Two Societies

1 W. L. Burn, *The West Indies* (London: Hutchinson, 1951).

2 Sarkin Ruwa Hassan and Mallam M. Shu'aibu, *A Chronicle of Abuja,* (Ibadan, Nigeria: University Press, 1952).

3 S. J. Hogben, *The Muhammadan Emirates of Northern Nigeria* (London: Oxford University Press, 1930).

4 *Colonial Reports, Northern Nigeria, 1900–1908* (London: H.M.S.O.).

5 R. Montgomery Martin, *History of the West Indies* (London: Whittaker, 1836).

6 C. Daryll Forde and R. Scott, *The Native Economies of Nigeria* (London: Faber, 1946).

7 Rev. G. W. Bridges, *Annals of Jamaica* (London: John Murray, 1827); John Stewart, *A View of the Past and Present State of the Island of Jamaica* (Edinburgh: Oliver & Boyd; London: Whittaker, 1823).

8 Henry Barth, *Travels and Discoveries in North and Central Africa* (2 vols.; London: Ward, Lock & Co., 1890); E. W. Bovill, *Caravans of the Old Sahara* (London: Oxford University Press, 1933); D. Denham and H. Clapperton, *Narrative of Travels and Discoveries in Northern and Central Africa* (London: John Murray, 1826).

9 Herman Merivale, *Colonization and Colonies* (1861) (London: Oxford University Press, 1928); L. J. Regatz, *The Fall of the Planter Class in the British Caribbean, 1763–1833* (New York: Century Co., 1928).

10 Barth, *op. cit.;* Denham and Clapperton, *op. cit.;* C. H. Robinson,

Hausaland (London: Low & Marston, 1897); J. F. Schon, *Magana Hausa* (London: Society for the Propagation of Christian Knowledge, 1906).

[11] Eric Williams, *Capitalism and Slavery* (Chapel Hill: University of North Carolina Press, 1944).

[12] Barth, *op. cit.;* M. G. Smith, *The Economy of Hausa Communities in Zaria Province,* Colonial Research Publications No. 16 (London: H.M.S.O., 1955).

[13] Martin, *op. cit.*

[14] *Colonial Reports, Northern Nigeria,* 1900–1908 (London, H.M.S.O.).

[15] F. W. de St. Croix, *The Fulani of Northern Nigeria* (Lagos: Government Printer, 1944); O. and C. L. Temple, *Notes on the Tribes, Provinces and Emirates of Northern Nigeria* (Lagos: Church Missionary Society, 1922).

[16] C. W. Cole, *Land Tenure in Zaria Province* (Kaduna, Nigeria: Government Printer, 1949).

[17] Stewart, *op. cit.*

[18] R. Bickell, *The West Indies As They Are* (London: Hatchard, 1825); Stewart, *op. cit.*

[19] W. J. Gardner, *A History of Jamaica* (1874) (London: Unwin, 1891); Ragatz, *op. cit.*

[20] E. J. Arnett, *Gazeteer of Zaria Province* (London: Waterlow & Sons, 1920); M. G. Smith, *Government in Zazzau, 1800–1950* (London: Oxford University Press, 1960).

[21] M. G. Smith, *The Economy of Hausa Communities;* Stewart, *op. cit.*

[22] M. G. Smith, *The Economy of Hausa Communities,* and *Government in Zazzau.*

[23] Thomas Cooper, *Facts Illustrative of the Condition of the Negro Slaves in Jamaica* (London: Hatchard, 1824); James M. Phillippo, *Jamaica, Its Past and Present State* (London: John Snow, 1843).

[24] Bridges, *op. cit.;* Ragatz, *op. cit.*

[25] T. P. Hughes, *Notes on Mohammedanism* (London: Allen, 1894); H. Lammens, *L'Islam, Croyances et Institutions* (Beirut: Imprimerie Catholique, 1926); A. S. Tritton, *Islam* (London: Hutchinson, 1951).

[26] F. H. Ruxton, *Maliki Law* (London: Luzac, 1916).

[27] David de Santillana, "Law and Society," in Sir T. Arnold and Alfred Guillaume, *The Legacy of Islam* (London: Oxford University Press, 1931), pp. 284–310; Ruxton, *op. cit.*

[28] Ragatz, *op. cit.*

[29] Williams, *op. cit.*

[30] Alexander Barclay, *A Practical View of the Present State of Slavery in the West Indies* (London: Smith, Elder & Co., 1828).

[31] T. S. Simey, *Welfare and Planning in the West Indies* (London: Oxford University Press, 1946); Williams, *op. cit.*

[32] Daryll Forde, *Family and Marriage among the Yako,* Monographs in Social Anthropology (London: London School of Economics, 1941).

[33] Smith, *The Economy of Hausa Communities.*

[34] Barclay, *op. cit.;* Bridges, *op. cit.;* Mrs. Carmichael, *Domestic Manners and Social Conditions of the White, Coloured and Negro Populations of the West Indies* (2 vols; London: Whittaker, 1833); H. N. Coleridge, *Six Months*

in the West Indies (London: Murray, 1825); Bryan Edwards, *The History, Civil and Commercial, of the British Colonies in the West Indies* (5 vols; London: Whittaker, 1819); Ragatz, *op. cit.;* Stewart, *op. cit.;* Williams, *op. cit.*

35 M. G. Lewis, *Journal of a West India Proprietor* (London: John Murray, 1845).

36 Simey, *op. cit.;* Williams, *The Negro in the Caribbean* (Manchester: Panaf Ltd., 1946).

37 Carmichael, *op. cit.;* Coleridge, *op. cit.;* Grenada Free Press, "Colonial Enquiry" (St. George's, Grenada, W.I.: The Grenada Free Press, 1832), pp. 238–239, 242, 256–257, 264–265; Lewis, *op. cit.*

38 R. S. Rattray, *Ashanti* (London: Oxford University Press, 1923).

39 A. R. Radcliffe-Brown and C. D. Forde, *African Systems of Kinship and Marriage* (London: Oxford University Press, 1950).

40 Sir H. S. Maine, *Ancient Law* (London: Routledge, 1905).

41 Bickell, *op. cit.;* Carmichael, *op. cit.;* Lewis, *op. cit.;* Stewart, *op. cit.*

42 Edwards, *op. cit.;* Lewis, *op. cit.*

43 M. G. Smith, "Some Aspects of Social Structure in the British Caribbean about 1820," *Social and Economic Studies,* Vol. 1, No. 4 (1953), pp. 57–79.

44 Stewart, *op. cit.*

45 Barclay, *op. cit.;* Bickell, *op. cit.;* Bridges, *op. cit.;* Cooper, *op. cit.;* Lewis, *op. cit.;* Stewart, *op. cit.*

46 Gardner, *op. cit.;* Phillippo, *op. cit.*

47 Bickell, *op. cit.;* Lewis, *op. cit.*

48 Barclay, *op. cit.;* Carmichael, *op. cit.;* Stewart, *op. cit.*

49 Burn, *op. cit.;* Coleridge, *op. cit.;* Ragatz, *op. cit.*

50 Bickell, *op. cit.;* Cooper, *op. cit.;* Lewis, *op. cit.;* Stewart, *op. cit.*

51 Carmichael, *op. cit.;* Cooper, *op. cit.;* Lewis, *op. cit.;* Stewart, *op. cit.*

52 Mary F. Smith, *Baba of Karo: A Woman of the Moslem Hausa* (London: Faber, 1954): M. G. Smith, *The Economy of Hausa Communities.*

53 H. Barth, *op. cit.;* M. G. Smith, *The Economy of Hausa Communities.*

54 Mary F. Smith, *op. cit.*

55 Ruxton, *op. cit.*

56 M. G. Smith, *The Economy of Hausa Communities.*

57 de Santillana, *op. cit.;* Guillaume, *Islam* (London: Penguin Books, 1954); Tritton, *op. cit.*

58 Mary F. Smith, *op. cit.;* M. G. Smith, *The Economy of Hausa Communities.*

59 Mary F. Smith, *op. cit.;* M. G. Smith, *The Economy of Hausa Communities.*

60 Ruxton, *op. cit.;* Mary F. Smith, *op. cit.*

61 Hassan and Shu'aibu, *op. cit.;* O. and C. L. Temple, *op. cit.*

62 M. G. Smith, *The Economy of Hausa Communities* and *Government in Zazzau.*

63 M. G. Smith, "Some Aspects of Social Structure in the British Caribbean."

64 Edwards, *op. cit.;* John Lunan, *Abstract of the Laws of Jamaica Relating to Slaves* (Kingston, Jamaica: 1819); Ruxton, *op. cit.*

65 Barth, *op. cit.*

66 Burn, *op. cit.*

67 Ragatz, *op. cit.;* Williams, *Capitalism and Slavery;* Sir William Young, *The West India Commonplace Book* (London: Phillips, 1807).

68 F. H. Ruxton, *op. cit.*

69 Williams, *Capitalism and Slavery.*

70 M. G. Smith, *The Economy of Hausa Communities.*

71 Martin, *op. cit.;* Ragatz, *op. cit.;* Young, *op. cit.*

72 M. G. Smith, *Government in Zazzau.*

73 Bridges, *op. cit.;* Gardner, *op. cit.*

74 Hassan and Shu'aibu, *op. cit.;* Hogben, *op. cit.;* M. G. Smith, *Government in Zazzau;* O. and C. L. Temple, *op. cit.*

75 Bickell, *op. cit.;* Bridges, *op. cit.;* Edwards, *op. cit.;* Gardner, *op. cit.*

76 Martin, *op. cit.*

77 C. G. Seligman, *The Races of Africa* (London: Butterworth, 1930); C. L. Temple, *Native Races and their Rulers* (Lagos: C. M. S. Bookshop, 1918 [printed in Capetown]); O. and C. L. Temple, *op. cit.*

78 Lewis, *op. cit.;* Stewart, *op. cit.*

79 *Ibid.*

80 Carmichael, *op. cit.;* Cooper, *op. cit.;* Lewis, *op. cit.;* Stewart, *op. cit.*

81 F. Edgar, *Litafi na Tatsunyoyi na Hausa* (Belfast: Mayne, 1913), 3 vols.; Mary F. Smith, *op. cit.*

82 de St. Croix, *op. cit.;* M. G. Smith, *The Economy of Hausa Communities.*

83 Sir H. Richmond Palmer, "The Fulas and their Language," *Journal of the Royal African Society,* Vol. 22 (1922), pp. 121–136.

84 Bickell, *op. cit.;* Carmichael, *op. cit.;* Lewis, *op. cit.;* M. G. Smith, "Some Aspects of Social Structure in the British Caribbean"; Stewart, *op. cit.*

85 Mary F. Smith, *op. cit.*

86 M. G. Smith, "Some Aspects of Social Structure in the British Caribbean"; Stewart, *op. cit.*

87 *Ibid.;* Williams, *The Negro in the Caribbean,* and *Documents on British West Indian History, 1807–1833* (Port of Spain, Trinidad: Trinidad Publishing Co., 1952).

88 M. G. Smith, "Some Aspects of Social Structure in the British Caribbean"; Williams, *The Negro in the Caribbean.*

89 Guillaume, *Islam;* Hughes, *op. cit.;* Mary F. Smith, *op. cit.*

90 Ruxton, *op. cit.*

91 Williams, *The Negro in the Caribbean.*

92 Ruxton, *op. cit.*

93 Mary F. Smith, *op. cit.;* M. G. Smith, *The Economy of Hausa Communities.*

94 Ruxton, *op. cit.*

95 M. G. Smith, *The Economy of Hausa Communities.*

96 Bickell, *op. cit.;* Carmichael, *op. cit.*

97 Lewis, *op. cit.*

98 Carmichael, *op. cit.;* Lewis, *op. cit.*

99 Stewart, *op. cit.*

100 Ruxton, *op. cit.*

101 de Santillana, *op. cit.;* H. A. R. Gibb, *Mohammedanism* (London: Oxford University Press, 1949); Guillaume, *Islam;* Hughes, *op. cit.;* Lammens, *op. cit.;* Tritton, *op. cit.*

102 de Santillana, *op. cit.*

103 Gibb, *op. cit.;* Hughes, *op. cit.*

104 Max Weber, *The Protestant Ethic and the Spirit of Capitalism,* trans. by Talcott Parsons (London: Allen & Unwin, 1930).

105 R. H. Tawney, *Religion and the Rise of Capitalism* (London: Penguin Books, 1940).

106 *Ibid.*

107 Merivale, *op. cit.;* Williams, *The Negro in the Caribbean.*

108 Carmichael, *op. cit.;* Gardner, *op. cit.;* Edward Long, *The History of Jamaica* (London: T. Lowndes, 1774).

109 Ragatz, *op. cit.;* Young, *op. cit.*

110 Burn, *op. cit.;* Gardner, *op. cit.*

111 Barclay, *op. cit.;* Bickell, *op. cit.;* Bridges, *op. cit.;* Carmichael, *op. cit.*

112 Long, *op. cit.*

113 Barclay, *op. cit.;* Bridges, *op. cit.;* Carmichael, *op. cit.;* Stewart, *op. cit.;* Williams, *Documents on British West Indian History.*

114 Thomas Carlyle, "The Nigger Question" (1849) in Carlyle, *English and Other Critical Essays* (London: Dent & Sons, 1925); Fernando Henriques, *Family and Colour in Jamaica* (London: Eyre & Spottiswoode, 1953); Madeline Kerr, *Personality and Conflict in Jamaica* (Liverpool: Liverpool University Press, 1952); Simey, *op. cit.*

115 Carmichael, *op. cit.;* Lewis, *op. cit.;* Williams, *Documents on British West Indian History.*

116 Barclay, *op. cit.;* Carmichael, *op. cit.;* Stewart, *op. cit.;* Edwards, *op. cit.*

117 Cooper, *op. cit.;* Ragatz, *op. cit.*

118 Barclay, *op. cit.;* Carmichael, *op. cit.;* Grenada Free Press, *op. cit.*

119 Edwards, *op. cit.;* Williams, *Capitalism and Slavery.*

120 Mary F. Smith, *op. cit.*

121 Schon, *op. cit.;* M. G. Smith, *The Economy of Hausa Communities.*

122 Cole, *op. cit.*

123 M. G. Smith, *The Economy of Hausa Communities.*

124 Mary F. Smith, *op. cit.,* p. 41.

125 M. G. Smith, *The Economy of Hausa Communities.*

126 Hughes, *op. cit.;* Lammens, *op. cit.;* Ruxton, *op. cit.*

127 Forde and Scott, *op. cit.;* M. G. Smith, *The Economy of Hausa Communities.*

128 *Ibid.;* M. G. Smith, *Government in Zazzau.*

129 Bickell, *op. cit.*

130 Barclay, *op. cit.*

131 Young, *op. cit.*

132 Carmichael, *op. cit.*

133 Ragatz, *op. cit.*

134 Williams, *Capitalism and Slavery.*

135 Stewart, *op. cit.*

136 Ragatz, *op. cit.*

[137] Lewis, *op. cit.*

[138] Stewart, *op. cit.*; Young, *op. cit.*

[139] Lewis, *op. cit.*; Ulrich B. Phillips, "A Jamaica Slave Plantation," *Caribbean Quarterly*, Vol. 1, No. 1 (1949), pp. 4–12; Stewart, *op. cit.*

[140] Carmichael, *op. cit.*; Williams, 1953, *op. cit.*

[141] Barth, *op. cit.*; Forde and Scott, *op. cit.*; Mary F. Smith, *op. cit.*; M. G. Smith, *The Economy of Hausa Communities.*

[142] G. E. Cumper, "A Modern Jamaican Sugar Estate," *Social and Economic Studies*, Vol. 3, No. 2 (1954), pp. 119–160; Simey, *op. cit.*; Williams, *Capitalism and Slavery, The Negro in the Caribbean.*

[143] Karl Marx, *Critique of Political Economy* (1859), trans. by N. I. Stone (London: K. Paul, Trench, Trubner and Co., 1859), p. 11.

[144] Burn, *op. cit.*; Ragatz, *op. cit.*

[145] Merivale, *op. cit.*, p. 303.

[146] Bickell, *op. cit.*; Bridges, *op. cit.*; Burn, *op. cit.*; Carmichael, *op. cit.*

[147] Bridges, *op. cit.*; Carmichael, *op. cit.*; Stewart, *op. cit.*

[148] Carmichael, *op. cit.*; Edwards, *op. cit.*; Long, *op. cit.*

[149] Cooper, *op. cit.*; Gardner, *op. cit.*; Phillippo, *op. cit.*; Ragatz, *op. cit.*

[150] Gardner, *op. cit.*; Ragatz, *op. cit.*

[151] Barclay, *op. cit.*; Carmichael, *op. cit.*; Coleridge, *op. cit.*; Gardner, *op. cit.*; Hall, "Sir Charles Metcalfe," *Caribbean Quarterly*, Vol. 3, No. 2 (1953), pp. 90–100.

[152] Gardner, *op. cit.*; Hall, "The Apprenticeship Period in Jamaica, 1834–8," *Caribbean Quarterly*, Vol. 3, No. 3 (1953), pp. 142–166.

[153] Sir Allan Burns, *History of Nigeria* (London: Allen & Unwin, 1949), p. 187.

[154] Arnett, *op. cit.*

[155] Sir F. D. Lugard, *Report on the Amalgamation of Northern and Southern Nigeria and Administration, 1912–19* (London: H.M.S.O., 1920), pp. 43–44.

[156] M. G. Smith, *The Economy of Hausa Communities*, and *Government in Zazzau.*

[157] *Colonial Reports, Northern Nigeria, 1900–1908.*

[158] Mary F. Smith, *op. cit.*

[159] M. G. Smith, *The Economy of Hausa Communities*, and *Government in Zazzau.*

[160] Arnett, *op. cit.*; *Colonial Reports, Northern Nigeria, 1900–1908.*

[161] *Ibid.*

[162] *Ibid.*

[163] Gardner, *op. cit.*; Hall, "The Apprenticeship Period in Jamaica."

[164] Hugh Paget, "The Free Village System in Jamaica," *Caribbean Quarterly*, Vol. 1, No. 4 (1950), pp. 7–19.

[165] Hall, "Sir Charles Metcalfe," and "The Apprenticeship Period in Jamaica."

[166] Gardner, *op. cit.*

[167] Paget, *op. cit.*

[168] F. Cundall, *Chronological Outlines of Jamaican History, 1492–1926* (Kingston, Jamaica: Institute of Jamaica, 1929).

169 Gardner, *op. cit.*

170 Richard Hart, *The Origin and Development of the People of Jamaica* (Kingston, Jamaica: Trades Union Congress, 1952).

171 Cumper, "Labour Demand and Supply in Sugar," *Social and Economic Studies,* Vol. 2, No. 4 (1954), pp. 37–86.

172 John Bigelow, *Jamaica in 1850* (London: George Putnam, 1851).

173 W. G. Sewell, *The Ordeal of Free Labour in the British West Indies* (New York: Harpers, 1861).

174 E. B. Underhill, *The West Indies* (London: Jackson, Walford & Hodder, 1862).

175 Amy K. Lopez, "Land and Labour to 1900," *Jamaican Historical Review,* Vol. 1, No. 3 (1958), pp. 289–301.

176 Cundall, *op. cit.*

177 Gardner, *op. cit.*

178 Cundall, *op. cit.*

179 Royal Commission, *Report Relating to the Disturbances in Jamaica* (London: H.M.S.O., 1866).

180 R. V. Sires, "Governmental Crisis in Jamaica, 1860–1866," *Jamaican Historical Review,* Vol. 2, No. 3 (1953), 1–26.

181 *Handbook of Jamaica* (Kingston, Jamaica: Government Printer, 1954), p. 29.

182 Lord Olivier, *Jamaica, the Blessed Island* (London: Faber, 1936).

183 Ronald V. Sires, "The Jamaica Constitution in 1884," *Social and Economic Studies,* Vol. 3, No. 1 (1954), pp. 64–81.

184 E. B. Underhill, *The Tragedy of Morant Bay* (London: Alexander & Shepheard, 1895).

185 Olivier, *The Myth of Governor Eyre* (London: Hogarth Press, 1933).

186 Olivier, *Jamaica, the Blessed Island.*

187 W. M. Macmillan, *Warning from the West Indies* (1936) (London: Penguin Books, 1938); Sires, "The Jamaica Constitution in 1884."

188 Royal Commission, *Report on the West Indies* (London: H.M.S.O., 1944).

189 Hart, *op. cit.;* Olivier, *Jamaica, the Blessed Island.*

190 Lopez, *op. cit.*

191 Olivier, *Jamaica, the Blessed Island.*

192 Sir F. D. Lugard, *The Dual Mandate in British Tropical Africa* (London: 1929); Margery Perham, *Native Administration in Nigeria* (London: Oxford University Press, 1937).

193 Forde and Scott, *op. cit.;* M. G. Smith, *The Economy of Hausa Communities.*

194 Barth, *op. cit.;* Denham and Clapperton, *op. cit.;* Mary F. Smith, *op. cit.*

195 Cole, *op. cit.*

196 M. G. Smith, *The Economy of Hausa Communities.*

197 Henriques, *op. cit.;* Kerr, *op. cit.;* Macmillan, *op. cit.;* Simey, *op. cit.*

198 Barth, *op. cit.;* Burns, *op. cit.;* Forde and Scott, *op. cit.;* Hassan and Shu'aibu, *op. cit.;* Lugard, *The Dual Mandate;* Perham, *op. cit.;* C. L. Temple, *op. cit.;* O. and C. L. Temple, *op. cit.*

[199] Mary F. Smith, *op. cit.*; M. G. Smith, *The Economy of Hausa Communities* and *Government in Zazzau.*

[200] M. G. Smith, "Secondary Marriage in Northern Nigeria," *Africa,* Vol. 23, No. 4 (1953), pp. 298–323.

[201] M. G. Smith, *Government in Zazzau.*

[202] M. G. Smith, "Secondary Marriage in Northern Nigeria."

[203] Simey, *op. cit.*

7: The Plural Framework of Jamaica Society

[1] Fernando Henriques, *Family and Colour in Jamaica* (London: Eyre & Spottiswoode, 1953).

[2] M. G. Smith, "A Framework for Caribbean Studies," *Caribbean Affairs,* Extra-Mural Department, U.C.W.I., (Jamaica: University College of the West Indies, 1955).

[3] Edith Clarke, *My Mother Who Fathered Me* (London: Allen & Unwin, 1957).

[4] G. E. Simpson, "Jamaican Revivalist Cults," *Social and Economic Studies,* Vol. 5, No. 4 (1956).

[5] C. A. Moser, *A Study of Levels of Living, with Special Reference to Jamaica* (London: H.M.S.O., 1957).

[6] G. E. Simpson, "Political Cultism in West Kingston," *Social and Economic Studies,* Vol. 4, No. 2 (1955), pp. 133–149.

[7] Madeline Kerr, *Personality and Conflict in Jamaica* (Liverpool: Liverpool University Press, 1952).

[8] Simon Rottenberg, "Entrepreneurship and Economic Progress in Jamaica," *Journal of Inter-American Affairs,* Vol. 7, No. 2.

[9] M. G. Smith, *Labour Supply in Rural Jamaica* (Kingston, Jamaica: Government Printer, 1956).

[10] W. R. Bascom, "The Esusu: A credit institution of the Yoruba," *Journal of the Royal Anthropological Society,* LXXII (1952), 63–69.

[11] Clarke, "Land Tenure and the Family in Four Communities of Jamaica," *Social and Economic Studies,* Vol. 1, No. 4 (1953), pp. 85–119.

[12] Sidney W. Mintz, "The Jamaican Internal Marketing Pattern," *Social and Economic Studies,* Vol. 4, No. 1 (1955), pp. 95–103.

[13] Mrs. Carmichael, *Domestic Manners and Social Customs of the White, Coloured and Negro Populations of the West Indies* (London: John Murray, 1833), 2 vols.

[14] Philip Curtin, *Two Jamaicas: The Role of Ideas in a Tropical Colony; 1830–1865* (Cambridge, Mass.: Harvard University Press, 1955), pp. 32–33, 114–116, 163, 169.

[15] M. G. Smith, "Slavery and Emancipation in Two Societies," *Social and Economic Studies,* Vol. 3, Nos. 3 and 4 (1954), pp. 239–290.

[16] Peter Evans, "Legal Aid to the Poor," *The Daily Gleaner* (Kingston, Jamaica), Nov. 30, 1956, p. 12.

[17] R. B. LePage, Personal Communication, 1956.

8: Community Organization in Rural Jamaica

[1] I wish to thank G. J. Kruijer, Sidney Collins, Sidney Mintz, and George E. Simpson for helpful comments on the first draft of this paper. Its substance was presented as a lecture at the summer school for the Co-ordinated Extension Services of the Jamaica Farm Development Program, held at the University College of the West Indies (hereafter referred to as UCWI), Jamaica in 1956. I am indebted to several of the officers for stimulating comments during the following discussion.

[2] Conrad Arensberg, "The Community Study Method," *American Journal of Sociology*, LX, 109–125; F. J. Wright, *Elements of Sociology* (London: University Tutorial Press, 1942), p. 203.

[3] Betty Starr, "Levels of Communal Relations," *American Journal of Sociology*, LX, 125–135.

[4] Sydney Collins, "Social Mobility in Jamaica, with Reference to Rural Communities and the Teaching Profession," *Transactions of the Third World Congress of Sociology*, Vol. 3 (1956), pp. 267–276; M. G. Smith, "Slavery and Emancipation in Two Societies," *Social and Economic Studies*, Vol. 3, No. 3 (1954), pp. 239–290.

[5] Edith Clarke, "Land Tenure and the Family in Four Communities in Jamaica," *Social and Economic Studies*, Vol. 1, No. 4 (1953), pp. 81–118.

[6] M. G. Smith, *A Report on Labour Supply in Rural Jamaica* (Kingston, Jamaica: Government Printer, 1956).

[7] *Ibid.*, "A Framework for Caribbean Studies," essay 3 of this volume, originally published in *Caribbean Affairs* (Jamaica: Extra-Mural Department, University College of the West Indies, 1955).

[8] Collins, *op. cit.*; E. P. G. Seaga, "Parent-Teacher Relations in a Jamaican Village," *Social and Economic Studies*, Vol. 4, No. 3 (1955), pp. 289–302.

[9] *Ibid.*

[10] E. N. Burke, "Jamaica Welfare" in *The Farmer's Handbook* (Kingston, Jamaica: Jamaica Agricultural Society, 1952), pp. 171–176; Collins, "Patterns of Adjustment to Economic and Social Projects in a Village Community in Jamaica" in *Report of International Conference on Regional Planning and Community Development* (London, 1957).

[11] G. O. Fox, "The Charlestown Extra-Mural Club," Newsletter No. 127 (Jamaica: UCWI, 1956); D. G. Hall, "Note on Extra-Mural Clubs," UCWI Newsletter No. 88: E. M. Liburd, "The Charlestown Extra-Mural Club," UCWI Newsletter No. 129.

9: Education and Occupational Choice in Rural Jamaica

[1] I very much appreciate the generosity of Mr. P. C. C. Evans of the Institute of Education, London University, for permission to use these survey findings.

[2] M. G. Smith, *Labour Supply in Rural Jamaica* (Kingston, Jamaica: Government Printer, 1956).

[3] C. A. Moser, *The Measurement of Levels of Living with Special Reference to Jamaica* (London: H.M.S.O., 1956).

[4] M. G. Smith and G. J. Kruijer, *A Sociological Manual for Extension Workers in the Caribbean* (Jamaica: Extra-Mural Department, University College of the West Indies, 1957), p. 42.

[5] Madeline Kerr, *Personality and Conflict in Jamaica* (Liverpool: Liverpool University Press, 1952).

[6] Lloyd Braithwaite, "Social Stratification and Cultural Pluralism" in Vera Rubin, ed., *Social and Cultural Pluralism in the Caribbean*, Annals of The New York Academy of Sciences, Vol. 83, Art. 5 (1960), p. 829.

[7] Dorothy L. Meier and Wendell Bell, "Anomia and Differential Access to the Achievement of Life Goals," *American Sociological Review*, Vol. 24, No. 2 (1959), p. 190.

[8] Talcott Parsons, *The Social System* (London: Tavistock Publications, 1952).

10: The Transformation of Land Rights by Transmission in Carriacou

[1] The field work reported here was carried out at Harvey Vale in November, 1953, with the assistance of F. A. Phillips, then District Officer, Carriacou. I am happy to acknowledge here the considerable help which I received from Mr. Phillips during my study of the island.

[2] Edith Clarke, "Land Tenure and the Family in Four Selected Communities in Jamaica," *Social and Economic Studies*, Vol. 1, No. 4 (1953), pp. 81–118.

[3] The sociology of Carriacou was investigated as part of a study of Grenadian society and its culture. Comparison of these two societies is instructive. For an account of Carriacou, see M. G. Smith, *Kinship and Community in Carriacou* (New Haven: Yale University Press, 1962). Certain aspects of the system of land tenure which receive scant attention in this paper are discussed in the monograph.

[4] *West Indian Census*, 1946, Part H (Kingston, Jamaica: Government Printer, 1950), p. 1, table 1.

[5] *West Indian Census*, 1946, Part G (Kingston, Jamaica: Government Printer, 1949), p. 49, table 43.

[6] *West Indian Census*, 1946, Part B (Kingston, Jamaica: Government Printer, 1950), p. 26, table 39.

[7] Although the areas of separate occupancy on each plot are correctly represented for 1953 by number and size, no attempt has been made to reproduce their spatial relations exactly on the map.

11: Structure and Crisis in Grenada, 1950–1954

[1] *West Indian Census*, 1946, Part B (Kingston, Jamaica: Government Printer, 1950), page 26, table 39.

[2] *Colonial Reports, Grenada*, 1952 and 1953 (London: H.M.S.O., 1955), page 15.

[3] *West Indian Census*, 1946, Part B, p. 43, table 55.

[4] *Report of the Labour Department*, 1953 (Grenada: Government Printer, 1956).

5 *Grenada Handbook and Directory,* 1946 (Grenada: Government Printer, 1946), pp. 41–42.

6 *Grenada Handbook and Directory,* 1946 (St. George's, Grenada: Government of Grenada, 1946), p. 45.

7 I.e., end of the cane crop, between May and July.

8 For a first-hand account of these relations, see M. G. Smith, *Dark Puritan* (Jamaica: Extra-Mural Department, University of the West Indies, 1963).

9 *Colonial Reports, Grenada,* 1952 and 1953, p. 33.

10 At 1952 exchange rates, £ sterling = $4.80 BWI or $2.80 U.S. To convert Grenadian cents to U.S. values, multiply by 7/12.

11 "Report of a Committee Appointed to Examine the Working of the District Boards and to Report What Amendments They Consider Necessary to Be Made to the Ordinances Relating to Local Government," Administration Department, Grenada, E. S. Christiani, chairman (Nov. 25, 1947), unpublished.

12 M. G. Smith, *Stratification in Grenada* (Berkeley and Los Angeles: University of California Press, 1965).

13 W. R. Bascom, "The Esusu: A Credit Institution among the Yoruba," *Journal of the Royal Anthropological Institute,* LXXII, 63–70, London.

14 *Council Papers, Grenada.* Report of a Commission appointed under the Commissions of Enquiry Ordinance to enquire into the economic condition of the various classes of wage-earners in Grenada, with special reference to the Agricultural Industry, and to obtain recommendations for their amelioration. (St. George's, Grenada: Government Printer, 1938).

15 *Council Papers, Grenada, 1954.* Report on the Labour Department, 1951, p. 3.

16 *Ibid.,* p. 4.

17 *Ibid.,* p. 1.

18 *Grenada Council Paper 3 of 1952.* Report on the Grenada Police Force, 1951.

19 *Ibid.,* p. 15.

20 *Council Papers, Grenada, 1956.* Report on the Labour Department, 1953.

21 *Council Papers, Grenada, 1956,* Report on the Labour Department, 1954.

22 Simon Rottenberg, "Labour Relations in an Undeveloped Economy," *Caribbean Quarterly,* Vol. 4, No. 1 (1955), pp. 61, 50–61.

23 *Ibid.,* pp. 54–55.

12: Short-range Prospects in the British Caribbean

1 For reasons apparent below, I do not believe that the date of composition determines the value of a reasoned prediction. I prepared this forecast in June, 1961, so that members of a forthcoming conference on The Political Sociology of the British Caribbean, which was held in December, 1961, could evaluate the forecast in the light of developments during the interval between the drafting and presentation of this essay. The Jamaican referendum on the West Indies Federation was held in September 1961—with the results anticipated here. The West Indies Federation dissolved in 1962.

2 M. G. Smith, *A Framework for Caribbean Studies* (Jamaica: Extra-Mural

Department, University College of the West Indies, 1955), and "Social and Cultural Pluralism" in Vera Rubin, ed., *Social and Cultural Pluralism in the Caribbean*, Annals of The New York Academy of Sciences, Vol. 83, Art. 5 (1960), pp. 763–777.

³ M. G. Smith, *Government in Zazzau, 1800–1950* (London: Oxford University Press for International African Institute, 1960), and "Kagoro Political Development," *Human Organization*, Vol. 19, No. 3 (1960), pp. 37–49.

⁴ David Lowenthal, "The Range and Variation of Caribbean Societies," in Rubin, ed., *op. cit.*, pp. 786–795.

⁵ *The Daily Gleaner* (Kingston, Jamaica), June 14, 1961, p. 1.

⁶ David Lowenthal, "The Social Background of West Indian Federation" in David Lowenthal, ed., *The West Indies Federation: Perspectives on a New Nation*, American Geographical Society Research Series No. 23 (New York: Columbia University Press, 1961), p. 76.

⁷ Leonard Broom, "The Social Differentiation of Jamaica," *American Sociological Review*, Vol. 19, pp. 115–123 (1954), and "Urbanization and the Plural Society" in Rubin, ed., *op. cit.*, pp. 880–891.

⁸ M. G. Smith, "Structure and Crisis in Grenada, 1950–1954," background paper for Conference on Political Sociology of the Caribbean, December, 1961, essay 11 of this volume.

⁹ M. G. Smith, "Slavery and Emancipation in Two Societies," essay 6 of this volume, originally published in *Social and Economic Studies*, Vol. 3, No. 3 (Jamaica, 1954), pp. 239–290, and "Ethnic and Cultural Pluralism in the British Caribbean," essay 2 of this volume, originally published in *Ethnic and Cultural Pluralism in Intertropical Countries* (Brussels: INCIDI, 1957), pp. 439–477.

¹⁰ *Ibid.*, *Government in Zazzau*, and "Kagoro Political Development."

¹¹ Eric Williams, "Race Relations in Caribbean Society" in Vera Rubin, ed., *Caribbean Studies: A Symposium* (Jamaica: University College of the West Indies, 1957), pp. 54 ff.

¹² Peter Newman, "The Economic Future of British Guiana," *Social and Economic Studies*, Vol. 9, No. 3 (1960), pp. 263–296; K. Berrill, A. P. Thorne, G. E. Cumper, and K. E. Boulding, "Comments on The Economic Future of British Guiana by Peter Newman," *Social and Economic Studies*, Vol. 10, No. 1 (1961), pp. 1–34; Peter Newman, "Epilogue on British Guiana," *Social and Economic Studies*, Vol. 10, No. 1 (1961), pp. 35–41.

¹³ Lloyd Braithwaite, "Social Stratification in Trinidad," *Social and Economic Studies*, Vol. 2, No. 3 (1953), pp. 5–175, and "The Problem of Cultural Integration in Trinidad," *Social and Economic Studies*, Vol. 3, No. 1 (1954), pp. 82–96.

¹⁴ Elliott P. Skinner, "Group Dynamics and Social Stratification in British Guiana" in Rubin, ed., *op. cit.*, pp. 904–916.

¹⁵ D. J. Crowley, "Plural and Differential Acculturation in Trinidad," *American Anthropologist*, Vol. 59 (1957), pp. 817–824; Morton Klass, "East and West Indian: Cultural Complexity in Trinidad," in Rubin, ed., *op. cit.*, pp. 855–861.

¹⁶ M. G. Smith, "West Indian Culture," essay 1 of this volume, originally published in *Caribbean Quarterly*, Vol. 7, No. 3 (1961), pp. 112–119.

17 Morley Ayearst, *The British West Indies: The Search for Self-Government* (London: Allen & Unwin, 1960); G. E. Cumper, ed., *The Economy of the West Indies* (Jamaica: Institute of Social and Economic Research, UCWI, 1961).

18 *Economic Survey for 1960* (Kingston, Jamaica: Central Planning Unit and Government Printer, 1961).

19 *A National Plan for Jamaica* (Kingston, Jamaica: Government Printer, 1957); *The Economic Development of Jamaica*, Report of a Mission of the International Bank for Reconstruction and Development (Baltimore, Md.: Johns Hopkins University Press, 1952).

20 Lowenthal, ed., "The Social Background of West Indian Federation."

21 M. G. Smith, "The Plural Framework of Jamaican Society," essay 7 of this volume, originally published in *British Journal of Sociology*, Vol. XII, No. 3 (1961), pp. 249–262.

22 C. Paul Bradley, "Mass Parties in Jamaica," *Social and Economic Studies*, Vol. 9, No. 4 (1960), pp. 375–416; O. W. Phelps, "The Rise of the Labour Movement in Jamaica," *Social and Economic Studies*, Vol. 9, No. 4 (1960), pp. 417–468.

23 George E. Simpson, "Political Cultism in West Kingston, Jamaica," *Social and Economic Studies*, Vol. 4, No. 2 (1955), pp. 135–149, "Jamaican Revivalist Cults," *Social and Economic Studies*, Vol. 5, No. 4 (1955), pp. 321–442; Philip D. Curtin, *Two Jamaicas: The Role of Ideas in a Tropical Colony* (Cambridge, Mass.: Harvard University Press, 1955); Peter Abrahams, *Jamaica, An Island Mosaic*, Corona Library (London: H.M.S.O., 1957).

24 M. G. Smith, "Politics and Society in Jamaica" (unpublished MS).

25 M. G. Smith, Roy Augier, and R. Nettleford, *The Ras Tafari Movement in Kingston, Jamaica* (Jamaica: UCWI, 1960).

26 M. G. Smith, "Slavery and Emancipation in Two Societies."

Index

Index

Date Due